British Intelligence

British Intelligence
Secrets, Spies and Sources

Stephen Twigge
Edward Hampshire
Graham Macklin

the national archives

First published in 2008 by
The National Archives, Kew,
Richmond Surrey, TW9 4DU, UK
www.nationalarchives.gov.uk

The National Archives brings together the Public Record Office,
Historical Manuscripts Commission, Office of Public Sector Information
and Her Majesty's Stationery Office.

A catalogue card for this book is available
from the British Library
ISBN 978 1 905615 00 1

Jacket design by Ken Wilson|point918
Page design and typesetting by Ken Wilson|point918
Printed in Malta by Gutenberg Press

Jacket images: *top*, John Drysdale, Getty Images;
bottom right, Christine Schneider / Zefa / Corbis

Contents

Introduction

Almost every modern state needs an intelligence service that can play a part in guaranteeing national security, and Britain is no exception. From its beginnings in the Elizabethan court to today's fight against international terrorism, acquiring reliable information on the intentions and capabilities of friend and foe has been an overriding objective of British diplomacy. For the majority of its existence the secret world has remained in the shadows, its activities known only to the initiated. Yet while life in the shadows provided the freedom to operate with few restrictions, it also had drawbacks. The inability of the agencies to argue their case publicly made it difficult for them to defend their position in the battle for resources, and the end of the Cold War exacerbated this dilemma. In the early 1990s the intelligence and security agencies were placed on a statutory basis which set out their functions and established formal arrangements for control and oversight. The legislation also had important implications for the intelligence records that could now be released to the National Archives.

The world of secret intelligence was for decades largely neglected by historians, denied access to the archives of the intelligence and security agencies. Without this lifeblood of history, our understanding of their activities has been shaped by a steady stream of lurid novels, sensationalist journalism and memoirs written by former practitioners and senior officials. Yet the position has now changed and restrictions covering intelligence records have been reviewed, allowing emphasis to be placed on openness rather than closure. The Waldegrave Initiative on Open Government, announced in 1993, represented the first step in the controlled release of intelligence material to the National Archives at Kew. Over the next few years a steady stream of formerly classified documents has been transferred to the National Archives and opened to public inspection. In 1997 a new Labour government encouraged agencies to be more proactive in their disclosure policy and in recent years all of the agencies, either directly or indirectly, have released a proportion of their historic records into the public domain. The security service, MI5, announced a phased release of its files in 1997, and was soon followed by GCHQ. In the following years thousands of records have been brought to the archives at Kew.

The range of intelligence material now available at the National Archives covers a large swathe of British history, ranging from the 18th century to the height of Cold War. Perhaps unsurprisingly, issues of peace and war predominate, with the events of the First and Second World Wars constituting a large proportion of the material released to date. This is not to say that other areas have been neglected, for, as we shall see, the intelligence world was involved in nearly every aspect of public life—from divination to flying saucers. This book identifies key topics that demonstrate the range and scope of intelligence material; individual chapters explore a particular theme rather than the work of individual agencies. The narrative of each chapter highlights important activities and developments, enabling key records to be illuminated in context. *British Intelligence* thus provides both a compelling guide to the National Archives' collection and a valuable framework for future inquiry.

Exploring security service records, as might be expected, is not always a straightforward process. For example, the public disclosure of historical material does not extend to the Secret Intelligence Service (SIS), the records of which remain closed. This policy was endorsed in 1998 by the then foreign secretary, Robin Cook, who argued that SIS's records must remain secret: individuals who cooperate with SIS are given an unshakeable commitment that their identities will never be revealed. However, such a commitment does not mean that material held by SIS is never put into the public domain. The records of the Special Operations Executive (SOE), which were inherited by SIS after the war, and a small collection of intelligence records predating the creation of the agency in 1909 have recently been transferred to the National Archives. A considerable amount of SIS material from the Second World War can also be found in the files of MI5 and GCHQ.

While the release of intelligence material has broadly been welcomed, only a small proportion of the archive has yet been opened, and our knowledge of Britain's intelligence and security services remains, inevitably, incomplete. The majority of intelligence material released to date concerns the events of the two world wars—and, with the exception of papers from the Joint Intelligence Committee (JIC) and the Defence Intelligence Staff, records relating to British operations in the Cold War remain largely closed. However, in examining those records that have been released, a number of common themes and key functions emerge. One characteristic is a vindication of Palmerston's dictum that nations have no permanent allies, only permanent interests. In its long and distinguished history, British intelligence has spied on almost every country in the world: America, during the war of independence; Spain, Germany, France and Russia (both imperial and Soviet) from the age of the Armada to the two world wars; China, the Soviet Union and the nations of Eastern Europe during the Cold War; the countries of the Middle East and central Asia during the 'Great Game'; and most states in Africa following European decolonization. Indeed, the list of countries that have not caught the attention of British intelligence must be very small.

While adversaries change, the intelligence agencies' requirements and priorities have remained fairly constant. The fight against terrorism is a prime example. From the creation of Scotland Yard's Special Irish Branch in the late 19th century to the establishment of the Joint Terrorism Analysis Centre in the early 21st, counter-terrorism has been a constant preoccupation for British intelligence.

The government's current counter-terrorism strategy, known as CONTEST, is designed to counter the global threat to British interests posed by al-Qaeda and its associates. The strategy has four key objectives:

- to prevent terrorism, by tackling the factors that make individuals, organizations and communities, both in the UK and elsewhere, prone to violent extremism
- to pursue terrorists and those who sponsor their campaigns by disrupting their activities
- to protect against terrorist attacks on UK citizens, key national services and UK interests abroad
- to prepare the UK to be as ready as it can be for the consequences of a terrorist attack.

These aims would have been readily understood by past generations of intelligence officers. The need to prevent and thwart attacks, track down networks, protect the public and prepare for the worst are all activities with a long heritage in British intelligence. Disrupting and infiltrating organizations that pose a threat to the UK is a core function of both the security service and SIS, using methods and techniques developed and refined from their beginnings in the Secret Service

Bureau. Despite the rapid changes in technology, therefore, it is only by looking back at the history of the intelligence services that we can really understand the present and prepare for the future.

The evolution of British intelligence

In exploring intelligence activities and those involved in them, some deep-rooted (and undeniably attractive) perceptions have to be challenged. The term secret intelligence, for example, is often associated with cloak-and-dagger operations undertaken at the dead of night behind enemy lines. The reality is more mundane, although no less important. Many activities that bear the name 'intelligence' do not involve agents; they are conducted from within well-lit offices with little of the glamour and excitement usually portrayed in books and films. In Britain, for example, the first permanently established intelligence organization was the Post Office, which from the 17th century maintained a Secret Office to intercept the mail of suspected plotters, and in the 18th century established a deciphering department to break the secret codes employed by foreign powers. The growth of the British Empire in the 19th century placed considerable strain on an already overstretched military. The need to protect supply lines, subdue nationalist revolt and secure frontiers against the designs of expansionist neighbours all required accurate and timely intelligence. Even here, however, the majority of intelligence was derived from open sources. The Admiralty, for example, was the first to establish a global reporting system which monitored the strength and deployment of the French and Russian fleets. The system relied primarily on naval attachés who gathered their information from the press and government publications and from observing the movements of ships in and out of docks and harbours. The creation of the Naval Intelligence Department in 1887 did not fundamentally alter the work of naval attachés, who were informed that under no circumstances should they run agents or obtain intelligence by covert means.

Military intelligence was treated in a similar fashion, with the majority of tactical information derived from field reconnaissance and foreign maps. It was only in 1873 that the War Office established its first intelligence branch, which in 1888 became the Directorate of Military Intelligence. Apart from the Post Office, the first civilian institution to possess an intelligence function was the Metropolitan Police; in March 1883 they established a Special Branch to gather intelligence on

Irish 'Fenian' terrorism on mainland Britain and overseas revolutionary groups based in the UK. It was only at the beginning of the 20th century that Britain's first truly secret intelligence organization was established. The impetus behind this move was due to a number of factors, including the perceived failure of intelligence in the Boer War, increased tension with Germany and the publication of a series of alarmist novels suggesting that Britain was awash with foreign spies. The need was made all the more apparent when it was discovered that there was not one single British agent operating in the whole of mainland Europe. In 1909, in an attempt to establish a credible intelligence network—and to reorganize the existing arrangements that had emerged as so inadequate—the government established the Secret Service Bureau. The bureau had two primary functions: to determine the nature and scope of espionage that was being carried out by foreign agents; and to build up and direct the work of British agents employed overseas. The formation of a single body to manage intelligence at home and abroad did not last long. The home section (MI5) was responsible for counter-espionage and placed under the control of the War Office, whereas the foreign section (MI6) came under the operational control of the Admiralty, which was the principal consumer of intelligence from overseas.

Britain was not alone in establishing a secret service. Imperial Germany possessed its own intelligence bureau (IIIb), which reported to the Prussian general staff and which by the turn of the century was staffed by 124 officers stationed throughout Europe. In France secret intelligence was gathered by the Deuxième Bureau of the General Staff, while in Russia the feared Okhrana (the 'protection section') was responsible for monitoring opposition to the tsar and the imperial regime both at home and abroad. Of all the major industrial nations, only the United States, which was yet to face any direct threat to its national security, did not possess a significant intelligence organization, with only five officers assigned to its Office of Naval Intelligence.

The First World War marked further reorganization of British intelligence, with the bureau's foreign section taken over by the War Office and placed within its directorate of military intelligence. It was only following the post-war review of intelligence requirements, conducted by the Secret Service Committee, that the Secret Intelligence Service as we know it today would emerge. The First World War also demonstrated the effectiveness of signals intelligence (SIGINT), with the Admiralty's Room 40 successfully intercepting and decoding German diplomatic and military telegrams. Following the war, all civilian and military SIGINT was combined into a single body, the Government Code and Cypher School (GC&CS), the precursor of the modern day GCHQ. In the inter-war period the three agencies, MI5, MI6 and GC&CS, began to consolidate their positions and working practices. The inter-war period also witnessed the first attempts to coordinate the work of the various intelligence agencies across government, with the creation in 1936 of the Joint Intelligence Committee (JIC). The JIC was chaired by a representative of the Foreign Office and soon established itself as the senior intelligence assessment body in the United Kingdom.[1]

In the Second World War the secret agencies increased in both scope and number. The three established agencies were joined by the Special Operations Executive (SOE), responsible for mounting sabotage operations behind enemy lines; the Ministry of Economic Warfare (MEW), which monitored Germany industry and selected vulnerable points in the supply chain suitable for attack; the Political Warfare Executive (PWE) responsible for black propaganda; MI9 with responsibility for escape and evasion; and British Security Co-ordination (BSC), which supervised intelligence operations in the United States. The Second World War again demonstrated the importance of signals intelligence, with the allies once again successfully breaking Germany's military and diplomatic codes. The intelligence was a crucial factor in the allied victory over Nazi Germany and is claimed to have reduced the length of the war by months, if not years.

If the First World War was a war of attrition and the Second World War a war of production, the Cold War between East and West, which dominated international relations for the second half of the 20th century, was a war fought primarily by the intelligence services. The development of the ballistic missile and the atomic bomb meant that whole societies could be destroyed in a matter a minutes. Knowledge of an adversary's nuclear capability, and the likelihood and imminence of attack, became of paramount importance to international security in the nuclear age. Monitoring Soviet capabilities and intentions was a prime objective of British intelligence during the Cold War, with scientific and technical intelligence playing crucial roles. Espionage still had an important part to play, with the intelligence services of both East and West vulnerable to penetration and defections.

The collapse of the Soviet Union in 1991 led many to question whether Britain still required a large and expensive intelligence organization. With no obvious enemy to monitor, and no immediate threat to international security, the agencies suffered budget cuts in line with reductions in the armed forces. Following the mass-casualty attacks of 9/11 in the US, however, they soon found themselves in the front line of the battle against al-Qaeda and its affiliates. Techniques developed during the Cold War, such as signals intelligence, agent running and covert operations, are now employed in the global war against terror. The need to protect the UK against attack and prepare the population for the consequences of failure is redolent of the Cold War, albeit on a smaller scale. While the threat of nuclear Armageddon may have receded, the concern expressed by Stanley Baldwin over 75 years ago 'that the bomber will always get through' remains a constant fear.

While there are similarities with the past, there are also differences. In the struggle against international terrorism, increased emphasis needs to be placed on human sources. The vast technical infrastructure of satellites, listening stations and computers that characterized the Cold War is of limited use against individuals and organizations that no longer communicate by phone, but instead prefer the security of passing messages by trusted couriers. Only eyes and ears on the ground can bring back intelligence on terrorists, on underground arms networks and the release of nuclear and biological materials on to the black market. This does not imply that technical intelligence is now redundant, but rather that its focus will shift increasingly towards internet-based communications and the potential dangers posed by cyber-terrorism to the nation's critical infrastructure. The challenges facing the agencies were starkly underlined by the director of GCHQ who recently described Web-based communication as a complete revolution and the biggest change in telecommunications technology since the invention of the telephone. The Web's sinister potential is fast becoming apparent. In Iraq violent attacks on US soldiers and the decapitation of Western hostages are regularly videoed and uploaded on to militant websites for propaganda purposes. Monitoring these sites and developing strategies to counter them will require techniques similar to those first deployed by the Political Warfare Executive during the Second World War.

The Iraq war also demonstrated the limits of intelligence. Prior to the allied invasion, it was claimed that the Iraqi regime possessed biological and chemical weapons systems that could be deployed within 45 minutes of receiving an order to use them. These claims were later proved false, leading to accusations that intelligence was being distorted for political ends. The Butler inquiry, established after the conflict to investigate the accuracy of the intelligence and examine the reasons for the discrepancy between its evaluation and subsequent use by the government, found no evidence of deliberate distortion or culpable negligence. Rather, it discovered that there was a tendency for worst-case estimates to become the prevailing wisdom, with the result that more weight was placed on the intelligence than it could bear. To ensure that the episode is not repeated, the committee concluded that if intelligence is to be used more widely to inform public debate, the government must be careful to explain its uses and limitations, and to establish a more effective dividing line between assessment and advocacy.

The requirement to monitor and to prevent the spread of nuclear, chemical and biological weapons has been an enduring commitment for British intelligence. For over half a century, since the explosion of the first nuclear weapon in 1945, successive governments have recognized the threat posed to British interests by the proliferation of weapons of mass destruction. During the Cold War, Britain—in conjunction with the international community—was largely successful in monitoring sensitive nuclear technologies and preventing their acquisition by other states. While the list of those countries that now possess nuclear weapons has increased beyond the five declared nuclear powers, it has not matched the alarmist predictions made by President Kennedy in 1963, who believed that by the end of the 1970s over 20 countries would possess atomic weapons, making nuclear conflict almost inevitable.

During the Cold War, the threat of surprise attack was a constant and inevitable concern. As a result, the intelligence community's major task was to assess the intentions and capabilities of the Soviet Union, particularly its nuclear arsenal. The British believed that a Soviet surprise attack with atomic weapons was unlikely, and that intelligence would provide sufficient warning of attack in order to mount a retaliatory strike. In retrospect, the majority of these assessments were vindicated. But the judgements of the future may not be so straightforward. In the words of James Woolsey, a former director of the CIA, the nuclear dragon may have been slain, but it has been replaced by a jungle of poisonous snakes. Catching these snakes before they can bite will be a major preoccupation of intelligence organizations for the next decades and possibly beyond.

Exploring the world of intelligence

The primary intention of *British Intelligence* is to highlight the rich and diverse collection of intelligence records that can be found at the National Archives. To achieve this, each chapter deals with a separate theme, with sources indicated in the footnotes, focusing primarily upon the material now available in the public domain. The historical narrative is interwoven with episodes from the past that highlight some of the greatest successes—and failures—along the way, as well as the motives and machinations of those who worked in the shadows of the secret world. The book seeks to shed light on some of the shadowy aspects of British history, and to provide a framework and guide for all those interested in the history of intelligence.

Chapter 1 charts the development of Britain's domestic intelligence services and the battle against enemy agents and subversive elements on home soil, from 19th-century Irish Republican terrorism to the end of the Cold War and today's post- 9/11 world. In chapter 2, the international dimension of intelligence is explored. As the records of SIS are not transferred to the National Archives as a matter of policy, this chapter relies on material available in the records of its sister agencies and other related organizations. Chapters 3–5 deal with military, naval and air force intelligence respectively. They show how the services' need for real-time tactical intelligence was often at variance with the drive for greater centralization—an issue that came to a head with the creation of the Defence Intelligence Staff in 1964. The role of special operations is the theme of chapter 6, which details some of the organization's great successes and notable failures alongside lesser-known aspects of its work such as the parachuting of Soviet 'pickaxes' into occupied Europe in the Second World War. The theme of chapter 7 is scientific and technical intelligence, from its beginnings in the First World War, countering the effects of poison gas, to its Cold War involvement with rockets, germ warfare and flying saucers. Chapter 8 explores the role of communications intelligence, revealing how reading the enemy's diplomatic and military traffic has played a vital role in both peace and war. Individual chapters also consider the machinery of intelligence, confirming that coordination, analysis and oversight are an often overlooked but vital aspect of intelligence. Chapter 9 looks forward to the future, and the changing role of intelligence in the 21st century.

Through the chapters a number of constant themes emerge: the bravery and ingenuity of individuals; the increasing use of science and technology; inter-agency squabbles; and the fight for resources within an ever-diminishing budget. Information, whether deriving from human or technical intelligence, is seldom cut and dried, neatly packaged and sealed from doubt, and the murky worlds of double or even triple agents create a hall of mirrors in which nothing may be what it seems. In the 21st century security concerns are acute, but dangers are no longer predictable or clearly defined. The need for fresh thinking is a view supported by Sir David Omand, the former security and intelligence coordinator, who has recently argued that 'intelligence structures, processes, co-ordination mechanisms that may have worked for nations in the past will have to be re-thought against the new threat and how it might develop'.[2]

One of the central foundations of nuclear strategy is the belief that states will be deterred from using nuclear weapons by fear of retaliation. The same is not true of terrorist organizations, especially those that embrace suicide as part of their ideology and who have neither land nor citizens to protect. Terrorist acquisition of nuclear weapons or materials is one of the most serious threats currently faced by the international community. In recent years Western intelligence has been successful in breaking up a number of clandestine nuclear operations. Among the most significant was the network associated with Abdul Qadeer Khan, the father of the Pakistani atomic bomb, who sold nuclear technology and information to Libya, Iran and North Korea. His activities soon came to the attention of the British and American authorities, resulting in a carefully planned intelligence operation that successfully intercepted a cargo ship loaded with nuclear components destined for Libya. Khan was later arrested and his operations halted.

Individual victories do not end the war, however, and a constant fear is that determined terrorists will manage to obtain nuclear material and detonate a crude device in a metropolitan area. To prevent this nightmare from becoming reality, Western governments will increasingly rely on intelligence to provide warning of attack and to assist covert operations. Intelligence, however—sporadic, patchy and intuitive as it can be—is merely a technique for improving the basis of knowledge. As demonstrated in Iraq, it has its limitations and can never give the whole picture. Such is the challenge facing those who work with harvested information, conscious that it can never truly reveal how a terrorist network would react in certain circumstances. Intelligence may uncover secrets—but it cannot reveal the future.

1 | Domestic Intelligence

On the afternoon of 13 December 1867 Richard O'Sullivan-Burke and Joseph Casey were languishing behind bars in Clerkenwell Prison. Yet these two senior members of the Irish Republican Brotherhood—a revolutionary group commonly known as the Fenians—were confident that they would not be confined for much longer. Shortly before 4 o'clock their comrades on the outside placed a barrel stuffed with gunpowder against the prison walls, intending to detonate the explosives while the two men exercised in the prison's yard. They sought to blow a hole large enough to allow their escape—and in this, as *The Times* commented the next day, they were to prove 'horribly successful'.

The magnitude of the explosion, which tore a 60-foot breach in the wall, was far greater than these inexpert bombers had anticipated. Had the prisoners been exercising as they were expected to be at the time, they might well have been crushed under an avalanche of masonry. So loud was the blast that it could be heard for miles around, while the narrow tenement streets in the surrounding neighbourhood were devastated. The house immediately opposite collapsed, others stood without windows and doors, bricks and glass littered the ground and some 40 men, women and children were reported injured. Four people died—one on the spot, two overnight and a fourth shortly afterwards, victims of what *The Times* described as a conspiracy bent on the creation 'of a terror throughout the United Kingdom' that had 'declared war on the Government and society of these isles'. In condemning the outrage the newspaper continued:

> With traitors and assassins such as these there can be but one course. We desire to say nothing which may aggravate the bitterness of English feeling, or increase the indignation which will burst forth to-day in every part of the land. We feel that the Fenians have filled to the full the cup of wrath, and that in dealing with them public opinion will need rather to be restrained than instigated. We would impress on our readers the duty of looking at these events with as much calmness as is consistent

with human nature, of remembering that not every Irishman—nay, not even every processionist and every listener to seditionist speeches—is a Fenian. The conspiracy to which these Clerkenwell assassins belong is probably directed by a few, and its active co-operators may be only some thousands in the whole kingdom. This leaven might, if left to itself, soon leaven the whole lump; and it is therefore necessary to remove it at once.[1]

In an instant this 'modern Gunpowder plot' had catapulted terrorism, and with it the importance of domestic intelligence, to the very top of the Victorian political agenda. Fearing a full-blown bombing campaign, the government authorized the foundation of a Secret Service Department (SSD). This was intended as an expansion into England of the extant anti-Fenian intelligence network, which had been run from Dublin Castle, to create an overarching 'British' intelligence network. Although the SSD lasted only until April 1868 and achieved little, its importance is to be located less in its achievements than in what it represented: the first flourishing of a codified domestic intelligence network on the British mainland.

The Fenian threat continued to loom large in the years that followed, a turbulent time troubled by political and labour unrest and fears over the number of foreign revolutionaries and radicals granted asylum in the country. In 1883, in the midst of a new round of bombings that saw Glasgow, Liverpool and London targeted, the Metropolitan Police Special Irish Branch was founded, with the express remit of combating Fenian terrorism. This small section within the Criminal Investigation Department was the forerunner of Special Branch; shortly after its formation, the word 'Irish' was dropped from its name and it became responsible for acquiring, assessing and interpreting a wider range of intelligence. It was also, where necessary, charged with taking executive action against political subversion, public disorder and terrorism within the United Kingdom. From 1892 onwards, for example, Special Branch (and in particular its star agent, William Melville) was involved in combating the threat deemed to emanate from a burgeoning anarchist movement. At the same time Special Branch also began providing diplomatic protection and as a result had nearly tripled in size by 1905.

A draft letter of 10 July 1909, written by the commissioner of police to the under-secretary of state and preserved at the National Archives, indicates the extent to which Special Branch had developed from its Irish roots in its first years of existence. Written shortly after the murder in

London by an Indian seditionist of Sir Curzon Wyllie, the letter asked for extra officers, stating:

> In consequence of the Indian agitation, culminating in a recent assassination, it has been necessary to detail Officers for the personal protection of Statesmen; to keep a close supervision over certain persons known to hold extreme views; and to carry out the numerous inquiries called for by the India Office and other Authorities. The forthcoming visit of the Emperor and Empress of Russia to this Country will necessitate the closest possible supervision over the large number of Russian and other Anarchists resident in London. In addition, the protection of Their Majesties the King and Queen has to be arranged for daily, and the agitation by the 'Suffragettes' has necessitated the assignment of two Officers of the Special Branch for the Protection of the Prime Minister from the importunity of women.[2]

The same file includes a number of similar letters, including one specifically focused on the suffragette menace, an issue that had lately been 'engaging the attention of the commissioner'. Dated 22 September, it argued that 'the persistence with which these women maintain their campaign against members of HM Government makes it necessary to take measures to combat their designs and to protect Ministers from insult, annoyance and violence'. Written in the same month that force-feeding was introduced to combat the growing practice of hunger-striking by imprisoned suffragettes, the letter called for a complement of officers. In light of the politically sensitive nature of the work the author noted:

> It is essential that only men of practical experience should be employed on this work, as any tactical mistake would be much criticised and would have the effect of promoting, instead of arresting, the progress of the Suffragette propaganda. Those employed on this duty will be at a distance from head-quarters and will be unable to apply for specific instructions for particular emergencies, and this denotes the desirability of employing experienced and resourceful officers.[3]

Special Branch, which had already conducted inquiries in this area, was seen as the outfit for the job, and an addition of 16 officers was agreed.

In the early years of the 20th century, however, as political and international tensions mounted, public anxiety about security issues continued to rise. Both the Secret Service Department and Special Branch had been founded to combat internal 'subversion', yet the climate of fear remained, along with a crisis of confidence in Britain's security apparatus. Popular concern was heightened by the publication of a series of alarmist novels, describing in graphic detail the threat posed from Germany and its network of spies. The first of these, *The Riddle of the Sands* by Erskine Childers, was a tale of two British yachtsmen who stumble across German invasion plans; it was followed in 1906 by William Le Queux's fictional account of a German invasion of England, a story serialized by the *Daily Mail* which became an overnight sensation. In book form *The Invasion of 1910 with an Account of the Siege of London* sold more than a million copies and was translated into 27 languages. Alarm was taking hold, and it had to be addressed.

The foundation of MI5

Bestselling author Le Queux continued to exert an unsettling influence, along with several authors publishing on similar themes. He followed his blockbuster with *Spies of the Kaiser: Plotting the Downfall of England*, claiming to have unearthed all manner of German espionage activity, from the surveillance of dockyards to the planned systematic sabotage of key industries following the declaration of war. To add authenticity to his account, the author claimed to possess secret documents that substantiated his story. Whatever Le Queux's motive, the book's publication in 1909 led to a torrent of questions from a concerned public.[4] The *Weekly News* even offered £10 to readers to provide information on German agents to its 'Spy Editor'—and was quickly inundated with letters reporting supposed German espionage activities across the length and breadth of the kingdom.

Response came from the highest levels. In October 1909 the British government asked the Committee of Imperial Defence to examine the espionage threat posed by Germany and to recommend any changes that were thought necessary. The committee assembled a small but high-powered subcommittee under the chairmanship of the secretary of state for war, Lord Haldane. Other members included the first lord of the Admiralty, the home secretary, the postmaster general, the permanent secretaries of the Foreign Office and Treasury and the commissioner of the Metropolitan Police. By July, the inquiry was able to forward its findings to the prime minister. The report, which was duly approved by the cabinet, contained four main recommendations. These were the creation of a system to control the movement of aliens, the introduction of measures to protect key military installations against sabotage, the revision of the 1889 Official Secrets Act and the creation of a Secret Service Bureau (SSB).[5] The last was to be responsible for dealing with offers of information from foreign spies; to act as an intermediary between the Admiralty, War Office and British secret agents working abroad; and to run agents within the United Kingdom in order to establish the nature and scope of the espionage being carried out by foreign powers.

The Secret Service Bureau was initially intended to consist of a military and a naval branch, each with considerable autonomy and staffed by retired officers. The first head of the military branch was Captain (later Sir) Vernon Kell, a 36-year-old officer in the South Staffordshire Regiment employed as an assistant to the Committee of Imperial Defence (plate 1). According to his letter of acceptance, preserved on microfilm at the National Archives, Kell was 'very glad' to accept the appointment, which in addition to a full pension offered him a salary of £500.[6] Commander Mansfield Cumming was appointed as the head of the naval section, and on 1 October 1909 the new bureau began its work. Within less than a year of its formation, the bureau was split into two: Kell was made responsible for the 'home section' of the SSB, covering domestic intelligence up to the three-mile limit, and Cumming for the 'foreign section' dealing with intelligence beyond this perimeter. Cumming's section was to become the forerunner of the Secret Intelligence Service (SIS), more commonly known as MI6.

Funded by the Secret Service Vote, Kell, or 'K' as he was known, had a staff of 10, many of whom were recruited after service in India, almost all through personal acquaintance. His hand was strengthened between 1909 and 1911 by a number of legislative measures, including the foundation of the D-Notice Committee in 1910. This gave newspaper proprietors the opportunity to censor themselves voluntarily in the interests of national security, in order that the military authorities would not have to order them to do so.[7] More crucial was the revision of the 1889 Official Secrets Act the following year; although sponsored by Lord Haldane, this overhaul was in reality largely the work of Kell. A particular concern, at a time when spies were seen to be lurking round every corner, was the lack of legislation to tackle espionage—for example, anyone found photographing, planning or sketching fortifications. In a letter to Haldane, Kell complained that unless the authorities could show that actual damage had been committed, the only law that he could currently use was one of trespass, 'in which case the punishment is practically a nominal one, amounting in most cases to a nominal fine, which for our purposes is useless as a deterrent'.[8] Working closely with Kell, Haldane drew up a legal rationale for the home section and its successors' existence. Most importantly this meant that, although Kell's organization itself lacked the power of arrest (this was and would remain the responsibility of Special Branch), espionage was now established as a felony; it could be investigated properly, prosecuted and, hopefully, deterred.[9] A half-empty House of Commons passed the new Act in under one hour on a humid afternoon.

In April 1914, with war looming, the home section of the SSB became a subsection of the War Office's Directorate of Military Operations, section 5 (MO5), and was given the designation MO5(g). Its foundation, the Committee for Imperial Defence hoped, would lock the civil authorities into the military machine, allowing them to play their part in opposing the 'German interest' on the east coast of England. In September 1916, as part of a broader reorganization by the General Staff (p. 95), MO5(g) was renamed Military Intelligence, section 5 (MI5), the name by which it is essentially known today. It was renamed again in 1929, this time becoming the Defence Security Service, and again in 1931, when it was officially designated as the Security Service. It is still called this today—though the title MI5 continues to exert a powerful hold on the popular consciousness.

The First World War

As war broke out the authorities confronted the task of controlling 'enemy aliens'—both those already living in Britain and those now entering and leaving the country were seen as potential sources of German espionage. The government's immediate response, as anti-German riots broke out across the country, was internment, and in little over a year (October 1915) some 32,000 people were being held in camps across the country.

Britain's security services were closely involved in identifying and monitoring foreigners. On 5 August 1914 an Order in Council had provided the basis for the War Office's secret registry of aliens, which required all foreigners to register with the police within 48 hours of disembarking. MO5(g) used these details—together with evidence from the 1911 census returns, to which they had secretly been granted access—as the basis for its 'central registry', a massive card index. By the spring of 1917 this stood at some 250,000 names, generating approximately 27,000 personal files on chief suspects. The central registry operated a rudimentary and faintly amusing classification comprising two parts: a 'civil classification' — B.S., A.S., N.S. or E.S., (British, Allied, Neutral or Enemy Subject) — followed by a 'general military (special intelligence) classification':

> AA: 'Absolutely Anglicised' or 'Absolutely Allied' — undoubtedly friendly.
> A: 'Anglicised' or 'Allied' — friendly.
> AB: 'Anglo-Bosche' — doubtful but probably friendly.
> BA: 'Bosche-Anglo' — doubtful but probably hostile.
> B: 'Bosche' — hostile.
> BB: 'Bad Bosche' — undoubtedly hostile.[10]

A 'Special Intelligence Black List' followed these initial headings, denoting various other misdemeanours of which an individual could be suspected. The Black List was compiled through a mix of surveillance and police reports together with censorship of cables, carried out by MO5d (later MI8), and of post, carried out (albeit in a more haphazard manner) by the Testing Department (MI9c). This 'vital element' in the MO5(g) armament was facilitated by the then home secretary, Winston Churchill, who ensured that the Post Office worked with Kell to supervise 'undesirable communications' with Germany.

The First World War also saw the introduction of passports, which were gradually phased in during 1915. Initially required only for passengers travelling from France and Holland, they became compulsory for all passengers on 30 November of that year. In addition, strict searches and interrogations were carried out at ports, as recorded in MI5's First World War branch reports, now preserved on microfilm at the National Archives:

> Passengers who could not give a satisfactory account of themselves were then submitted to a careful search. Much information was provided by M.I.5. as to enemy methods of concealment. Hiding places for messages were looked for in the seams of ladies under clothing, in the lining of boxes of sweets, in the handles of umbrellas, sticks and shaving brushes, in fountain pens, tins of blackening and artificial flowers. Many were devices for conveying invisible ink. Warnings were issued against soap and scents, toilet preparations such as hair-washes, and dentifrices, articles of clothing which might be soaked in solutions for secret writing, as well as books, and luggage labels and other articles on which invisible messages might be written.[11]

During this period, Kell's organization was credited with a series of successes against agents such as Mata Hari (Margaretha Zelle), executed for espionage by the French on 13 February 1917 (though there was little real proof of her treachery), and the Irish revolutionary Sir Roger Casement who, having been stripped of his knighthood, was hanged for treason (of which there was more solid proof) on 3 August 1916.[12] Another notable—though less famous—case, described in files at the National Archives, is that of Carl Friedrich Muller, arrested and executed in June 1915 (plates 2 and 3). Muller had arrived in England in January of that year and was active for a mere month before his apprehension. His communications with Germany, some sent through an English-born intermediary of German descent called John Hahn, were all intercepted by British intelligence. They appeared innocuous enough until it was discovered that they were written in invisible ink concocted from a mixture of formaldehyde and lemon juice. The letters—and, indeed, the offending lemon (exhibit 43: 'one whole lemon')—are preserved in his files.[13]

Another set of files at the National Archives details the exploits of Karl Hans Lody, a junior lieutenant in the German Naval Reserve. He spoke fluent English and had volunteered to work for the Naval Intelligence Department in May 1914, but despite his enthusiasm and patriotism the young man proved a rank amateur; he received little training and appears to have had scant flair for espionage. After arriving in Edinburgh in August, his very first message to his German controllers was transmitted through 'Adolf Burchard' via an address in Stockholm known to be an intelligence front. It was promptly intercepted by Postal Censorship and passed to MI5. Subsequent telegrams were sent uncoded, which made the task of the security services even easier. Tasked with spying on Royal Naval activity in the Firth of Forth, many of Lody's telegrams were allowed to reach their destination—not least because they contained seriously inaccurate and misleading information. One particularly valuable nugget was the false claim he repeated in a letter dated 4 September 1914 that: 'great masses of Russian soldiers have passed through Edinburgh on their way to London and France ... it is estimated here that 60,000 men has passed, a number which seems greatly exaggerated. I went to the depot (station) and noticed trains passing through at high speed, blinds down. The landing in Scotland took place at Aberdeen.'

Travelling under an American passport in the name of 'Charles A. Inglis' and posing as an American tourist, Lody stayed in Edinburgh before travelling to Ireland. On his way to Ireland he passed through the thriving port of Liverpool, taking time to send his controllers his impressions. Like his previous missives, this was intercepted and it proved to contain information that, at a time of war, could be construed as genuinely sensitive. Lody's arrest was ordered. Apprehended in his hotel in Killarney, County Kerry, in October, he valiantly stuck to his Inglis cover story—which was gravely dented by the discovery in his jacket of a tailor's ticket bearing the name C. H. Lody and the address Job Steinberg, Berlin, N.W. Neustadtischer Kirchstr. 15.

The War Office was insistent that Lody be publicly tried by court martial at the earliest possible opportunity for 'war treason', an offence that was considered a 'war crime' and thus carried the death penalty. Found guilty, Lody was shot by firing squad in the Tower of London on 6 November 1914—the first German spy of the war to be executed. His patriotism and the bearing with which he conducted himself during the trial won not inconsiderable public admiration—and may account for the fact that subsequent trials were held in secret. 'I suppose that you will not care to shake hands with a German spy,' Lody reputedly said to the officer detailed with escorting him from his cell to the execution ground. 'No,' replied the officer, 'but I will shake hands with a brave man.'[14]

As the Western front became static, government concerns switched from monitoring the mobilization of German troops to the potential threat posed to munitions production. A series of accidental explosions at armaments factories in 1915 led the authorities to fear sabotage. On 16 February 1916, with the assistance of MI5, the Ministry of Munitions founded its own 'intelligence section' to vet 'aliens' employed in munitions factories and related industries. In March 1917 the unit, which had been christened the Ministry of Munitions Labour Intelligence Division (MMLI), was renamed the Parliamentary Military Secretary Department, no 2 section (PMS-2), an anodyne name deliberately designed to obscure its functions, which had come to include monitoring 'labour unrest'. The department was later reabsorbed into MI5 as A Branch, tasked with investigating industrial unrest, particularly in the shipyards of 'Red Clydeside'.

At the same time, MI5's work during the war had gradually evolved from detecting cases of espionage to actually impersonating one of the German agents it had captured and executed, and then feeding back false information to Germany, in a role that would prefigure perhaps the service's greatest triumph, the Double Cross system. It would be easy to exaggerate MI5's successes, however. On the one hand, there is the extent to which Kell's organization overreacted to the issue of 'enemy aliens'. Kell's own imagination had been fired by fantasies of

Le Queux and he had come firmly to believe in a vast interlocking German conspiracy that sought to subvert king and country. His judgement was not aided by the fact that MI5 had arisen out of the SSB, an organization that had been formed to counter a perceived German threat, not a real one.

Having failed to formulate a realistic appraisal of the threat posed by German espionage prior to the outbreak of war, MI5 then failed to conduct a more sober assessment on its outbreak. It is also worth noting that, despite the tens of thousands of names on the central registry, only 37 transpired to be genuine spies. Of these, all were treated with the utmost severity and 12 were secretly executed, mainly within the closed confines of the Tower of London. MI5 was also extremely lucky that its chief rival, Gustav Steinhauer's 'N' organization, a part of German naval intelligence, was equally deficient in exploiting MI5's weaknesses. In the opinion of one historian, German intelligence was so deficient that it 'would have failed regardless of the existence or non-existence of MI5'.

The post-war period

The end of the First World War saw MI5 at the peak of its organizational influence. By 1918 it had 844 members of staff (133 officers, the remainder support staff), divided into six branches: A—monitoring aliens; D—Imperial Overseas Intelligence including Ireland; E—Ports and Frontier Control; F—Preventative Security; G—Investigation; H—Secretariat and Administration. This change in both the scale and size exacerbated the need to coordinate the work of the various agencies, avoid duplication of effort and establish priorities. No longer was intelligence collected and analysed by two organizations—the Admiralty and the War Office—as it had been in 1900. Now MI5, SIS, the Government Code and Cipher School (GC&CS) and the intelligence branch of the RAF were involved, and the potential for overlap and confusion had dramatically increased.

Initially the role of monitoring fell to the Secret Service Committee, which first met in January 1919 under the chairmanship of Lord Curzon, the lord president of the council. Its terms of reference were to enquire into the current activities of the various secret service branches of government and to determine how best to organize this work. However, such coordination was relatively low priority. Day-to-day operations were conducted by the individual services as approved by ministers, with overall objectives set by the prime minister in discussion with cabinet colleagues. In practice, successive prime ministers preferred to keep intelligence matters at arms length, leaving questions of policy to be determined by the Secret Service Committee constituted specifically for the purpose.

The committee's final report, which was issued in February, praised the wartime contribution of the secret service, which had produced intelligence 'equal if not superior' to that obtained by any other country. The report also sounded critical notes over the 'overlapping of activity and responsibility' which ought to be reduced to a minimum, although it still recommended keeping the distinction between the military and civilian intelligence branches. The main thrust of the report, however, was concerned with countering the dangers of Bolshevism — which the committee believed threatened the very fabric of British society.[15] To address the perceived menace of international communism, the committee recommended the creation of a Directorate of Home Intelligence (DIHO)under Basil Thomson, assistant commissioner of police at Scotland Yard. The directorate proved to be short lived, lasting only two years before the hopeless confusion caused by Thomson's ego and turf wars with the police and MI5 led to its abolition.

The Secret Service Committee was reconvened in 1921, under the chairmanship of Sir Warren Fisher, permanent secretary to HM Treasury and head of the home civil service. Other members included Sir Eyre Crowe, permanent under-secretary at the Foreign Office and Sir Maurice Hankey, the cabinet secretary, and between them they sought to identify areas for budgetary savings at a time of financial stringency for all government departments. The committee met five times between May and June and issued its report in July. The main loser was Basil Thomson whose directorate was abolished; criticism was also directed at the War Office for its failure to identify any areas in which savings could be realized. The report was generally sympathetic to both MI5 and SIS, with the committee finding no sign of culpable extravagance or mismanagement and claiming to be 'unable to discover any point at which the secret intelligence organisation encroaches upon, or is encroached upon, by any other'. Despite these findings, the committee had to face economic realities, and it recommended that the secret vote be reduced by over a third from £475,000 to £300,000.

The cuts seemed harsh, but funding had to be justified in a climate of recession. The end of the First World War had seen off the threat of German espionage, and Irish republican terrorism also ceased to be a prime concern after the Irish civil war ended in 1923. The civil war had been a momentous conflict for the security services, throwing up one of British intelligence's greatest adversaries, Michael Collins, the director of intelligence for the Irish Republican Army (IRA).

Collins, whose surveillance file can be found at the National Archives, was born in Cork in 1890 and rose through the ranks of the Irish Republican Brotherhood (IRB) to play a part in the bloody Easter Rising of 1916. He was lucky not to have been executed when it failed, but was instead interned, whereupon he emerged as one of the leading figures in a small nationalist party called Sinn Fein. After his release he stood for parliament, and was duly elected as MP for West Cork.

His election and subsequent appointment as minister for finance, in January 1919, coincided with the outbreak of the civil war in Ireland. Secretly elected as both president of the IRB and IRA director of intelligence, Collins extensively penetrated the British establishment in Ireland, and in particular its intelligence centre at Dublin Castle. His objective was to blind the British to what was going on in the country, noting that 'Without her spies England is helpless'. His methods were brutal in their simplicity: as one of his hit men later recalled, 'two or three of us would go out with an [IRA] intelligence officer walking in front of us ... His job was to identify the man we were to shoot ... He would take off his hat and greet the marked man ... As soon as he did this we would shoot.'[16] The ruthless apogee of Collins's plan came on 21 November 1920—'Bloody Sunday'—with the simultaneous assassination of 14 British intelligence officers in Dublin—a triumph for the IRA and a disaster for British security services. Less than two years later, in August 1922, Collins was killed during an ambush by an opposing Republican faction in County Cork. Ironically, the Special Operations Executive (chapter 6) would later use many of the irregular warfare methods he pioneered in their own guerrilla war against the Nazis.

In the aftermath of both conflicts MI5 experienced swingeing cuts and saw staffing numbers plummet; by 1929 its staff levels were reduced to 16 'officers and civilian officials'. Its fortunes were to be revived, however—though this might not have been apparent at the time—by events in Russia.

'Reds under the bed'

In March 1919, the Third International established the Comintern, with the stated aim of fomenting world revolution. The affiliation of the Communist Party of Great Britain (CPGB) to this organization in

August 1920 raised the spectre of a political party dedicated to seizing power in Britain through the same revolutionary methods. Despite such worries, MI5's monitoring of the Bolshevik threat was initially constrained, domestic 'subversion' being the preserve of Special Service Department (SSD) of the CID. Since 1913, the SSD had been led by the assistant commissioner of the Metropolitan Police, Sir Basil Thomson, a former assistant premier of Tonga and governor of Wormwood Scrubs. As MI5 did not have the power of arrest, it had fallen to Thomson and CID to arrest and interrogate spies detected by MI5, though officers of the latter were often present. As MI5's official history dryly noted, this division of labour caused a certain amount of rivalry and jealously and 'may therefore be said to have had marked disadvantages'.

Appointed DIHO head in 1919, Thomson added the Home Office's Special Irish Secret Service to his intelligence portfolio the following year, taking control of monitoring Irish Republican activity. For its part, MI5 was confined to monitoring Bolshevism in the armed forces, the unit appearing parochial in comparison with Thomson's far more vibrant work combating domestic 'revolutionary movements' in the wake of the Bolshevik revolution.[17] Unlike Kell, who preferred anonymity, Thomson relished the limelight, often examining agents himself and revelling in his status as a 'spy catcher'. His tenure as Britain's security supremo was brief, however. In 1921 he 'retired' after losing Lloyd George's confidence and in 1925 was arrested and fined for committing an act of indecency with the splendidly named Miss Thelma de Lava. In the aftermath of Thomson's fall from grace it was Kell who filled the void, taking control of both domestic and military security.

Without the spectre of Communism stalking the land it is doubtful whether MI5 would have continued to exist. Fears of Communist subversion grew to be conceived of in similar terms to the 'invasion' fear rampant at the turn of the century. The security services themselves detected the hidden hand of Communism seemingly everywhere, including behind the General Strike of 1926. And yet in their frantic search for 'reds under the bed' MI5 proved surprisingly pedestrian in its choice of subjects to investigate: the Labour movement, the armed forces and the CPGB, which never had more than 17,500 members between its foundation in 1921 and 1940, and certainly no more in the post-war period prior to its demise in 1991. To their eternal embarrassment, MI5 ignored early reports of Communist activity in British universities. This was a failure that was to haunt them in the form of the 'Cambridge Five'. Indeed, the problem of gauging Soviet intentions was never resolved.

As the intelligence community, with the assistance of MI6, began investigating the Soviet presence in their midst so, too, did the Soviets begin watching the watchers. Recently released files show that intelligence operations were in fact compromised from the outset: two Special Branch officers, Sergeant Charles Jane and Inspector Hubert van Ginhoven, had been recruited to Soviet intelligence by W. N. Ewer, foreign editor of the *Daily Herald*. Between 1919 and 1929 Ewer was perhaps the pivotal figure in Soviet intelligence operations in London, which he orchestrated through the Federated Press of America, a Soviet 'front' organization. Both Jane and van Ginhoven were dismissed from the police force in April 1929, though their files reveal an interest in the pair until 1950, noting that Jane in particular, regarded by the service as 'an ardent Communist at heart', had fallen upon hard times after his dismissal.[18]

Throughout the 1920s and 1930s the security services focused their attentions on the CPGB, led by Harry Pollitt.[19] In May 1921 Special Branch raided the CPGB offices at 16 King Street, Covent Garden, arresting its secretary, Albert Inkpin, and confiscating several tons of documentation. Inkpin was charged with having illegally procured the National Labour Press Ltd to print the 'Theses of the Communist International', deemed likely to cause sedition and disaffection under the terms of the Emergency Regulations, 1921.

One event with potentially more serious ramifications for the intelligence services occurred on 12 May 1927, when 150 officers of the Metropolitan Police and Special Branch, acting on a tip-off, raided the premises of the All-Russian Co-operative Society (ARCOS), at 49 Moorgate Street, Moorgate, London. The impetus behind the raid came from a disaffected ex-employee of ARCOS who informed officials that a classified War Office training manual had been photocopied at its offices. This and other intelligence convinced the authorities that ARCOS was a front for Soviet espionage. The building, which also housed the offices of the Russian Trade Delegation, was raided with the express permission of the home secretary, Sir Williams Joynson-Hicks, who commanded MI5: 'raid ARCOS; do you want that in writing?'

On entering the building the police discovered officials hastily burning papers and a mass of documents were seized. Foreign Office interpreters aided Special Branch officers in rigorously poring over the seizure and MI5 was left in no doubt that 'members of ARCOS and the Russian Trade Delegation are directing and carrying on the work of *military espionage* and *subversive propaganda* from 49 Moorgate'.[20]

The immediate success of the raid, however, was more than out-weighed by the intelligence disaster that followed in its wake (p. 250). In the aftermath of the raid the Bolsheviks were alerted to the fact that their diplomatic traffic was being read, leading them to adopt 'one-time pads' for their communications, which defied the attentions of British cryptanalysts for some years to come.

The raid's impact was also disastrous in other ways. In the end no evidence of espionage was found, and the resultant acrimony led to a break in diplomatic relations with Moscow. The whole affair brought the shortcomings of British intelligence, in particular its coordination (or lack of it), into sharp relief, and the Secret Service Committee was asked to look into the affair. Hugh Sinclair, director of SIS, saw a renewed opportunity to press his case for greater unification of the intelligence agencies, especially Special Branch, and submitted a long memorandum on the case 'showing the danger which is caused by the absence of any central control or authority, in matters of this sort'. The committee, however, remained unwilling to take the action recom-mended by Sinclair, believing that 'cooperation had been good on the detective plane, although there had been some impetuosity higher up.'

ARCOS grabbed the headlines, but the Secret Service Committee had interrupted other investigations to review it, and several problems remained unresolved. Although the committee had decided against drastic reorganization after a series of meetings held through 1925, it still had concerns about Scotland Yard's role in the intelligence world, in particular the function of the Special Branch sections SS1 and SS2, whose business was liaison with the agencies.[21] There was concern that in monitoring the activities of Labour activists and Trade Union officials, the police might be perceived as working for the interests of the Conservative government. This prospect led Baldwin to reconvene the Secret Service Committee early in 1927 to discuss the activities of Special Branch, including the proposal that SS1 and SS2 might be transferred to SIS.

During the 1930s, MI5 and Special Branch maintained files on tens of thousands of individuals. And while MI5 has released many of its PF (personal) files to the National Archives, Special Branch has proved markedly more reluctant to release its own files on individuals, many of which appear to have been routinely destroyed. One of the few Spe-cial Branch files open to public scrutiny is that covering the author of *Animal Farm* and *Nineteen Eighty-Four*.[22] The files at the National Archives reveal that on 22 February 1936 Wigan police contacted

Special Branch to ask for help in establishing the identity of one 'Eric A. Blair or George Orwell' ('about 35yrs, slim build, long pale face') and in ascertaining whether he was known to be associated with the CPGB. Orwell had aroused the local constabulary's suspicions by attending a Communist meeting on the day of his arrival and by reading what appeared to be a foreign Communist newspaper. He was known to be staying in a poor part of town, was in receipt of 'an unusual amount of correspondence' and had been seen collecting 'an amount of local data'. The letter suggested, 'from his mode of living [it would appear] he is an author, or has some connection with literary work as he devotes most of his time in writing'. Orwell was at the time researching his book on the conditions of the working classes in the north, *The Road to Wigan Pier*.

The chief constable's letter prompted a four-page Special Branch report, which established that Orwell was a nom de plume and that the author himself was the Eton-educated son of a former Indian civil servant. It noted that he had served for a time in the Indian police service, before moving to France where he had worked as a freelance journalist, living rough for a period while he researched his book *Down and Out in Paris and London*. In terms of his politics, he was known to have taken an interest in the activities of the French Communist party, but information was not yet available to show whether he was 'an active supporter of the revolutionary movement in France'.

By 1942, Special Branch's opinion of Orwell seems to have hardened. A further report, dated 20 January of that year, drew attention to the fact that he dressed 'in a bohemian fashion both at his office and in his leisure hours', before baldly stating that 'this man has advanced Communist views' — the latter prompting a question mark to be added to the margin of the document by MI5. Indeed, Orwell's MI5 file, which is preserved at the National Archives alongside that compiled by Special Branch, begins with the following note:

> In view of the report at serial 7a which rather contradicts the impression given by Orwell's writings, I spoke to Inspector Gill of Special Branch asking whether his Sergeant could elaborate on the question of Blair's 'advanced Communist views'. Mr. Gill rang me up this morning to say that Serg. Ewing described Blair as being 'an unorthodox Communist' apparently holding many of their views but by no means subscribing fully to the Party's policy. I gathered that the good Sergeant was rather at a loss as to how he could describe this rather individual line, hence the expression 'advanced Communist views'. This fits in

with the picture we have of Blair/Orwell. It is evident from his recent writings, 'The Lion and the Unicorn' and his contribution to Gollancz's symposium, 'The Betrayal of the Left', that he does not hold with the Communist Party nor they with him.[23]

While both Special Branch and MI5 kept Orwell under surveillance up to the time of his death in 1950, MI5 recognized that his views were a long way removed from orthodox Communism. They thus made no attempt to bar his employment with the BBC in 1941 or to prevent him working as a correspondent to the allied forces.

The long game

The security services monitored extremist revolutionary organizations using a variety of methods, including the use of paid informers, augmenting their knowledge through the active penetration of such organizations with their own agents. MI5's chief 'agent runner' was Charles Maxwell Knight, head of MS Section, later to become known to millions of young radio listeners as 'Uncle Max' through his natural history programmes for the BBC.[24] Recruited to MI5 by Kell in 1925, Knight had been intelligence director of the British Fascisti, a group founded by Miss Linton Orman to 'combat Red influences in the country and Empire'. Knight would maintain his membership until 1930, two years before the majority of the party transferred their allegiance to Sir Oswald Mosley's British Union of Fascists (BUF). During the course of his career, Knight came to the conclusion that there was 'a very long standing and ill-founded prejudice against the employment of women as agents'—one that he felt held little water, though he was no believer in 'Mata Hari methods'. Indeed, many of his most effective agents were women, including Joan Miller, who penetrated the anti-Semitic underworld of British Fascism, and Olga Gray, whom he infiltrated into the CPGB in 1931.

Gray in particular proved an astute choice. Beautiful and resourceful, the 19-year-old Gray succeeded in gaining the trust of senior officials within the CPGB, including Percy Glading and Harry Pollitt, its general secretary. To maintain her cover, Knight insisted she move only at the invitation of the party itself. This came in June 1934, when Pollitt used her as a courier to take documents given to her by Glading to Indian Communist leaders. This was followed in February 1935 by an invitation to become Pollitt's personal secretary. Though ill health forced her to resign not long afterwards, Gray maintained her social contacts with both men, which was to prove invaluable. In February 1937, Glading invited her to take a flat in London, rent-free, which he would use from time to time to develop photographs of—it transpired —classified documents pilfered from the Woolwich Arsenal by Glading's associates. Gray agreed. 'Mr Peters' (senior Soviet agent Theodore Maly) then arrived to vet her. Having suitably impressed 'Mr Peters', she was cleared to assist Glading and his espionage ring. They were arrested on 21 January 1938. In court Gray, who was identified only as 'Miss X', provided watertight testimony against her 'comrades'. Although now fatally compromised, her seven years as an MI5 'sleeper' agent had not been wasted. Glading was sentenced to six years' hard labour for breaching the Official Secrets Act.[25]

Although the Woolwich Arsenal case was a success, it was a success of a low order. Only minnows had been caught in the net. The larger fish, including Maly, escaped the dragnet—though not Stalin's paranoia. ?
Having returned to Moscow in June 1937, Maly was 'liquidated' during the purges. On the other side of the balance sheet was the connected case of John Herbert King, revealed in his fascinating files at the National Archives (plates 4 and 5). King was recruited and run by the flamboyant Dutch artist and architect Henri Christiaan Pieck— who had himself become a member of the Soviet Intelligence Service (the GPU) after a visit to Moscow in 1929. Pieck was subsequently charged with penetrating the British Foreign Office, a longstanding target of Soviet espionage; his task appears to have been simplified by the department's near total lack of internal security. In 1930 the Soviets had gained access to large quantities of telegrams and code books following a 'walk-in' at the Soviet embassy in Paris—by a debt-ridden, alcoholic cipher clerk, thoroughly unsuitable as an agent. King, however, was a different kettle of fish and the two files covering his case at the National Archives provide a fascinating insight into the workings of the GPU.

With a view to working up a connection with members of the Foreign Office, Pieck was established in Geneva, where he set about trying to create an introduction to the various Foreign Office delegations to the League of Nations. These attempts extended to hiring a room above that of the British vice consul and dropping a silver pencil on to his balcony. His break came when a hard-up British subject approached him for a loan, allowing him to go to the consulate and ask whether the man was 'all right' for the money. For the next two and a half years, according to a subsequent report titled 'Leakage from the Communications Department', Pieck 'sedulously and with considerable success' cultivated the British official community:

> With the thoroughness in detail characteristic of the G.P.U. he wormed his way into the acquaintance and even affections of a considerable number of British officials and successfully allayed suspicion by posing as the prince of good fellows, habitué of the International Club, always 'good' for a drink, a motor expedition, or a free meal—a histrionic effort worthy of a better cause.[26]

Pieck became well known for the freedom with which he distributed his money, a point highlighted in the report, which estimated that his entertaining had cost the GPU the 'not inconsiderable sum' of £20,000. One of those into whose affections Pieck insinuated himself was cipher officer R. C. Oake, whom he met at the International Club in late 1933. To Oake he was a 'likeable, big-hearted and rather simple fellow', something of a playboy and a 'good mixer', who had come to Geneva to gain commissions to paint portraits. Through him, Pieck met King, whom he quickly identified as a suitable target. Pieck followed King back to London and, through an introduction from Oake, established a legitimate business in Buckingham Gate that would be the front for his activities. It was at this point that he fully ensnared King. According to a report by an unnamed former agent, in which King is referred to as 'X':

> Pieck got hold of him by saying that the Dutch Banks had formed a bank amongst themselves which bank had the aims of investing monies abroad and catering for loans. For these ends they had to have forward political information. Pieck offered X a number of shares in the Bank, and a sum of money if he would just give him tit-bits of information about what was going to happen. That might have sounded very innocent to a man like X. The information X was giving was not very important to that man. As Pieck was well introduced I suppose he fell for this. He was given shares, printed for the purpose, and £500 a month. Pieck has been able to get hold of weekly bulletins, which he calls weeklies and monthlies. They were marked 'Secret. To be returned to H.M. Government'—and Pieck finally got X to work. He has met him not only in London. Pieck has actually been inside the F.O. with X. He himself instructed X to use a Leica camera. [27]

In 1936 Pieck was recalled to Moscow and was replaced with the doomed Theodore Maly, whom King later descried as 'a very tall, cadaverous man of about 40'. Maly ran him until his own abrupt—

and fatal—recall to Moscow the following year. Unlike the professional tradecraft displayed by MI5 in dismantling the Woolwich Arsenal spy ring, King was unmasked largely by chance. Following his defection to the West, Colonel Walter Krivitsky published an article in New York's *Saturday Evening Post* alleging that a man named King, who worked in the Foreign Office Communications Department, was a Soviet spy. MI5 was initially dubious, though King was placed on a three-week sick leave. On 25 September 1939 he was asked by Detective Inspector William Rogers of Special Branch to account for £1,300 deposited in a Chancery Lane safe deposit box. King made a statement, largely to exonerate his mistress, claiming 'it is mostly the proceeds from gambling'. On 28 September, however, King changed his story:

> I am not a permanent civil servant and am not entitled to a pension.
> I felt that by this means I could obtain some money to provide for
> when I retired without in any way endangering the security of the
> State. I handed to Pieck, from time to time, copies of telegrams coming
> in from Embassies—for example, reports of conversations between
> Hitler and Sir Neville Henderson or between Kemal Ataturk and the
> ambassador in Turkey or some such persons. There were sometimes
> eight or nine pages of roneoed matter—sometimes three or four—
> never more than ten. They were never of any great political import-
> ance. The telegrams were always decoded copies, and never in cipher.
> They were spare copies that were available in the room.[28]

The authorities took a far dimmer view of his actions (plate 6). King was charged under section 2 (1) of the Official Secrets Act (1911). He pleaded guilty and was sentenced at the Central Criminal Court in October 1939 to 10 years' imprisonment, a conclusion that Kell described as 'satisfactory' in a letter to Air Vice Marshal Sir Philip Game of New Scotland Yard.[29]

Throughout this period MI5 was helped in its attempts to prevent Soviet penetration of the British establishment by a combination of strong anti-aliens legislation and the strictures of passport control. Both of these significantly hindered the operation of agents for prolonged periods of time. Added to this was the paranoia of the Stalinist system itself, which scored a series of spectacular own goals, liquidating many of its best agents and exiling an even greater number to the gulags as the revolution consumed its own children. Others such as Walter Krivitsky and Alexander Orlov, who refused to go meekly to their fate, simply defected, providing a further boon to MI5 and SIS (though Krivitsky soon committed suicide).[30] The net effect of Stalin's evisceration of the Soviet intelligence system was that for prolonged and crucial periods prior to and during the Second World War those agents who had been infiltrated successfully were left to their own devices.

The Nazi menace

MI5 maintained its focus on the Communist threat for most of the 1930s, despite the rise of Nazi Germany. Indeed, MI5 officers even visited the newly installed Nazi regime in 1933 to peruse some of the material seized after the Nazis had stormed Karl Liebknecht House, headquarters of the German Communist Party.[31] Domestically MI5 did not begin issuing monthly intelligence reports on Mosley's BUF, which had grown significantly, until April 1934.[32] They were hampered in this work, however, by the refusal of the Home Office to grant intercept warrants for senior Fascist leaders (granted for Robert Gordon-Canning in 1938 and Archibald Findlay in 1939), despite evidence that Mosley was receiving regular payments from Mussolini.

The problems presented by the rise of Nazi Germany (and to a lesser extent Mussolini's Fascist Italy) were myriad, ranging from a lack of intelligence about the Nazi party and Hitler's general intentions to the question of actual German espionage and the activities of German *Ausland* organizations, all of which were closely scrutinized by B Division. MI5 gained much useful intelligence from contacts in touch with the Nazi propaganda ministry through the German embassy in London, which it had succeeded in penetrating through the recruitment of several of its officers, including the press attaché Jona 'Klop' Ustinov, father of the actor Peter Ustinov, as well as the embassy counsellor Theodor Kordt and the junior embassy secretary, Wolfgang zu Putlitz.[33] Major coups, such as learning of the Nazis' decision to invade Prague several days beforehand, were deadened by the inability of the British state to put this information to any practical use.

In fact, the overwhelming volume of raw intelligence flooding into Whitehall not just from MI5 but from all its intelligence structures soon became a major problem. This had led to the formation in 1936 of the Joint Intelligence Committee (JIC), the purpose of which was to make sense of it all. It was the JIC that designated Nazi Germany the 'ultimate enemy'. Despite this belated realization what emerges, however, is a general failure across the breadth of the British intelligence community to appreciate both the logical conclusions of Nazi ideology and the threat it posed.

May 1940 and the subsequent fall of France occasioned a security revolution. The chiefs of staff hurriedly convened a grim-faced meeting on 27 May, concluding that Britain could carry on the war without France but only so long as civilian morale held. Consequently they recommended that potential 'fifth columnists' be dealt with harshly. Churchill's cabinet accepted the recommendations without question, establishing, as an offshoot of the Home Defence Executive—itself founded to ensure the prompt meeting of military needs during wartime—the Home Defence (Security) Executive (HD(S)E).[34] Chaired by former air minister Lord Swinton, the object of HD(S)E was, 'principally to consider questions relating to defence against the 5th Column and to ensure action'.

The foundation of HD(S)E coincided with the circulation of Lord Hankey's report on MI5, which urged that 'the fullest possible weight' be given to MI5's recommendations to counter subversion.[35] MI5, however, was ill prepared for the task in hand. At the end of 1938 it had 30 officers and 103 administrative and registry staff, all of whom laboured under an intense workload, vetting personnel and chasing the largely chimerical 'fifth column'. Its surveillance section had a mere six men. Maxwell Knight's MS Section was similarly restricted, with only 14 agents operating within 'subversive' organizations in 1939; while as late as July 1939 Special Branch had a fleet of only four cars with which to cover the entire Metropolitan Police district—and one of these, a Hillman Minx, was being rented from a private car hire firm. These were hardly ideal circumstances as British intelligence struggled to cope not only with an impending world war, but also with a sudden flurry of IRA activity across the capital.

With fears of invasion imminent, MI5 lobbied for action to be taken against the potential 'fifth column' activities of the BUF and its leader. During this period MI5 had other subversive organizations under investigation, including the Right Club. This anti-Semitic and pro-Fascist organization was led by Captain A. H. Maule Ramsay, Conservative MP for Peebles. His activities, together with those of the Russian émigré Anna Wolfkoff and Tyler Gatewood Kent—a cipher clerk at the US embassy—served as a trigger both for their own arrest and for the internment of Mosley and his key deputies on 22 May under Defence Regulation 18B (1A). They were joined by hundreds of British fascists as the Nazi threat to Britain appeared at its most grave. It was the end of the line for British Fascism. Although the majority were released by 1941, and Mosley himself in November 1943, British Fascists continued to be monitored for the remainder of the war by regional security liaison officers (RSLOs), who maintained 'suspect lists' of those to be detained in the event of an invasion until September 1944.[36] In the immediate aftermath of the war British Fascism (and indeed British Communism) remained under intense scrutiny.

The main victim of the security revolution was Kell who, after 31 years in charge of MI5, was summarily 'retired' by Churchill, on the advice of Lord Swinton, as was his faithful deputy Sir Eric Holt-Wilson. The task of rebuilding MI5 fell to Sir David Petrie, a former head of Indian Political Intelligence (IPI). Petrie was regarded as an exceptional man-manager and under his stewardship MI5 expanded, as it had done during the First World War, to 868 staff (634 of whom were women), including 233 officers. However, although Petrie had agreed to the position on the basis that he would be 'master of his own house', this was not entirely the case. The wartime diaries of Guy Liddell, Head of B Division, reveal that throughout the war MI5 was periodically riven by internal tensions—not to mention jealousy over the encroachment of a burgeoning group of competing agencies, including the Special Operations Executive (SOE) and the Political Warfare Executive (PWE). A greater challenge to its organizational autonomy was presented, however, by the suggestion, made in 1942, that the majority of B Division should be transferred to reinforce Section V of SIS, led by Valentine 'Vee Vee' Vivian, thus forming a new organization, the Directorate of Counter-Espionage (DOCE).

Further tensions between MI5 and SIS arose over the management of the Twenty Committee and the Radio Security Service (p. 253). MI5 also found itself having to liaise with a plethora of foreign allied intelligence services, including officers from the French Deuxième Bureau exiled in London, officers from the Russian NKVD, and, not least, the operations of the British Security Co-ordination (BSC) in New York. MI5, through seconded security officer John Senter, also played a vital role in providing security for the newly formed—and, within the intelligence community, frequently disparaged—SOE, the secret sabotage and subversion apparatus created by Churchill in the darkest years of the war.

Camp 020 and the Royal Patriotic School

The 'fifth column' panic prompted the establishment of two secret security establishments in which MI5 could interrogate recalcitrant

British Fascists, captured Nazi spies and suspect refugees. These were Camp 020, at Latchmere House on Ham Common, Richmond, which was opened in July 1940, and a reserve detention centre, Camp 020R, at Huntercombe Place, Oxfordshire. The former was run by the formidable Colonel R. W. G. 'Tin Eye' Stephens, a former Indian Army officer seconded to MI5 in 1939.

Although the wholesale internment of the majority of 'alien' refugees was doubtless an overreaction, there was little doubt that the Nazis were attempting to infiltrate spies. The first of these arrived in September 1940 and 'the real work began', noted MI5 historian John Curry. From then until 12 November some 14 enemy agents landed in Britain, while another seven surrendered on arrival (plate 7). MI5 had little problem rounding up these agents, of whom five were subsequently executed and another committed suicide, while three became part of the Double Cross system (p. 41). Only one, a Czech intelligence officer working for the Gestapo called 'Wilhelm Moerz' (Werner Mikkelsen), described by MI5 as 'undoubtedly one of the cleverest secret agents the Germans have at the present time', is believed to have eluded capture. MI5 officially gave up looking for him in 1941.[37] The initial failure of the Abwehr to insert agents into Britain led its leader, Admiral Wilhelm Canaris, to begin experimenting with mixing his agents in amongst the many genuine refugees fleeing Nazi-occupied Europe.

Alongside the internment of leading British Fascists in 1940, Churchill famously ordered the wholesale internment of 26,000 alien refugees—the majority of whom had fled persecution in continental Europe—with the words 'collar the lot'. Churchill soon executed a volte-face, rounding on the 'witch-finding activities' of MI5, which he himself had instigated. The HD(S)E then required MI5 to vet the tens of thousands of internees with a view to their release, placing an intolerable strain on its meagre resources. However, the blunt tool of internment proved strikingly effective. By the end of 1940, Petrie noted that 'practically every potentially dangerous person, whether British or foreign, had been swept into the net'. Non-enemy aliens meanwhile had to convince the authorities they had every reason to be in Britain. However, the conditions in which these security measures were undertaken were rudimentary: interviews with Port Security Control 'examiners' were conducted wherever space could be found.

To cope with the flood of paper occasioned by the internment, interrogation and release or detention of thousands of foreign refugees (many of who were Communists and thus monitored by F2B, the section concerned with foreign Communist and Trotskyist movements), the British authorities established a network of clandestine interrogation centres to weed out potential enemy agents. This situation was remedied on 10 January 1941 with the establishment by the HD(S)E of the Royal Patriotic School (RPS), also known as the Royal Victoria Patriotic School, a reception and processing centre for all aliens, who were legally required to attend after disembarking.[38] The RPS operated on two sites: Trinity Road, Wandsworth, for men, and nearby Nightingale Lane for women. As well as weeding out possible enemy agents and obtaining useful recruits, the RPS allowed information to be gleaned in a systematic manner from refuges on conditions prevailing within Nazi-occupied Europe.

MI5 regarded the RPS 'not as a detention camp, but as a comfortable and well equipped centre' and stated in March 1941 that 'the conditions there should be as good as they can possibly be made'. In October 1942 it was reorganized into the London Reception Centre (LRC) and although nominally under Home Office control was operated by officers from MI5's section B1D, processing some 33,000 individuals during the course of its existence. MI5, and more specifically B Division, was determined to detect and prevent the penetration of British intelligence organizations through the RPS/LRC and liaised closely with SIS, SOE and the LRC to prevent such an occurrence. Such was the scrutiny that a dedicated MI5 officer was given the job of liaising with SOE, with a brief to monitor the arrival of returning SOE officers who had not passed through the LRC but who might have been turned to 'play back' to German intelligence.[39]

Double Cross

Perhaps the greatest of MI5's wartime successes was the Double Cross or Twenty Committee, chaired by the historian John Masterman, provost of Worcester College, Oxford (1946–61), who had been Dick White's tutor. White, a senior MI5 officer, became the only man to head both MI5 and MI6. The pivotal role played by the Twenty Committee was a closely guarded secret and only became public knowledge in 1972, following the publication of Masterman's book *The Double Cross System*. The book, which was actually Masterman's internal report on running double agents, had been written for the director general of MI5 following the end of the war.[40]

The Twenty Committee, which was founded in January 1941, was a subcommittee of the W Committee, which aimed:

> To keep our agents sufficiently well fed with accurate information so as not to lose the confidence of the enemy;
>
> To control as many of the agents in this country as we can, in order to make [the enemy] feel that the ground is covered and they need not send any more of whose arrival we might not be aware;
>
> By careful manoeuvring of these agents and a careful study of the questionnaires, to mislead the enemy on a big scale at the appropriate moment.[41]

The Twenty Committee was tasked with carrying out day-to-day oversight to ensure this goal. It was a startling success. Indeed, within a short space of time MI5 could boast that 'we actively ran and controlled the German espionage system in this country'.

Once an enemy agent had been 'turned' by the interrogators of the LRC and Camp 020 he or she was handed over to the Special Agents Section (B1A) run by Colonel Thomas Argyll 'Tar' Robinson, under whose watchful eye the double agents would do their best 'to mislead the enemy, and perhaps deflect his plans, by handing out false information'. Ultimately MI5 operated a total of 120 double agents during the course of the Second World War, though some were of no great import. In this task Robinson worked closely with the Twenty Committee, which in turn utilized British intelligence's ability to read Nazi wireless traffic to deadly effect in deceiving the Nazis about British intentions.

The greatest triumph of the Double Cross system was undoubtedly Juan Pujol Garcia, a young Spaniard (plate 8). He had volunteered his services to the British during the war, though the British authorities were reluctant to have anything to do with him. So Pujol took it upon himself to become a German agent, practising numerous deceptions on them in the process, with the ultimate intention of being a more tangible asset to the British. Eventually, after a number of approaches, the British finally accepted him in 1942, though not before a wrangle between MI5 and MI6 as to whose asset he should be. Code-named Garbo (Bovril by MI6), Pujol and his MI5 case officer Tomás Harris wove an intricate web of deception. Together they invented a network of fictitious agents and fed the German High Command a carefully constructed trail of false intelligence that misled them for years (plates 9 and 10). His greatest coup, however, came with Operation Bodyguard and its attendant Fortitude deception plans to divert the German military's attention away from the Normandy beaches and towards Pas de Calais during the D-Day landings of 6 June 1944.

Garbo radioed his controller stating that 'it is perfectly clear that the present operation, though a large-scale assault, is diversionary in character'. His intervention made a significant contribution to the success of Operation Overlord. The 1st SS and 116th Panzer divisions, then on their way to Normandy, were redirected towards Calais. A measure of his success could be found in the confidence the Germans retained in his information, awarding him the Iron Cross on 29 July 1944.[42] On 21 December Pujol was awarded an MBE, followed by lunch at the Savoy. 'I think he was extremely pleased,' noted Liddell in his diary.[43] It certainly placed Pujol in the novel situation of being one of the few people ever to have been awarded such distinction by both sides.

The Cold War

After 1945 MI5 was left to tie up many of its loose ends, such as chasing Fascist renegades. Many of them were former members of Mosley's BUF, who were at large in Europe and who were to be brought home to face justice—though very few, with the exception of William Joyce who broadcast for the Nazis as 'Lord Haw Haw' and John Amery, the son of Churchill's friend and fellow cabinet minister Leopold Amery, were to pay the ultimate price for their treachery.

As the war drew to a close MI5 was faced with processing a mass of captured intelligence officers, 'stay-behind' agents and 'line crossers'. Those who had fought on the Eastern front were particularly eagerly sought for the intelligence they could provide about the capabilities of the former Soviet ally as hot war began its inexorable slide into Cold War. The detainees were initially taken to Camp 020, which proved increasingly inexpedient, leading to the establishment of two forward interrogation centres. One was in Dienst, near Brussels, alias 1 Det. CSDIC (Combined Services Detailed Interrogation Centre [UK]), 'a medieval sort of place ... with dungeons and moats and excellently suited for the purpose', which was founded in November 1944. This existed until 30 September 1945 when it was absorbed into no. 74 CSDIC (WEA) (Combined Services Detailed Interrogation Centre [Western European Area]), a converted bath-house in the spa town of Bad Nenndorf, near Hanover, which had been established in June 1945. The centre closed soon afterwards, and has been dogged ever since by allegations of mistreatment and torture. The facility was at the forefront of gathering intelligence during the early onset of the Cold War and many senior Nazis, including figures such as Gestapo intelligence officer Horst Kopkow, who had led the investigation into Die Rote Kapelle (The Red Orchestra—p. 78) and Rote Drei (Red Three), passed through its doors.[44]

The end of the war saw further rumblings about the proposed unification of British intelligence, the proposal that MI5 and SIS should share headquarters and suggestions that the Metropolitan Police should take over certain MI5 functions.[45] Although MI5 saw off these challenges it could not escape the imposition of a new director general, on 30 April 1946, in the form of Sir Percy Sillitoe, a senior policeman. Not everyone within MI5 greeted his appointment with equanimity. Although Liddell was elevated to deputy director general, 'Tar' Robinson, the mastermind behind the Double Cross operation, resigned, moving to Government Communications Headquarters (GCHQ). Further changes stemmed from the report submitted by the cabinet secretary, Sir Norman Brook, in March 1951, which recommended that henceforth MI5 should be subordinate to the home secretary.

Spy versus spy

The discovery in the aftermath of the war that scientists Allan Nunn May and Klaus Fuchs had been selling nuclear secrets to the Soviets, together with the unearthing of the Cambridge spy ring (p. 81), created panic on both sides of the Atlantic. In America, the near-hysteria ushered in the era of virulent anti-Communism most associated with Senator Joseph McCarthy and the House Un-American Activities Committee. Britain was spared the worst excesses of the anti-Communist witch-hunts, but behind the scenes the government acted quickly, authorizing MI5 to begin systematically vetting potential civil servants. This built on the procedures established in May 1946 when Labour prime minister Clement Attlee established the secret GEN 183 committee on 'subversive activities' to weed out Communists and Fascists from sensitive civil service positions. This process of 'positive vetting' was conducted by C Division, which liaised with similar security units in the Foreign Office, led by George Carey-Foster, and the Commonwealth Relations Office, led by Sir Phillip Vickery. Stung by the activities of Nunn, May and Fuchs (p. 227), the Atomic Energy Authority was already alive to the threat and had appointed Liddell as its security adviser after his retirement from MI5. Between 1948 and 1955, 167 civil servants were removed from their posts, 25 were dismissed, 24 resigned, 88 were transferred to non-sensitive work and 33 were eventually reinstated. Attlee robustly defended MI5 against the withering criticisms of its detractors, but could not disguise the fact that the damage had already been done.

The various spy scandals of the early 1950s led some to conclude that the British intelligence services had been penetrated at the highest level. This belief led to the establishment of the joint MI5/MI6 Fluency Committee, which embarked upon a morale-sapping internal 'mole hunt', focusing upon White's successor as director general in 1956, Sir Roger Hollis. Questioned as to whether Hollis was a Soviet agent, KGB defector Oleg Gordievsky replied: 'Of course not. But when the KGB saw the chaos caused by the allegations against Hollis, their laughter made Red Square shake.' Although Hollis was eventual cleared by the Trend inquiry, the stigma continued to hang over the service like a pall. Indeed, his immediate successor, Martin Furnival Jones, inherited a service deeply demoralized. In 1977, in an attempt to reinvigorate the service, prime minister James Callaghan introduced a major overhaul of MI5's recruitment procedures.

Not everything was doom and gloom, however. The 1960s witnessed a number of important counter-espionage coups for MI5, leading to the imprisonment of MI6 double agent George Blake, though he later escaped from Wormwood Scrubs on 22 October 1966, re-emerging in Moscow, where his exploits were much feted.[46] Equally significant were the arrest of Admiralty clerk John Vassall, and the detection in 1961 of the Portland spy ring that through Harry Houghton, a former sailor and civil servant employed by the Admiralty Underwater Weapons Establishment, was gaining intelligence on a hitherto top secret Royal Navy facility (p. 134). Surveillance revealed that Houghton passed the information to 'Canadian businessman' Gordon Lonsdale (Konon Trofimovich Molody), who in turn passed it on to an antiquarian bookseller and his wife, Peter and Helen Kroger. Sentenced to long terms of imprisonment, Lonsdale and the Krogers were later exchanged for British citizens held by the Russians.[47]

Between 1960 and 1970 investigation of Soviet intelligence activities led to the conviction of 12 British subjects, with a number of others avoiding prosecution. One of the most infamous was the chief technician Douglas Britten, who in 1968 was sentenced to 21 years in prison for passing highly secret information to his Soviet controller, Alexander Ivanovich Borisenko, counsellor in the Cultural Department of the Soviet embassy, who returned to Russia shortly after the arrest. Sentencing Britten, Mr Justice Davies stated that the information he had

passed on could undermine 'and to some extent already had undermined the defence of this country and might in certain eventualities
endanger every man, woman and child'.

This counter-subversion effort continued throughout the decade,
focusing increasingly on the detrimental activities of Soviet diplomats
in Britain. Numbering 150 (including working wives), this figure was
higher than in any other country in the Western world, with the exception of the United Nations in New York. A handful of diplomats were
expelled, but not on a scale that prompted the remainder to curtail
their activities. The British government periodically made discreet
approaches to the Soviet Union about the scale of 'unacceptable' activity in the United Kingdom, but with no tangible effect. The defection
of a member of the Soviet Trade Delegation, Oleg Lyalin, precipitated
by his arrest on a drink-driving charge, gave British intelligence not
just a window on the identity of their intelligence counterparts 'but, in
addition, he provided carefully documented evidence of planning for
sabotage in times of tension'.

The revelations infuriated the prime minister, Edward Heath, who
summoned a high-level meeting attended by Furnival Jones and his
counterpart in SIS, Sir John Rennie. In framing a response, Furnival
Jones agreed that the current position was intolerable and that the aim
'should be to get rid of the people we knew to be spies'.[48] He also
expressed a note of caution, believing that the Russians would react
badly if they were forced to remove 100 intelligence officers from the
country and would doubtless retaliate. Rennie was more sanguine and
contended that 'our allies in western Europe, far from viewing our
action badly would probably welcome it'. A memorandum drafted
jointly by the home secretary Reginald Maudling and foreign secretary
Alec Douglas-Home placed the number of Soviet intelligence officers
operating in Britain at 120, possibly 200. This was more than MI5
could contain. Maudling and Douglas-Home's memo, which can be
found among the records of the Prime Minister's Office at the National
Archives, estimated the potential damage already caused as considerable, stating that 'Known targets during the last few years have
included the Foreign Office and Ministry of Defence; and on the commercial side, the Concorde, the Bristol "Olympus 593" aero-engine,
nuclear energy projects and computer electronics.'[49] Two courses of
action were suggested to the prime minister:

> The first would be the drastic one of telling the Russians that a specified
> list of some 100 intelligence officers must be removed at an early date;

that their numbers both inside and outside the Embassy would thereafter be limited to the reduced establishments thus created; and that this
new ceiling would thereafter be reduced by one every time an official
was caught in intelligence activities and required to leave the country.

The second would be to impose parity between our Embassies and
enter into negotiations over the size of the Soviet official community
outside the Embassy; and this would be made more effective if we
asked the Russians at the same time to remove the 100 specified intelligence officers but presented it to them in a way which would avoid put-
ting their prestige at issue — by offering to keep this list of 100 names
confidential and dealing with the matter publicly on the basis of a
straightforward reduction in numbers, provided that they undertook
to co-operate in arranging that the people who left were those named
in the list.[50]

Edward Heath agreed that the current position could not continue and
must be 'firmly and speedily settled … at one blow'. On 24 September
1971 the British government acted and expelled 90 Soviet diplomats
resident in the UK and revoked the visas of a further 15 who were
abroad at the time. Operation Foot as it was codenamed was a significant coup in the intelligence war against Russia, an act from which
Soviet intelligence never fully recovered.[51] Lyalin was given a new identity and went into hiding. He died in 1995.

Operation Foot had specifically excluded representatives of Soviet
Military Intelligence (GRU) working out of the Soviet embassy in
order to avoid retaliation against Moscow-based British attachés.
Three Soviet attachés in London came to the attention of MI5, however, when they were observed 'cultivating British citizens with the clear
intention of recruiting them as agents'. The 'most flagrant case' was
that of the Soviet military attaché himself, Colonel Chelpanov, who
'offered money in return for classified information to a young English-
man who had recently left the Army and is writing a book on infantry
weaponry'. The man in question reported Chelpanov to MI5, who
used him to ensnare the military attaché. However, neither the expulsion of the *Rezidentura* nor a warning to the Soviet ambassador about
the conduct of GRU officers ended the problem of Eastern bloc espionage. In July 1972 there were still approximately 137 East European
intelligence agents in Britain working at the behest of the KGB, a
quantity the prime minister considered 'far too large a number' and
that 'must be reduced as speedily as possible'.[52]

Although MI5 maintained its focus on Soviet subversion it also maintained its watching brief on other domestic organizations, including a

raft of 'subversive left' organizations, not to mention the Provisional IRA (PIRA), which had been increasingly active since the 1960s. Both Special Branch and MI5 were also engaged in examining the 'subversive' influences supposedly behind industrial unrest. Other targets, which emerged during the early 1980s, included terrorist activities associated with the Iranian embassy siege (1983) and the Libyan People's Bureau (1984).

Despite the enhanced vetting procedures and wider recruitment following the scandal of the 'Cambridge Five', individuals could still be a cause for concern. In 1983 one of MI5's officers, Michael Bettaney, was jailed for 23 years for betraying secrets to the KGB. The Security Commission inquiry into the affair criticized MI5 and led directly to the appointment of Sir Anthony Duff, a former cabinet and Foreign Office official, in 1985. Further unwanted publicity was occasioned by the revelations of another former MI5 officer, Cathy Massiter, that MI5 F Branch, led by Charles Elwell, was spying on both the Campaign for Nuclear Disarmament (CND) and the National Council for Civil Liberties (now Liberty), maintaining files on two of its officers, Patricia Hewitt and Harriet Harman.

Coming in from the cold

The implosion and collapse of the Soviet empire in 1989 forced MI5 rapidly to reorient itself following the overnight disappearance of its principal enemy. That same year MI5's statutory basis was finally enshrined in the Security Service Act (1989).[53] This placed the service on a legal footing, complying with a ruling by the European Court of Human Rights that stated that, although an intelligence agency could infringe a citizen's privacy for reasons of national security, there must be a means of legal redress for those who felt themselves to have been wrongly investigated. This was followed in 1994 by the Intelligence Services Act, which provided a further legal underpinning for the service, and the establishment of the Intelligence and Security Committee, an oversight committee consisting of senior parliamentarians tasked with overseeing the expenditure, administration and policy of MI5, SIS and GCHQ. The post-Cold War world also saw an expansion of the role of MI5 to encompass responsibility for combating Irish Republican terrorism on the mainland in 1992 and fighting 'serious crime' in 1996.

In tandem with these developments MI5 embarked on a large-scale public relations exercise to show that, since the end of the Cold War, the service had become more transparent. This openness was marked in 2001 with the publication of *Open Secret*, an autobiography written by its former director general, Dame Stella Rimington, the first woman to have held the post. The drive towards limited public transparency had begun in July 1993 with the publication of *The Security Service*, a short and not particularly informative brochure. Its importance, however, was symbolic, allowing MI5 to acknowledge publicly (albeit in a limited fashion) its duties, methods and operations. Journalists attending the accompanying press conference and photo-call, the first to be given by a senior MI5 official in its then 84-year history, were warned not to expect 'a great avalanche of openness'. Ironically, the publication of Rimington's memoirs coincided with the imprisonment, upon his return to England, of MI5 officer David Shayler, whose very public criticisms of MI5 'bureaucracy' led to his imprisonment for breaching the Official Secrets Act. 'Openness' was not to be universal.

Following the terrorist attacks of 9/11 in the United States, government funding for MI5 was increased, with staff numbers increasing by 50 percent over three years. The primary focus is now counter-terrorism. Speaking in November 2006, the director general of MI5, Dame Elizabeth Manningham-Buller, presented a stark picture of the terrorist threat facing the United Kingdom. She revealed that the service had identified 200 groupings or networks, totalling over 1,600 identified individuals, who were actively engaged in plotting acts of terror in Britain or overseas. This stark warning was reinforced by Jonathan Evans, the new director general, who in his first public speech, in November 2007, warned that the service was facing 'the most immediate and acute peacetime threat' in its 98-year history. As the service prepares to mark its centenary, the threat of terrorism remains as prevalent today as it was in 1867 when the death and destruction at Clerkenwell Prison so dramatically placed the public in the front line of politically motivated violence.

2 | International Intelligence

Britain, in common with other states, has a long tradition of engaging in espionage to gather intelligence on foreign powers' capabilities and intentions. For several centuries its agents were adventurers or military officers—sometimes both—but the Secret Service Bureau, founded in 1909, introduced more formal arrangements under the watchful gaze of Vernon Kell and Mansfield Cumming. These grand old men of British intelligence—the original 'K' and 'C'—established the prototypes of MI5 and MI6 which flourished in the chaos and carnage of the First World War. International intelligence was essential in a volatile, shifting Europe, with reliable information on Soviet Russia's intentions becoming a priority following the armistice.

As tensions rose again through the 1930s, the Secret Intelligence Service—operating under cover in Passport Control offices—was struggling to cope. In reaction, the secret Z Organization was established under former MI5 man, Claude Dansey, running agents under cover of commercial firms operating throughout Europe. A German double cross saw the capture of Major Richard Stevens and Captain Sigismund Payne Best, heads of SIS and Z Organization in Holland, devastating both intelligence networks at the start of the Second World War. Yet this conflict—and the Cold War that followed—was to see the resurrection of the SIS and other intelligence-gathering units, with new ideas sweeping into play. As the stakes grew ever higher in the nuclear age, loyalties became commodities and agents targets for spymasters on both sides of the Iron Curtain. In a climate of fear and suspicion, acts of individual espionage—the Cambridge spy ring, Soviet agents Penkovsky and Gordievsky—could shake an organization to its roots and threaten the confidence of the world's most powerful nations.

One thousand years of espionage

One of the first examples is recorded in the *Anglo-Saxon Chronicle* and describes an early example of intelligence gathering in Britain. In

865 a large army of Vikings—commanded by the Danish chieftain Guthrum—landed in East Anglia, eventually capturing the city of York. The only resistance to the invasion came from Alfred, King of Wessex, who managed to keep the Vikings out of his territory. Anxious to discover Danish war plans, Alfred disguised himself as a minstrel and successfully gained entry to Guthrum's camp. Once inside, he headed for Guthrum's tent where a meeting of the war council had been convened. Standing outside the tent with other minstrels, Alfred was able to overhear the Viking high command as they plotted their military campaign. This intelligence proved decisive, enabling Alfred to rout the Danish forces at the Battle of Edington in 878. Whatever the truth of Alfred's daring raid, successive British monarchs have sought to consolidate their grip on power by gathering intelligence on their enemies abroad and opponents at home.

One of the fathers of modern intelligence was Sir Francis Walsingham, the spymaster of Queen Elizabeth I. Born in 1532 to a well-known Protestant family, Walsingham spent his early years abroad, cultivating contacts from within the Huguenot community in France and among leading Protestant statesmen in Italy and Switzerland. Following Elizabeth's ascension to the throne, Walsingham returned to England where he was soon appointed secretary of state and privy councillor. One of his first tasks was to establish a network of agents operating both at home and abroad, reflecting the queen's concern to gain information on the activities of Catholic plotters and foreign papists, particularly King Philip II of Spain.[1] Walsingham soon proved his worth. In 1586 he uncovered a conspiracy led by Anthony Babington, a young Catholic nobleman, to overthrow Elizabeth and replace her on the throne with her cousin Mary, the Roman Catholic former queen of Scotland. The disruption of the Babington Plot, one of a series uncovered by Walsingham, was made possible by the use of a double agent, Gilbert Gifford, entrusted with carrying messages between Mary and Babington. With Gifford in place, Walsingham was able to intercept and copy Mary's correspondence, including a letter of 6 July 1586 which contained Babington's plan for the assassination of Elizabeth and her chief ministers. On receiving Mary's reply, Thomas Phelippes, forger and Walsingham's chief code-breaker, added a short postscript encrypted in Mary's cipher. This postscript, now in the State Papers Scotland Series at the National Archives along with Mary's ciphers, asked Babington for 'the names and quelityes of the six gentlemen which are to accomplish the dessignement, for that it may be I shall be able uppon knowledge of the parties to give you some further advise necessarye to be followed therein'—essential information for the authorities.[2] In August 1586 the conspirators were arrested and sentenced to death for treason; Mary herself was executed at Fotheringhay Castle on 5 February 1587, in front of 300 witnesses.

Walsingham's network of agents abroad also proved invaluable in providing Elizabeth with information about Spanish naval construction and movements before the Armada set sail for England in 1588. One of his main sources of intelligence was the spy Antony Standen, a Catholic adventurer who had settled in Florence and was known to be close to the Tuscan ambassador to Spain, Giovanni Figliazzi. Employing the pseudonym 'Pompeo Pellegrini', Standen wrote regular reports to Walsingham on developments in Spain. His reports were evidently well received, earning him a pension of £100 a year, which he used to good effect in recruiting agents within the Spanish navy. Standen's network was almost certainly the source of a list of all the ships, men and supplies in the Spanish navy that was passed to Walsingham in 1587, revealing that the Armada would not be ready to set sail until 1588 at the earliest.[3] In 1590 Standen visited Bordeaux, where he assumed the identity of André Sandal, but—in an event graphically illustrating the complex life of an agent—he was soon arrested as a Spanish spy, to be released only after the intervention of Anthony Bacon (a fellow British agent and close relative of Lord Burghley, Lord Treasurer of England). His cover now blown, Standen returned to England, where he was briefly imprisoned in the Tower of London. Following his release, he resumed his travels in Europe, spending his final years in Rome.

During the reigns of William III and Anne, the focus of intelligence activity on the continent switched from Spain to France. A primary motive was the need to uncover the intrigues of the Jacobites and their foreign backers as they attempted to restore the Catholic Stuarts to the British throne. The wars with France and the continued activities of the Jacobites during the Hanoverian period led to an increase in intelligence work of all kinds, including the acquisition of information from intercepted correspondence. The advent of the Napoleonic Wars which followed the short-lived peace concluded at Amiens in 1802 saw a further increase in British intelligence operations. A major triumph occurred in 1807 when the British government received prior knowledge of Napoleon's intention to draw Denmark into the Franco-Russian alliance against Britain. The intelligence derived 'from so many and such various sources' enabled the British navy to take prompt and effective action against the Danish fleet at Copenhagen. In the course of the battle over 14,000 artillery rounds and phosphorus rockets were fired into the city, resulting in the deaths of 2,000 civilians and the destruction of over 30 per cent of the buildings.[4]

Following the outbreak of the Peninsular War in 1808, the British received a regular stream of intelligence from both Spanish and Portuguese sources on the dispositions of French military forces, which greatly assisted Wellington's campaign. Outside Europe, the East India Company, which administered Indian affairs in conjunction with the government's Board of Control, began its operations in Persia to counter French (and later Russian) influence in the country, which was designed to undermine British interests in the subcontinent. These activities marked the beginnings of the 'Great Game'—a phrase first coined by Arthur Conolly, an intelligence officer of the British East India Company's Sixth Bengal Light Cavalry. The term was later used by Rudyard Kipling in his novel *Kim* to describe the covert operations conducted by Britain, Russia and China during the 19th century in order to gain influence in Central Asia.[5]

The need for foreign intelligence diminished after the defeat of Napoleon at Waterloo in 1815, with a corresponding reduction in the funds allocated to it by parliament. This allocation, known as the Secret Vote, was used for a variety of purposes. Ambassadors were provided with modest sums for secret purposes, including the payment of informers and the bribing of foreign officials. In 1839, for example, the British ambassador in Paris was instructed to use 'a modest application of secret service money' to ensure that members of the French Chamber of Deputies ratified an Anglo-French commercial agreement.[6] A number of freelance operations were also funded via the Secret Vote. In one, the author and traveller Lawrence Oliphant was sent by the foreign secretary on various missions abroad to report on matters of political interest, such as Denmark's dispute with Prussia over Schleswig-Holstein and the 1863 revolt in Russian Poland. Secret funds were used to influence the press in foreign countries and persuade newspaper proprietors to feature pro-British articles. The Reuters news agency was particularly helpful and received an annual sum of £500 for its services. Money was also required to pay pensions to former agents and individuals who had assisted the British at various times. The fact that none of this was disclosed led some to believe that secret service money was being diverted for other purposes.

In the 1880s the prime minister, William Gladstone, was forced strongly to defend the Foreign Office in its management of the Secret Vote.[7] He later informed parliament that the foreign secretary's declaration that the money had been properly expended was sufficient and that no further particulars should be given.[8] In similar style, the foreign secretary, Sir Edward Grey, responded to proposed cutbacks in the aftermath of the Boer War, describing the Secret Vote as his 'purdah lady', who should remain veiled from the lascivious gaze of grasping Treasury clerks. Nonetheless, records show that the secrecy surrounding the fund allowed some monarchs and senior officials to plunder it for their own personal advantage. King Edward VII's 'personal' donation to a relief fund for victims of a fire in Constantinople is perhaps the best-known example. In 1907, the fund was used to purchase a majority shareholding in the Constantinople Quays Company, a major shipping and trading organization, believed to be in danger of falling under German control.[9] In an attempt to stop further misuse, the Secret Vote was audited by the Treasury and accompanied by a sworn statement that the money had been spent 'according to the intent and purpose for which it had been given'.

A new era — the Secret Service Bureau

By the end of the 19th century, the world's second oldest profession was still viewed as a job unfit for a gentleman. Those enticed into the world of espionage had no career structure, no central organization and no long-term strategy. This changed in 1909 with the Committee of Imperial Defence's report on Germany's potential espionage threat; it offered four main recommendations including the formation of a Secret Service Bureau, and was duly approved by the cabinet in the summer. Intelligence machinery had entered a new phase.

The Secret Service Bureau was initially intended to consist of a military and a naval branch, each with considerable autonomy and staffed by retired officers. The former was headed by Captain Vernon Kell, the latter by Commander Mansfield Cumming, a 50-year-old retired Royal Navy officer. Exactly why Cumming was identified for the position is unclear. His career in the navy appears relatively uneventful and in the years preceding his appointment he seems to have been mainly concerned with the construction of boom defences at Southampton. Nonetheless, Rear Admiral Sir Alexander Bethell, the director of naval intelligence (DNI), chose Cumming personally for the post, offering it to him in a letter of 10 August 1909. Cumming replied that he was 'exceedingly keen' to take up the challenge and was 'determined to make it a success'.[10]

The new head of the bureau's naval section quickly settled into his role, developing a fondness for disguises, mechanical gadgets and secret inks. He is remembered as initiating the practice of writing exclusively in green ink, a tradition continued to this day by his successors. Located in a small office in Victoria Street and funded via the Secret Vote, the new bureau began its work on 1 October 1909. After the SSB was divided in 1910, with Kell as head of the home section (the ancestor of MI5) and Cumming as head of the foreign section (later to become the Secret Intelligence Service (SIS) or MI6), the two sections began to establish their own separate identities. The Foreign Office still retained financial control through the Secret Vote, with payments to 'C' and 'K', as the heads of SIS and MI5 became known within Whitehall, being recorded in the Foreign Office secret service accounts.[11]

Intelligence in the First World War

The outbreak of the First World War placed considerable demands on the intelligence services, with information required on military and political developments within Germany and elsewhere. Despite attempts to remain autonomous, Cumming's foreign section was soon absorbed into the War Office's Directorate of Military Intelligence, which assumed overall control of army intelligence during the war. Initially, the foreign section was listed as Section 6 of the Directorate of Special Operations, from where it gained the name MI6 by which it is popularly known today. Section 6 was redesignated as MI1c in January 1916, staying under that designation for the duration of the war.[12]

The first goal of allied intelligence was to gain information on German troop movements. This was achieved by establishing a network of train watchers, supplemented by information obtained from agents operating behind German lines. The best known of these networks was 'La Dame Blanche' (The White Lady) which by January 1918 had over 400 agents reporting on German troop movements in occupied Belgium and France. Equally important to information on military deployments, however, was information on German trade movements. Of particular interest to the allies was the network of trading companies that had been established by Germany in neutral countries in response to the blockade of its ports by the Royal Navy. In recognition of the need for such information, and on the recommendation of the Committee of Imperial Defence, the War Trade Intelligence Department (WTID) was established on 1 January 1915. It soon began issuing its Secret Weekly Bulletin of Trade Information from Confidential Reports, which can be found among the records relating to the department held at the National Archives. These were compiled from the various communications of government departments, intercepts by censors, articles in the foreign press and intelligence obtained from British companies and trade attachés. The breadth of information covered appears to have been huge, from rumours of contraband trade, sudden notable increases in exports and imports, changes in the German exchanges, and additions to the Prohibited Lists, to slightly more bizarre entries. For example, the very first bulletin commented:

> Negotiations for a Conference with the Meat Packers are proceeding, but at present there is not complete agreement between the parties concerned as to the basis of discussion. It is agreed that the discussion should include the subject of future shipments of Meat Products to European neutral countries … Meanwhile there are some reasons for thinking that German buyers do not yet despair of obtaining further supplies of Meat Products from the United States. Some recent notable fluctuations in the Chicago Pig Market have been attributed to German buying …[13]

Similarly, the bulletin for 20–26 November 1915 recorded that 'German Hospitals at the Front are running short of Cognac, Rum and Port, which in the past reached them in large quantities from Denmark and Sweden'. Alongside these were reports that 'shoe blacking' with a particularly high fat content was being imported into Germany (the fat then being re-extracted for food), and mention of the embarrassment experienced in certain districts of Germany due to a shortage of small change. This shortage was believed to be due to 'the collection of nickel coins by the Government'.

In March 1916 the department was transferred to the Foreign Office and placed under the control of Lord Robert Cecil, operating from temporary accommodation erected in the drained lake at St James's Park. This location appears to have resulted from wartime pressures on office space. According to a wonderfully testy memorandum from October of that year, the department was initially housed in a building that was not only far too small for its needs but also unhygienic to the point of risking the health of its 'employés'. To address these concerns, the Office of Works suggested a move to the Westminster Palace

Hotel, but these premises were soon taken over by the National Liberal Club after their own building was occupied by the cabinet. The whole sorry tale was conveyed to senior officials in the following terms:

> There does not appear to exist any other building suitable for the Department; the Windsor Hotel is altogether unsatisfactory and would be very costly, and the St. Ermin's Hotel, which has also been suggested, is very much too big. The only other possibility is to build some premises in St. James's Park. Apart from other objections to this way of dealing with the difficulty, it would cause a delay of at least two months, which is very undesirable. It thus appears that the only reason why a Government Department, essential for the conduct of the war, should not be housed in a suitable building immediately is that the building is wanted by a political club.[14]

Despite such hardships, the work conducted by the department proved to be of remarkable value, providing raw information and analysis that was, according to a navy report, of 'the greatest possible value in conducting the economic and blockade aspect of the war'. The WTID ended its life under the Department of Overseas Trade, its officials, who included numerous academics, assisting the Historical Section of the Foreign Office in the publication of handbooks for the British delegation at the Paris peace conference.

Germany was not the only country on which information was sought. The intentions and capabilities of both Ottoman Turkey and Russia were major priorities for British intelligence. In 1917 the British government received secret correspondence that elements within the Turkish leadership were prepared to enter into a separate peace deal with the allies. The source of this information was Basil Zaharoff, a Middle-Eastern entrepreneur and arms dealer who had a reputation for private wheeler-dealing. Zaharoff's knowledge of the Balkans and his links with the Turkish government made him a useful agent for the British. Through Zaharoff, Britain was informed that Enver Bey, the Ottoman Minister of War, and forty of his 'Young Turk' associates believed Turkey was 'ruined and lost'. Moreover, for a substantial sum of money and their safe passage to America, they would be prepared to open the Dardanelles to the British fleet. Lloyd George, the British prime minister, was so impressed with the intelligence provided by Zaharoff that he contemplated a payment of $25 million to buy Turkey out of the war. An initial payment of $5 million was promised in return for opening the Straits to British submarines, with a further $2 million guaranteed once Turkish forces had withdrawn from Palestine

and the Hedjaz railway. Zaharoff advised the British to be cautious and
not to place reliance on Bey or 'any of this Forty Thieves'.[15] Exactly
what money was paid to whom and when is, as yet, unclear. According
to Zaharoff, seven million Swiss francs were deposited in Enver's bank
account and probably hurried the surrender of the Turks by several
days.[16] In April 1918 Zaharoff was informed by the British ambassador
in Paris that the king was pleased to award him the Grand Cross of the
British Empire in recognition of his 'eminent services to the cause of
the Allies'.

Events in Turkey were eclipsed by developments taking place in Russia. In October 1917 the Bolsheviks seized control of the capital, St
Petersburg, bringing Lenin and his Communist party to power. The
revolution and the country's descent into civil war increased the urgency
of obtaining reliable intelligence on Russia's future intentions. Acquiring accurate information on Russian affairs presented challenges. The
strict censorship of the press made the task more difficult than in other
European states. Russian officials, however, were poorly paid and were
willing to supply information on a host of subjects for modest remu-
neration from secret service funds. To supplement their own sources,
British intelligence employed a number of freelance volunteers. The
most notable of these was Sidney Reilly, a captain in the Royal Canadian Flying Corps, whose exploits became known to a wider British
public due to the success of the television series *Reilly Ace of Spies*,
first screened in 1983.

Reilly, who had been born in Odessa in 1874, and whose real name
was Sigmund Rosenblum, was a virulent anti-Communist and before
the revolution had been employed as an arms dealer on behalf of the
Russian government. In April 1918 he arrived in Murmansk on a mission to make contact with anti-Bolshevik opposition groups. His
enthusiasm quickly overcame him and he soon became involved in
organizing a counter-revolution. In July and August 1918, Lenin survived two attempts on his life. The latter was almost successful, with
Lenin being hit by two bullets at close range. In the reprisals that followed almost 8,000 counter-revolutionaries were summarily executed.
Reilly, who had been implicated in the plot, managed to escape to
Helsinki and was later awarded the Military Cross for his exploits.
The use of private adventurers such as Reilly soon proved embarrassing to the British government, which sought to normalize relations
with the Soviet Union. In 1921 Reilly was formally dismissed from the
service, his close association with anti-Bolshevik conspiracies now a

liability rather than an asset. His position within the service was conveyed to senior staff in January 1922 by Major Desmond Morton, head of SIS office organization: 'Reilly is not a member of our office and does not serve C in that he is not receiving any pay from us. He worked at one time during the war in Russia for C's organisation and is undoubtedly of a certain use to us.'[17] Reilly's fate was effectively sealed the following year when Colonel Stuart Menzies, then head of SIS's military section, made it clear that he wanted no further contact with Reilly. According to a note in a file compiled by MI5, now held at the National Archives, Menzies regarded him as 'an extremely clever but absolutely unscrupulous person'.[18]

Despite his dismissal from the service, Reilly remained in close contact with Russian counter-revolutionaries and he was soon involved in further intrigue. In 1925 he travelled to Finland to meet representatives of the Trust, a supposedly anti-Communist organization. Flattered by the attention he received from a female member of the group, Reilly took little persuasion in accompanying her to Moscow to meet with the Trust's leadership. Reilly had walked into a trap. The Trust was not a counter-revolutionary organization bent on bringing down the regime but a front established by the Soviet secret police to identify subversives. On his arrival in Moscow, he was arrested and imprisoned in the Lubyanka. In September 1925 the Soviet press published an official statement 'that a certain Captain Reilly of the British Army, an alleged spy, was arrested by the GPU and finally shot'. While capturing public imagination, Reilly's exploits were not typical of the new breed of intelligence officer, who was expected to demonstrate political judgement and discretion rather than military prowess.

The Political Intelligence Department

By the end of the war Britain had established an effective military and naval intelligence system. The Foreign Office, however, was concerned that it was not always receiving information it required in order to consider the impact of political events around the world. There was also a need to coordinate the various sources of political intelligence and control its distribution to government departments. In 1918, to address these requirements, the Foreign Office established the Political Intelligence Department (PID). To provide the necessary staff, who were in short supply due to the war, the Foreign Office turned to the Department of Information's Intelligence Bureau (DIIB). Headed by the novelist and politician John Buchan, author of *The Thirty-Nine Steps*, DIIB was responsible for furnishing the government with information on political developments in foreign countries and for providing the various propaganda sections with effective material and suggestions as to its use.[19] The proposal to transfer the staff of the DIIB to the Foreign Office did not meet with the approval of Lord Beaverbrook, the owner of the *Daily Express* and head of the Department of Information. Beaverbrook was furious and initially blocked the move, but later relented when the entire staff of the DIIB threatened to resign in protest.

The first head of the PID was Sir Wiliam Tyrrell, a Foreign Office veteran noted for his single-mindedness and ability to achieve results. Day-to-day running of the department was largely undertaken by his deputy, James Headlam-Morley, a diplomatic historian who later became historical adviser to the Foreign Office. Known informally as the 'Department of all the Talents', other members of PID included Lewis Namier, Arnold Toynbee, Alfred Zimmern, the brothers Allen and Rex Leeper, Harold Nicolson and Robert Vansittart, all of whom rose to become distinguished academics, diplomats and administrators. The experts employed by PID were organized on a geographical basis and received information from overseas missions supplemented by material supplied from naval and military intelligence. In addition to serving the needs of the Foreign Office, PID also acted as the clearing house for political intelligence to other government departments. Unlike its service counterparts, PID did not have its own agents in the field. It is evident, however, that informal contacts existed with the world of secret intelligence. Rex Leeper, PID's Russian expert, was a close friend of Sidney Reilly and acted as the unofficial link between the Foreign Office and the Bolshevik representative in London, Maksim Litvinov.

The basic work of the department appeared in the form of memoranda and special reports that analysed political developments in various countries.[20] The PID also covered events in friendly and neutral states, including France and America. The department was assigned a crucial role in the post-war Paris peace conference, for which it produced a series of country handbooks, now preserved at the National Archives, that addressed the historical, economic and political questions that would be faced by the British delegation. The reports produced by the PID were required reading for senior officials and ministers, with Lord Balfour describing them as very able and useful documents. PID's continued existence, however, was short-lived. Following the end of the war, the Treasury sought to reduce expenditure and demanded the closure of all 'temporary' wartime bodies. The PID fell into this category, and despite the best attempts of the Foreign Office to maintain its control over political intelligence, the PID was broken up with its members either leaving or transferred to regional departments within the Foreign Office.[21]

Changes after 1918

For Cumming, a naval officer, the virtual absorption of his organization by the War Office was not a happy experience. Indeed, following the armistice, many questioned the need for a separate overseas intelligence section and advocated its absorption into the service intelligence branches. To justify SIS's continued existence, Cumming argued that in an uncertain world obtaining political intelligence by covert means was vital to Britain's continued security and foreign policy objectives. His lobbying proved persuasive. In 1919 the cabinet established a Secret Service Committee, chaired by Lord Curzon, to advise on the most appropriate structure to meet Britain's peacetime intelligence needs. The committee made three major recommendations. First, MI5 was given the responsibility for countering espionage and sedition within the United Kingdom and her colonies and dominions overseas. Second, to deal exclusively with Bolshevik-inspired subversion, Sir Basil Thomson's short-lived Directorate of Intelligence was established. Third, 'in order to keep the distinction between military and civilian intelligence', Cumming was given overall responsibility for the collection of secret information in foreign countries likely to be of interest to His Majesty's Government.[22] Not until 1921, however, after further deliberations by the Secret Service Committee, was SIS given exclusive responsibility in this area.

Throughout the early 1920s, the government's financial position remained stark. Stringent economies were sought, with defence spending singled out for wide-ranging cuts. The Geddes Committee on National Expenditure proposed reducing the defence budget and the Secret Vote. This view was supported by the Treasury, who contended that military demobilization—following the end of the First World War and the Anglo-Irish Treaty of 1921, in which British forces were withdrawn from the Irish Republic—made economies not only sensible but also essential. The Treasury thought it absurd that, three and a half years after the Armistice in 1918, the country still possessed an intelligence organization based on wartime levels. This opinion was challenged by Winston Churchill, who as secretary of state for war argued that too severe a reduction would damage the whole system at a time when 'the situations all over the world are so complex that greater vigilance on the part of SIS is required than in 1914'. To examine the various options, the Secret Service Committee was once again reconvened. The committee was directed to find 'less elaborate and costly means of obtaining intelligence' and told that the present system 'involved a certain amount of waste and overlapping'. After lengthy discussions, the budget was cut by a further third to £200,000, of which £90,000 was to be allocated to SIS.

The monopoly of conducting espionage abroad came at a price in that its main consumers, the War Office, the Admiralty and later the Air Ministry soon transferred liaison officers from their own intelligence departments to SIS headquarters. These officers acted independently, often issuing their own requirements and circulating reports to their home departments. In order to operate abroad, SIS was required to work closely with the Foreign Office. This posed a problem for senior Foreign Office officials who were determined that diplomats would not be used as spies. To placate these concerns, the Passport Control Department was established. Its officials (SIS officers working under cover) would be employed by the Foreign Office, but would not enjoy diplomatic status. The arrangement also had advantages for the Foreign Office, enabling officials to keep abreast of SIS activities and to monitor its reports sent back to London. By the early 1920s the Passport Control Office had established stations in over 25 countries. The majority of these were in Europe, with only five stations (Beirut, Buenos Aires, New York, Vladivostok and Yokohama) covering the whole of Asia and the Americas.[23] In contrast to the present day, the number of staff employed by SIS was small, amounting to 200, a large proportion of whom were retired naval officers. In 1923 Cumming died in office, to be replaced as chief of SIS by Rear Admiral Hugh 'Quex' Sinclair, the former head of naval intelligence.

The Zinoviev letter

In the aftermath of the First World War, Soviet Russia replaced Germany as the principal target of SIS operations. The British establishment viewed Moscow as the main potential source of insurrection within the Empire, particularly India. Immediate concern was focused on the activities of the Communist International (Comintern), which had been established in 1919 with the explicit aim of spreading revolutionary Marxism throughout the world. The Comintern was headed by Grigori Zinoviev, a close confidant of Lenin, who went on to establish strong links with the Communist Party of Great Britain (CPGB). The scale and nature of this relationship became a major preoccupation of the British security services.

Matters came to a head in 1924, the year that saw both the death of Lenin and the election of Britain's first Labour government under prime minister Ramsay MacDonald. One of the Labour government's first tasks was to re-establish diplomatic relations with the new regime in Moscow. The outcome was an Anglo-Soviet treaty that sought to settle all outstanding questions between the two countries and which included the provision of a government loan. The Conservative Party was strongly opposed to 'bailing out' the Soviets and mounted a concerted campaign against the treaty, which had still to be ratified by parliament, seeking to portray the Labour government as soft on Communism. In October, the government was defeated on a vote of no confidence and a general election was called for 29 October 1924.

No sooner had the election been announced than rumours began to circulate concerning an intercepted letter from Zinoviev to the central committee of the CPGB. The letter, brought to the attention of SIS by Sidney Reilly, was sent to SIS headquarters in London from its station in Riga on the Baltic coast. In the letter Zinoviev urged the party to intensify its agitation in support of the Anglo-Soviet treaty, to infiltrate its members into the armed forces and to prepare for violent insurrection. The letter was dated 15 September 1924 and was received in London on 24 October. A copy mysteriously found its way to Fleet Street, and its publication in the *Daily Mail*—alongside headlines such as 'Civil War Plot By Socialist Masters', 'Moscow Order To Our Reds' and 'Mr MacDonald Would Lend Russia Our Money'—severely undermined MacDonald's position. It suggested that in its dealings with Moscow the Labour government was at best naive and at worst untrustworthy. MacDonald immediately condemned the Zinoviev letter as a crude hoax, but the damage had been done and the Conservative Party under Stanley Baldwin was returned to power.

For many on the left, the Zinoviev letter represented a blatant attempt by the British establishment to discredit the Labour Party. What role, if any, the intelligence services played in the affair was a recurrent question. In 1998, in an attempt to discover the truth behind the letter, the foreign secretary, Robin Cook, sanctioned an inquiry.

Undertaken by Gill Bennett, chief historian at the Foreign and Commonwealth Office, the inquiry concluded that the letter was in all likelihood a forgery, most probably written by White Russian émigrés opposed to the Soviet regime.[24] The role played by the intelligence services was more equivocal. There was no evidence to suggest that a coordinated campaign was conducted by SIS to undermine the Labour government. However, the possibility that individual members of SIS, with links to the Conservative Party, had passed the letter to the press could not be ruled out.

The political fallout from the Zinoviev affair through the autumn of 1924 brought into question the actions of the intelligence agencies. To establish the facts behind the affair, the new prime minister, Stanley Baldwin, directed the Secret Service Committee to hold an enquiry 'into the existing organisations and their relationship to one another' and to recommend any changes that 'would conduce to the greater efficiency of the system'.

The committee met on 26 February 1925 and began by questioning the heads of all the organizations concerned with intelligence. The new head of SIS, Hugh Sinclair, had strong views on the way forward. He strongly believed that the existing agencies should be amalgamated and directed by a single individual, preferably himself. Sinclair had already succeeded in attaching the Government Code and Cypher School (GC&CS) to SIS in September 1923 within months of taking up his post and had attempted to do the same with Indian Political Intelligence, though this remained under the control of MI5.[25] The committee was not convinced by Sinclair's ideas, believing that the concentration of so much power in one individual would disturb the balance of ministerial responsibility. In their final report, issued in December 1925, the committee merely recommended 'that efforts should be made to concentrate the various secret organisations in the neighbourhood of Whitehall' and 'that all sections of the intelligence community should make an effort to co-operate more closely'. It was further recommended that the Secret Service Committee should remain in existence 'to which any fundamental differences of opinion arising between the various branches could, if necessary, be referred for advise or settlement'.

The Committee reconvened once more in 1931. This time the issue under consideration was SIS's employment of agents within the UK. Sir John Anderson, permanent secretary to the Home Office, was concerned that SIS was undertaking work that was clearly the responsibility of Special Branch or MI5. Sinclair made it clear to the committee that in his view the distinction between espionage and counter-espionage was an artificial one, and that SIS required access to information about domestic subversion in order to prosecute their struggle against Bolshevik activities overseas. Anderson strongly believed that there should 'be only two organisations dealing with secret service work, C covering foreign countries and MI5 the Empire.'

The committee accepted this position and recommended that Scotland Yard should be stripped of its intelligence functions, a proposed reorganization that was soon implemented. SS1, Scotland Yard's anti-Communist section, was transferred to MI5, with SS2 relocated to the Home Office where it acted as 'a central bureau of information about suspects for the whole of the country'. SIS also lost control over its own network of domestic agents, the 'Casuals', recruited to infiltrate Communist organizations with the intention of corroborating reports obtained from Moscow. The 'Casuals' were transferred wholesale to MI5, where they became known as 'M Section'; they continued to co-operate closely from their new base with the counter-espionage section of SIS under Valentine Vivian. This would be the last occasion on which the Secret Service Committee was convened in its inter-war form. It continued to meet occasionally during the war years, but its role was diminished; its primary function of coordination was now carried out by the Joint Intelligence Committee.

The rise of Nazism

In employing the bulk of its resources against the Soviet Union, SIS had little or no spare capacity to focus on other developments, notably the rise of the Nazi party in Germany. Already overstretched, the SIS cover as the Passport Control Office further hampered its ability to obtain high-grade intelligence on German intentions. Rather than gathering intelligence, staff in Berlin, for example, were primarily involved in issuing visas to Jewish applicants who wished to enter Palestine. The Nazi persecution of the Jews increased these numbers dramatically, bringing many stations to the point of breakdown. The inability of SIS to provide timely intelligence of Italy's invasion of Abyssinia in 1935 further eroded its credibility within Whitehall.

With the threat of war apparent, the need to obtain accurate intelligence on Germany's economic and military capabilities became pressing. To provide this information, the government turned increasingly

to the Industrial Intelligence Centre (IIC) which had been established
in 1931. Headed by Major Desmond Morton, a former SIS officer, the
IIC was a semi-independent organization tasked with collecting, interpreting and distributing industrial intelligence and coordinating its
activities with the Admiralty, War Office and Air Ministry.[26] A major
focus of IIC activity was the German aircraft industry. In this work it
was assisted by the SIS air section, which had been established in 1930
under Wing Commander Frederick Winterbotham. One source of
intelligence on the German aeronautics industry was provided by
debriefing British engineers who had recently visited German factories
and air shows. A further source was provided by businessmen who were
asked to pass on 'useful and important information' on production,
indicating possible targets for air attack.

Between 1934 and 1939, 12 reports were compiled on the German
air force, with additional reports prepared on the strength of the German army and navy. The conclusions were: that Germany was rearm-
ing for war; that it was impossible to guarantee peace beyond January
1939; and that in any future conflict with Germany, Britain's prospects
would be extremely grim unless she obtained substantial assistance in
loans and materiel from the United States. The Anschluss of Austria
and Germany in March 1938 convinced many that war with Germany
was inevitable and that obtaining accurate intelligence on Hitler's intentions was now more critical than ever. The prospect of SIS providing
this intelligence, however, was less than encouraging. For one thing,
the SIS Passport Control Office cover was well known to the German
authorities. For another, the head of the SIS station in Vienna had been
arrested and interrogated by the occupying German forces, which
meant that other SIS operations abroad were potentially undermined.

In response to these developments, and to provide an additional
source of intelligence, Sinclair began to construct an entirely separate
network. Headed by Claude Dansey, a former MI5 officer with extensive business contacts, the role of the Z Organization was to recruit
agents and place them under cover using a network of shipping companies, holiday firms and business organizations. It is claimed, for
example, that Dansey and the Z Organization bankrolled Alexander
Korda's London Films company in order to enable its agents to travel
through Europe under the cover of looking for suitable film locations.
Dansey, who would later serve as deputy chief of SIS, was a controversial figure, being variously described as 'ruthless', 'the only professional in SIS' and 'an utter shit'. Dansey held a low opinion of most

SIS officers, believing them incompetent, complacent or both. He held an equal disdain for Sinclair whom he regarded as 'a half-mad paranoid', who communicated with his staff via messages left in a locked box to which his 'equally half-mad sister' had the only key. The Z Organization was equally controversial, its existence a secret even to most members of SIS.[27] This situation was soon to change. On the outbreak of war, Z agents were directed to make themselves known to their local Passport Control Office and to combine forces. The existence of two parallel organizations, each with its own network of agents, soon proved disastrous, as events in the Netherlands were to show.

Following the closure of the Berlin Passport Control Office in August 1939, the station at The Hague, headed by Major Richard Stevens, became the main centre for anti-Nazi operations in Europe. On 4 September 1939, a day that saw the death of Hugh Sinclair and London HQ thrown into turmoil, Stevens received a visit from Captain Sigismund Payne Best, a businessman and well-known member of the British expatriate community. Stevens was astonished to learn that Best has been recruited by Dansey and was his chief Z agent in the Netherlands. After initial hesitation, Stevens agreed to combine their forces in the common fight against Nazi Germany. One of the agents employed by Best was Dr Franz Fisher, a businessman who claimed to have made contact with a small but influential group of disaffected German officers planning to overthrow Hitler and stop the war. The prospect of removing Hitler from power proved irresistible: Stevens and Best demanded a meeting with the ringleaders of the plot.

On 9 November 1939 Stevens and Best, accompanied by Lieutenant Dirk Klop, a Dutch intelligence officer, set off for the Dutch border town of Venlo to meet a shadowy German general whom they understood to be the chief conspirator. The meeting was scheduled to take place at the Café Backus, only a few hundred yards from the German border. All was not as it seemed. Fisher was a double agent working for the *Sicherheitsdienst*, the Gestapo's own intelligence service. On arriving at the café, the three men were ambushed by the Gestapo, with Klop receiving a fatal wound to the chest. According to Best's own account, they were then frog-marched over the border and hustled into the customs office, 'where we were made to stand with upraised arms facing a dirty whitewashed wall. Behind each of us stood a man, pistol in hand.'[28] Best and Stevens were then handcuffed, bundled into waiting cars and driven to Düsseldorf for interrogation.[29] The decision to kidnap the British intelligence officers was allegedly carried out on the express orders of Hitler, who believed the British were behind the unsuccessful attempt to assassinate him at the *Burgerbraukeller* in Munich the previous day (8 November). For SIS, the abduction of Stevens and Best was a disaster. Under interrogation both men revealed information about British espionage operations, with the result that all the networks run by SIS and the Z Organization in Europe were totally compromised.

SIS goes to war

The long-expected war with Germany was now a reality and SIS entered it rudderless and ineffective. Its chief of 15 years, who had staunchly defended the independence of SIS, had just died in office and, following the Venlo incident, its networks in Europe were essentially non-existent, the information obtained from Best and Stevens enabling the Gestapo to arrest British agents in occupied territories. The person chosen to lead SIS and revitalize the service was Sir Stuart Menzies, who had been Sinclair's deputy for over a year. A former guardsman and son-in-law to Rupert Beckett, chairman of the Westminster Bank, Menzies was well connected and was formally confirmed in post on 28 November 1939.[30] The organization he took over was ill equipped and in no position to cope with a major war against a resurgent Germany. The London organization inherited by Menzies was comprised of ten sections, the most important being the political, military, industrial and counter-espionage sections. Menzies also had direct control over the Government Code and Cypher School (GC&CS), which had been transferred to SIS in 1923.

Menzies's first priority on taking office was to increase the SIS presence in Europe, now reduced to just three stations, in Stockholm, Lisbon and Berne. Outside Europe the position was little better, with most intelligence derived from either MI5 or naval intelligence. In May 1940, following the fall of France, Neville Chamberlain was replaced as prime minister by Winston Churchill, who became leader of the new wartime coalition and quickly moved to instil a sense of urgency into British intelligence. The first to feel the firm hand of leadership was Vernon Kell, the long-serving head of MI5, who was summarily dismissed, while SIS lost control of section D, a quasi-military unit established in March 1938 and specializing in clandestine warfare. The purpose of this shake-up soon became apparent. Churchill was determined to take the war to Germany. To achieve this he created the Special

Operations Executive (SOE). Its mission was to undertake sabotage operations behind enemy lines and to assist the various resistance movements throughout Europe. SOE comprised three distinct elements: MIR, the War Office's guerrilla warfare unit; section D; and Electra House, the black propaganda department of the Foreign Office. The activities of SOE and its relationship with SIS are described in chapter 6. As the war progressed, SIS was required to coordinate its activities with an increasing variety of other intelligence organizations. These included the Ministry of Economic Warfare, the Political Warfare Executive and British Security Coordination.

Intelligence machinery in the Second World War

If the First World War was a battle of attrition, the Second was a battle of industrial production. Gaining knowledge of German industrial output and its need for raw materials was central to British war plans. The responsibility for acquiring such intelligence was given to the Ministry of Economic Warfare (MEW), which was established on 3 September 1939 under the control of Sir Ronald Cross, the former minister of shipping. The directive given to MEW was constantly to monitor Germany's economic potential for war, to estimate strengths and weaknesses in industrial production and to select vulnerable points in the supply chain suitable for attack by land, sea or air. One of the principal architects of MEW was Sir Desmond Morton, the former head of the Industrial Intelligence Centre. The organization drawn up by Morton consisted of seven departments of which the Intelligence Department, with Morton as its head, was by far the largest. The Intelligence Department consisted of two sections, Blockade Intelligence and Economic Warfare Intelligence.

In January 1939, with the international situation rapidly deteriorating, the efficient organization of intelligence bodies became paramount. The chiefs of staff contended that the Joint Intelligence Committee (JIC) would be more effective if chaired by the Foreign Office and provided with political intelligence on which it could produce 'a reasoned analysis of international affairs'. The Foreign Office was initially reluctant to get involved, believing the work of the JIC to be primarily military. However, it later agreed to send a representative to the Situation Report Centre, established in April 1939 to pool all military and political intelligence requiring immediate response.[31] The Situation Report Centre issued weekly reports on the international situation and daily bulletins on specific events needing urgent ministerial action. In July, with the full agreement of the Foreign Office, the centre was amalgamated with the JIC. The subsequent reorganization gave the JIC its form and functions for the next six years.

On the outbreak of war in September 1939, it became a subcommittee of the war cabinet, with a membership expanded to include the heads of SIS, MI5 and the Ministry of Economic Warfare's Intelligence Directorate. The JIC soon found itself over-burdened with administration and unable to meet all the chiefs of staffs' requirements, so in November 1940 the Future Operations (Enemy) Section (FOES) was created. This inter-departmental intelligence organization, reporting directly to the chiefs of staff, was responsible for preparing military appreciations and plans from the enemy point of view.[32] It was not greeted with universal acclaim, and soon gained a reputation 'for crystal gazing and guesswork'; in March 1941 FOES was disbanded and replaced by the Axis Planning Section (APS) as an integral part of the JIC.

In the early months of the war, the relationship between MEW and the service ministries was less than satisfactory. This was primarily due to the service departments preferring to rely on their own sources of economic intelligence rather then placing faith in a newly created ministry staffed largely by civilians. Following the fall of France, this position changed. The largely ineffective Cross was replaced by Hugh Dalton, a future chancellor and creator of SOE, with the MEW given full representation on the JIC. The Intelligence Department was renamed the Enemy and Occupied Territories Department, which was soon shortened to the Enemy Branch. Throughout the war, MEW produced a weekly intelligence review that detailed the production of armaments and the availability of raw materials, including oil, in both Germany and German-occupied countries.[33] The steady stream of intelligence was used by the joint planners to mount attacks on known bottlenecks, intercept cargoes and disrupt the German wartime economy. Following the defeat of Nazi Germany, the MEW was disbanded, with responsibility for economic intelligence transferred to the newly formed Joint Intelligence Bureau in the Ministry of Defence.

Hearts and minds — the Political Warfare Executive

German military success at the start of the war was matched by an equally strident public relations campaign directed by Joseph Goebbels, the Nazi minister for public enlightenment and propaganda. To sustain public morale at home and bolster resistance abroad, an equally effective allied propaganda machine was required. At the outbreak of war, the British propaganda effort was confined to a small team located in Electra House under the direction of Sir Campbell Stuart, former deputy director of propaganda during the First World War. The team at Electra House was responsible for producing leaflets which were dropped over Germany. A draft of the first of these, *Warning! A Message from Great Britain*, can be found among the files at the National Archives. Addressed to the men and women of Germany, it informed them that Britain did not want war and would work with any peace-loving German government.[34] But Churchill demanded results and fresh thinking. In 1940 Stuart resigned, with responsibility for propaganda transferred to the newly created SOE.

These arrangements did not meet with the approval of the Foreign Office, which was anxious to mount propaganda operations of its own. The closure of most diplomatic posts in Europe meant that diplomacy could play little part in the conduct of the war. It was only through the medium of propaganda that the Foreign Office could reassert its influence. For some, regaining control over the future direction of political warfare was essential to the success of the war. This view was forcibly conveyed to the foreign secretary, Sir Anthony Eden, by Rex Leeper, now assistant under-secretary of state.

> Total warfare is a combination of armed forces and civilian morale. The two are intimately related so much so that armed forces alone will not win this war for us. We have got to influence civilian morale in Europe in such a way as to get the population doing what we want them to do. That is political warfare, an integral part of total warfare. To call it merely propaganda obscures people's vision as to the real nature of the task; to entrust this task to a department such as the Ministry of Information shows a lack of understanding. The representative of Political Warfare on the highest plane can only be the Foreign Secretary with his control over foreign policy and his seat on the Defence Committee ... He could see to it that Political Warfare actively assisted the strategic conduct of the war.[35]

These views evidently met with the approval of Churchill who, in August 1941, created the Political Warfare Executive (PWE) as the sole authority for conducting all aspects of psychological warfare with the objective of destroying the German war machine.

Political control of PWE was directed by a ministerial troika comprising Anthony Eden, Hugh Dalton, the minister of economic warfare, and Brendan Bracken, minister of information. The role of coordinating policy directives for 'Pee Wee', as the organization became known within Whitehall, was given to Sir Robert Bruce Lockhart, a senior Foreign Office official, who later assumed the title of director general. A secret organization, PWE operated under the cover of the Political Intelligence Department of the Foreign Office and consisted of two discrete elements: regional directorates based at Woburn Abbey and responsible for operational matters; and a central nucleus of functional departments based in London. In 1942 the London headquarters relocated to Bush House, which already housed the European Service of the BBC. Ministerial oversight was also streamlined, with Eden given responsibility for policy and Bracken placed in charge of administration.

The primary directive given to PWE was 'to split the German people, not to do Goebbels' job and unify them'. To achieve this aim the country directorates employed the dark arts of black propaganda and subversive rumour to undermine enemy morale. Within PWE a 'rumour' committee concocted outlandish tales then spread by agents and leaflet drops. To be successful the stories had to be plausible and to play on existing prejudices. Great care was taken to insert reliable information gleaned from returning agents and enemy interrogations. The key to a good story was often sex. Nazi leaders were portrayed as deviants or sexual predators. German front-line soldiers were targeted with lurid tales of wives and girlfriends being seduced by leading Nazis while they served heroically in the trenches.

The doctoring of German newspapers to feature bogus headlines was a commonly used technique. Hitler's proud boast in October 1941 that Russia would be defeated by the end of the year was a propagandist's dream. Millions of copies of the Nazi newspaper *Völkischer Beobachter* were produced with banner headlines ridiculing the campaign in the east and dropped over Germany during 1942. PWE also operated a number of clandestine radio stations, the best known of these being Gustav Siegfried Eins, which came on the air shortly after the flight of Rudolf Hess to England in 1940. The station, which claimed to be operating from within Germany, featured 'Der Chef', an unrepentant Nazi who directed his vitriol against both Churchill, who was described as a 'drunken old cigar-smoking Jew', and corrupt Nazi party officials who were betraying the German people. The station was the brainchild of Sefton Delmer, a former announcer on the BBC's

German service, who had been recruited by PWE in 1940. The role of 'Der Chef' was played by Peter Seckelmann, a German defector. In 1943, the station was closed in a blaze of gunfire after a fictitious Gestapo unit stormed the station while it was still broadcasting, apparently shooting 'Der Chef' dead on air.

As the war began to turn in Britain's favour, PWE began to focus its operations in support of the D-Day landings. Millions of leaflets were printed and dropped over enemy lines. The purpose was to exaggerate allied successes, create panic within the German ranks and induce surrender. For those contemplating surrender, Allied Safe Conduct Leaflets were a particularly sought-after item. In total over 32 million leaflets covering six European languages were printed and distributed by the British and American air forces. Another venture was *Nachrichten fur die Truppe* (News for the Troops), which was a daily newspaper aimed at German forces. The paper was edited by Harold Keebel (later the feature editor for the *Daily Mirror*) and featured news stories, sports results and even pin-ups. The purpose was to provide the German foot soldier with a readable alternative to the censored newspapers supplied by the German High Command. It was hoped that such stories would sap the will to resist further allied advances. The daily print run soon reached one million copies, with final production figures reaching a staggering 160 million. In the final months of war, the majority of PWE staff were transferred to the Psychological Warfare Division of SHAEF under the control of General Eisenhower. PWE was finally wound up in 1946 with a small unit retained for the re-education of German prisoners of war.[36]

Operation Mincemeat

In the run-up to D-Day, a number of deception operations were carried out by the London Controlling Station under Colonel Oliver Stanley. One of the most famous, ingenious and macabre was Operation Mincemeat, which was designed to convince the Germans that the allies' main military thrust would be through the Balkans, rather than their main objective which was the island of Sicily. The deception plan relied on convincing the Germans that they had accidentally stumbled across secret British papers (plate 11). To achieve this, a plan was devised in which a recently deceased corpse would be dressed in military uniform, handcuffed to a suitcase carrying military plans and washed up on a Spanish beach. The deception, as recorded in documents at the National Archives, relied on convincing the Germans that the body on the beach was one of the passengers aboard a military plane that had crashed off the Spanish coast. To execute the plan, the cadaver of a 34-year-old man was discreetly obtained from St Stephen's Hospital, Fulham. The body was that of a labourer of no fixed abode who had recently committed suicide by swallowing phosphorus rat poison. In the absence of an elaborate post mortem, of which the Spanish 'as Roman Catholics had a dislike', his death would be consistent with an air crash at sea.[37]

The body was given the false identity of William Martin, a major in the Royal Marines, and dressed in full battledress uniform. To further bolster the deception, a variety of items were placed with the body from money and cigarettes to theatre ticket stubs and personal letters. These were used to build up a personality, and included a demand for settlement of a £79.19.2d overdraft from Lloyds Bank; a photograph of his fiancée; a letter from his father to the family solicitor concerning imminent nuptials; and a receipt for an engagement ring, unpaid in light of his overdraft (plates 12 and 13). To preserve the body it was packed in dry ice and placed in an airtight container from which most of the oxygen had been removed. The container was then placed aboard the British submarine HMS *Seraph*. To conceal from the crew the fact that there was a dead body on board, the container was labelled 'Handle with Care—Optical Instruments—For Special FOS Shipment'. On 30 April 1943 'Major Martin's' body was released from the submarine a mile off the Spanish coast. The operation was relayed to London by the captain of HMS *Seraph*, Lieutenant N. L. Jewell:

> The canister was opened at 04.15 and the body extracted. The blanket was opened up and the body examined. The brief case was found to be securely attached. The face was heavily tanned and the whole of the lower half from the eyes down covered with mould ... The body was placed in the water at 04.30 in a position 148 degrees and 1.3 miles from the beach and started to drift inshore. This was aided by the wash of the screws going full sped astern. The rubber dinghy was placed in the water blown up and upside down about half a mile further south of this position. The submarine then withdrew.[38]

To give the deception operation further credence, the death of Major Martin following a plane crash was announced in *The Times*. By good fortune, his name appeared in a list of persons mainly killed in accidents. The body was eventually discovered washed up on the shore. It was taken to the local morgue where a doctor certified that death was due to asphyxiation through immersion in the sea while still alive. The personal effects, including the briefcase, were then removed and the body was buried in a Catholic cemetery at noon on 2 May. As expected, German intelligence was informed of the incident and made copies of all the documents before they were returned to the British naval attaché in Madrid. Intercepted communications revealed that the High Command in Berlin had received the false documents and believed them to be genuine. A report of the incident was sent personally to Admiral Dönitz; it concluded that 'the genuineness of the documents is above suspicion' and that 'the enemy is unlikely to know that they have been captured or to start their operations earlier than they had intended'. A cable was immediately sent to Churchill who was then in the United States: it consisted of only three words, 'Mincemeat Swallowed Whole'.

When the allies eventually landed in Sicily, they were met by only two German divisions. No measures were taken to reinforce the island, while a build-up of German forces in the Balkans waited in vain to repel an attack that never materialized. The British post-war report on the operation concluded:

> There can be no doubt that Mincemeat succeeded in achieving the desired effect of dispersing the German effort. It is probable that it was largely responsible for the fact that the East end of Sicily, where we landed, was much less defended both by troops and fortifications than the West end near Sardinia.[39]

After the war, the story of Operation Mincemeat was brought to public attention in the 1955 film *The Man Who Never Was*.

America enters the war

To defeat Germany, Britain required the active support of the United States. The fall of France in May 1940 made such assistance all the more imperative. Churchill was determined to end American isolationism and set upon establishing a covert organization in the United States to further British interests. The man chosen to head the organization, which became known as British Security Co-ordination (BSC), was William Stephenson, a Canadian industrialist and trusted confidant of Churchill, who assumed the code name Intrepid. Operating out of offices in the Rockefeller Center in New York, Stephenson soon began to recruit his team, which included Roald Dahl, who became better known for his children's books, and Ian Fleming, the creator of

James Bond.[40] BSC had three declared objectives: to investigate German activities; to thwart the threat of sabotage against British interests; and to influence American public opinion in Britain's favour. There was also a fourth undeclared objective: to ensure American participation in secret activities throughout the world in the closest possible collaboration with the British. To pursue these goals, Stephenson established alliances with J. Edgar Hoover of the FBI and Colonel William Donovan, President Roosevelt's newly appointed co-ordinator of information.

Propaganda was directed against organizations that were thought to be pro-Nazi or avowedly isolationist, such as the America First Committee, whose membership included the aviator Charles Lindbergh, the actress Lillian Gish and the film producer Walt Disney. To further its aims, BSC ran its own radio station, WRUL, and press agency, the Overseas News Agency, which was used to plant stories in American newspapers such as the *New York Post*, *Herald Tribune* and *Baltimore Sun*. Every tactic in the propaganda handbook was exploited to the full. In one of its more bizarre operations, BSC employed the services of Louis de Wohl, a Hungarian astrologer who became a minor celebrity with his claims that Hitler's astrological chart showed nothing but disaster (p. 194). A more sophisticated operation was to plant the suggestion in American minds that Hitler's plan for global domination included occupation of the South American continent. This was achieved by the use of a forged map which showed South America divided into five new states under Nazi control. It was claimed that the map was stolen from a German courier's bag in Buenos Aires. The news of its discovery caused a sensation, with President Roosevelt denouncing Nazi Germany as posing a clear threat to the interests of the United States. His views were made clear in a speech to the American public on 27 October 1941:

> I have in my possession a secret map, made in Germany ... It is a map of South America as Hitler intends to reorganize it ... into five vassal states, bringing the whole continent under their domination ... One of these new states includes the Republic of Panama and our great life line the Panama Canal ... This map makes clear the Nazi design, not only against South America but against the United States as well.[41]

The Japanese attack on Pearl Harbor in December 1941 and America's entry into the war allowed BSC to function more openly, especially in its relations with American special forces. In June 1942 Donovan met with the British war cabinet and reached agreement on the future of Anglo-American covert operations. The British would be responsible for Europe, India and East Africa, with the Middle East and the Balkans a joint concern. America would conduct operations in China, Korea, the South Pacific and North Africa. To provide a more offensive capability, Donovan was placed in charge of a new organization, the Office of Strategic Services (OSS), which specialized in intelligence and sabotage operations. OSS, the forerunner of the CIA, was organized into five divisions: SI (Secret Intelligence); SO (Secret Operations); R&A (Research and Analysis); MO (Propaganda); and X-2 (Counter-intelligence). New recruits received initial training at BSC's Camp X in Whitby, Ontario, the first school for clandestine operations established in North America. OSS also established new headquarters in London, located in Grosvenor Street, close to the US embassy.

The first overseas operations of OSS were conducted in North Africa, where it had already established a strong network in support of the allied landings in November 1942. Following the allied invasion of Europe, OSS conducted joint missions with British forces. To assist the French resistance, so-called Jedburgh teams were formed, which consisted of an American, a British and a Free French soldier. In all 93 Jedburgh teams were dropped into France following the Normandy invasion. Their purpose was to provide communications, direction and assistance to the local guerrilla forces. The close relationship between OSS and its British counterparts was recognized after the war. Stephenson was knighted by the British in the 1945 New Year's Honours list and in 1946 was awarded the Presidential Medal of Merit, becoming the first non-US citizen to receive such an award.[42]

The Cold War

Following the defeat of Germany and Japan in 1945, the majority of intelligence organizations that had grown up during the war, such as SOE and PWE, were either disbanded or absorbed into the Foreign Office, the military or the intelligence agencies. The division of Europe into allied and Soviet spheres of influence was soon transformed into a Cold War, with both sides distrusting the other's intentions. Information became a prized currency as tensions grew.

Rich sources of intelligence on the Soviet Union were found both through exploiting the numerous Russians who found themselves on the wrong side of the Iron Curtain and by penetrating the files of Nazi

intelligence, captured at the end of the war. Key among the latter were
those covering the 'Rote Kapelle'—the Abwehr cover-name for operations carried out against a series of Russian intelligence cells operating in Belgium, France, Holland, Switzerland and Germany itself. Of
these, seven networks were discovered and broken by the Germans
who appeared to have succeeded in penetrating, if not entirely eliminating, the main Russian organization in Western Europe. Offering
the possibility of real insight into the methods of the Russian intelligence service, this source was of huge potential value and prompted
the production of a three-volume US/UK report in 1949, entitled 'The
Case of the Rote Kapelle'.[43] Only recently released to the National
Archives, the report begins by underlining the difficulty of producing a
simple and coherent account given the scale and complexity of the
organizations in question.

Alongside the narrative of Soviet activities in Europe from 1935 to
1945 is an index of personalities involved, complete with biographies
and photographs. Much emphasis is placed on individuals throughout
the text, not least because events to date had indicated that the experienced 'professional Russian spy' was apt to re-emerge despite previous
detection and even imprisonment. Prime among these was the
'extremely resourceful and capable' Leopold Trepper (plate 14), whose
activities had focused on France and the UK before they were turned
against Germany. Trepper had initially operated under the commercial
cover of a number of different firms in Belgium and later France,
including the Foreign Excellent Raincoat Company, which exported
raincoats to Scandinavia. Responsible for a number of espionage rings
(plate 15), his arrest in a dentist's chair in December 1942 was due in
part to the pressures involved in operating in occupied territory, oblig-
ing hitherto separate organizations to abandon pre-war security measures and establish contact with each other. Once captured, with operations compromised, Trepper offered to work as a double agent and
provided information on many of his compatriots, though, as the
report speculated, possibly only on those whom he believed the Germans were bound to discover for themselves:

> It is extremely likely that Trepper intended from the moment he was
> captured to practice a triple-cross. An instance of this kind of activity
> was when he succeeded in obtaining from the German Intelligence in
> 1943 an up-to-date statement of their knowledge of British resources
> in the Mediterranean, which he sent to Moscow ostensibly to create
> confidence. In fact the information was needed by the Russians in their

concern for a second front. It is also almost certain that he had outside lines of communication with the Russian Intelligence Service during his period of captivity.[44]

Trepper used the comparative freedom of an 'honour prisoner' to his advantage. Ever resourceful, he managed to evade his captors, escaping from Paris in January 1945 as Vladislav Ivanovitch Ivanowski.

Though the German files undoubtedly proved a boon to the intelligence services, they did contain some notable gaps, not least with regard to Soviet operations within the UK. This was in part because Henri Robinson, one of those responsible for operations in the UK, revealed very little to his German captors under interrogation. This saved the lives of many of his agents and subsequently hid their identities from the British intelligence services. Equally frustrating was the knowledge that Trepper himself had visited the UK on a number of occasions, including a series of visits made in 1938; the purpose of these visits was not known, since, as the report conceded, 'they did not interest Trepper's German interrogators'.

In 1945, as at the end of the First World War, the intelligence machinery developed during the war came under review following the defeat of Germany and Japan. While there was general agreement that the growing Soviet threat required a continuing provision of intelligence, the size, function and organizational structure needed in the future were not yet certain. A variety of reports were undertaken to address these issues, among them a review of intelligence organizations by Air Chief Marshal Sir Douglas Evill in 1947.[45] In his review — which was to prove one of the most far-reaching — Evill concluded that current knowledge of Russian intentions, scientific capability and technical progress was 'seriously inadequate' and that 'the only hope of satisfactory progress' lay in the 'very careful planning of our intelligence offensive'. To achieve this, he recommended that the JIC should be reconstituted as a full committee of the chiefs of staff (rather than a subcommittee); that the status of the JIC chairman should be raised to the rank of under-secretary in the Foreign Office; and that a new charter, emphasizing its new authority, should be jointly approved by the minister of defence and the foreign secretary. The government accepted these recommendations as part of a new order of intelligence organization to suit the emerging post-war world.

The new demands imposed by the Cold War also resulted in a reorganization of the SIS command structure. In place of the ten semi-

autonomous sections, five new directorates were created. These were
(I) Finance and Administration; (II) Production, responsible for operational intelligence and divided along geographical lines; (III) Requirements, responsible for analysis and distribution and divided into nine
subject areas, the most important being R5, the counter-intelligence
section; (IV) Training and Development; and (V) War Planning.[46] The
GC&CS at Bletchley Park was also made independent of SIS and placed
under direct Foreign Office control. The service's primary directive
was to provide strategic intelligence on the Soviet Union.

The West was concerned that Stalin, far from consolidating his territorial gains made at the end of the war, was determined to press on
and impose Communist rule over the whole of Europe. The Communist party's seizure of power in Poland and Czechoslovakia confirmed
these fears. To contain Soviet expansionism, the West sought to bolster its armed forces and mount a concerted campaign aimed at win-
ning hearts and minds. In January 1948 the British foreign secretary,
Ernest Bevin, presented his ideas to the cabinet. Bevin proposed the
creation of a small dedicated unit working within the Foreign Office to
collect information on Communist policy, tactics and propaganda and
to provide material for anti-Communist publicity abroad. The unit,
which was named the Information Research Department (IRD),
would also act as a counter against the Cominform, the Soviet Union's
own propaganda department, created by Stalin in October 1947. The
first head of IRD was Ralph Murray, a former BBC employee who had
served in PWE during the Second World War.[47]

Due to its specialist nature, and to avoid the unwelcome scrutiny of
parliament, a proportion of IRD's funding came from the Secret Vote.
Over the next months, IRD rapidly increased its staff; recruits included
the novelist Fay Weldon, the academic Robert Conquest and the journalist Brian Crozier. The primary aim of IRD was to produce non-
attributable anti-Communist material which was then recycled by
unsuspecting journalists. To achieve this IRD established a publishing
house, Ampersand, a number of news agencies and a radio station.
The cultivation of opinion-formers, such as journalists, politicians and
trade unionists, formed a significant element of IRD's work. Major
successes in these early years included the publication of a Russian edition of George Orwell's *Animal Farm*, the commissioning of articles
by well-known figures on the left such as Harold Laski and Richard
Crossman and the inclusion of IRD material in the left-wing magazine
Tribune. Those countries in which the Communist party had strong

support were priority targets. France and Italy were prime examples in which IRD material was handed over to party organizers and others of influence who could make good use of it. The aim was to undermine the credibility of the Communist party by supplying material on the 'realities' of life under Stalinist rule. Character assassination and the circulation of scurrilous rumours were also favoured tactics. In undertaking its work, IRD worked in close contact with the Colonial Department, the Central Office of Information and the Overseas Services of the BBC. Its relationship with the intelligence agencies was particularly strong. One organization with which IRD enjoyed a close working relationship was the anti-Soviet section of SIS, which had been established in 1944 and which soon became the principal department within SIS, consisting of a headquarters staff of 60 officers, with an equal number stationed overseas. All of these, significantly, came under the control of one Harold 'Kim' Philby.

The Cambridge spy ring

During the 1930s Philby, in common with many intellectuals, joined the CPGB in the belief that it represented the best defence against Fascism. Marxist societies were soon established at both Oxford and Cambridge. The majority of these had an open membership; however, a small number remained secret. One of these, known as the Apostles, was based in Trinity College, Cambridge, and attracted recruits who, in addition to Philby, included Guy Burgess, Donald Maclean, Anthony Blunt and John Cairncross. In their zeal to further the cause of international Communism, the Cambridge five sought actively to assist the Soviet state. All were soon recruited by Russian intelligence and instructed to conceal their Marxist sympathies. Philby took his orders to the extreme and travelled to Spain where he wrote a series of newspaper articles in support of Franco and the Nationalists.

Following the outbreak of the Second World War, the five found positions at the highest levels of government. Philby was recruited by MI6 and worked in Section V (counter-espionage), taking command of the Iberian department where he worked closely with SOE. Among the agents recruited by Philby were Malcolm Muggeridge and Graham Greene. At the end of the war, Philby was posted to Istanbul as MI6 head of station and later to Washington, where he acted as liaison officer with the newly formed CIA. From his position at the heart of Western intelligence, Philby supplied a wealth of classified information to

Moscow, resulting in the deaths of numerous agents. Of the other members of the spy ring, Cairncross joined the Foreign Office and became private secretary to Maurice Hankey, the minister responsible for overseeing the intelligence services, and was later assigned to GC&CS. Maclean also joined the Foreign Office and was posted as first secretary to the British embassy in Washington where he was privy to the secrets of the Manhattan Project, the code name for the Anglo-American atomic bomb programme. Burgess joined MI6 and worked in the office supervising SOE operations. After the war he was posted to the British embassy in Washington. Blunt joined MI5 where he represented the service at the weekly meetings of the JIC.

The Cambridge five are regarded by many as the most successful spy ring of modern times, achieving remarkable levels of penetration before they were eventually exposed. The intelligence that they passed to Moscow revealed the innermost secrets of the British state and would have been more effective had Stalin not regarded them with suspicion as possible double agents. In 1949 Maclean came under suspicion of passing classified information to Moscow. The method by which he was unmasked was based on analysis of Soviet diplomatic traffic which had been partially deciphered by US code-breakers (p. 258). The messages showed that between 1944 and 1946 a member of the British embassy, who was given the code name Homer, had passed information to Soviet intelligence. The list of possible suspects was narrowed down to three or four individuals. One was Donald Maclean. The list of names was forwarded to the embassy's SIS liaison officer, Kim Philby. In order to warn Maclean that he would soon be unmasked as a Soviet agent, Philby arranged for Guy Burgess to return to London. Yuri Modin, Maclean's Soviet handler, was also informed and he made arrangements for Maclean's defection to Moscow. On his return to London, Burgess visited Maclean and agreed to accompany him to the coast, where he was to board a ship to France. Anxious that Burgess might also be exposed and interrogated by MI5, Modin insisted that he should also defect. On 25 May 1951 Burgess and Maclean left England for the last time, never to return.[48]

The disappearance of two high-ranking diplomats caused consternation within Whitehall. It soon became apparent to investigators that they had been tipped off and the search for the 'Third Man' began in earnest. A close associate of both men, Philby quickly became a prime suspect. Despite intensive questioning, nothing incriminating could be found. He was nevertheless tarnished by the episode and forced to resign. In 1955 Philby was named in the press as chief suspect for the 'Third Man'. He immediately called a press conference at which he strongly asserted his innocence. He was eventually cleared of suspicion by Harold Macmillan, the foreign secretary, who in an ill-judged statement to the House of Commons declared that there was no evidence 'to conclude that Mr Philby has at any time betrayed the interests of his country, or to identify him with the so-called "Third Man", if indeed there was one'. After leaving SIS, Philby found employment as *The Economist*'s Middle East correspondent. Despite Macmillan's statement, many remained suspicious of Philby's loyalty. In 1961 the Soviet defector Anatoly Golitsyn provided fresh evidence of Philby's guilt. Confronted with this new information, Philby finally defected to the Soviet Union in January 1963, slipping out of Lebanon on the Soviet freighter *Dolmatova*.[49]

The remaining two members of the Cambridge spy ring, Anthony Blunt and John Cairncross, remained at large but were eventually uncovered. In 1945 Blunt left MI5 to became director of the Courtauld Institute and was appointed surveyor of the king's pictures, receiving a knighthood in 1956. All seemed well until 1964, when Blunt was confronted with new evidence of his wartime activities. In exchange for immunity from prosecution and a promise of secrecy, he made a full confession and was allowed to continue in public life. In 1979, however, following the publication of Andrew Boyle's book *The Climate of Treason*, Margaret Thatcher named Blunt as the 'Fourth Man'.[50] Now in public disgrace, he was forced to resign from his many positions and stripped of his knighthood. The identity of the 'Fifth Man' remained a public mystery until 1990 when his name was revealed by the KGB defector Yuri Modin.[51] Cairncross strenuously denied the charges and retired to the South of France, where he died in 1995 aged 82.

Penkovsky and Gordievsky

The penetration of the adversary's intelligence service was not the sole preserve of Moscow. In the early 1960s, Oleg Penkovsky, a colonel in Soviet military intelligence, made contact with Greville Wynne, a British businessman in Moscow who had contacts with SIS. Penkovsky, who was disillusioned with life in Soviet Russia, offered his services and handed Wynne a package of confidential documents. Initially the British were reluctant to believe their good luck, assuming Penkovsky was a Soviet double agent. In April 1961 Penkovsky visited

Britain as the head of a Soviet trade delegation. He was eventually contacted by British intelligence and agreed to a meeting at which he was cross-examined by both SIS and the CIA. His credentials verified, Penkovsky agreed to work as a 'defector in place' and over the next 18 months supplied a wealth of material to his British and American handlers. One of these was Janet Chisholm, the wife of Ruari Chisholm, reportedly SIS head of station in Moscow, who agreed to meet Penkovsky in a local park while walking with her children. When Penkovsky arrived he proceeded to engage her in seemingly casual conversation. At the end of their meeting he gave her youngest child a box of sweets; it contained seven rolls of exposed Minox microfilm revealing secret information about the Soviet nuclear arsenal.[52] The intelligence was instrumental in demonstrating that the Soviets did not possess the number of ballistic missiles claimed by Khrushchev.

In October 1962 a U2 spy plane discovered Soviet missiles in Cuba. Penkovsky's intelligence was instrumental in enabling US analysts to identify the missiles before they became operational. Photographic evidence of the deployment was presented to the United Nations and proved invaluable in forcing the Soviets to dismantle the sites. As the crisis reached its climax, Penkovsky was arrested, found guilty of high treason and executed. Some reports claim that he was tied to a board with piano wire and cremated alive. During his interrogation, Penkovsky named Greville Wynne as one of his contacts. A few days later, Wynne was arrested in Budapest and sentenced to eight years in prison for espionage. In 1964 he was exchanged for the Soviet spy George Lonsdale.[53]

The Soviet Union's humiliating withdrawal of its missiles from Cuba led to the removal of Nikita Khrushchev and his replacement as Soviet leader by Leonid Brezhnev. The foreign policy agenda pursued by Brezhnev was one of consolidation. In 1968 he ordered Warsaw Pact forces to invade Czechoslovakia and eliminate the liberal reformist regime of Alexander Dubček. The crushing of the Prague Spring dismayed many members of the Communist party. One of these was Oleg Gordievsky, a colonel in the KGB. After joining the KGB in 1962, Gordievsky was posted to the Soviet embassy in Copenhagen. Following the invasion of Czechoslovakia he offered his services to British intelligence. In 1982 he was posted to London as the KGB resident-designate responsible for all Soviet intelligence and espionage activity in the UK. Over a two-year period he passed over hundreds of classified documents to his British handlers and was instrumental in unmasking Michael Bettaney, an MI5 officer working for the Soviets. In 1985

Gordievsky was ordered back to Moscow and arrested. It appears that his cover had been compromised by Aldrich Ames, a senior official in the CIA, who had been recruited by the KGB. Gordievsky was questioned for several weeks but no solid evidence could be found to implicate him. He was eventually released and allowed to return to his family in Moscow. MI6 was concerned for his safety and hatched a plan for his safe return to London. Gordievsky was instructed to catch a train to the Finnish border where he was met by two British agents and smuggled across the border in the boot of a car. His entry into Finland was theatrically marked by the opening strains of Sibelius's *Finlandia* playing loudly on the car's stereo.[54]

The Franks Committee

In April 1982, the Argentine military invaded the Falkland Islands, catching the British authorities by surprise. In response, a British naval task force was rapidly assembled and sent to the South Atlantic. Following a brief but intense military campaign, in which 225 British and 750 Argentine servicemen lost their lives, British sovereignty over the islands was restored. In the political aftermath of the campaign, the government of Margaret Thatcher took the decision to review the diplomatic, military and intelligence dimensions to determine whether lessons could be learnt for the future. A committee of five privy councillors under Lord Franks, a senior civil servant and former ambassador to Washington, was convened for the purpose. The other members of the committee were Lord Barber, a Conservative peer and former chancellor of the exchequer; Lord Lever of Manchester, a Labour peer and former paymaster general; Sir Patrick Nairne, a senior civil servant with a background in the Admiralty and MoD; Merlyn Rees, a Labour MP and former home secretary; and Lord Watkinson, a Conservative peer and former transport minister.

The committee, officially known as the Falklands Islands Review Committee, took evidence in private and met between July and December 1982. A primary concern for the committee was the paucity of intelligence prior to the Argentine invasion. To determine the reasons for this apparent intelligence failure, the committee took evidence from the Sir Colin Figures, chief of SIS, Sir Brian Tovey, the director of GCHQ, Sir Anthony Duff, the intelligence coordinator, Patrick Wright chairman of the JIC and Robert O'Neill, head of the assessment staff. The committee's main conclusion was that the government 'could not have foreseen' the invasion and that it would not be justified to attach 'any criticism or blame to the present government for the Argentinean junta's decision to commit its act of unprovoked aggression in the invasion of the Falkland Islands on April 2 1982'.[55]

In relation to intelligence, the committee was more critical, expressing its surprise that events in the first three months of 1982 did not prompt the JIC to reassess Argentine intentions. It was particularly concerned that the assessment staff attached greater significance to secret intelligence rather than information derived from open sources such as diplomatic exchanges and the wealth of material published in the Argentine press—which, in the view of the committee, provided ample evidence of Argentina's desire to recover Las Malvinas using force if necessary. Franks recommended closer liaison between the assessment staff, the Foreign Office and the Ministry of Defence to ensure that open source intelligence and relevant diplomatic and political developments were taken fully into account. The composition of the JIC was also criticized in that 'it was too passive in operation to respond quickly and critically to a rapidly changing situation which required urgent attention'. The committee believed that the chairman of the JIC should be full-time, be appointed by the prime minister and have more independence from government departments.

These recommendations were accepted by the government, with the result that the chairmanship of the JIC was removed from Foreign Office control and transferred to the intelligence co-ordinator in the Cabinet Office. In 1985, the chair of the JIC assumed the role of the prime minister's foreign policy advisor, a position held by Sir Percy Craddock until his retirement in 1992. In absolving the government of blame for its failure to anticipate the invasion, the Franks report was strongly criticized by members of the opposition. The former prime minister, James Callaghan, was particularly scathing of both the report and the role played by its chairman, Lord Franks: 'For 338 paragraphs he painted a splendid picture, delineated the light and the shade, and the glowing colours in it, and when Franks got to paragraph 339 he got fed up with the canvas he was painting, and chucked a bucket of whitewash over it.'

Out of the shadows

Throughout the 20th century, the exploits of Britain's SIS became embedded in the popular consciousness. The glamorous adventures of

James Bond, embellished by the memoirs of former officers and the imagination of journalists, gave the organization an almost mythical status. Officially SIS did not exist; even its name was regarded as an official secret. Following the collapse of the Soviet Union, the need to maintain this pretence became counterproductive as the service sought to justify its role (and budget) within the new world order. On 6 May 1992 the prime minister, John Major, publicly avowed the existence of SIS to the House of Commons and named its chief, Sir Colin McColl. In 1994 parliament passed the Intelligence Services Act which placed SIS and GCHQ on a statutory footing. The Act defined the role of SIS: to obtain and provide information relating to the actions or intentions of persons outside the British Islands; and to perform other tasks relating to the actions or intentions of such persons. It also established a tribunal to investigate complaints and an oversight committee, the Intelligence and Security Committee, consisting of nine MPs reporting directly to the prime minister.

The new policy of openness became more apparent in 1994 when SIS moved into its new headquarters at 85 Vauxhall Cross, vacating the drab tower block at Century House that it had occupied since 1965. Designed by Terry Farrell, and costing over £240 million, the new building has become a major landmark on the London waterfront and was even featured in the 1999 James Bond film *The World is Not Enough*. SIS now has a presence in cyberspace, with its own website going live in 2005.[56] Despite such openness, SIS has no immediate plans to transfer its files to the National Archives. To mark the centenary of the service in 2009, the foreign secretary has agreed to the preparation of a volume of SIS official history covering 1909 to the early Cold War. Professor Keith Jeffery of Queen's University Belfast has been appointed as the author and publication of the volume is planned for 2010. As the service prepares to celebrate its 100th birthday, public interest in espionage and intrigue, whether real or imagined, remains as strong as ever.

3 | Military Intelligence

An integral part of successful operations, military intelligence is as old as war itself. John Churchill, the first Duke of Marlborough whose own military career spanned the 17th and 18th centuries, famously stated that no war could be conducted successfully 'without early and good intelligence'. Many have agreed, not least Churchill's great admirer, the Duke of Wellington, who placed much reliance on his daring agent Colquhoun Grant. Yet the gathering of intelligence on an enemy's strengths, weakness and strategic objectives was not always maintained: decades later, the British—incredibly—found themselves without maps of the Crimea at the start of the Crimean War.

The foundation of the Intelligence Branch in 1873 first placed military intelligence on a professional footing. It proliferated during the First World War, spawning a variety of MI units, including MI5. In the Second World War, MI14 provided early intelligence of Hitler's intention to target Russia in the run up to Operation Barbarossa, while MI9 and MI19 exploited the intelligence potential of escapers, evaders and captured enemy prisoners of war. Despite drives towards centralization and pressure to cut costs, the authorities continued to support acquisition of military intelligence in the Cold War years. It was crucial to numerous operations, including those in Cyprus and Kenya, where field intelligence officers carried out 'thrilling work' in combating Mau Mau rebels. Intelligence also informed British attempts to monitor Russian intentions and technologies in East Germany through the long-running BRIXMIS reconnaissance operations.

The Duke of Wellington's spies

Within the British army, the responsibility for gathering military intelligence was first assumed by the implausibly named scoutmaster-general —responsible for a network of scouts and agents seeking to obtain information on an enemy's plans and dispositions. In 1686 the position of scoutmaster-general was abolished, and the gathering of military intelligence transferred to the post of quartermaster-general. During the Napoleonic Wars Major General Sir Robert Brownrigg, then quartermaster-general and later governor of Ceylon, successfully established the Depôt of Military Knowledge, uniting all information relating to military plans, maps and publications in one organization.[1] The creation of the depôt in 1803 marks the first in a long line of organizations responsible for providing intelligence to the British army.

The Napoleonic Wars also demonstrated the need for prompt and accurate field intelligence. The commander of British forces, the Duke of Wellington, readily appreciated its value and established a network of intelligence officers and local spies. These provided him with both strategic information, gathered by the interception of enemy letters, and tactical intelligence, gathered by men in the field known as 'exploring officers' or 'army guides'. Placed under the command of George Scovell, Wellington's chief code-breaker, the guides were recruited for their local knowledge, language skills and ingenuity in the field.[2]

One of the early recruits was Colquhoun Grant—the product of a quite extraordinary family who could count a governor of Trinidad and a distinguished lieutenant colonel in the Madras army among his siblings. Colquhoun's career would prove no less remarkable. In 1808, during the Peninsular War, he undertook intelligence-gathering missions behind enemy lines and narrowly avoided capture by French forces, escaping half-dressed and abandoning his horse and papers. During Wellington's blockade of Ciudad Rodrigo, a small cathedral city in western Spain, Grant was once again infiltrated behind enemy lines, bringing back intelligence that French forces were unable to mount a successful counter-attack to relieve the siege. In 1812, in another foray behind enemy lines, Grant was captured by French dragoons and imprisoned in Salamanca. The circumstances of his detention are described in an intercepted letter from General de la Martinière, the original of which is preserved at the National Archives among a file of dispatches. This states that Grant had been discovered alone with one servant on the flank of the French columns, dressed in 'the uniform and badges of an English officer'. He was found to be carrying 'papers and notes which indicate clearly the role of a man of importance to the English army, having the most accurate and the most detailed ideas of the marches, the composition, the strength and the movement of the French army'.[3]

Transferred by his captors to Bayonne in southern France, Grant managed to escape and travelled to Paris. Once there, he made contact with a British secret agent and remained in the city for several weeks, during which time he continued to gather intelligence for Wellington. As Paris became too dangerous, Grant returned to Spain in the guise of an American sailor. After Napoleon's return from exile in Elba, Wellington placed Grant in charge of the army's intelligence department, promoting him to the rank of assistant adjutant-general.[4]

Grant's exploits were still being related a century later, forming part of a lecture on intelligence in European warfare that was delivered by Lieutenant Colonel James Edmonds in 1908 and is now held at the National Archives. Edmonds devoted some space to Wellington's use of agents disguised as peddlers or musicians to gather intelligence on enemy troop movements—a tactic he believed Germany could well be deploying in contemporary Britain given the numbers of unregulated foreign aliens residing in the country. He then turned to the duke's most trusted officer, using the following story from 1815 to illustrate the importance of passing on information from agents in the field—however trivial or unlikely it may seem:

> lying out in France in front of the army and employing various agents,
> some actually located in the French War Office, Grant discovered
> that Napoleon was moving on the 13th June and sent in a message;
> it had unfortunately to pass through the Head Quarters of General
> Dornberg, commanding a cavalry brigade, who not knowing Grant
> and deeming the message incredible, not only did not send it on, but
> sent it back. The Duke heard it only on the morning of Waterloo, the
> 18th, when Grant himself came in. Had it reached him on the 14th, the
> course of the campaign would no doubt have been less hazardous. It is
> said that Wellington was reluctant to move at all because no message
> from Grant had reached him.[5]

The Crimean War and its aftermath

Following the defeat of Napoleon in 1815, the Depôt of Military Knowledge was starved of resources and fell into disuse. The parlous state of military intelligence was starkly revealed in 1854 when Russian troops invaded Turkey, leading to the Crimean War. The British army were caught completely unprepared: no maps of the area were available and knowledge of Russian forces and tactics was virtually non-existent. Fortunately for the British, Major Thomas Best Jervis of the Royal Engineers—enjoying a holiday in Belgium—accidentally discovered a Russian map of the Crimea and a number of Austrian maps of Turkey in a second-hand bookstore. Realizing the importance of his find, Jervis returned to London and reproduced copies of the maps at his own expense. In recognition of his work, he was promoted to lieutenant colonel and made director of the newly established Topographical and Statistical Department.

A collection of Jervis's reports and memoranda from 1855 and 1856 relating to the department are preserved at the National Archives. In a letter to Sir Robert Peel dated 31 May 1855 he laid out the dual purpose of the new department, which was modelled on the French Depôt de la Guerre. In peacetime the aim was to produce maps, plans and surveys of vital interest to the army; in wartime it was to act as a secret intelligence corps, operating outside the constraints and distractions of a purely military service. The department's role was to seize every opportunity to acquire valuable local knowledge, to take plans, surveys and exact military drawings, and to obtain the most accurate statistical, physical and sanitary information. Progress was summarized in the Topographical and Statistical Department's annual report for 1855, a 50-page document, in which Jervis outlined the key achievements of his first year in charge. He was clearly keen to investigate cutting-edge developments including the potential applications of photography, a technique that 'may deservedly be taken up at some future time'. It was, Jervis recognized, an art still 'in its infancy' and as yet of 'very limited application', but one that might prove the most economic and effective means of copying documents, from detailed maps to state papers. Alongside this and the department's more normal work, Jervis also devoted space in his report to a glowing description of a model of Sebastopol that he had recently seen to completion. Built on a scale of 10 inches to a mile, it extended:

> from the Vernutta and Baidar river on the South East, to the Heights of Inkerman, including the site of the last action, and thence westward to the Khersonese Lighthouse:- the heights true to scale. The entire ground work of this model was completed this evening; and has been pronounced, after a very careful examination by General Sir Colin Campbell, Gen Dickson, the Staff of Major General Jones, Col Hamilton, and Colonel Rollo, to be a very faithful and valuable representation of the ground, insomuch that numerous officers have come and pointed out instantly and with delight and satisfaction particular

localities, which may give every confidence to his Lordship in regard of its accuracy.[6]

Despite such endeavours, the Topographical and Statistical Department could only provide marginal assistance to the conduct of the Crimean War. Badly organized from the start, the campaign was characterized by dreadful conditions for the troops, including a lack of food and inadequate medical supplies. Significantly, the advent of the telegraph meant that this was also the first military campaign covered 'live' by the press. A series of articles by *The Times*' celebrated war correspondent, William Howard Russell, graphically portrayed the hardships and daily horrors encountered by British forces. Growing public disquiet brought down the government and sparked a series of enquiries into the conduct of the war. The most important was the select committee chaired by John Roebuck, a close friend of John Stuart Mill and radical MP for Sheffield. Published in 1855, Roebuck's five-volume report, 'The Army before Sebastopol', was severely critical of both the army and the political establishment for waging a war for which they were completely unprepared. Lord Raglan, commander of British forces in the Crimea, was singled out for particular criticism: 'he foresaw nothing, provided nothing, left everything to chance and found himself encompassed with the horrors of a Polar winter before he had taken a single precaution.'[7]

The army was slow to respond to these criticisms and it was only after the Franco-Prussian War of 1870 that urgent reform was undertaken. The scale of the Prussian victory demonstrated to the British army that military strength was determined not by the regular forces in uniform, but rather by an ability to deploy trained reservists to the ranks after mobilization. The architect of the reforms was Edward Cardwell, secretary of state for war under Gladstone, and he reorganized the army into regimental districts based on county boundaries. All infantry regiments would now be composed of two battalions, one serving overseas with the other stationed at home forming a reserve. To support the new regimental structure, the Topographical and Statistical Department was directed to concentrate its resources into obtaining information on the strength, organization and equipment of foreign armies and new developments in military science.[8]

Military intelligence was now acknowledged to be an essential component of any modern army, and in 1873 Cardwell announced the creation of the Intelligence Branch. Under the command of Major

General Sir Patrick MacDougall, this would take over responsibilities formerly carried by the Topographical and Statistical Department. The Intelligence Branch moved in 1882 into new premises in Queen Anne's Gate, where it would remain until 1901. To underline its growing importance, the head of the Intelligence Branch, Major General Henry Brackenbury, was in 1887 given the title director of military intelligence (DMI), with direct access to the commander in chief. Following Brackenbury's promotion to lieutenant general in 1888, the Intelligence Branch was renamed the Intelligence Division, now comprising five country sections, a map section and a library.[9]

The Directorate of Military Operations

In March 1896 Major General Sir John Ardagh, former private secretary to Lord Lansdowne, the viceroy of India, was appointed to the position of DMI. In his rise through the army, Ardagh had established close friendships with senior political and military figures and maintained cordial working relations with the Admiralty, Colonial Office and Foreign Office. His appointment as DMI was well received. In 1899 Ardagh was dispatched to The Hague as a military adviser to the first peace conference that sought to establish procedures for settling international disputes without the need for war, but no sooner had the conference ended than South Africa declared war on Britain.

In the ensuing campaign against the Boers, a variety of field intelligence units were established. These included Rimington's Tigers—a force of irregulars so named because of the distinctive wild-cat fur worn around their hats—and Lovat's Scouts, largely composed of crofters and shepherds from the northern highlands of Scotland, skilled in stalking, riding and shooting.[10] The responsibility for directing these various units and analysing the information they obtained was given to Colonel C. V. Hume, a career soldier who was appointed in 1901 to head up the South African section. Under Hume's leadership, the number of field intelligence officers increased from two to 132, but nevertheless the campaign in South Africa soon ran into trouble: Ardagh and the Intelligence Division in London faced fierce criticism for their failure correctly to assess the numerical strength of the Boers. They were also accused of ignorance of the enemy's armaments and strategy, and of providing insufficient warning of the conflict to the government of the day.

In the aftermath of the campaign a Royal Commission was appointed under Lord Elgin to enquire into the conduct of the war in South Africa and the perceived failings of the Intelligence Division. The commission soon discovered that—far from failing in their duty—the Intelligence Division had not only issued a succession of reports highlighting the likelihood of war with South Africa, but had also produced estimates of Boer military preparations which were 'remarkably accurate'.[11] It was soon discovered that these reports had been deliberately excluded from cabinet discussion by senior officials who wished to downplay the talk of war with South Africa. These revelations vindicated the work of the Intelligence Division, which now received praise rather than condemnation from the press and public alike.

To ensure that intelligence assessments were acted upon in the future, the decision was taken in 1904 to integrate the Intelligence Division within the Directorate of Military Operations (DMO), located in the War Office building in Whitehall.[12] The directorate was eventually composed of six sections: MO1 Strategic; MO2 Europe (less France), the Middle East and the Americas; MO3, France, Russia, Scandinavia and the Far East; MO4, Topographical; MO5, Special Duties, from which the Secret Service Bureau would soon emerge; and MO6, Medical Intelligence. It was still not considered necessary to possess a permanently established intelligence unit for field operations. Consequently, as documents in the National Archives show, when war was declared on Germany a motley collection of journalists, teachers and policemen were summoned to the War Office and informed that they were to join a new unit known as the Intelligence Corps.[13] After three weeks' basic training, the unit was moved to France with individual intelligence officers assigned to various headquarters. The Intelligence Corps was composed of a mounted section, a motorized section and a security section, the last helping to ensure that the rear areas and lines of communication remained free from subversion, espionage and sabotage.

As the First World War progressed, the Intelligence Corps, like most of the British army, became bogged down in the network of trenches covering France and Belgium. To obtain up-to-date information on German troop deployments, the head of the Intelligence Corps, Major Dunnington Jefferson, turned to the Royal Flying Corps (RFC), which was able to photograph German positions from the air and provide intelligence on troop movements and artillery locations. Aerial photography was first used during the battle of Neuve-Chapelle in 1915, when pilots of the RFC were ordered to fly at 800 feet, allowing the observer to lean out of the cockpit and take photographs while under fire. Three members of the Intelligence Corps were attached to each squadron of the RFC to analyse the images they took, and they were not short of work (p. 140). The output of the RFC photographic squadrons was prolific, with over 19,000 photographs produced and analysed during the Battle of the Somme alone.[14]

As the war continued, the volume of military intelligence increased dramatically. In 1916, in order to manage its collation and dissemination, military intelligence was once again separated from operations, with Brigadier General Sir George Macdonogh appointed to the reintroduced position of director of military intelligence (DMI) at the War Office.[15] The reorganization created sections designated by the prefix MI, including MI1, the secretariat section responsible for administration and secret intelligence. MI1(a) undertook clerical duties; MI1(b) was responsible for enemy ciphers; MI1(c) was the precursor of the Secret Intelligence Service (SIS), with headquarters in Northumberland Avenue; and MI1(d) was responsible for the production of intelligence summaries. MI2 and MI3 were country sections dealing with Europe, the Middle East, the Far East and the Americas. MI4 was responsible for the production and storage of maps; and MI5 dealt with counter-espionage. MI6, not to be confused with the later SIS, dealt with trade policy, international law and arms traffic. MI7 covered press control and propaganda, while MI8 and MI9 were responsible for cable and postal censorship respectively.[16] Section MI10 was established in 1917 to deal with foreign military attachés and missions, and in 1918, following the Russian revolution, a new section, MIR, was created. This section had responsibility not only for Russia but also for the Caucasus, Asia and the Far East.[17]

The inter-war years

The DMI ended the war with its reputation enhanced and in possession of an efficient headquarters staff and well-organized field networks. Following the signing of the armistice in November 1918, however, the directorate's work was gradually scaled down, with more experienced staff transferred to other duties. DMI also lost responsibility for gathering secret intelligence, transferred to SIS, and signals intelligence, passed to the Government Code and Cypher School (GC&CS). Following the war the primary roles of the Intelligence Corps, until it was disbanded in 1929, lay in policing the colonies, particularly India, and forming part of the occupying Rhine army. The intelligence directorate also worked closely with the Colonial Office, preparing reports on leading activists and political organizations. An example of their work, completed in the early 1930s and now at the National Archives, is a report on leading mullahs on the border of the North West Frontier Province.[18]

The rise of Hitler and the Nazi party led to enlargement of the German section. One of its new recruits was Frank Davies who, in the mid-1930s—in anticipation of a future war with Germany—prepared a report on the most efficient organization and working methods for the Intelligence Corps. Following the remilitarization of the Rhineland and occupation of the Sudetenland in 1938, the intelligence directorate quickly produced a revised edition of the *Manual of Military Intelligence*, replacing the previous version published in 1922.[19] Over 60 pages in length, the manual contained sections on organization, the interrogation of prisoners, security, censorship and propaganda. The primary role of military intelligence was 'to identify and locate every enemy unit and study their activities in order that no important movements or concentrations may go unmarked'. In relation to the interrogation of prisoners of war, it was noted that 'the most valuable prisoners from an intelligence point of view are officers and the better educated NCOs provided that they can be persuaded to talk'. It was also made clear that it was 'forbidden to penalise prisoners in any way for refusing to reply to questions, or for giving false information'.

The Second World War

Following the outbreak of war in September 1939, military intelligence was placed under the command of Brigadier General Francis Davidson.[20] One of his key objectives was to re-establish the Intelligence Corps, disbanded in 1929. Taking advantage of the report prepared by Davies, suitable recruits were first interviewed at the Intelligence Corps Depot before being sent to the Intelligence Training Centre (ITC) at Matlock in Derbyshire, where, as course outlines held in the National Archives reveal, they received specialized training in field intelligence, security and prisoner interrogation.[21] When the British Expeditionary Force deployed to France it had within its ranks 31 Field Security Sections, and by the end of the war a staggering 10,000 recruits had been through the ITC's doors.[22] Once the training was satisfactorily completed, officers and NCOs were posted to staff headquarters or to other organizations such as SIS and the Special

1. Sir Vernon Kell in January 1920. Kell battled threats to national security for more than 30 years as head of the Secret Service Bureau's home section and its successor MI5. He was summarily retired by the newly appointed prime minister, Winston Churchill, in June 1940.

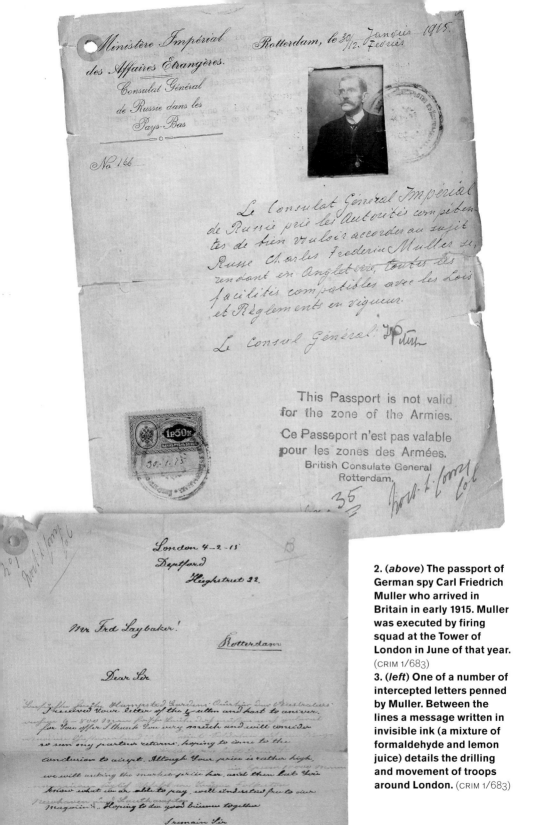

2. (*above*) **The passport of German spy Carl Friedrich Muller who arrived in Britain in early 1915. Muller was executed by firing squad at the Tower of London in June of that year.** (CRIM 1/683)

3. (*left*) **One of a number of intercepted letters penned by Muller. Between the lines a message written in invisible ink (a mixture of formaldehyde and lemon juice) details the drilling and movement of troops around London.** (CRIM 1/683)

4. (*right*) **Vernon Kell's letter of thanks to the head of Scotland Yard, written on the conclusion in 1939 of the case against John Herbert King. The Foreign Office employee was unmasked after a Soviet spy defected to the West.** (KV 2/815)

5. (*below*) **A photograph of King, 'a very weak man' according to his controller Henri Christiaan Pieck, through whom he passed confidential telegrams and dispatches to the Soviets.** (KV 2/816)

6. Part of an official report on the King case, including his meetings with Pieck. It notes that although King might not have known for which country his information was destined, there was 'no doubt that he acted from purely mercenary motives'. (KV 2/816)

SECRET

1287

P.F.47815/B.14.

20th October, 1939.

My dear Commissioner.

With reference to the recent case against John Herbert KING, which concluded satisfactorily last Wednesday, I should like to let you know how very much I appreciate the admirable work that has been done by the officers of the Special Branch and their co-operation with us in connection with this case.

Inspector Rogers and Sergeant Jones and the officers working with them have handled this matter with the greatest keenness and efficiency, and I should be very grateful if you would convey to them my high appreciation of their work and co-operation.

Yours sincerely,
V.G.W.Kell.

Air Vice-Marshal Sir Philip Game,
GCVO., GBE., KCB., KCMG., DSO.,
New Scotland Yard.

4.

Sir Nevile Henderson or between Kemal Ataturk and the Ambassador in Turkey or some such persons. There were sometimes eight or nine pages of roneoed matter — sometimes three or four — never more than ten. They were never of any great political importance. The telegrams were always decoded copies and never in cipher. They were spare copies that were available in the room."

KING said that he met PIECK in various places, including the office in Buckingham Gate where one room had a trestle table, a lamp and a camera. KING said that the telegrams he gave PIECK were for his retention so that there was no need for these to be photographed. PIECK paid him sums of money varying between £50 and £200 at a time.

In 1936 PIECK left, but before doing so introduced KING to a man named PETERSON (this man has been identified as Paul HARDT @ PETERS who occurs in the GLADING case). The introduction took place in the office in Buckingham Gate. PIECK told KING that PETERSON would carry on instead of him. KING kept in touch with PETERSON for about 18 months until June 1937 when he told KING that he had to go away for a month or so. KING stated that he had not seen or heard of PETERSON since. During the 18 months he handed to PETERSON copies of Foreign Office telegrams in the same way as he had to PIECK. PETERSON gave him various sums of money, generally £100 or £150.

Though PIECK had never asked KING to obtain a Foreign Office cipher, PETERSON did so on many occasions. KING swore that he refused and at no time transmitted to anyone any cipher or re-cipher tables. All the documents he gave to PIECK and PETERSON were, he said, already decoded.

7. (*left*) Photographs from a December 1940 report showing German spies caught in Britain. (KV 3/76)

8. (below) Double agent Juan Pujol Garcia, codenamed Garbo, built up an imaginary network of sub-agents to feed a carefully contrived blend of false and genuine intelligence back to Berlin. He and his controllers achieved the greatest triumph of MI5's Double Cross system in the Second World War, diverting attention away from the Normandy beaches during the D-Day landings. (KV 2/64)

GARBO TRAFFIC   (2 Cop

Date of Letter: 16/10/42

Date and Place of Posting (Postmark):

Addressed to:
(Name & address)   Sra. Dona Maria do Ceu Pereira
                    Rua Coelho da Rocha, 82-1 da
                    Lisbon

(COVER LETTER)

My own darling Maria,
    I cannot tell you how happy I was to get your beloved letter.
I just ate the words and I have kissed every page of it and carried
it about in the pocket over my heart. How silly and sentimental,
I can hear you say, but I cannot help it for you know I worship the
very ground you walk on. It is miserable to be so many miles away
from you but darling, I think of you all the time and I swear I
never look at another woman. I can hear you laughing at that knowing
me, but my sweetheart it really is true. These Scotch girls of ours
are all very wellm but don't know what love is, not real love - our
sort I mean. Sweetheart, how I long with all my being to hold you in
my arms again. A thousand kisses to my beautiful Maria.
    But I must try and be sensible and tell you what I have been
doing. Not much to interest you, my dearest one, I am afraid. Work
mostly and damned hard work. However, we Scotsmen rather like work,
it is a kind of hobby with us. I know you are laughing but then I
like to pretend that I hear that silvery laugh of yours. Do you re-
member that time you laughed at me when you said I was so serious
about my career and I stopped you. Kisses did it, didn' they? There
I am being all sloppy again. Back to the work. I hope you will be
proud to hear that I have had another rise.Mind you I deserved it.
thing like blowing one's own trumpet but I really have

(SECRET WRITING)

Observations made from the time I left London on 25/9 until
now. Part of my journey I "hitch-hiked" so as to get all
possible information. I met en route some soldiers of the
Tank Corps who were returning to Warminster after 18 days
leave (one weeks leave and a further 10 days embarkation leave).
One of them said he had been undergoing special training in
Scotland during which he had to swim in his kit. They spoke
of a great number of Americans being at Warminster as well as
a regiment of Guards. A soldier with them said that the
Americans had taken over the whole of Southern Command. A
railway official in Manchester told me that there is an important
centre for the training of parachute troops at a place called
Ringway. He said that there is always very great activity
there and that many thousands of men must be trained and
that they used two-engined bombers for dropping the parachutists.
At Crewe there were three or four hundred troops in or
around the town and I was told that about thirty air-borne
officers had recently been staying there. The men had been
undergoing training in air-borne landings on the sandy beaches
near Southport. These men wear ordinary uniform with a
plum red coloured beret and a shoulder badge of the same
colour with the word "Air-borne" in blue. A great number
of American troops in the Warrington district including some
negro battalions. They are also stationed at Bellevue,
Manchester, which is a big pleasure ground. In Carlisle there
are a lot of troops, most of them Pioneers, R.A.S.C., R.E.,
Loyals, Borders, London Irish Rifles, Black Watch and Scottish
infantry regiments. There were also a few Royal Armoured
Corps men in the town, some driving Bren carriers. I saw
a convoy of five 3.5 guns passing through the town and they
took the Kingstown road. I heard in conversation that there
are a few tanks here but I could not find out the number or
where they are stationed. I also heard that there are about
two hundred and fifty troops billeted in corrugated iron
huts (not camouflaged) to the west of Kingstown. I have
heard from my brother who writes a lot about Dunoon, about
its possibilities as an invasion port and of their being a
number of invasion barges and ships there.
    A few days ago a large floating dock moored at the mouth
of the Gareloch. 20 or even more merchant ships at anchor down
the river and with them destroyers and light naval craft.
A large dock being constructed on the east side of the Gareloch
and there are controls on the road between Shandon and Gare-
lochhead. 2 small merchant-ship unloading at the dock and a
small aircraft carrier was there. There is a torpedo testing
range at the tope of Loch Long.
    On return to Glasgow I heard that a large battleship,
believed to be "Repulse", was in the Firth of Clyde about 18/9.
I have a lot to write but my chief in London told me to keep
my letters short and only write once in ten days. I will
therefore write the rest to London.

                                        Pedro.

9, 10. (*opposite*) Written by 'Angus' to his darling Maria, this sentimental *billet doux* is a transcript of one of Garbo's cover letters from October 1942. The message it concealed (*above*) was written in invisible ink and attributed to sub-agent 'Pedro'. It was produced at a time when Garbo traffic was contrived to hint at a planned allied invasion of Norway. (KV 2/64)

11. (*right*) The hook in Operation Mincemeat. This 1943 letter was in the possession of a body that was obtained by the British, dressed as an officer and dropped by submarine off the Spanish coast. Believing the fictitious Major Martin to be the victim of a plane crash, German High Command were successfully misled about the forthcoming invasion of Sicily. (WO 106/5921) **12, 13.** (*below*) A list of items placed with Major Martin's body to build a believable personality and create the impression of a trusted but careless man; (*below right*) Martin's identity card and a snapshot of his fiancée (WO 106/5921)

TELEPHONE, WHITEHALL 9400.

WAR OFFICE,
WHITEHALL.
LONDON, S.W.1.

23rd April, 1943

PERSONAL AND MOST SECRET.

My dear Alex —

        I am taking advantage of sending you a personal letter by hand of one of Mountbatten's officers, to give you the inside history of our recent exchange of cables about Mediterranean operations and their attendant cover plans. You may have felt our decisions were somewhat arbitrary, but I can assure you in fact that the C.O.S. Committee gave the most careful consideration both to your recommendation and also to Jumbo's.

        We have had recent information that the Bosche have been reinforcing and strengthening their defences in Greece and Crete and C.I.G.S. felt that our forces for the assault were insufficient. It was agreed by the Chiefs of Staff that the 5th Division should be reinforced by one Brigade Group for the assault on the beach south of CAPE ARAXOS and that a similar reinforcement should be made for the 56th Division at KALAMATA. We are earmarking the necessary forces and shipping.

        Jumbo Wilson had proposed to select SICILY as cover target for "HUSKY"; but we have already chosen it as cover for operations "BRIMSTONE". The

/C.O.S.

General the Hon. Sir Harold R.L.G. Alexander,
    G.C.B.,C.S.I.,D.S.O.,M.C.,
      Headquarters,
      18th Army Group

13
12

PERSONAL DOCUMENTS AND ARTICLES IN POCKETS

Identity discs (2) "Major W. MARTIN, R.M., R/C"
                  attached to braces.

Silver cross on Silver chain round neck.

Watch, wrist.

Wallet, containing:-

             Photograph of Fiancee
             Book of stamps (2 used)
             2 letters from Fiancee
             St. Christopher plaque
             Invitation to Cabaret Club
             C.C.O. Pass   In cellophane
             Admiralty Identity Card   container
             Torn off top of letter.
             1 £5 note - March 5th 1942 C/227 45827

             3 £1 notes X 34 D 527008
                    W 21 D 029293
                    X 66 D 443119

1 Half crown

2 Shillings

2 six pences

4 pennies

Letter from "Father"

Letter from "Father" to McKenna & Co., Solicitors

Letter from Lloyds Bank

Bill (receipted) from Naval & Military Club

Bill (cash) from Gieves Ltd.

Bill for engagement ring

2 bus tickets

2 counterfoil stubs of tickets for Prince of Wales' Theatre 22.4.43

Box of matches

Packet of Cigarettes

Bunch of keys

Pencil Stub

Letter from McKenna & Co. Solicitors.

Issued in lieu of N: 09650 lost

NAVAL
IDENTITY CARD No. 148228

Surname MARTIN

Other Names WILLIAM

Rank (at time of issue) CAPTAIN, R.M.
        (ACTING MAJOR)

Ship (at time of issue) H.Q.
      COMBINED OPERATIONS

Place of Birth
      CARDIFF

Year of Birth 1907

Issued by

At

Date 2nd February 1943.

Signature of Bearer
W. Martin

Visible distinguishing marks
NIL.

T.6.

PF 68258

[TREPPER, Leopold or Liebch.]

PF 68258

ALIAS:

TREPER, Leiba ben Zeharya
MIKLER, Adam   (cover in Belgium 1939-40)
GILBERT, Jean   (cover in France, 1940-42)
IVANOWSKI, Vladislav Ivanovitch (for travel
        from Paris to Moscow, 1945)

de WINTER
SOMMER
Grand Chef
Le General
L'Oncle
Onkel Otto

- 3 -

TREPPER's Group.

Chapter I. Introduction.

1.   Leopold TREPPER was an extremely resourceful and capable man, who
eventually became a director of the Red Army Intelligence in Western
Europe, and responsible for several espionage groups. The particular
network described here is named after him since he founded it early in
his career and it was composed of people immediately connected with him.
TREPPER's Group operated, under the control of the 4th Department of
the General Staff of the Red Army, in Belgium, and later in France, from
1936 to 1942. It owed its success very largely to TREPPER's dynamic
personality.

2.   It is believed that TREPPER first made contact with Soviet
espionage agents in Paris in 1932. Thereafter he was sent to Moscow to
be trained for three years. He returned to Western Europe in about 1936
and began recruiting a network of agents. Little is known about the
activity of his group between 1936 and 1940, apart from what TREPPER
chose to reveal to the Germans after his arrest in 1942. It is thought
that it concentrated mainly on France and the United Kingdom, and that it
was only turned against Germany at a later date. These enterprises
appear to have been successful.

3.   TREPPER operated his group under the cover of various firms. At
first it was centered on Brussels, but shortly after the German invasion
of the Low Countries, TREPPER moved his headquarters to Paris and left
Victor SUKOLOV behind in charge of the remaining network. The Germans
made several arrests in Brussels towards the end of 1941 which eventually
led to the capture of TREPPER in 1942. TREPPER offered his services to
the Germans and revealed the names of most of his group, besides the
identities of certain other persons with whom he was in contact. It is
believed that he did so only because he knew that their capture was
inevitable. The Germans appear to have been taken in by his apparent
good faith and TREPPER was able to carry out a successful triple-cross.
He managed to escape after about nine months.

4.   It is highly probable that TREPPER did not disclose the whole
of his network. Some of his agents may still be active, while others,
including TREPPER himself, are believed to be still alive and may
re-appear.

5.   We have little evidence by which to assess the value of TREPPER's
group to the Russians. However, consideration of the movements and
general activities of those concerned, and of the lines of communication
known to have existed, suggest that the network did obtain intelligence
of considerable value.

Chapter II. Pre-war Activities (1936 - 1939).

1.   In December 1936, having completed his training in Moscow, Leopold
TREPPER was despatched on a mission to France. He was instructed to
report on the general situation and draw up plans for the establishment of
an espionage network which it is believed was to be directed mainly against
the United Kingdom. He returned to Moscow to report in 1937 and 1938
using on each occasion false papers in a different name. In 1937 he
travelled to Brussels and met Leon GROSSVOGEL, a Communist whom it is
believed he had previously known in Palestine. Leon GROSSVOGEL had been

/General

14. (*above*) Leopold Trepper, leader of the Soviet Rote Kapelle spy ring. Arrested by the Germans, he played a successful triple cross on his captors. (KV 3/351)
15. (*left*) Details of Trepper's remarkable career, from files based on captured German documents and recently released to the National Archives. The British hoped that analysis of these documents would provide insight into the Soviet Intelligence services as Second World War ally became Cold War enemy. (KV 3/351)

52. New East German 'Tellurometer' - 9 Mar 71

53. New East German 'Tellurometer' with possible signal lamp - 9 Mar 71

54. Complex box bodies - 11 Mar 71

55. BTR 60 PB with probable bent dipole - 23 Mar 71

16. (*above*) Examples of covert pictures taken in 1971 by the British commander-in-chief's Mission to the Soviet Forces of Occupation in Germany, or BRIXMIS. Travelling on 'tours' allowed by the 1946 agreement, the three-man liaison teams attempted to chart the deployment and capability of Soviet forces in East Germany. (wo 208/5266) **17. (*right*) A member of one of the liaison teams posing in a mission car.** (wo 208/5256)

Operations Executive (see chapter 6). Members of the Intelligence Corps were also involved in the formation of special forces, including the Long Range Desert Patrol Group and the Special Air Service.

Within the London headquarters, the most important organizational change occurred in May 1940 when a new section was established to provide intelligence on Germany and Nazi-occupied Europe. Known as MI14, it attracted the ablest officers, such as Kenneth Strong, the future head of the Defence Intelligence Staff, Alan Pryce-Jones, later editor of *The Times Literary Supplement*, Eric Birley, professor of ancient history at Oxford and compiler of the 'Birley Bible' — a who's who of the German army — and Noel Annan, a future Labour peer and vice chancellor of London University.[23] One of the first tasks given to MI14 following the fall of France was to assess the most likely date for a German invasion of Britain. To do this, it relied on Ultra (p. 253) and information provided by the Polish underground, concluding, against the prevailing wisdom, that the invasion would be postponed indefinitely: Hitler's real target was Russia. On 22 June 1941 Hitler launched Operation Barbarossa with the aim of eliminating Stalin and the Soviet Communist state. MI14's reputation for providing reliable assessments of German intentions rose accordingly.[24]

As the war progressed, other sections were created within military intelligence to cover a variety of roles. In mid-1940 MI10 was established, with responsibility for technical intelligence. MI10 was composed of three subsections: MI10(a), which dealt with armoured fighting vehicles; MI10(b), which covered engineering equipment; and MI10(c), responsible for transportation (railways and canals), oil and military science.[25] Other branches established included MI11, which dealt with field intelligence and was responsible for protecting troops against enemy agents hidden among the civilian population, and MI12, concerned with postal censorship and liaison with MI5.[26] In December 1941 a new post of deputy director (DDMI) was established with responsibility for prisoners of war and overseeing the work of two further sections, MI9 and MI19. Although these two departments came under the military intelligence directorate, their tasks also included operations, transport and supply in addition to gathering intelligence.

Prisoners of war

MI9 was established in December 1939 under the command of Colonel Norman Crockett, the former head of the London Stock

Exchange. Initially based at the Metropole Hotel in London, MI9 was soon relocated to Camp 20, a country house in Wilton Park near Beaconsfield.[27] The organization had two roles: preparing British and allied servicemen so that they might be better able to escape or avoid capture and disseminating any information that might be gleaned from those who returned. To achieve this, Intelligence School 9 (IS9) was established: it trained intelligence officers in the principles of escape and evasion so that they in turn might train those men most at risk of capture. Escape aids were also manufactured, from compasses hidden inside pens and buttons to maps printed on silk and stitched into clothing. The importance of these was emphasized on the very first page of the *MI9 Bulletin*, now among the War Office's files at the National Archives. It offered a dramatic cautionary tale:

> He was in plain clothes, his instinct was to escape. Here was the risk; as he appeared on the top of the wall shots might ring out. He heaved himself up ... his waistcoat hooked on to something ... he freed it ... a sentry lighting a cigarette ... He dropped into the garden and crept into some bushes. To his horror he realized he had left his food tablets, map and compass on the wrong side of the wall, as a result of which he later suffered considerably. This prisoner, who escaped in the Boer war is now the BRITISH PRIME MINISTER BUT THE MORAL IS STILL THE SAME. *ALWAYS CARRY YOUR ESCAPE AIDS WITH YOU.*[28]

The *MI9 Bulletin* contained morale-boosting tales of escape and information intended to help others do so. It also devoted a certain amount of space to standard techniques employed by interrogators should you be unlucky enough to get caught, as well as ruses to watch out for and basic mistakes to avoid. For example, while it was important to try to restrict comment under interrogation to confirmation of name, rank and number, it was equally important to ensure the destruction of papers. According to a German intelligence officer cited in the bulletin, 60 per cent of his information came from captured documents compared to 15 per cent from interrogation itself.

In addition to its work aiding escapers and evaders, MI9 was also charged with extracting intelligence from enemy POWs in the first years of the war. In December 1941 the division of MI9 with responsibility for this was hived off as a new section, MI19, and placed under the command of Captain A. R. Rawlinson.[29] Interrogations were carried out at the Combined Services Detailed Interrogations Centre (CSDIC), known as the London Cage. The chief interrogator was the feared Lieutenant Colonel Alexander Scotland, later appointed head of the War Crimes Investigation unit. CSDIC operated facilities at Trent Park, near Barnet, Hertfordshire, known as Cockfosters Camp, which housed senior officers; Latimer House, Buckinghamshire, known as No 1 Distribution Centre, housing mainly German POWs; and Wilton House, Beaconsfield, Buckinghamshire (No 2 Distribution Centre), used primarily for Italian prisoners.

Those destined for the London Cage or other CDSIC-run institutions were selected by the POW Interrogation Service (PWIS), which subjected enemy POWs to preliminary questioning after capture.[30] An insight into this process is given by a file at the National Archives relating to a proposed reception camp at Kempton Park intended to deal with prisoners captured during Operation Overlord. Speed and efficiency were cited as essential and officers and NCOs in charge were to note any detail, however small, which was causing delay.[31]

The camp was to contain a total of 26 interrogation rooms, each manned by two orderlies, and was to handle a shuttle service of four trains a day, each containing 500 prisoners. All 2,000 of these had to be dealt with and evacuated within 24 hours. Within this period, each 'P/W' had to be 'detrained, fed, received, searched, medically examined, their clothes disinfested, bathed, re-clothed in their disinfested clothing, interrogated, accommodated for the night, provided with meals, and entrained for base Camps'.

The following items would be impounded:

(i)   Maps and Military Documents, printed or written.
(ii) All publications acquired before or after capture.
(iii) Visiting Cards, odd names and addresses scribbled on scraps of paper. All written or printed material, including letters, postcards, diaries, notebooks, photographs etc.
(iv) Cameras, compasses, binoculars or any other types of precision instrument.
(v)   Cigarette lighters.
(vi) Knives, scissors, razor blades, razors (cut throat), manicure sets, etc.
(vii) Pay books.[32]

Interrogation was to be carried out on an individual basis intended to sort prisoners into one of two groups. 'S's were special prisoners, to be set aside for further interrogation, segregated and taken to special segregated sleeping quarters. 'N.R.'s were prisoners not required for further interrogation who could be taken back to sleeping quarters in the main tented compound. The distinction was crucial, and the proposal noted that 'Great care must be taken to see that no 'S' P/W is trans-ferred to a Base Camp instead of to the L.D. Cages.'

The Joint Intelligence Bureau

Following the end of the Second World War, the Intelligence Corps was demobilized with spending on defence reduced across the board. In the new era of austerity, the service departments were expected to improve efficiency by pooling resources wherever possible. One result of this drive for greater centralism was the creation of the Ministry of Defence in 1946, designed to coordinate the work undertaken by the three separate service ministries. It was preceded in these efforts by the Joint Intelligence Bureau (JIB), established in August 1945 to carry on work previously undertaken by the MEW Intelligence Directorate and the Inter-Service Topographical Department.[33] Placed under the direction of Kenneth Strong, formerly of MI14, and located at Bryanston Square with the Joint Scientific and Technical Intelligence Committees (p. 222), the JIB was given wide-ranging responsibilities. These included producing and analysing intelligence on transportation, static and coastal defences, anti-aircraft defences, airfield intelligence, enemy war potential (both economic and industrial) and telecommunications.[34] The JIB was one of the first organizations to use all source intelligence, employing both overt and covert sources, and to employ a high proportion of civilian staff, including economists, engineers and scientists.

The creation of the JIB was not welcomed by the service departments, which regarded it as a competitor, rather than an addition, to their own intelligence organizations. To increase collaboration, a Service Liaison Section was established within JIB, with DMI contributing two officers. The JIB also had close relations with the Foreign Office, in particular its Economic Intelligence and Research Departments. Foreign Office posts abroad also received questionnaires compiled by JIB covering items such as topography, communications and industrial developments.[35] In addition to its London office, JIB established offices in the Middle East and Singapore to provide intelligence for the regional defence authorities.

BRIXMIS

In contrast to its fate after the First World War, military intelligence was not run down following the end of hostilities. Rather, it played a major role in supporting British forces deployed overseas while responding to new demands imposed by the creation of the allied Control Commission for Germany and the developing Cold War with Russia. Provisional arrangements for the military occupation and division of Germany had been agreed during 1944 in a series of meetings between Stalin, Roosevelt and Churchill, envisaging that Berlin would be split into zones of occupation with a military liaison mission stationed in each of the zones. In September 1946 an agreement governing the exchange of military liaison missions was signed in Berlin by General Brian Robertson, commander of the British occupation forces in Germany, and his Soviet counterpart General Mikhail Malinin.[36] Now held in the War Office records at the National Archives, the Robertson-Malinin Agreement laid down ground rules to be followed by the British and Soviet liaison teams. Its main provision allowed for reciprocal arrangements covering freedom of travel in each zone, with the exception of a number of restricted areas to be agreed in advance. The mission buildings were also granted full diplomatic immunity.

The UK mission, officially known as 'The British Commander in Chief's Mission to the Soviet Forces of Occupation in Germany' and soon shortened to BRIXMIS, had its main office in the British sector of West Berlin. A mission compound was also located in a small close just off the main Geschwister-Scholl-Strasse, near Potsdam railway station. Its Soviet counterpart, known as SOXMIS, occupied premises in Bunde, in North Rhine-Westphalia.[37] In the following year, similar liaison agreements were reached with the French and American forces stationed in Germany, but BRIXMIS was by far the largest of the allied liaison missions, with a staff complement equal to the French and US missions combined. Initially given a liaison role, BRIXMIS was not expected to become involved in covert reconnaissance, but following its transfer from the Foreign Office to the Ministry of Defence in 1950 it developed a technical intelligence capability with a specialist map-making team and electronic, signals and photographic experts. The British mission also had the right to fly a light aircraft, a two-seater Chipmunk, which was based at the RAF Gatow airfield in Berlin. The plane was allowed to fly anywhere within the Berlin Safety Zone and used the opportunity to photograph Soviet barracks and equipment.

The primary role of BRIXMIS was to chart the deployment and capability of Soviet forces. To achieve this required detailing the location of regiments and air squadrons, including information on their equipment, battle-readiness and military plans. The main bulk of intelligence was acquired via three-man liaison crews, allowed by the terms of the 1946 agreement to travel throughout East Germany in designated vehicles which afforded liberty of movement and diplomatic immunity (plates 16 and 17). These regular tours were, of course, always followed and harassed by Soviet and East German security forces that monitored every action. To improve their effectiveness, 'unauthorized' tours were sometimes conducted in restricted areas, with predictable results — car chases, collisions, rammings and harassment were common. A situation in which a mission crew was trapped at front and back by Soviet vehicles became known as a 'BRIXMIS sandwich'. The 1974 annual report, the most recent to be released to the National Archives, recorded some 20 separate incidents, from routine accusations of 'being behind signs' to the more dramatic:

> On 29 September 1974, a tour was observing a flying programme in two OPs in the woods north-east of Rothstein. Observation was commenced at 0930 hours from the first of the two OPs and the tour had moved to a second position after having seen a civilian moving in the area. At 1200 hours the tour reoccupied their first OP and continued monitoring the programme. At 1245 hours the crew was assaulted by a party of some twelve Soviet soldiers, tied-up and thrown into the back of a ZIL-130. There they remained bound for fifty minutes after which they were untied and the atmosphere became less tense. The tour car was entered and personal kit belonging to the tour was taken by the soldiers.[38]

Escorted to Wittenberg Kommandatura, they were released at a quarter to midnight. Other incidents recorded in the same report included a tour apprehended after their car became mired in mud in the woods north of Havelberg; a tour blockaded in a railway siding after they had stopped to investigate 'sounds of armour being unloaded'; and a tour officer floored by a punch to the jaw from an off-duty Praporshchik in a café in Neustrelitz. In rare cases, the violence spiralled out of control. At the height of the second Cold War in the mid-1980s, Sergeant Philippe Mariotti, of the French mission, and Major Arthur Nicholson, a member of the American mission, were both involved in fatal accidents.[39]

In addition to the tours, intelligence on the Soviet military was obtained by more covert methods. These included hiding at the end of runways in order to photograph the attached missiles as aircraft took off, penetrating live training areas to retrieve unexploded bombs and shells, and breaking into Soviet hangars to discover the dimensions of tank barrels and the composition of armour plating. In one unsavoury episode, a small BRIXMIS team was sent to recover toilet paper from a military latrine. The reasoning behind this operation, codenamed Tamarisk, soon became apparent. In large-scale Soviet field exercises, the supply of toilet paper often ran out, forcing soldiers to use anything to hand, including military manuals and other classified paperwork. The 'shit-diggers', as the team inevitably became known, soon proved their worth by recovering a series of Warsaw Pact order of battle booklets and numerous technical documents.[40]

The working relationship between BRIXMIS staff and their Soviet counterparts was often dictated by the wider geopolitical environment. During the period of détente in the early 1970s, for example, entertaining Soviet delegations at social events became more commonplace and a good means of obtaining an insight into the Soviet mindset. The BRIXMIS annual report for 1973 describes once such encounter with a Soviet delegation:

> Although not great party givers, they are certainly great party goers. They seem to enjoy contact with the Missions and in most cases are quite prepared to discuss topics of general interest. At party time, the Soviets usually behave in an exemplary manner. They seem intelligent, courteous and good-humoured and, unlike other nationalities, readily get the point of British humour. Socially, therefore, the cold war image of tight-lipped surliness on the part of the Soviets has now almost entirely disappeared. We do, however, still encounter the odd difficult individual, but he is something of a rarity and confines his Stalinist demeanour to allied junior officers struggling masterfully to interpret.[41]

At its height, BRIXMIS produced over 200 reports a year, which often corroborated material gathered from other sources. Once analysed by Tech Int(Army) and Tech Int(Air) in London, the information was circulated to allied intelligence agencies.[42] The mission also housed a detachment from 22 SAS Regiment whose role—thankfully never required—was to operate behind enemy lines in any future battle with Warsaw Pact forces. Following the fall of the Berlin Wall and the reunification of Germany in 1990, all allied and Soviet liaison missions stationed in the country were deactivated.

Counter-insurgency operations

Keeping tabs on the Russians was not the only preoccupation of military intelligence. Throughout the 1950s it was required to assist in a number of counter-insurgency operations in support of regular forces, responding to nationalist uprisings and Communist-inspired revolts that had broken out in Britain's restive colonies abroad. These included the Malaya Emergency (1948–60), the Mau Mau uprising in Kenya (1952–60) and the Cyprus Emergency (1954–59).

The Malaya Emergency was declared by the British colonial government in June 1948. The background can be found in events following the end of the Second World War, when the Malayan Communist Party (MCP), which had successfully waged a guerrilla campaign against the Japanese (p. 204), sought to free the country from British rule. To achieve this, the MCP organized a series of strikes and rebellions within Malaya's tin and rubber industries, and in June 1948 three European plantation owners were killed during disturbances. The British authorities responded by declaring a state of emergency, outlawing the MCP and other left-wing groups. To avoid imprisonment, the leadership retreated to the jungle and began a guerrilla campaign against the British under the name of the Malayan National Liberation Army (MNLA).

The MNLA was composed primarily of ethnic Chinese, although it did enjoy some support from the indigenous Malay population. In the early stages of the conflict, the British authorities sought to counter MNLA influence by launching special operations aimed at disrupting supply routes and training camps. These operations were conducted by irregular forces composed of ex-SOE personnel with previous jungle experience in Burma and Malaya. Known as the 'Ferret Force', these units operated outside the normal command structure and antagonized both the military and civilian authorities. The Ferret Force was soon disbanded and replaced by a small SAS contingent called the Malayan Scouts. The Scouts were commanded by Lieutenant Colonel Michael Calvert, a veteran of Chindit operations in Burma, who took over responsibility for all special operations within Malaya.[43]

Disorganization in the establishment of special forces was reflected in the state of the regional intelligence community. It consisted of a variety of conflicting interests, including Security Intelligence Far East (SIFE), staffed largely by MI5 officers and answerable to London; the Malayan Security Service (MSS), controlled by the local Malayan government; the Malay Police Force and Special Branch, controlled by the commissioner of police; and Military Intelligence, which reported to Far East Land Forces in Kuala Lumpur.[44] To coordinate the activities of these various bodies and provide clarity of leadership, the Colonial Office was given full membership of the JIC. Problems were still encountered on the ground, leading to the creation at local level of a Joint Intelligence Advisory Committee which reported to a newly appointed director of intelligence.[45]

In October 1951 the high commissioner of Malaya, Sir Henry Gurney, was killed in an MNLA ambush. To replace Gurney, Winston Churchill, who had recently been returned to power in the general election, appointed General Sir Gerald Templer, the head of Eastern Command and a former director of military intelligence. In addition to his powers as high commissioner, Templer was also appointed director of military operations and, as the records of the Colonial Office at the National Archives show, given a free hand to combine the disparate elements under his command into a single, well-organized force.[46] One of Templer's first actions was to step up operations against the MNLA leadership. To achieve this, he established an integrated intelligence staff and appointed Jack Morton, the head of SIFE and MI5 representative in Malaya, as his intelligence supremo.[47] Working in conjunction with RAF forces stationed in the Far East, Templer targeted MNLA headquarters and communications.[48] He also initiated a 'hearts and minds' propaganda offensive that sought to discredit the MNLA and its Communist sponsors, while members of the MNLA prepared to defect and provide intelligence against their former comrades were given financial incentives. The plan was a great success, with many deserters placed into a Special Operational Volunteer Force which led British patrols to MNLA camps hidden deep within the jungle.[49] The defections were also used in a series of psychological operations in which millions of leaflets aimed at demoralizing the MNLA's core support were dropped over the jungle from the air.[50]

Under concerted attack from all sides, the MCP began to sue for peace. In 1955 a meeting was arranged between the MCP leadership and the Malaysian authorities, but collapsed due to MCP demands for a complete amnesty for its members.[51] In 1957 Malaya was granted independence from British rule, removing the rationale behind the MNLA's anti-colonial struggle, and the Malayan government declared an end to the emergency on 31 July 1960. It had been a bloody conflict, with 1,438 Malayan troops, over 350 members of the British security forces and 2,400 civilians killed by the MNLA, who in return had suffered 6,700 dead, with 1,200 members captured or missing.

The difficulties encountered by British forces in Malaya were compounded by events in East Africa and the Mediterranean. Recently released MI5 files show that Britain had long been concerned by the move to independence in Kenya, and had kept nationalist leader Peter Mbiu Koinange under surveillance. In 1952 the Kikuyu tribe in Kenya began to demand greater land rights for indigenous Africans and mounted a rebellion against British colonial rule, including the murder of white settlers. This was followed in 1954 by violent revolt on the island of Cyprus, with the Greek Cypriot community demanding political union (*enosis*) with the Greek mainland. In both cases military intelligence played a crucial role. In Kenya, Special Branch was expanded and worked in conjunction with the army's Field Intelligence units, which acquired information through interrogation of suspected Mau Mau insurgents and paid informers.[52] A Kenya Intelligence Committee, supported by a network of provincial intelligence committees, was also established.[53] As in Malaya, money persuaded many Mau Mau to turn against their former compatriots and lead British forces to rebel camps and hideouts.[54]

The rules for carrying out these and other 'Special Methods', defined as 'any trick or stratagem by which intelligence may be obtained from the enemy', were laid out in 1956 in a proposed Training Pamphlet for the Operational Element of Special Branch. In assessing those most suited for the work, the pamphlet notes that 'the man who joined the gangs from a spirit of adventure, or for the prospect of plunder is the best man for the job'. The recruitment process for employing former Mau Mau members was to take place in camps run by Special Branch field intelligence officers (FIOs) and be divided into three phases. In the first phase, described as 'taming', it was suggested that the former rebels should undergo a re-education programme to instil them with 'respect for the government'. This would last for several weeks and would gradually be replaced by the second phase of training, in which 'the student should be given an idea of the job in store'. To provide an incentive, the best students could be given 'a few shillings, now and then, with which to buy certain luxuries such as a handful of beans or some meat'. Once the preliminary phases were completed successfully, the new recruits would undergo full training and be taken on active patrols. To demonstrate trust, they should be provided with a weapon and paid a regular wage. To conceal their new identities, the patrols would disguise themselves as rebels. The suggested process was described in some detail in the Special Branch training manual:

> If a forest or bush gang is being impersonated members of the party must smell as if they have not washed. This can be achieved by keeping

dirty clothes for the job and by not washing for a period prior to the patrol. In this connection it may be necessary to introduce lice and other vermin to the body.[55]

The training manual contained further advice for white Europeans accompanying the patrols, who were advised to black both their faces and hands using blacking supplied for theatrical use. If blacking was in short supply, 'camouflage cream, boot polish and burnt cork are less effective'. For intelligence officers, life in the patrols was often dangerous but rewarding. Writing in February 1956, the head of Special Branch in the Rift Valley, Major Stewart, spoke for many when he declared that 'there is no more thrilling work to be done anywhere in Kenya than that of an FIO. He is his own boss on operations, he plans his own work and the success he gets depends entirely on how good his planning has been.'

On 24 April 1954 the army launched Operation Anvil in which the city of Nairobi was placed under military control. During the operation, over 17,000 Africans were arrested on suspicion of being active members of Mau Mau or assisting in the rebellion. Thousands of Kikuyu were either interned or deported to the Kikuyu reserves in the highlands west of Mount Kenya.[56] By October 1955, in actions redolent of the Boer campaign 50 years earlier, over one million Kikuyu had been concentrated into 854 government-controlled villages. In recent years, the conditions in these detention centres have been the centre of controversy, with the British accused of condoning systematic human rights violations, including torture and rape.[57]

In October 1956 Dedan Kimathi, the last Mau Mau leader still at large, was captured by Kikuyu Tribal Police and subsequently hanged in early 1957.[58] His capture and execution marked the effective end of the Mau Mau uprising, although the emergency remained in effect until January 1960. Following the suppression of the uprising, the British sought a political solution to satisfy the growing demands of the African population. In December 1963 Kenya was granted independence, with Jomo Kenyatta, one of the leaders of the Mau Mau revolt jailed by the British in 1953, becoming president of the newly independent Republic of Kenya.[59]

In tandem with events in East Africa, British forces also faced an uprising in Cyprus involving the majority Greek Cypriot community on the island. The leader of the Greek Cypriots was Archbishop Makarios who, unknown to the British, was also the head of a revolutionary group committed to political union with Greece. The *Enosis* movement had a military wing, known as EOKA, commanded by Colonel George Grivas, who had a reputation for extreme violence and involvement in far-right politics. The flash point for the rebellion was Britain's announcement in July 1954 that, following its withdrawal from Egypt, Britain's new military headquarters in the Middle East would be situated on Cyprus. The strategic significance of the deployment meant that talks on Cypriot independence were indefinitely postponed. In April 1955 EOKA marked the beginning of its military campaign by exploding 16 bombs across the island.[60] In the following months, numerous attacks were carried out against British property and military facilities. The Intelligence Report for the first week of June 1956, preserved in one of a number of files relating to the *Enosis* movement, illustrates the level of violence encountered by British forces:

> ARMED ATTACKS. Security forces' patrols were ambushed on three occasions, an automatic weapon being used in two of these and shotguns in the other.
>
> ASSASSINATIONS. A Turkish-Cypriot police constable, a Greek-Cypriot Assistant District Inspector and a British expatriate government schoolmaster were murdered. Two British expatriate soldiers and the son of a warrant officer were ambushed while returning from bathing, one soldier was killed, the youth was tied up and fired at with a shotgun at close range but survived.
>
> Grenades were thrown on 37 occasions as follows:
> > 20 at military patrols, two of which failed to explode
> > One at a police station
> > Two at police patrols
> > Eight at the residence of service families or British expatriates
> > Six at other targets.
>
> SABOTAGE. On five occasions sabotage of military buildings under construction was attempted with explosives. Two bombs with time fuses failed to explode. Arson of a government elementary school and a house occupied by a serviceman's family was attempted.[61]

In an attempt to halt the violence, Makarios was arrested and deported to the Seychelles, with a bounty of £5,000 offered for information leading to the arrest of Grivas. In common with events in Malaya, the British appointed Field Marshal Sir John Harding as governor of Cyprus with full military powers. A Cyprus Intelligence Committee was also established which brought together in one organization the police, military and civilian authorities.[62]

The new structure soon brought rewards. In June 1956 a cache of arms and documents was discovered, including Grivas's diary which contained extensive details of EOKA operations and organizational structure. The importance of the find was relayed to London in the following terms:

> Second group is almost certainly Grivas' HQ group and special arrangements have been made to cordon and search the area ... where contact was first made with second group much material was found, including seven weapons, ammunition, bombs, clothing and food. Also found Grivas' diary for 10th May to 9th June, and many documents. Translation of any of importance will be signalled soonest.[63]

Initial successes were curtailed by the Suez operation, during which EOKA was able to regroup and mount further attacks on British forces, which were now stationed all over the island. In November 1956, following the increase in EOKA activity, a formal declaration of emergency was declared. To counter the upsurge in violence, Harding employed a similar strategy to that undertaken in Malaya and Kenya, in which captured or disillusioned members of EOKA were formed into small groups, known as Q-Patrols, and used to locate arms dumps and safe-houses. The intelligence obtained by the Q-Patrols led directly to the detention of over 100 EOKA guerrillas and the recovery of numerous weapons and explosives. In March 1957 EOKA's second in command, Gregory Afxentiou, was killed in a firefight. The continued success of the Q-Patrols led EOKA to call a ceasefire and begin negotiations with the British authorities.

The declaration of a ceasefire coincided with a new government in Britain, under Harold Macmillan, who favoured a political solution to the Cyprus problem leading ultimately to some form of independence. One manifestation of this new approach was Harding's replacement as governor by Sir Hugh Foot, the former governor of Jamaica and brother of Michael Foot, the Labour MP.[64] The government's preference for a negotiated settlement led to a decrease in military operations, with more emphasis placed on intelligence gathering to assist the British delegation in the forthcoming talks on independence. In 1958 John Prendergast, the former head of Special Branch in Kenya, was appointed director of intelligence throughout Cyprus. The overriding objective for Prendergast was to locate Grivas and ensure he did not commit any actions that would undermine the negotiations. Employing a network of informers, Grivas was eventually tracked down to a hideout in Nicosia. A snatch squad was prepared to arrest

Grivas but was stood down on the express orders of Macmillan, who feared that the death or detention of Grivas would derail the entire peace process. In 1960, after years of difficult diplomacy, Cyprus was granted independence, with Britain retaining two sovereign bases on the island. In 1964 British forces returned to the island, this time to separate the Greek and Turkish communities and prevent a full-scale civil war.[65]

The Defence Intelligence Staff

In 1964 the incoming Labour government began to reorganize the armed services along lines first proposed by the outgoing Conservative administration. The rationale behind the reforms was to achieve greater efficiency by eliminating duplication and increasing centralization wherever possible. The individual service ministries were abolished and replaced with a unified Ministry of Defence, represented at cabinet by a secretary of state. The intelligence organization was treated in a similar fashion, with the JIB merged with the individual services' intelligence staffs to form the Defence Intelligence Staff (DIS). Located in the old War Office on Whitehall, the DIS was organized on functional rather than service lines, its first director general being Sir Kenneth Strong, the former head of the JIB. Immediately under the director general was the post of deputy chief of the defence staff (intelligence) (DCS(I)), a military appointment that was rotated between the three services. Its first holder was the former head of naval intelligence, Vice Admiral Sir Norman Denning. The DCS(I) was responsible for four directorates: Service Intelligence, Scientific and Technical Intelligence, Economic and Logistic Intelligence, and Management Support. In 1984, in a further round of reorganization, the two positions of director general and DCDS(I) were abolished and replaced with a single post of chief of defence intelligence (CDI).

As presently constituted, the CDI is responsible for the overall coordination of defence intelligence throughout the armed forces and single-service commands. The CDI is supported by a deputy CDI, who is responsible for intelligence production, and a director general of intelligence collection (DGIC). He or she oversees the work of the Defence Intelligence and Security Centre (DISC), located at Chicksands, Bedfordshire, and the Intelligence Collection Group (ICG), which was established in June 2006 and is responsible for the provision of geographic, image and signals intelligence. The ICG is comprised of four elements:

THE DEFENCE GEOGRAPHIC CENTRE (DGC) based at
Feltham, responsible for the provision of geographic information. DGC is a largely civilian organization headed by a
director from the civil service. It maintains a large collection of maps, air charts and atlases and provides expert
advice on international boundaries, geographic names and
geophysical matters.

THE JOINT AIR RECONNAISSANCE INTELLIGENCE CENTRE
(JARIC), located at RAF Brampton, Cambridgeshire,
responsible for image intelligence. JARIC is a joint military
and civilian organization under the command of a group
captain and employs a total of 514 staff, of which 294 are
military. The majority of its personnel are employed on one
site at RAF Brampton.

THE JOINT AERONAUTIC AND GEOSPATIAL ORGANIZATION
(JAGO) based at Hermitage, Berkshire, Mönchengladbach
in Germany and Northolt, Middlesex. JAGO is a tri-service
organization commanded by an army colonel and responsible for the integration of in-theatre geographic support to
UK, UN and NATO operations.

THE JOINT SERVICES SIGNALS ORGANIZATION (JSSO) based
in Cyprus, Digby, Lincolnshire, and Cheltenham. The JSSO
is a tri-service organization responsible for signals intelligence and providing specialist support to military operations. As part of its remit, JSSO conducts research into new
communications systems and techniques to provide ongoing operational support to British forces at home and
abroad. The JSSO is under the command of a group captain of the RAF Operations Support Branch and has a staff
of 1,600 drawn from all three services.[66]

Following the terrorist attacks of September 2001, DIS has placed
increased emphasis on weapons of mass destruction and counter-
proliferation. Further to focus its intelligence resources, it has been
suggested that the DIS should be removed from the Ministry of Defence
and become a separate agency, adopting a similar relationship to its
parent department to that enjoyed by SIS in its dealings with the Foreign
and Commonwealth Office. This proposal was rejected by the Butler
inquiry, which contended that the DIS was so integral to defence planning and operations that its separation would be counter-productive.

It nevertheless considered that further steps were needed to integrate the work of the DIS more closely with the rest of the intelligence community. The view that DIS should serve wider national priorities in addition to its defence role was accepted by the government, with the result that DIS is now included in the distribution of SIS reports and directly involved in the central intelligence requirements and priorities process. In its long history, military intelligence has moved a long way from its beginnings in the corps of scouts to its current role as an integral asset in the global war against terror.

4 | Naval Intelligence

Naval intelligence grew increasingly important during the 16th to 18th centuries, as England's—and later Britain's—prosperity and power depended upon maritime trade. The Royal Navy's ability to protect such trade required a variety of intelligence, ranging from information on an enemy's intentions—and the disposition, equipment, supply, training and morale of its forces—to physical details of the seabed, winds and coastline. Gathering intelligence became part of the navy's day-to-day operations, aided by spies like the Huguenot Peter Fontaines, employed by the secretary of state in the reign of William III. A more professional approach emerged with the foundation of the Naval Intelligence Department (NID) in the late 19th century; under the celebrated William Reginald 'Blinker' Hall, its code-breakers played a key role in the First World War, creating the first British crypto-analytical organization. Several of them returned to interpret German radio communications during the Second World War, as decrypts from Bletchley Park helped to shape the course of the Battle of the Atlantic. The intelligence challenges of the Cold War, from tracking submarines on the seabed to monitoring the latest Soviet warships, brought major technical advances, as well as an intriguing return to coastal surveying—this time on the shores of Britain itself, in case of Soviet attack. Successes were, however, again mixed with failures, such as the high-profile disappearance of MI6's Commander Crabb and the loss of crucial information to the Soviets, who balanced their technological inferiority with the application of old-fashioned espionage.

Naval intelligence in the age of sail

Understanding an enemy's coast and its individual mix of shallows, depths, currents, tides and winds was vital, and such information was collected by every naval ship. Not only did the captain ensure the upkeep of a ship's log for submission to the Admiralty, he also had charge of remark books describing the coast and including space for illustrations. Such records for the 18th century, currently being transferred to the National Archives, provide an incredible body of information on the coasts of Europe, Africa, Australia, South America and the East and West Indies. The standard remark book contained entries on soundings and measures of depth taken by the vessels, suitable places for anchoring, the availability of fresh water, wood, provisions and other forms of refreshment ashore, details of fortifications, potential landing places and any other relevant intelligence. The books were accompanied by crew members' sketches of the coast, including significant landmarks and points of interest. From the mid-18th century both books and drawings provided the Admiralty with an intelligence archive to help plan future operations, and today offer insight into 18th-century coastal life and economy across the globe.[1]

Naval intelligence in this period did not just come from the diligent recordings of naval officers aboard ship. Diplomats and politicians were also involved in what Sir James Harris, British minister at The Hague, called the 'dirty work' of paying informants in foreign countries for information. Distressing as this might be for the diplomatic corps, such activities could yield vital intelligence on the intentions or preparations of potential adversaries. As Harris himself sniffed, 'when one is employed to sweep chimneys one must black one's fingers.'[2]

Perhaps the most remarkable of these intelligence agents paid by government office-holders was Peter Fontaines, a Huguenot spy employed by the Earl of Nottingham, secretary of state in the reign of William III. Nottingham, a former supporter of the deposed Stuart dynasty, was a high Tory of the old school with a very pronounced pragmatic streak. Fontaines, who hailed from a Protestant Norman family of some repute, became a surgeon in the French navy, before coming over to the British when the Revocation of the Edict of Nantes by Louis XIV in 1685 caused him to lose his position and his lands.[3] Entering the Royal Navy as an ordinary surgeon on the 30-gun *Lively*, his spying career started in 1689 when the *Lively* was captured by the French at the start of King William's War. In an incident that indicated a surprising naivety in a future spy, Fontaines noticed a former acquaintance on the crew of the capturing ship and introduced himself. The former acquaintance informed the captain of the French vessel and our hero was not exchanged like the other officers, but arrested as a traitor and sent to the French dockyard town of Brest:

> Being arrived at Brest I was sent ashore chained hands and feet under
> the guard of a lieutenant, a sergeant and six soldiers, who carried me
> before Monsieur Desclouseaux, Intendant [senior crown official] of
> Brest, who without having any regard to humanity, which forbids the ill
> treating of prisoners, fell upon me with his cane and beate me till he
> raised pitty in my guards, leaveing me halfe dead upon the place, so
> that they were forced to carry me by four men into prison.[4]

He was then chained in a dark dungeon and sentenced to death before
being taken manacled on board seven or eight ships, chest and back
inscribed 'behold a renegado against God and his king'. The interces-
sion of sympathetic naval officers brought about his transport to the
Court of Appeal at Rennes. Fontaines' noble background and relations in the town helped in dramatically reducing his sentence to five
years' service in the French navy as a surgeon—at his expense. His conditions now improved as well: on the journey back to Brest, 'I was
treated better, for I did eate and drinke with those that conducted me,
also lodged in the innes, onely had a chaine at my foot.'

At Brest his remaining chain was removed and Fontaines was placed
under house arrest with some English officers. Once again in the
French fleet, he happened upon the brother of the surgeon who had
betrayed him in the first instance, fought a duel with him and was
thrown in gaol again. Fontaines managed to escape, only to be recap-
tured and sent back to Brest by sea. By a stroke of luck, he finally
ended up in England after the ship on which he was being transported
was captured by two English warships. Back in England once more, he
offered to tell what he knew and provide his services as a spy.

Fontaines proved immensely useful to William III's government at a
time when Britain and France were at war. His adventures provided
detailed descriptions of the coast and defences around Brest and the
best ways to attack them, as well as of the coastal towns between Brest
and St Malo. He wrote a report on how to improve the quality of the
Royal Navy's surgeons along the lines of the French navy. At the government's behest he also spent periods of the next four years incarcer-
ated with French prisoners of war, masquerading as a captive to discover vital intelligence from fellow officers. For his services Fontaines
was granted an annual pension of £80 combined with the salary of a
'midshipman extraordinary'. It is also possible that he was the same
Lieutenant Fontaines of the fifth-rate man of war *Scarborough*, who in
July 1694—outgunned by two French warships and following the
death of the captain and first lieutenant—was obliged to order her

surrender to the enemy. If so, he was not noticed as a Frenchman this time, and he and his crew were released. By 1696 Fontaines appears to have fallen from favour in government circles, perhaps because of the *Scarborough*'s loss; given leave to sail to the Netherlands, he vanishes from the record.

Fontaines is one of the more colourful spies employed by 17th- and 18th-century politicians and diplomats, but there were plenty of others. Many are known only from the chance survival of papers, comments and asides in private and public collections across the country. However, another named example comes from the reports of the Wolters intelligence ring in surviving letters, now in the National Archives, sent to the secretary of the board of Admiralty.[5] Richard Wolters of Rotterdam ran a network stretching from Paris to Madrid, covering many ports in between. By operating at one remove from the British government, the network offered the Admiralty and the secretary of state added security. Wolters made sure that any reports received from his agents were copied by his own clerk before being sent on to London, thus ensuring that each end of the operation—the customer and the collectors—had as little information about one another as possible. After Wolters' death the work was continued by his widow, Marguerite. The reports of the network surviving in the National Archives cover a period of more than 35 years, from 1749 to 1785—perhaps one of the longest-lasting intelligence networks of the modern era.

The Naval Intelligence Department

Coastal survey information continued to be used in Victorian times, particularly during the Crimean War. The details of tides and winds were used to great effect in reducing the vital Russian fort on the island of Sveaborg defending St Petersburg harbour, ultimately forcing the Russians to surrender. By the later 19th century, however, traditional methods of paying informants for vital 'human intelligence' had largely died out, leaving the Admiralty with no form of clandestine intelligence-gathering capacity beyond the few naval attachés posted to foreign representations. As rivalry with France built up and interested lobby groups pointed out the growing strength of the French and other European navies, pressure to create a professional naval intelligence organization increased. John Colomb, the prominent naval strategist, was one of the first to call for a naval intelligence department. He complained in a speech to the Royal United Services Institute in 1881 that in the event of war the navy would have no way of tracking the progress of enemy sea raiders. Two years later, following a Royal Commission on imperial defence and commerce, a small Foreign Intelligence Committee (FIC) was established within the Admiralty secretariat with a staff of two officers, two clerks and a copyist.[6]

It was not until 1886, however, when Captain Lord Beresford became one of the lords of the Admiralty and began to express concern about a lack of intelligence collection capability that the small FIC was eventually turned into a proper Admiralty department. A junior member of the Board of Admiralty, Beresford was initially ignored, but he took his concerns over the board's head direct to Lord Salisbury, the prime minister. Salisbury, aware that the War Office's Intelligence Branch had proved a success, ordered the Admiralty Board to create a proper Naval Intelligence Department (NID), under Captain William Henry Hall, head of the FIC. The Admiralty took its revenge a year later by drastically reducing the department's budget and salaries. As a result, the NID's first attempts to find out if a press scare about the French fleet's mobilization at Toulon had any truth to it ended in embarrassing failure. The naval attaché to Paris was absent and in the end the Foreign Office had to approach other nations, such as Germany and Italy, to confirm or deny the story, so lacking was the NID in its own agents or sources of information. A follow-up investigation of the French fleet by Hall's number two, Royal Marine Captain Aston, became farcical when Aston, travelling to France without any disguise, attempted to communicate with bewildered locals in stilted schoolboy French. Struggling with basic pronunciation the British naval officer, trying to ask directions to the sea, was thought to 'want his mother'.

Despite such inauspicious beginnings, the NID became increasingly professional and important in the development of naval strategy. Its raised profile was partly because, unlike the army, the navy had never developed a professional 'general staff' and had indeed actively resisted the idea. It thus lacked a core of officers trained in processing operational information, presenting strategic and operational alternatives and suggestions to leaders, and helping to implement them through appropriate orders and commands. As a result the NID increasingly fulfilled this role in the late 19th and early 20th centuries. Under Sir Cyprian Bridge (head of naval intelligence 1889–94), it gained awareness of history and historical understanding in framing strategic and policy decisions, as well as the need for good public relations and an understanding of naval matters to assist policy-making. Aside from the emergence of the vocal 'navalist' pressure group the Navy League, Bridge also helped support and sponsor the creation of the Navy Records Society, a much more subtle benefit to the navy and to intelligence. It was established by the eminent historian Sir John Knox Laughton to make papers and manuscripts on naval history more accessible to historians. Many of the transcribed and published documents came from the Admiralty's own records, often still closed to most researchers. Where the Navy League was populist and rabble-rousing, the Navy Records Society, with just 500 distinguished 'opinion-forming' members and the support of eminent historians, was more of a behind-the-scenes organization seeking to focus debate about naval expenditure and policy. As a result during years of 'naval scares' and Naval Defence Acts one of Britain's intelligence services helped found a learned historical society that is still publishing and active today. [7]

The First World War and Room 40

Following two decades of arms races, when Europe finally plunged itself into the First World War, the head of naval intelligence was probably one of the most able naval officers of his generation. William Reginald 'Blinker' Hall (so named because of his constant blinking) was the son of William Henry Hall, the first head of the NID. He had been an outstanding naval officer whose rise to the senior echelons of the service had appeared assured. When war broke out he was commanding the new battle-cruiser *Queen Mary*, not only turning her into the best gunnery ship in her squadron but also installing the first cinema, bookshop and chapel in a British warship, dramatically improving the stokers' washing facilities and abolishing the ship's police. For all these reasons the *Queen Mary* was considered not just the happiest but also the most effective ship in the fleet, and Hall acquired the reputation of being a good leader — strict in discipline but with a genuine concern for those under his command. Unfortunately Hall's health broke down in the first months of the war and he asked to be relieved of his command. Ironically, this probably saved his life as the *Queen Mary* went down with almost all hands at the Battle of Jutland in 1916. [8]

Hall was fortunate that the post of director of naval intelligence had recently become available, and his appointment in November 1914 proved to be an inspired choice. He had already done some clandestine spying work in the past when, posing as a civilian motor-launch owner, he faked a breakdown of his engines just outside the new naval building slips at Kiel harbour, allowing two young officers below decks to take photographs. Hall inspired devotion in his staff and had an ability—unusual for a naval officer of the time—to think laterally and unconventionally, although he also had a ruthless streak and could be prone to bursts of anger, with an occasionally cruel sense of humour.

Installed in Room 40 of the Admiralty in Whitehall, Hall's naval intelligence team was largely taken from civilian life and Hall's personal contacts.[9] It included an eccentric mix of art historians, schoolmasters, Cambridge dons, junior diplomats, a Presbyterian minister, stockbrokers and barristers, but they soon managed to break one of the German navy's codes and began to pass the operational information they contained to the Admiralty and naval commanders. Hall's NID began to break diplomatic codes as well, developing into the first dedicated British crypto-analytical organization. Details of Room 40's crypto-analytical work are described in chapter 8, including the interception and use of the Zimmermann telegram to bring the United States into the war (p. 244). Hall managed the entire process—the greatest intelligence coup of the war—largely by himself, initially without Foreign Office approval and in the final stages despite the misgivings of Foreign Office officials. He ensured that the US would enter the war with the result that—although mobilization took a long time—it occurred just in time to achieve the final exhaustion of the German war effort.

'Blinker' Hall's individual approach to intelligence—not least his independent network of spies and selective sharing of information with other intelligence services—caused resentment and suspicion within sections of the navy and Foreign Office. Proposals were even afoot to abolish the position of director of naval intelligence; this did not in the event occur, but although the director retained access to the first sea lord, the importance and influence of the NID diminished in the inter-war years.[10]

As a result the NID was in a poor state at the start of 1939. Its new head, Rear Admiral John Godfrey, found the existing staff of 50 wholly inadequate in terms of both numbers and quality, a legacy of a prevailing attitude to intelligence in the services as a career backwater, not something for which an ambitious or bright officer would volunteer. Godfrey decided to consult his First World War predecessor, 'Blinker'

Hall. One of the first pieces of advice he took was to trawl the city of London for possible intelligence officers, as Hall had done at the start of the previous conflict. After contacting the governor of the Bank of England and various scions of city banking families such as the Rothschilds and Hambros, Godfrey managed to bring in another 20 officers from the civilian world. One of these was a stockbroker named Ian Fleming, recommended by the governor and Sir Edward Peacock, another senior banker. Godfrey invited Fleming to join the NID over lunch at the Carlton Grill; he accepted, and later became Godfrey's planning officer and personal assistant. Godfrey also recruited veterans of Room 40 such as Jock Clayton and Captain Thring, hired to lead the resurrected Operational Intelligence Centre (OIC) and the Submarine Tracking Room of the OIC respectively.[11]

Godfrey had realized that recruiting from outside the navy often found people able to think laterally, make unexpected connections and transcend the standard Royal Navy approach. Aside from the stockbrokers and former Room 40 men, by the summer of 1939 his team in the coordinating section of NID included an artist, a book collector, a classics don from Oxford, a judge, a journalist and a schoolmaster. Describing the coordinating section as rather like a 'commune', he found the noise they made in their office so loud that he had a green baize door placed in the doorway between his office and the coordinating section. It was a wise precaution; by the end of the war over 1,000 people would be working in the NID.

Ultra and Communications Intelligence

The NID had many roles during the Second World War, but communications intelligence—interpreted through the NIC and used at sea—has received by far the most attention. The existence of Ultra—the British decryption of German coded radio communications produced by Bletchley Park—was unknown by the general public until 1974, when F. W. Winterbotham's book *The Ultra Secret* exposed this codebreaking capability[12]. The breaking of the silence over Ultra—the existence of which had been known only to a handful of officers and political leaders in the British, Canadian and US armed forces—resulted in a number of books written by those involved in decoding, interpreting and using Ultra decrypts, along with a multi-volume official history. Films, television and the internet have celebrated Ultra's importance—almost creating the impression that decoding intelligence won the

Battle of the Atlantic and perhaps even the war itself.

Work by Professor David Syrett, the leading historian of the operational use of Ultra at sea, has shown that this is an exaggerated view of Ultra's importance. Code-breaking needs to be put into perspective. It certainly gave important assistance in fighting the Battle of the Atlantic, but codes were not broken at all times, and code-breaking itself could take so long that information revealed was no longer of operational use, let alone tactical relevance. Furthermore, the Germans were able to read British coded messages sent in the Combined Cipher 3 for part of the war, which allowed them to work out allied convoy schedules. As David Syrett has observed:

> Communications intelligence did not make German U-boat operations an open book to the Allies. In the first years of the war, the Allies could not read coded German U-boat radio messages and throughout the war the Germans prudently excluded certain types of information from radio transmissions to U-boats. And the best intelligence could not overcome Allied shortcomings in material, organisation or strategy … Communications intelligence did not win the Battle of the Atlantic by itself, but it greatly increased the effectiveness of Allied naval and air forces, shortening the conflict by months if not years.[13]

The story of Ultra and the war against Dönitz's U-boats is therefore more complex than films and even some historians have suggested. Code-breaking was, for example, only one of four types of communications intelligence used during the Battle of the Atlantic. The first was direction finding: intercepting signals from U-boats and locating the source of the signals to find a U-boat by triangulating a number of interceptions from different direction-finding sets. As reports in the National Archives reveal, there were great hopes for direction finding early on in the war. Commander Kemp, who had led the direction-finding plotting section (NI8(X)) of the OIC, explained the sequence of events:

> With the Norwegian campaign in 1940 came the first real burst of activity and early enthusiasms, such as impelled one plotter to broadcast to the fleet the position, course and speed of an enemy unit, were soon damped when the limitations of HF/DF [high frequency direction finding] plotting were exposed as the campaign proceeded. It very quickly became apparent that D/F could never, except in exceedingly rare cases, give more than a reasonably accurate area in which the transmitter could be found.[14]

In the first years of the war the allies set up 51 stations, using the most modern high frequency direction finders, on the eastern and western Atlantic coasts to intercept U-boat signals. According to a history of naval intelligence in the Second World War at the National Archives, there were 15 high frequency stations and 13 medium frequency stations in the United Kingdom by September 1942.[15] Many more were located abroad in British colonies and dominions, and in the United States. From 1942 the allies even began to fit high-frequency direction finders on some selected convoy escorts, giving escort commanders bearings on which they could steam down, force the U-boat to dive and therefore lose contact with the convoy. Incredibly, German naval intelligence did not discover this innovation until the end of the Second World War.

The second form of communications intelligence was 'operator fingerprinting'—the identification of individual enemy signals operators from the way in which they tapped the Morse key. Requiring highly skilled Morse 'listeners', this enabled individual ships or boats to be tracked. Fingerprinting provided useful ancillary intelligence when combined with the Ultra decrypts, as German signals did not include the name of the U-boat but just that of its captain. This technique could therefore help locate a single boat, even if its captain had changed.

The third form of communications intelligence involved analysing the characteristics of a transmission, even if the code could not be broken. From the length of the message, the type of message and some of the patterns of the code, it could be discerned whether a message related to a sinking, contact, position or even a weather report.

The most useful form of communications intelligence, however, was the ability to decipher the message itself. The location of the sender, his 'fingerprint' and the general character of the message all contributed some useful information, but the decoded content was the most operationally important for those fighting the Battle of the Atlantic. This was especially the case with Dönitz's U-boat fleet. Having complete confidence in his codes, he decided to fight the battle using a centralized command and control approach dependent on signals, and also to transmit most of the U-boats' missions once the boats were at sea. This gave Dönitz considerable flexibility in allowing for changes in operational orders, but it also left the U-boats much more dependent on coded communications than they might otherwise have been.

German naval codes relating to the U-boat fleet in the Atlantic were not being regularly broken until February 1941, and the code-breaking was not consistently successful until June of that year (plate 21).[16] Up to that time the OIC had had to rely on the first three types of intelligence. An enormous number of intercepted signals were received by the OIC until February 1942, estimated to have saved up to 1.5–2 million tons of shipping. Unfortunately the Germans then modified the Enigma code machines issued to U-boats in the Atlantic to include a fourth wheel. The new machine, codenamed 'Shark' by the British, caused the 'great blackout', leaving the OIC dependent on the other three forms of communications intelligence until December 1942, when the codes were broken once again.

In practical terms, the time taken to break a particular message's code often meant that the Ultra decrypts were too late to influence an engagement's outcome. One example highlighted by Syrett demonstrates the problem. A message from the Commander in Chief U-boats called 14 U-boats to establish a patrol line in a section of the mid-Atlantic at 11.16 German time on 14 December 1942. It was not decoded until 17.45 British time on 16 December, by which time Convoy ON 153 had been intercepted by a U-boat on the patrol, with the loss of merchant vessels and a destroyer.[17] Such outcomes were not uncommon, but the decoding time could often be quicker and—even if a convoy could not be rerouted—a message could at least be sent warning the escorts of U-boats in the vicinity. A completely successful operational use of an Ultra decrypt described by Syrett was on 19 May 1943, when a command to establish a U-boat patrol line a few days hence was decoded 30 hours before the line was fully established; all the relevant convoys were rerouted.

Ultra also provided some vital intelligence of other types, not least the knowledge that the Germans could read Combined Cipher 3. This allowed the allies to phase out that code and close the one major German intelligence window on allied navies. Ultra decrypts also indicated when new U-boat technologies—such as the *schnorchel* and new types of torpedo—were being trialled. Towards the end of the war, U-boat hunting groups made up of escorts, and even including small aircraft carriers converted from merchant ships, were able using Ultra decrypts to hunt and destroy particular U-boats.

The decryption of German signals was a closely guarded secret both during and after the war. In the Royal Navy only members of the OIC and no more than eight other very senior officers, including the first lord of the Admiralty and the first sea lord, were aware of its existence. Intelligence derived from Ultra was generally distributed by the OIC under the pretext of having deriving from other intelligence means. This also meant that the naval command operated two plots in its main operation rooms at the 'Citadel' in the Admiralty. As Patrick Beesly, a former member of the OIC, described:

> One side effect of these arrangements was that the great majority of important operational decisions were not taken in the main operational rooms in the Admiralty and the other commands, whose plots could not show enemy dispositions in detail. They were taken instead in Rooms of the OIC, or in small side offices at Western Approaches and Coastal Commands.[18]

Betrayal in the Baltic

As the Cold War took shape, the intelligence services reoriented their operations eastwards. Partisans in Latvia and Estonia were still holding out against the Soviets and MI6 wanted to aid their cause by sending trained émigrés to help them. A means of infiltrating agents into the Baltic states without the attention of an airdrop was sought. NI16, the branch of naval intelligence that after the Second World War took over the running of Frank Slocum's 'private navy' of fast craft used to drop off agents on the continent, was the perfect organization to run such operations. Commander Anthony Courtney, Head of NI16, was aided by David Wheler, a Baltic specialist, and John Harvey-Jones, a recent arrival in naval intelligence and a future chairman of ICI and television business 'troubleshooter'.[19]

Courtney recruited a former German E-boat captain with a visceral hatred of Communists who had undertaken similar operations for the Abwehr in the closing years of the war. He picked a crew of like-minded former E-boat sailors, and a former German E-boat was stripped down and rebuilt with silent underwater exhausts and more powerful engines. The boat, under British command, was officially part of the fishery protection service of the British government, and the mission, Operation Jungle was launched in May 1949.

Unfortunately, the Soviets had planted a double agent, Vidvuds Sve-ics, with the émigrés and he betrayed his colleagues. A second mission similarly ended in failure as the agents landed in Lithuania were immediately ensnared in an elaborate Soviet network of hoax guerrillas, feeding false information back to MI6. In fact, the armed resistance movement in the Baltic states was all but exhausted, and although the navy ran many more missions into the Baltic each failed in turn, its agents being killed or 'turned' by the waiting Soviets. Even as late as

1953 MI6 still believed it had a working link with the Baltic resistance movements—little knowing that they had all been betrayed by Kim Philby back in the West and by successful infiltration by the MGB (the KGB's predecessor).

The fate of Buster Crabb

Unsurprisingly in the Cold War climate of suspicion about capability and intent, the Soviets were very secretive about their newest warships. When the Sverdlov class cruisers first emerged in the early 1950s they caused immense concern; armed with a large battery of medium calibre guns, they represented the largest and most powerful vessels built by the USSR since the war. When the *Sverdlov* herself passed through the Dover Straits, naval intelligence made sure that her radar and sonar 'image' was recorded, as well as many hundreds of photographs. Following a request by the Admiralty, MI6 asked Commander Lionel 'Buster' Crabb to undertake an underwater investigation of her hull to see whether the ship had sonar or noise-reduction devices. Crabb, a former Royal Navy diver awarded the George Medal in the war for underwater bomb disposal work—in particular disabling limpet mines attached to the underside of vessels—had worked for the Admiralty since 1948.[20] An adviser on underwater, salvage and diving matters, he had also undertaken some MI6 work on the side. The involvement of MI6, which at the time did not officially exist, theoretically helped the Admiralty to ensure 'deniability' if such work were discovered.[21]

Crabb's examination of the *Sverdlov* proved useful and was undetected. When the *Sverdlov*'s sister ship, the *Ordzhonikidze*, undertook a similar voyage to Britain in 1956, this time for a goodwill visit with the Soviet leadership on board, the Admiralty and naval intelligence decided to undertake the same inspections, again using Crabb. The prime minister, Anthony Eden, made it clear that no such risky intelligence collection should take place due to the potential diplomatic repercussions, but either this message did not reach naval intelligence or MI6, or it was ignored. The Foreign Office was informed, but it has been alleged that Michael Williams, the Foreign Office official told of the operation by MI6, had just learned of his father's death and in the resulting confusion may not have passed the information on to his masters.

The problematic background complemented other ill omens to the operation. The day before the two dives Crabb's MI6 linkman, Ted Davies, had a heart attack. Crabb himself, a heavy smoker and starting to age, was not in the best of health. In the event he did not return from the second dive, and the remains of his headless corpse were discovered a year later in Chichester harbour. The Admiralty's initial response to press speculation—to give as little information as possible—did little more than fan the rumours. The possibility was raised that Crabb had been killed by Soviet guards, but it seems more likely that his death was natural—an unhealthy man either being swept away by the tide or suffering a heart attack while diving. The files held by the National Archives shed little light on how he met his end, and it seems probable that no one will ever know for certain.[22]

The US invasion of Britain

Back in the United Kingdom a programme to survey all of Britain's beaches had got underway after a request by the US Navy in 1946.[23] Codenamed Operation Sandstone, it would last for almost 20 years. Not just a benefit in its own right, the survey also sought to assess the practicality of allied military landings in the event of a Soviet attack. In effect, the survey team, part of NI11, was planning for the re-invasion of, or at least the insertion of raiding parties or agents into, the United Kingdom following a Soviet conquest. The files on Sandstone at the National Archives include hundreds of individual beach surveys with annotated maps of the coast and measurements of depth at different tide levels; there are also details of places to land military equipment.

After the Soviets exploded their first nuclear weapon the fear of conventional attack receded, but the work continued, albeit at a lower level of intensity. This time it investigated the possibility of creating artificial harbours along the coast in the event of a nuclear attack on Britain's ports. The survey team included not just photographers, land surveyors and a naval survey group, but also a small team driving an amphibious military vehicle—designed to test the practicality of military landings and the ability of local roads and streets of coastal towns to take military vehicles. For example, an innocuous portion of the Welsh coast near Caernarfon was assessed for its defensibility and one subsection specifically dealt with the potential for 'Assault':

> The whole of the L.W. [low water] line of the beach is fringed with stones and large boulders up to 6ft in diameter. At the northern limit of the beach the boulders from the L.W. to the H.W. [high water] line cease abruptly and give way to firm sand up which an amphibious jeep was landed from seaward without difficulty.[24]

Positions for potential arms dumps and stores depots were also described: one survey proposed setting aside a seaside hotel car park as an arms and stores base.[25]

Other surveys were undertaken abroad. One of Ireland was undertaken by the Irish authorities, with results apparently passed direct to the US without being revealed to the British. Surveys were also undertaken of the eastern Mediterranean, the German coast and the Suez area.[26] By 1965 the national beach survey—now under DI19 within the Defence Intelligence Staff—had been wound up altogether, although the staff continued work on surveys required for various defence purposes, such as hovercraft landing slips, well into the 1970s. During this time DI19 itself was absorbed by 'L' Section of DI32, which undertook similar work.[27]

Listening for the Soviet fleet

The clandestine operation of submarines directly off the Soviet coast had been considered in the early post-war years, but for operations more dramatic than intelligence gathering. Newer versions of the wartime 'X Craft'—used to fix mines to German warships—were built, officially for training purposes. In reality one of their tasks was to place nuclear devices just off Leningrad in the event of war, and it was feared that the Soviets had similar plans with their miniature submarines.[28]

In July 1955 the Admiralty had extracted from a reluctant Foreign Office an agreement that activities to collect communications, electronic, photographic and underwater intelligence did not need any prior approval from the Foreign Office or other government department, provided that such operations did not enter the other countries' territorial waters and that precautions were taken to avoid 'incidents'. This gave the navy considerable flexibility in conducting clandestine submarine operations off the coast of the Soviet Union. Begun some years before, these had involved the tracking of Soviet submarines and signals intelligence work in the North Sea. Similar US naval activities in the northern seas and in the Pacific had been concealed from the British until the institution of reciprocal arrangements and intelligence sharing in 1956, although these were quickly cut off by the US following the embarrassment of the Crabb incident.[29]

The introduction of the ultra-quiet Porpoise and Oberon class submarines into the British fleet in the late 1950s created new opportunities for tracking and surveillance work. Their silent running capabilities were so impressive for their time that one surfaced by the Statue of Liberty completely unnoticed by US defences or warships.[30] Sitting off Murmansk in the freezing Northern Sea, the new boats undertook signals intelligence work, picking up sonar and underwater communications traffic; such work continued until the end of the Cold War. Security was tight, with the boats' crews not knowing their destination before they set off from port; they then rendezvoused with a harbour tug, the crew of which would paint out the boat's pennant number and weld shut the hatches. Welding the hatches was intended to help keep the boat watertight if she were rammed; it also had the unsettling result of making the vessel difficult to escape from if damaged and forced to surface.[31]

Such dangers were a real possibility. The British were forced to admit to the Norwegians in 1963 that one of the Porpoise class vessels had been in the Barents Sea on an intelligence-gathering mission when it accidentally found itself in the middle of a Soviet naval exercise. She was identified by a Soviet helicopter with a 'dipping sonar' and pursued by surface vessels; she then seems to have been rammed, perhaps accidentally, and had to surface, her batteries exhausted, and make at high speed for Norwegian waters. This vessel had a lucky escape, but the missions off Murmansk continued until the end of the Cold War. It is highly probable that British conventional submarines were regularly close to the Soviet shoreline, dockyards and enemy warships.

While conventional submarines such as the Porpoises and Oberons sought to collect signals and other intelligence on submarines and warships leaving and entering Soviet bases, nuclear submarines increasingly played cat and mouse with Soviet boats. When tracking Soviet vessels the dividing line between what was legitimate and what was not was a difficult one in a period of tense armed peace between the two great power blocs. Submarines, Soviet as well as British, found within territorial waters would not expect to be given any quarter. In 1967 a Soviet submarine—probably a Whiskey class conventional submarine—was unlucky enough to be caught up in a British anti-submarine exercise just off the coast from the Londonderry anti-submarine training school.[32] According to a file covering the incident, which can be found among the records of the Prime Minister's Office at the National Archives, the exercise involved three frigates and three submarines, one of which was the Royal Navy's first nuclear submarine, HMS *Dreadnought*. On board, observing the exercise, happened to be the commander in chief of the home fleet. On hearing that a Soviet submarine had been detected, the local flag officer in operational command of the exercise immediately ordered a general chase and hunt for the vessel.

The hunt was only called off when the defence secretary himself ordered the ships to desist and return to the planned exercise, the risk of causing a diplomatic incident just prior to the visit to Britain of Alexei Kosygin, the premier of the Soviet Union, being considered too great. The defence secretary's private secretary, reporting the incident to the prime minister, made it clear that such aggressive action was not an isolated event: 'It has been usual practice to hunt any submarine that our ships or aircraft find—and, while naturally avoiding any action that could be open to criticism in relation to another warship on the high seas, to shadow the submarine contact until the boat has to surface.'

Tracking the Soviet fleet

The Soviet fleet was tracked by many and various means during the Cold War, ranging from allied submarines and surface fleet to maritime patrol aircraft, satellites and SIGINT. As tracking Soviet naval activities could be carried out over international waters, a significant amount of electronic, technical, photographic and acoustic intelligence could be gathered simply by shadowing. In parallel with submarine tracking, the Admiralty undertook a series of air photo-reconnaissance operations using naval and RAF Coastal Command aircraft. In the late 1950s these included the multi-faceted Operation Grape, which consisted of a series of sub-operations following a perhaps ill-considered alcoholic theme: Operation Sherry involved RAF Canberras photographing Soviet warships in the Atlantic and North Sea; Operation Moselle tracked Soviet warships between the UK and Malta; Operation Claret was an electronic reconnaissance mission in the Atlantic; and Operation Chianti the same in the Mediterranean.[33]

Such operations continued throughout the Cold War and the tracking, photographing and assessment of the signals and sensors of Soviet warships and aircraft became a routine part of every British warship's life. Soviet submarines, ships and aircraft were analysed for technological information about their weapons, radar, sonar and electronic countermeasures technologies. Photographs were taken of these vessels and their equipment, and forces assigned to locate and track ballistic and cruise missile-carrying submarines to ensure their destruction if war broke out. A few examples in the National Archives give a flavour of the Royal Navy's routine work in the Cold War. A file covering the tracking work of the aircraft carrier *Ark Royal* in the mid- and late 1970s reveals that it was often the centrepiece of various exercises and deployments. Soviet frigates and missile cruisers were tracked, aircraft would overfly and take photographs, and the ships' sensors would be read and specific data recorded. The information required was set out in instructions from DI17, the section of Defence Intelligence that supervised and coordinated the tracking of Soviet vessels. Radar and sonar signals were recorded, as were the signals from any electronic countermeasures and wireless traffic. In addition, the course and tactical deployment of the vessels were noted, as were other markers such as navigation lights and the visibility of crew members on deck.[34]

Naval intelligence also used non-military vessels to undertake surveillance of Soviet warships, including through Norwegian intelligence's Operation Delfinius. Funded by MI6 and the CIA, Norwegian intelligence built up networks of informers from the large numbers of their countrymen employed as merchant seamen across the globe. MI6 maintained links with these Norwegian networks via the Scandinavian interests of Hambro's merchant bank; they also ensured that the head of station in Norway was a naval specialist, such as Frank Slocum or Ted Davies, a former member of Slocum's wartime fast-boat unit (p. 124). When Norwegian vessels visited Soviet, Eastern bloc or Chinese harbours, the intelligence authorities would try to include either a Norwegian officer disguised as a sailor or a Norwegian sailor recruited as an agent. They were instructed to look for new harbour works, investigate the depth of the harbour and report anything unusual. By 1956 some Norwegian merchant vessels were even fitted out with hidden cameras and monitoring equipment.[35]

British naval intelligence was engaged in similar activities in the North Sea. Trawlermen from Hull or Aberdeen were recruited via Operation Hornbeam to provide information on Soviet naval capabilities. They were trained to handle specialist cameras and identify Soviet warships, and were sometimes accompanied on the trawlers by listening teams of GCHQ or other intelligence units. In the early 1950s, shadowing of Soviet naval exercises by trawlers resulted in at least five incidents where the trawlermen risked arrest and possible imprisonment, and these operations lasted until at least the mid-1970s. The famous loss of the modern stern trawler *Gaul*, which vanished with all hands in February 1974, was thought at the time to be possibly linked to her involvement in clandestine spying work. However, such speculation has not been substantiated by any of the opened records at the National Archives, or by the official inquiries conducted to investigate the loss.[36]

Corsair and SOSUS

Before the Second World War it had been realized that detecting submarines with sonar—effectively emitting sound waves and listening for their return after they bounce off an object in the sea, such as a submarine—was a much more complex matter than originally envisaged, particularly as submarines became capable of diving ever deeper. Calculations were by no means straightforward. Sound waves in water move at a quarter of the speed they do in air, but that speed is modified by factors such as pressure and the temperature and salinity of the water. The signal's strength is also affected by the spreading and dissipating of the sound wave and the reflection of the signal from matter (or changes in density) in the water other than submarines or manmade objects. For example, the sea surface and the sea bed reflect sound waves, as do even more problematic bodies such as groups of air bubbles, solid particles or shoals of fish. Interpreting signals from sonar is therefore much more complex than with radar.[37]

A discovery just before the war held the potential for a revolution in detection at sea, but it was not fully exploited until after the war. In the deep ocean, at around 4,000 feet, there exist 'Sound Fixing and Ranging' (SOFAR) channels created by the heavy pressure and changing temperature in these conditions. Such channels allow low frequency sound waves, say from an explosion, to be carried enormous distances across the deep ocean.

Soon after the war, US researchers discovered that submarines made lower frequency noises than previously thought, and that such noises could be detected over great distances via SOFAR channels. Placing hydrophones (underwater microphones) on the continental shelf at the SOFAR level could thus enable the capture of these sound waves thousands of nautical miles away. The challenge now lay in finding the right technology to collate and analyse all the sound signals picked up from the SOFAR channels in order to identify which were submarine noises, and then to use this information to locate the submarines. The US and the UK took different approaches to the same problem. In the UK, project Corsair adapted methods used by astronomers to correlate signals over a long period to produce an average, which would then give the location of a submarine. Experiments with arrays of hydrophones up to 1,200 feet long were undertaken off the coast of Cornwall, Northern Ireland and the Shetlands, but heavy interference from fishing vessels, a maximum detection range of 70 nautical miles and difficulties in interpreting the results led to its cancellation. The arrays laid down were preserved on a 'care and maintenance' basis.[38]

The US project Jezebel proved more successful. Using a narrowband spectrum analyser originally developed by Bell Laboratories for speech analysis, it enabled the recording, analysis and storage of each submarine's or ship's unique 'acoustic signature'. Initially ranges of 100 miles were achieved, but this soon multiplied to thousands of miles with gradual developments in the technology, as Jezebel was developed into the SOSUS (Sound and Surveillance System) network of seabed hydrophones.[39] By the mid-1970s SOSUS had expanded into a sophisticated network laid across the both the American and European continental shelves of the North Atlantic. There were similar systems in the Pacific and across the key 'Greenland–Iceland–UK gap', which Soviet submarines had to cross if they wanted to break out into the Atlantic.

Up until the early 1970s SOSUS receiving stations had been built across the eastern and western seaboards of the US and Canada, and on British colonies such as Bermuda, Bahamas and Barbados. However, none had been installed in the UK, despite the US having some success in tracking submarines from the other side of the Atlantic. In 1973 the super-station at RAF Brawdy in Pembrokeshire was completed—the product not just of the reorientation of British naval strategy towards home waters following the withdrawal from worldwide commitments, but also of a programme of improving the SOSUS network's data-processing capabilities. Although conspiracy theorists have suggested that it was a secret base for UFO studies, and anti-nuclear protesters in the 1980s mistakenly thought that it was a nuclear facility, the base housed over 300 US servicemen working on the SOSUS system. It was probably the receiving station for much of the network on the eastern Atlantic continental shelf.[40]

During the 1980s the SOSUS network was augmented by the development of shipboard 'passive sonars', usually in the form of arrays of hydrophones towed behind warships. The British first took passive towed arrays to sea in converted Leander class frigates, placing the processing equipment needed for the arrays either in the ship's former helicopter hangar or in space created by removing the medium-calibre gun. Later ships of the Broadsword and Norfolk classes were similarly fitted with increasingly effective towed systems. Meanwhile, the US developed a dual approach to towed arrays. Like the British they equipped medium-sized warships to tow such arrays for tactical purposes (TACTASS: tactical towed array sensor system), but they also developed specially constructed unarmed twin-hull towed array vessels. These were designed to fill the gaps and augment the seabed SOSUS system with much more capable devices, satellite-linked to receiving stations (SURTASS: surveillance towed array sensor system). The first vessel of this type, the USS *Victorious*, was commissioned just as the Cold War ended. Since then, the SOSUS system has been maintained and upgraded, and its declassification by the US in 1991 has enabled its civilian use by scientists for oceanographic research, and to track the movements of large sea creatures such as whales.[41]

The intelligence war on the seabed resulted in both sides developing unusual technologies. In the early 1980s evidence started to emerge of the Soviets' release, from specially adapted Whiskey class submarines, of tracked vehicles on to the seabed. As to their use, the author of an article discussing these special submersibles, Captain John Moore (a former submarine captain and then editor of *Jane's Fighting Ships*), coyly suggested that the laying of 'navigational markers' may have been their main role. Moore would have known about SOSUS (and about probable Soviet equivalents) and would also have known that it was highly secret, but he was probably coming as close as he could to indicating that the Soviets had equivalent lines of detection/beacon devices, whether to help navigation through the islets of the Baltic or to track approaching enemy vessels.[42] By the late 1980s the Soviets had developed the specialist Uniform class submarines with a similar submersible-carrying role, while the British had built the highly sophisticated diving vessel, HMS *Challenger*. One of *Challenger's* roles was to be locating and disabling Soviet seabed hydrophones and arrays.[43]

Spies in the navy

The Soviet Union had always been far behind the West in the development of cutting-edge technology. Western fears of vessels such as the Sverdlov class cruisers were generally misplaced, as they often proved to be little more than copies of pre-war designs. The Soviet economic system made innovation difficult, resulting in a premium being placed on acquiring Western technology by any means possible. The next generation of warships, adapting the guided rocket technology captured from the Germans after the war (p. 218), began to show the leaps to be made from adapting Western designs. Sometimes this was extremely obvious even to the casual observer: by the late 1970s vertical take-off aircraft (codenamed Forger by NATO) bearing an uncanny resemblance to the Harrier jump-jet started to appear on the decks of Soviet carriers. In that case, however, the technology transfer was not completely successful. The Forger was never able to perform effectively and rarely operated out of sight of its mother ship; it was withdrawn after only 14 years with a production run of only 100.[44]

Often the Soviets could gain what they needed from nothing more than entering into civilian partnerships with Western companies. They never developed an effective microchip industry, so even civilian technologies could prove useful for the enormous Soviet military-industrial complex.[45] In many cases, however, acquiring military technology and information could only be achieved by placing and cultivating agents in the West. The navy seemed to suffer more than its fair share of these sorts of agents. The case of the Admiralty civil servant John Vassall, blackmailed into spying for the Soviets in the mid-1950s, is well known and chronicled in documents at the National Archives. Two other cases, also with records in the Archives, have been paid less attention, and are outlined here.[46]

The Portland spy ring was the first of a number of naval or Admiralty-related spy scandals during the Cold War.[47] Harry Houghton had been a chief petty officer in the navy, but after the Second World War had been employed as a clerk by the Admiralty. A posting to the British embassy in Warsaw gave him the chance to become involved in highly profitable black-market trading, selling Western goods to Poles. Spotted by Polish intelligence, he was lured into compromising himself with certain women and from then on was run as an agent. Houghton soon returned to Britain, his alcoholism, evident to his employers, causing his posting to be brief and not repeated. Among the Admiralty files at the National Archives is a character sketch by the former naval attaché in Warsaw, Ronald Mills, and shows the impression the 'unsuitable' Houghton made: 'he was self-confident, affable and easy going, rather objectionably familiar with the girls of the Embassy staff, obviously fond of a drink to judge by the smell of his breath in the early mornings.'[48] Unfortunately he does not appear untypical. Mills described Houghton as just one example of the 'low-level, brainless male clerks whom the Admiralty were recruiting' to work in naval attachés' offices at the time—a worrying conclusion given the sensitive role of the attaché at an embassy in the Soviet bloc.

The Admiralty then placed Houghton at the Underwater Detection Establishment at Portland, from where he began to pass back the limited information to which he had access to his handler, now the KGB's Konon Trofimovich Molody, who was operating in Britain under the false name of Gordon Lonsdale. To gain higher-quality information, Houghton started an affair with Ethel Gee, who later became a clerk at the Drawing Office Records Section. He and Molody persuaded the gullible Gee that 'Lonsdale' was in fact spying for the Americans and encouraged her to pass plans to them. The most important secrets leaked were the plans for the new Type 2001 sonar, currently being designed for the *Dreadnought*, Britain's first nuclear-powered submarine. In 1960 Houghton was unmasked by information supplied by a Polish defector and he, Gee, Molody and two other agents—from whose house Houghton had communicated with Moscow—were arrested, tried and imprisoned. Incredibly, naval intelligence had been told by the welfare officer at Portland four years previously that Houghton's wife thought he had been selling secrets, while the local probation officer had heard similar rumours, but no action had been taken.[49] On release from prison Houghton married Gee and wrote his memoirs, recounting incredible exploits of receiving Soviet agents dropped off by submarine and assignations in Austria and Ireland. While Houghton could have spiced up his spying career to increase book sales, his treachery undeniably ensured the transfer of important naval technology to the Soviets.

Equally interesting is the case of Sub-Lieutenant David Bingham (plate 18), whose activities came to light a decade later. Bingham was a naval officer who had been brought up 'through the ranks' as a 'special duties' officer. A character assessment by one of his commanding officers, Commander Clapp (who, as Commodore Clapp, 11 years later led the amphibious landings at San Carlos harbour during the battle to retake the Falkland Islands), damned him with faint praise. Although intelligent and 'professionally very adequate', he had never adjusted well to his elevation to commissioned officer status and had 'a slightly immature sense of proportion'.

Bingham had accumulated considerable debts: an early move from council housing to a mortgage, coupled with a perhaps unrealistic understanding of what he could afford, had left him with more than a few thousand pounds owing to banks. His statement to police after he had given himself in to the authorities noted that his wife had first 'jokingly' suggested selling secrets to the Soviets to help their debt situation. The first time he laughed it off, but after she raised it for the second time, he eventually agreed. To all intents and purposes his wife simply knocked on the door of the Soviet embassy; on gaining admittance, she explained her and her husband's financial predicament and handed over a letter from Bingham setting out his position and access to sensitive material. Mrs Bingham was asked to return for a 'film show and tea party' at the embassy; shortly afterwards Sub-Lieutenant Bingham visited a flat near Lancaster Gate in London. Fortifying himself at the bar of the Lancaster Hotel, he asked staff for directions. Once at the flat he was confronted by a Russian who invited him inside and ushered him to a table bearing some cocktail-party food and pens and paper.

Bingham was asked to supply information on various naval sonars and given a sketch of the place in the Surrey countryside where he would drop his findings (plates 19 and 20). He was given £600 as an upfront payment, £100 of which was to pay for a camera to photograph documents, the specifications of which he was given by the Soviet agent. Bingham duly supplied the information and repeated this work a number of times over the next year or so, rendezvousing with his handler and dropping his intelligence in the mundane surroundings of the A25 near New Malden Golf Club. Each time the payment grew less, ensuring that Bingham's debts were never totally paid off and the Soviets could keep a grip on him. Bingham finally cracked after the Soviets threatened him once too often; he handed himself in and was tried and imprisoned, as was his wife.[50]

The seriousness of the secrets he gave away is made clear in a note sent by the first sea lord to the chief of defence staff, preserved in one of the four Admiralty files at the National Archives that deal with the Bingham case:

> Of the national documents compromised the loss of the Fleet Operational and Tactical Instructions (FOTIs) represents the most urgent threat to the Fleet since these instructions were to form the basis of the impending major national Exercises HIGH WOOD and CURTAIN CALL, which are due to commence in November. The value of such exercises could be seriously prejudiced by an observer's knowledge of the basic documents which ships and aircraft will be using.[51]

The first sea lord's note ended with the helpful suggestion that 'you may feel that Ministers should be aware of the details of the Bingham affair before it again hits the national Press headlines'. The assessment of the head of naval technical intelligence at the Defence Intelligence Staff (DIS), also now in the National Archives, made clear the long-term seriousness of the exposure of the FOTIs:

> From the DIS point of view, the security breach is very serious; the Soviet Union now has a very good insight into our methods and capabilities in the field of Naval Technical Intelligence generally. However, there is no action the DIS can take to ameliorate the situation. (Director of Naval Warfare will no doubt be considering what action he can take to reduce the tactical consequences to the Fleet).[52]

One of the most significant elements compromised was FOTI 116—the rules of engagement for maritime forces. Admiral Ashmore, the commander in chief of the Western Fleet, stated that 'these rules of engagement have been compromised in toto. They were based on the SACLANT [Supreme Allied Commander, Atlantic] NATO rules of engagement, and there are therefore grave implications for this system also. The Russians will be able to monitor the Political and Military direction of any exercise in which they are used.' Just as serious was the compromise of FOTIs 301, 302 and 304, which covered naval defences against chemical, biological and nuclear attack; the breach of security 'gives away the paucity of our defences and our proneness to these forms of attack'. Also revealed were the 'inadequacy of our counter-measures' against anti-ship guided missiles, the inability to counter Soviet radar jamming, the operational capabilities of the Valiant class hunter-killer submarines, the Ikara anti-submarine missile system, the Nimrod anti-submarine aircraft and the navy's only ship-borne jamming radar.[53] In the Cold War games of cat and mouse across the ocean, and in any potential 'hot war', the Soviets had been handed three vital advantages: an aid to understanding how the enemy would probably react to situations; an improved knowledge of his weakest points and an understanding of some of his most sophisticated equipment.

From the age of sail to the age of nuclear Armageddon, information in these three areas has been sought by intelligence services. Together with knowledge of the enemy's intentions and geographical and physical intelligence, they form the basic aims of any intelligence organization, although the development of naval intelligence over the last three centuries reflects the dramatic changes in information availability. In the 18th century physical intelligence—the knowledge of landfalls, tides, depths and currents—was vital; every naval ship was expected to report on them. The descendants of these gatherers of physical information were the Sandstone surveyors and the oceanographers in the

Cold War era, but by then resources and interest had shifted towards technical intelligence, driven by the need of NATO and the Soviet Union to understand one another's capabilities. With this end in view, satellites, photo-reconnaissance aircraft, submarines, spies and even civilian shipping were called into service by both sides. Yet whatever success either side had in assessing the other's capabilities, Cold War intelligence could not produce effective answers about the adversary's political and grand strategic designs. For all its sophistication, naval intelligence, like other intelligence services, failed to foresee the collapse of the Eastern bloc and the Soviet Union. Old certainties crumbled with the Berlin Wall, and intelligence organizations were obliged to re-invent their roles and to respond to a radically changing world.

5 | Air Intelligence

The ability to harness hot-air balloons to lift people into the air transformed man's perception of land and sea. Photography made it possible to record this new experience, the famous image of French photographer Nadar in a balloon emphasizing the close association between the two. It was not until the start of the 20th century, however, that air photography was first used in a military context for intelligence purposes.

The merits of air reconnaissance were established in the First World War, as pilots from the RFC produced increasingly useful images of trench networks, batteries and fortifications, but its potential was more fully exploited in the Second World War, under the auspices of the Air Intelligence Branch. As the accuracy of bombing raids became critical, each side strove for intelligence on the other's technological advances, and by November 1943 a specialist radio intelligence and countermeasures group had been set up within Bomber Command. Photographic and electronic reconnaissance retained a key role in Cold War intelligence, fuelled by concern over intentions and capability, and the importance of obtaining accurate information prompted the accelerated development of high-altitude jets such as the British Canberra and the RB-45 of the US. As the Cold War intensified, the dangers of overflights of hostile terrain became more acute, encouraging the development of photo-reconnaissance satellite technology—in which Britain's resources were soon to be surpassed by those of the US. The gigantic costs of satellite systems providing even a fraction of the United States' and the Soviet Union's capability led Britain to near-complete dependence on the US for satellite-produced images by the 1960s. Nor was this the only risk associated with this development; by presenting apparently 'objective' information—albeit of a kind requiring skilled interpretation—satellite images could override other forms of intelligence obtained through more traditional, but not necessarily unreliable, ways.

The beginnings of air intelligence

According to a 1941 RAF staff lecture, now among the Air Historical Branch's files at the National Archives, photographs taken from the air were first applied to military purposes in 1900 during the Boxer rebellion. These could only have been achieved through the use of a balloon and were taken 'by an officer of the French army, Colonel Renard, who managed with very modest material and a great deal of initiative to secure a few good photographs of enemy fortifications during the Chinese campaign'.[1] Only after another decade had passed could useful photographs be obtained from powered flying machines such as aircraft and airships. The nascent Royal Flying Corps (RFC) showed interest in the intelligence role of aircraft, and further files reveal that at least two RFC officers were sent on War Office intelligence and reconnaissance courses in 1913.[2] The first experiments with air photography by British airmen were undertaken—on its own initiative—by No 3 Squadron RFC at the beginning of 1914. Officers bought their own cameras and took photographs of the Isle of Wight; they also developed negatives while still in the air, although it is difficult to imagine how this was done.[3]

Photographic reconnaissance grew from modest beginnings before the First World War into a strategy vital to both sides' understanding of enemy trench networks. The development of air intelligence and air power were integrally linked: one of the first battlefield uses of aeroplanes was for reconnaissance and spotting for artillery, supplementing and gradually replacing tethered balloons. The need to defend these reconnaissance aircraft against enemy predators led to the development of the air defence fighter aircraft. However, pilots in the early days of aerial reconnaissance were often challenged by far more basic issues, not least the problems of navigation and adverse weather conditions, as demonstrated during very first use of an aircraft for reconnaissance by the RFC in wartime. In August 1914 Lieutenant G. W. Mapplebeck of No 4 Squadron RFC reported on return from his mission to reconnoitre the small town of Gembloux in Belgium:

> 'Left Maubeuge 9.30 A.M. Using a large scale map, I followed Bleriot
> [almost certainly a Bleriot XI aircraft; both the British and French
> armed forces had a few at the start of war]. I did not pick-up my
> position on the map, so depended on Bleriot's pilot for correct route,
> intending to branch off on arriving at Nivelles. Missed Nivelles &
> arrived at a big town, but could not place it on the map (on my return
> I discovered this to have been Brussels).'[4]

Although Mapplebeck eventually found Gembloux, observing some cavalry in the vicinity, he appears to have spent much of the rest of his journey lost in cloud. After two hours in the air he attempted to return to Maubeuge but missed it completely, landing instead at Wassigny and then flying another half hour back to base. In his report he commented 'I found great difficulty in reading the large scale map, though very little with the small. The latter having the rivers, canals and railways more clearly marked is much simpler to use for cross country flying, though not so good for detailed observation.'

Mapplebeck was followed by many others during the opening days of conflict, but Britain was lagging behind. The fortuitous capture of a German Zeppelin alerted the British and French to the advanced nature of German photo-reconnaissance. According to reports in the National Archives, the Zeppelin 'was found to be carrying a camera the like of which had never been seen before. The quality of the negatives found exposed in it, and the details of the camera itself brought at least the French General Staff—and ours—to the exact realisation of what had been done by Germany, and the extent of our own neglect.'[5]

The first British use of air photography in a battlefield context occurred during the Battle of the Aisne in September 1914, when Lieutenant Pretyman took five photographs of enemy positions. However, the results proved disappointing—blurred, indistinct and of little use.[6] French expertise was required, and by building on French practice the British learned how to organize and conduct an air photographic intelligence operation. An experimental unit was set up to develop more effective cameras and processing facilities, and in March 1915 the first truly useful reconnaissance photographs were produced. These were taken at the Battle of Neuve Chapelle, alerting commanders to the digging of an extensive network of additional enemy trenches.[7]

Nevertheless, air reconnaissance was still in its early stages of development; balloons were still widely used and the problem of communicating with the ground had not yet been solved. As files at the National Archives show, experiments were made with different systems. Attempts were made to use lamps installed on artillery spotting aircraft, perhaps in imitation of their use at sea, to flash Morse signals to those on the ground. A report from February 1915 indicates that the results did not compare favourably with the use of wireless: 'Exclusive assistance of an aeroplane equipped with a lamp, only succeeded in registering 3 targets; whereas the 130th Howitzer Battery which shares the services of a "wireless" aeroplane with the artillery of 3rd and 5th divisions, has already registered 8 targets since 28th January.'[8] The report expressed several practical reservations, noting that on: 'a rough day it is very difficult to use a lamp and direct it on the battery. The lamp appears to be much more liable to get out of order and is more difficult to read against the sun' than the wireless. If wireless were adopted then 'the fatigue and difficulty of keeping the aeroplanes under observation [by staff on the ground waiting for lamp signals] is done away with'.[9] Lamps were quickly abandoned as a means of air-to-ground communication.

By April 1915 the RFC had defined four types of mission for aircraft. Significantly for the connection of early air power and reconnaissance, three of these related to reconnaissance. They were destruction (of enemy aircraft or ground targets), artillery observations and reconnaissance for immediate front-line forces, 'close' reconnaissance conducted by individual armies for tactical or operational purposes, and 'distant' reconnaissance ordered by the General Headquarters of British forces.[10] It is worth noting that the bombing role and the fighter role were still in such infancy that they had not yet been identified as different tasks.

Air power and air reconnaissance both developed dramatically as the First World War progressed (plates 23 and 24). The growth in aircraft capability and the increasingly crowded skies above the battlefield increased the RFC's interest in 'destruction'—initially destroying enemy reconnaissance aircraft or aircraft sent to protect them, and then discharging weaponry on to the ground, whether this consisted of bombs or machine-gun fire. During 1918 the Independent Force was formed to mount long-range strategic bombing attacks against targets in Germany, a forerunner of Bomber Command's strategic bomber offensive in the Second World War. Consideration was also being given to mounting an air attack on the German fleet in its harbour at Wilhelmshaven—an intriguing foretaste of the Taranto and Pearl Harbor raids of 1940 and 1941. From the point of view of air reconnaissance, an increasingly highly trained cadre of photographic interpreters started to build up—as early as 1916 the general staff had issued photo interpretation guidance—and methods used to support interpretation also developed considerably.[11] For example, files in the National Archives show that during the war Dr G. H. Niewenglowski, a professor at the Lycée Carnet in Tunis, developed methods for the stereoscopic examination of photographs.[12] Two photographs taken at the same time, from cameras mounted as a pair, produced a three-dimensional effect when viewed through a device that presented one photo to

one eye and the other photograph to the other eye. This distant ancestor of the 3-D glasses worn by cinema-goers in the 1980s and 90s made
the photographs much easier to interpret and understand. Dull marks
and lines turned into trenches, emplacements and batteries, enabling
military planners to appreciate the depth and quality of the enemy's
defences and fortifications. Air photo-reconnaissance and interpretation came of age during the First World War, influencing the conduct
of the first total war of the machine age.

Developments between the wars

As F. H. Hinsley notes in his official history of intelligence in the Second World War (to which the following sections are indebted)[13] the Air
Intelligence Branch (AIB) was the Cinderella of the Air Ministry during the 1920s and 1930s. Soon after the end of the First World War its
numbers were reduced to a mere 10, and—as with the other services at
this time—intelligence was considered a useful backwater for ineffec-
tual or ageing officers.

In 1925 the School of Photography at Farnborough introduced the
first standard film camera, the F.24, thus rendering plates obsolete. The
employment of these new cameras tended to be confined to photographing the Empire where there was an urgent need for accurate mapping and surveying. Aerial photography greatly assisted ground forces
in Somaliland and the North-West Frontier of India, and also helped
in surveying badly mapped regions. Despite these efforts, there was a
decline in the application of aerial photography. The War Manual of
1928 reflected this decline, defining a division of responsibility
between the RAF, tasked with taking and developing the photographs,
and the army, responsible for their interpretation. When used, aerial
photography was valued primarily for straightforward tactical work,
to be obtained by local commands and used for immediate or near-
immediate tactical purposes. The inter-war years did see an increase in
the operational ceilings for aircraft, while the resolution of photography improved, allowing high-level photographs to be interpreted for
more wide-ranging purposes. However, this was not exploited effectively by the RAF until after the start of the Second World War.

From 1935 the importance of aerial photographic intelligence began
to be recognized by the Air Ministry, and funds were provided to
improve its potential. Photographs were taken of Italy and its colonies
during the Abyssinian crisis (1934–5)—when it was feared that British

Egypt and the Suez Canal could be affected—and more money was thrown at the problem. However, although the new resources went to research and development, new equipment and training—including recruiting and training intelligence officers down to squadron level—it did not actually result in much new useful photographic intelligence. Part of the trouble was the prevailing RAF culture, which at all levels saw the pilot as a 'generalist'. This attitude, apparently dating back to the First World War, is indicated in a letter from a file of general air reconnaissance correspondence held at the National Archives (plate 22). Written 'in the Field' in July 1916, it passes on the following complaint from an unnamed photographic officer:

> the instruction of Photography at Reading has got to such a pitch of efficiency that the pilots know too much, and one of the questions apparently asked [by] the pilot is: "How do you adjust the lens of an aerial camera?", as also [is] "How do you load the plates for aerial camera?".
>
> Although all knowledge is valuable, yet the cause of the complaint is that this knowledge is sometimes put into practice with dire results as far as the adjusting of lenses is concerned. The complaint apparently is that many pilots arriving now from home are "trying to teach me my job and interfering very seriously with my arrangements as to cameras."[14]

Two decades later, the idea that aerial photography was not a specialist role persisted. Pilots were expected to fulfil the task in addition to their primary responsibilities. As a result, it was believed, a dedicated photo-reconnaissance programme was not required. Nor, given the competing demands for new aircraft types, was a specialist photo-reconnaissance aircraft given high priority.

As tension rose in Europe, acquiring aerial photographs of Germany posed additional problems for the RAF. Such photography required penetration of German airspace—a difficult situation to explain away if the Luftwaffe spotted an aircraft with RAF markings. The solution came in the form of Sidney Cotton, a maverick Australian pilot, inventor and entrepreneur who had flown with the Royal Naval Air Service in the First World War. The ingenious Cotton had created a process for developing colour film, invented a new type of high-altitude flying suit and run commercial aerial photographic businesses; he would also, less edifyingly, later run guns for the Nizam of Hyderabad. A cavalier and charismatic innovator, Cotton seemed the ideal candidate for this particularly risky and dangerous method of collecting intelligence.

The Secret Intelligence Service (SIS) had begun to develop an interest in aerial photography after working as a conduit for air intelligence photographs between France and Britain. French photo-reconnaissance pilots flying high over the German border had taken useful photographs of the borderlands and the Siegfried Line, and Squadron Leader F. Winterbotham, the SIS's linkman with the RAF, was keen to build on these beginnings. After negotiations with the Deuxième Bureau of the French air force, Winterbotham recruited Cotton—well known as a commercial flyer over European airspace—to take surreptitious photographs on behalf of the French and SIS. An American Lockheed 12A aircraft was purchased in early 1939, enabling Cotton to take photographs over western Germany and Italian colonies in Africa in sorties at 5,000 and 5,800 feet.

The sorties were a great success, and by May 1939 Cotton was working solely for SIS. He had begun to use three cameras arranged as a fan, the outer ones placed at 40 degrees to the central camera so as to create a single composite long image. Cotton was by now also flying at 15,000 feet and later 21,000 feet—higher than any other photo-reconnaissance aircraft—and his triple camera arrangement was able to take remarkably good-quality photos of 11½-mile-wide strips. The resourceful Australian had also solved the problem of glass in front of the camera frosting up at high altitude by passing warm air from the cockpit interior over the exposed surface of the glass to keep it warm.[15]

By July, Cotton had managed to develop business contacts in Germany to sell his method of colour film development, providing effective cover for trips into and out of Berlin. Cotton exploited such opportunities, managing to take photographs of the German fleet at its base in Wilhelmshaven, as well as targets in Mannheim and north of Berlin. A week before war started he even offered to fly Hermann Goering to London for last-ditch peace talks, using his business contacts in Germany and operating apparently without Winterbotham's knowledge. Hitler is understood to have vetoed the flight at the last minute, and Cotton proudly stated that his journey back to Britain was the 'last flight out from Berlin'.[16]

The onset of the Second World War

In 1939 Air Intelligence Branch suffered from a number of shortcomings.[17] Not least of these was an ongoing lack of understanding about the need for specialist photographic aeroplanes. Despite Cotton's incredible results, the RAF was still clinging on to the belief from the First World War that standard aircraft, rather than fast high-flying reconnaissance planes, were best for taking photographs. This resulted in disastrous loss rates of slow Blenheim bombers adapted for photo-reconnaissance in early sorties over Germany, coupled with very few usable photographs. Not until February 1940 did the first sortie over Germany by 'Cotton's Club' take place, flying in specially adapted Spitfires fitted with the triple camera system.

Before the war, Cotton had developed links with a private concern, the Aircraft Operating Company (AOC), drawing on its expertise to develop the specialized art of interpreting photographs. Such expertise did not exist within the RAF, largely because an agreement after the end of the First World War had given the Air Ministry responsibility for *taking* intelligence photographs and the War Office responsibility for *interpreting* them. As photo-reconnaissance declined between the wars, so did the War Office's interest, but when the RAF unilaterally decided to take over interpretation of its own photographs in 1938, it found a lack of skilled people to do the work. Cotton, initially working for SIS rather than the RAF, swiftly took the initiative and developed contacts with the private sector.

The simmering inter-service rivalry between the RAF and the Royal Navy that had dominated much of inter-war Whitehall military politics then intervened. The Admiralty made an approach to take over the AOC, impressed by its useful work in photographing the German battleship *Tirpitz* under construction. The Air Ministry, anxious to maintain Cotton's relationship with the AOC, made a counter-offer, and the AOC eventually became the Photographic Interpretation Unit (PIU) within Cotton's outfit. The RAF had to merge its own interpreters with Cotton's, with the result that both sides were required to learn from each other. A report on the PIU in the National Archive's files noted that 'when the unit was first formed most of the interpreters belonged to the Aircraft Operating Co. Ltd and were expert in the use of stereoscopic and photogrammetric methods of mapping from air photographs. They had little knowledge however of military interpretation except in the case of naval detail in the enemy ports.'[18] From the AOC perspective, the RAF interpreters were only 'slightly versed in interpretation of detail for RAF purposes' and had not had access to the equipment and expertise of the AOC. To resolve these problems a training programme was put in place to instruct interpreters in the different types of aircraft and airfield buildings. It included exhaustive handbooks (now in the National Archives) showing sample photographs and drawings of aircraft, ships and building types.[19]

Inter-service rivalry over photographic intelligence was somewhat reduced by the creation of the Combined Intelligence Committee (CIC), an offshoot of the cabinet Joint Intelligence Committee (JIC). Development of the CIC stemmed from the failure of intelligence to predict the German invasion of Norway and the need to avoid any such recurrence. The CIC was tasked with the coordination of intelligence sources to produce daily appreciations of the invasion risk. One of its first achievements was the prioritization of the competing requirements within the ministries for photo-reconnaissance work. The CIC managed to gain the agreement of the Admiralty, War Office, Air Ministry and SIS that it would become the sole authority capable of authorizing photo-reconnaissance missions. The Air Ministry also agreed to transfer Cotton's unit, renamed the Photographic Reconnaissance Unit (PRU), from AIB to Coastal Command, where it would emphasize reconnaissance along the enemy's coast.

Cotton's career with the RAF was in any case coming to a close. Despite having pioneered the art of photo-reconnaissance, the Air Ministry had always tolerated rather than embraced the unconventional Australian. Dismissed from active service with an OBE, Cotton continued his swashbuckling life after the war, dabbling in the less seemly end of Indian princely politics, prospecting for oil and civil engineering.[20] Cotton's creation, the PRU, continued to undertake vital air reconnaissance work. In late 1940 it photographed German Baltic ports, Norway and south-west France, using Spitfires modified to a range of more than 1,500 miles.

At the outbreak of war the AIB had increased its numbers to 40, and this increased to 240 in the first year of war. It was to be a year of significant change, with defeat in France resulting in a major reorganization of air intelligence. Old geographical subdivisions, reasonable enough in peacetime when most intelligence was sourced via attachés in foreign embassies across Europe, made little sense when Germany controlled most of the continent, and air intelligence was gradually rearranged along functional lines. The Air Ministry proved to be the most forward-looking of the three services in this area, and by April 1941 different directorates existed for strategic and operational intelligence and for signals intelligence, as well as assistant directorates for photo-reconnaissance and scientific intelligence. The old directorates covering Germany, Italy and other nations had become absorbed into the strategic and operational intelligence directorate.[21]

As far as scientific intelligence was concerned, the Air Ministry was certainly the most dynamic of the services, proposing the establishment of a joint scientific body as early as February 1939.[22] On the recommendation of Sir Henry Tizard, chairman of the Aeronautical Research Committee, it had also moved to bridge the gap between research and intelligence. In May of that year the Air Ministry agreed to the appointment of a scientific officer to the director of scientific research's staff who would liaise with Air Intelligence Branch. Scientific analysis itself would shortly be transported from backroom shadows to a high-profile intelligence sector, a change in outlook precipitated by two separate events. The first was a speech made by Hitler on 19 September 1939 that apparently referred to secret weapons being developed by the Germans to win the war with Britain. In fact, Hitler's badly translated speech had stated nothing of the sort, an analysis commissioned by the Joint Intelligence Committee concluding that the 'unnamed weapon' to which Hitler had referred was simply German air power.[23] It did, however, result in a flurry of interest in enemy technological developments, most importantly radar. This was followed in November 1939 by a genuine intelligence coup: the delivery of an anonymous report to the British naval attaché in Oslo in November 1939 (p. 215), which in a few short pages pointed out many of the most important scientific developments being undertaken in the military sphere in Germany.

Cooperation between the services on scientific matters continued to be poor throughout much of the war, with the Air Ministry's attempts to further cooperation often resisted by the Admiralty. However, Professor R. V. Jones, eventually appointed to the scientific research position, was able to make great advances—not least using information gleaned from the Oslo report—to surmise that the Germans had developed their own (much less effective) version of radar (initially Freya, then Würzburg, Giant Würzburg and Mammut), as well as the Knickebein and X-Gerat beam systems.

Signals intelligence and the Battle of Britain

The decryption of German Enigma codes (p. 120), used first in the Norway campaign and then from the Luftwaffe during the battle for France, provided useful intelligence on German operations, but not enough materially to affect the outcome of these campaigns.[24] Some of the most important information gleaned from Luftwaffe Enigma decrypts included an understanding of the German anti-aircraft organization—run by the Luftwaffe—which provided flak defences not just for the air force, but also for the army. However, as Hinsley notes, the first warnings that the Battle of Britain was about to commence came from a variety of sources, not just Enigma. Photo-reconnaissance indicated that runways and airfields were being expanded in France and the Low Countries. Enigma itself was also picking up by late June that enemy bomber and dive-bomber squadrons were being redeployed to these areas. The Y Service, responsible for intercepting enemy air voice transmissions and based first on the Sussex coast and then in Kent, also began to pick up information on the redeployment of Luftwaffe units.

At the start of the war, knowledge of enemy radio traffic had been almost completely lacking—short-range transmissions between Luftwaffe aircraft and their ground controllers were out of range of British receivers. After the fall of France German forces were only a few miles away over the Channel, and the interception of enemy air force communications soon became feasible. Particularly important were the very high frequency operational voice communications of Luftwaffe fighter pilots speaking to one another and to their ground-based controllers. Incredibly, as late as May 1940 AIB had no German-speakers assigned to Y Service. With the changing situation in France, six German-speaking members of the WAAF were hastily dispatched to the coast, joining the Y Service at Fairlight. As one of the six WAAFs, Aileen Clayton, wrote more than 30 years later in her history of the Y Service, *The Enemy is Listening*:

> Under normal peacetime circumstances, as a happy young daughter of middle-class parents, I would most probably have been thinking about the next tennis party or perhaps planning a weekend picnic by the sea. Now it was June 1940, and although on that fine summer's day I did indeed find myself going to the seaside, I was very apprehensive. I had been told the post was 'hush-hush', and I had a feeling that it must be some form of intelligence; but I had no idea what would be involved, other than that it was obviously connected with my knowledge of German.[25]

Aileen Clayton would go on to a varied war career with the Y Service, at home and in the Mediterranean. She became the highest-ranking female intelligence office in the Second World War and was awarded an MBE for her work.

The women quickly began to piece together an understanding of how the Luftwaffe operated, information which—combined with other intelligence sources on the Kent coast—would prove extremely important in the coming months of the Battle of Britain. As July wore on, it became clear, from combining Y Service, Enigma and photo-reconnaissance intelligence, that the RAF was facing two Luftwaffe commands: Luftflotte 2 in Belgium and the Netherlands and Luftflotte 3 in France. The total numbers of aircraft within these commands were gradually being revised downwards from AIB's alarmist estimates in June of over 2,500 bombers and nearly the same number of fighters. In reality, the figures were closer to 1,000 bombers and 900 fighters. Below this, as Clayton describes, Y Service had built up a relatively accurate picture of the German order of battle, the composition of their groups and wings, squadron call-signs and even the voices of individual squadron commanders.[26]

Intelligence always has its limitations, however: what it could not do at this stage was provide information on the rate of losses by the enemy. Between 9 August and 2 October it was thought that over 1,100 Luftwaffe aircraft had been destroyed when the real number was only 635. This was the result of cumulative AIB over-estimates of total numbers of aircraft, combined with over-optimistic claims of losses from Fighter Command and Anti-Aircraft Command. Enigma intelligence could also be partial or fragmented, often not supplying information on the Luftwaffe's detailed plans, objectives and methods. Most operational orders travelled over landline wires from Germany and not via wireless telegraphy; without timely access to these wires interception was impossible. Nor could last-minute changes in major raids or operations be picked up—which occasionally led to a loss of confidence in Enigma as an intelligence source. For example, Enigma encrypted messages revealed a large air raid on London planned for 13 September. Later decrypts found that this had been changed to 14 September, but in the event the raid took place on 15 September, with no Enigma warning. Another example, the air raids of 15 August, saw the Luftwaffe suffer heavy losses after attempting diversionary raids in the north of England with a main attack in the south. This attack was later considered to be the turning point in the Battle of Britain, but Fighter Command received no Enigma or Y Service intelligence predicting it. Last-minute radar signals provided the only advance warning of it, and one can only imagine the panic that ensued. A further problem with Enigma traffic during the Battle of Britain was that AIB had not expected Enigma or other high-grade sources to provide tactical intelligence. The AIB desk receiving the results of Enigma decrypts did not have the manpower or training to process and distribute tactical intelligence requiring rapid turn-round.

The German speaking WAAFs of Y Service were able to provide extremely useful tactical information towards the end of the Battle of Britain, as Luftwaffe pilots increasingly began to ignore radio security. The women could work out from translating voice transmissions which groups were forming up where, just outside the range of radar. They could confirm the planes' altitude, help radar plotters work out which were fighter and which bomber groups, and specify where the return rendezvous after the raids would be. All of this intelligence—Enigma intercepts, voice intercepts, as well as the less glamorous sources such as direction finding—contributed, alongside radar, to Fighter Command's defeat of the Luftwaffe in the Battle of Britain.

As the Luftwaffe turned its attention to attacks on civilian centres and Britain's capacity to fight the war (i.e. industrial and port targets), aircraft of the Wireless Intelligence Unit (WIU) identified the first of the 'beams'—the Knickebein navigation system (p. 214). This success, which allowed the AIB and the scientists to develop counter measures and 'bend the beams' away from intended targets, was followed by the identification of the X-Gerat and later Y-Gerat. These sought to guide bombers via VHF 'beams' from different base stations intersecting on the target. In the first of the Blitz's big city raids in which Coventry was devastated, the intersection of the beams over the city was only interpreted correctly on the afternoon of the raid. However, air intelligence began to improve at an incremental rate. Hinsley describes how Enigma decrypts and Y Service voice intercepts gradually combined with interception of X-Gerat beams allowing prediction of the targets for forthcoming raids. Another German device was the Elektra homing beacon to guide aircraft back to their bases. 'Masking beacons' or 'meacons'—originally developed by the Post Office—were used by the RAF to prevent the surreptitious use of German beacons planted by spies on British soil. These could deflect beacon signals on to random or pre-assigned points, causing aircraft to crash, thinking they were landing at their bases. The intelligence gathered from exploiting and analysing the German navigation beams led to the development of the RAF's own blind-bombing aid, Oboe, which helped to improve dramatically Bomber Command's bombing accuracy.

Reconnaissance and Bomber Command

As the Blitz ended and German aircraft were increasingly diverted to the eastern front, intelligence began to forecast the growing strain that the war was having on the German air force.[27] Enigma disclosed the Luftwaffe's manpower shortage, particularly as army regiments were now being formed out of Luftwaffe airmen and ground crew to fight on the eastern front. Increasing effort was put into understanding the signals and codes of the German defensive night-fighter organization, headed by General Kammhuber. Signals and transmissions collected by the Y Service were interpreted by the Government Code and Cypher School. Photo-reconnaissance was used to take images of radar sites and track the growth of German anti-aircraft defences and their sophisticated system of night-fighter control based on radar stations controlling 'boxes' of 40 miles radius.

Although this intelligence could help understanding of the German defensive network, little could be done initially to improve the effectiveness of bombing raids on German soil. German air-defence measures moved Bomber Command towards night-time bombing, which meant that pinpoint targeting was much more difficult to achieve. This resulted in the gradual drift by the air staff towards area bombing of large cities, seeking to sap morale and disrupt the economy to bring the war to a faster end. Photo-reconnaissance of some of the first targets of night-time raids showed that, although much damage was caused, the targets were often missed or only partially damaged. In April 1941 the Directorate of Bomber Operations had to concede that an accuracy of 300 yards was unobtainable and that 1,000 yards (with 600 yards in the best conditions) was more realistic.

In August 1941 analysis of Bomber Command's operational surveys showed that the first bombing offensive had largely been ineffective. In the Ruhr valley—the centre of Germany's heavy industry, and also its most heavily defended area—only seven per cent of aircraft had attacked within five miles of their targets. Nor were the results much better for less well defended areas. Despite conclusive photo-reconnaissance that towns targeted in raids had barely been touched, initially the photo-reconnaissance was doubted rather than the bomber crews' accounts, so important was the bombing campaign for the Air Ministry. Hinsley observes that the campaign continued mainly because it tied down air defences and manpower in the west rather than allowing them to be committed against the Russians in the east. The impact on Germany was also seen as a morale booster for the British public.

Strenuous attempts were made to increase accuracy. The Gee navigation system, introduced in March 1942, enabled aircraft to navigate to their targets and improved bombing accuracy somewhat; but photo-reconnaissance showed that still only 40 per cent of aircraft had bombed within five miles of their targets. The increasing use of incendiary bombs increased effectiveness, but at a terrible human and material cost. The medieval centre of Lübeck was destroyed in one such raid, causing Hitler to order retaliations against the historic British cities of Canterbury, Norwich, Exeter, Bath and York in the so-called 'Baedeker raids'. Although revenge attacks had been expected by AIB, the first raids came as a complete surprise: the Germans had deliberately flown low to avoid radar and maintained strict radio silence, and AIB had been unlucky in receiving no Enigma intelligence.

With the inaccuracy of high-level bombing still considerable, and the political need to be seen to be causing damage still strong, Bomber Command gained permission to move its whole force towards mass bombing, with raids by 1,000 bombers at a time. The May 1942 raid on Cologne was the first such attack: 45,000 people were made homeless, 3,300 houses were destroyed and nearly 500 people killed. The city was functioning normally within two weeks, however, and later mass raids on Essen and Bremen managed to miss most of their targets. Photo-reconnaissance revealed that in the former city the enormous Krupp defence works were left unscathed, and in the latter the port was almost untouched. Accuracy remained a pressing concern.

Operation Biting

Photo-reconnaissance proved to be vital to the allies throughout the war; numerous squadrons were dedicated to it and it played a key role in all theatres. Crucial for the planning of the D-Day landings, photo-reconnaissance was also involved in a huge variety of different operations from locating V1 and V2 launch sites later in the war to laying the groundwork for raids such as that on the Wurzburg radar at Bruneval. The radar was first located by a Spitfire reconnaissance aircraft, and a daring and unusual raid on the enemy coast followed in early 1942. The intention was to steal components from the radar at Bruneval for scientific assessment by the Telecommunications Research Establishment (TRE) back in Britain. It demonstrates both the importance attached to gaining an understanding of enemy radar and the resources that the British High Command was willing to devote to doing so. Now in the National Archives, the report on Operation Biting by Major-General Browning—commanding officer of the Airborne Division—sets out the genesis of the raid: 'The Air Ministry had information that the Germans had a new type of 53 cm RDF [radar] equipment, which was playing an important part in the control of German "flak" and probably in the control of searchlights. It was a serious menace to our aircraft.' Browning continued:

> The above information was given to Commodore Combined Operations (Commodore the Lord Louis Mountbatten, GCVO, DSO) who, after consulting GOC [general officer commanding] Airborne Division, obtained the approval of the Chiefs of Staffs Committee to an operation by parachute troops to capture this RDF set. The Chiefs of Staff agreed on 21 Jan '42 that one operational Whitley [bomber] Squadron from Bomber Command RAF, one company of parachute troops and sufficient light naval craft to evacuate the force by sea, should be made possible.[28]

The paratroopers were split into teams named after famous naval heroes (almost certainly a touch by Mountbatten). 'Nelson' was tasked with clearing beach defences to ensure that the group could get away; 'Hardy' and 'Jellicoe' were to take a nearby house and the German radio location set, respectively; 'Drake' was to create a diversionary attack and cover a nearby German encampment known by the planners as the 'rectangle'; and 'Rodney' would be a reserve unit covering any German counter-attack.

The operation was a near-complete success. The drop was largely successful, the aircraft encountering no anti-aircraft fire and the troopers meeting with little initial resistance, although some from 'Nelson' and 'Rodney' were dropped too far from the planned zone, which meant that clearing the beach defences took longer than planned. The 'Hardy' team took the nearby house with ease, killing the only German soldier inside.

> 'Jellicoe' surrounded the Radio location set; the crew of 5 men offered little resistance but all were killed with the exception of one Luftwaffe man who was taken prisoner. From him it was learnt that there were 100 Germans in the Rectangle and approximately one company in the Bruneval area. The lighthouse at Cap d'Antifer had warned them that a parachutist raid was taking place.[29]

Browning noted that 'After the RE [Royal Engineers] and RAF RDF experts had taken what was required from the RDF set, "Hardy",

"Jellicoe" and "Drake" withdrew southwards about half way to the beach.' After the obstacles had been cleared '"Hardy" and all technical experts, with the equipment which they had collected, also moved down to the beach. The remainder of the company was arranged in defensive positions near the beach while contact was made with the Navy.' A landing craft took off most of the troops whilst a fast motor-gunboat sped back to Spithead carrying the captured equipment and three Germans, including the Luftwaffe officer. Only one British soldier was killed and seven injured, and although seven soldiers who had been dropped too far from the zone and did not get to the beach in time had to be left in France, it was estimated that more than 40 Germans were killed. The operation enabled large parts of a German radar system, considered to be of 'great value', to be taken back to Britain for inspection. It also proved to be one of Mountbatten's earliest successes as head of Combined Operations, and was a forerunner of the much more ambitious St Nazaire raid of 28 March, in which the dry dock at that port was destroyed.

Resources and countermeasures

Through 1943, new devices helped to improve bombing accuracy. Gee was improved and upgraded, the bombing aid Oboe was installed in pathfinder aircraft and a device (H2S) was developed to show the ground beneath a bomber. The release of metallic strips into the air to confuse enemy radar—known as 'Window'—prompted controversy on its first use through concerns that Germany would copy it and retaliate. It was first used on the Hamburg raid (24 July 1943), drastically reducing bomber losses on the previously costly Ruhr offensive, and contributed significantly to the spoof raid directed at the Pas de Calais on D-Day.

By 1944 the allies were able to devote increasing resources to various electronic countermeasures and other equipment to support the bombing offensive. At the end of 1943, 100 Group was set up as a specialist radio intelligence and countermeasures unit within Bomber Command, consisting of Mosquitoes equipped with the Serrate homing device and more than a dozen Flying Fortresses equipped with a full suite of radio-jamming equipment. Recent research by Wing Commander John Stubbington has revealed the background to this most unusual RAF Group, at the core of which was 192 Squadron, operating under the direct control of Air Intelligence and in effect forming part of the Y Service, but collecting enemy signals from the air rather than from ground-based receivers. The signals intelligence equipment of 192 Squadron included the 'Bagful' recorder (explained below), which enabled analysts to record every single enemy signal encountered during a mission, for later assessment on the ground. 192 Squadron undertook over 2,088 sorties, the most of any 100 Group squadron, largely operating in support of major bombing missions over Germany. The squadron was lucky to suffer only five losses in nearly a year and a half of wartime operations, but enabled vital intelligence to be collected, feeding into the growing understanding of enemy air defence organization and operations.[30]

A glossary of the code names for various countermeasures used by 100 Group and other units, compiled in July 1944 and now in the National Archives, runs to more than five pages. A few examples provide a flavour of the range of technologies available to the allies in the last months of the war:

ABDULLA: 'A receiver to enable an aircraft to home on to an enemy radar ground station of the Würzburg type with a view to attacking it.'

BAGFUL: 'A receiver which can be carried either in operational or special navigational aircraft and which records automatically on a paper strip the wavelength of signals reaching the aircraft [and] also the time and duration of reception. This gives an automatic preliminary watch on enemy radar stations etc. on which a more detailed investigation can be based later.'

HANGOVER: 'Ground jamming transmitters are used to jam the enemy ground receiver which picks up the IFF [interrogation: 'friend or foe'] signals from his aircraft.'

MACCABOY: 'An airborne homer equipment designed to home on to enemy aircraft carrying jammers to interfere with our low flying warning chain.'

TINSEL: 'A simple method of jamming enemy HF R/T [high frequency radio/telegraph] control of his night fighters by transmitting engine noise from the ordinary communications transmitter of a bomber.'[31]

By the end of the Second World War over 700 servicemen were working in AIB, almost all of them being 'hostilities only' officers and ranks. A rapid retrenchment after the conflict brought numbers much lower than this, but still higher than the pre-war position, reflecting the new importance that air intelligence had assumed.

Photographic intelligence in the Cold War

Only a few years after the end of the war, in August 1949, the air intelligence Cold War started with a bang—more specifically an explosion on the Steppe, as the Soviet Union detonated its first atom bomb near Semipalatinsk, in modern Kazakhstan. A year later North Korea invaded South Korea, causing the deployment of hundreds of thousands of Western troops, airmen and sailors—and a dramatic increase in British defence spending, as the government feared an imminent Third World War.

Two issues weighed most heavily in air intelligence officers' minds. The first was that Soviet Tu-4 bombers, if modified to take nuclear bombs, could now drop them over much of Europe. They could also attack the continental United States if they flew over the North Pole on a one-way 'suicide' mission. This therefore created an urgent need for photo intelligence on bomber airfields and air-defence radar stations in the Russian Arctic and the west of the Soviet Union, in addition to the various nuclear facilities and test sites across the great expanse of the Soviet interior. It was an additional irony that the Soviets' capability had been achieved through US technology: the Tu-4 was a reverse-engineered copy of the US B-29 'Super Fortress' bomber and the Soviet air-defence radar system used wartime radar systems, supplied and built by the US.[32]

The second issue that intelligence officers had to grapple with was that new Soviet built MiG-15 jets, operating over North Korea, were now shooting down US Air Force's main reconnaissance aircraft, the piston-engined RB-29. Urgent requirements for reliable photo intelligence on enemy installations and equipment, combined with obsolete intelligence-gathering aircraft, led to a rapidly accelerated development of high-altitude reconnaissance jets, able to out-fly Soviet fighters and fly above the maximum height at which Soviet radar could detect targets. The long-term British solution was the adaptation of the Canberra light bomber with an operational ceiling of 50,000 feet. The photo-reconnaissance Canberra was still in service with the RAF until the middle of 2006, having served in both Gulf Wars, and so impressive was the aircraft that the US built its own version, the RB-57, which entered service in 1956.

From 1951 both the US and Britain undertook overflights of the Soviet Union to gather intelligence. Cooperation between the two countries' air forces was close—to the extent that RAF pilots flew photo-reconnaissance missions over the Soviet Union in US RB-45C jets, temporarily given British markings.[33] The Cold War could be a real shooting war for these crews. An account by the pilot of a British-manned RB-45C of an overflight of the western Soviet Union in April 1954 gives a flavour of the dangers they faced. Squadron Leader John Crampton recounted some strange phenomena he observed as he brought his aircraft back home high over the Ukraine after completing a photo-reconnaissance mission:

> Occasionally I saw, reflected on the cloud cover, flashes from the ground similar to lightning or an active bombing range at night. It was causing us no harm — just puzzling, that's all. Having taken nearly all our photos we were heading south towards Kiev at 36,000 feet and Mach 0.7 when the electric storm or bombing range flashes seemed to be getting more frequent — and always directly beneath us, which was odd for a random phenomenon. Had it not been for the absolute certainty with which the briefing officers had dismissed the possibility of flak I would have been a shade suspicious because it all closely resembled the German variety I had seen a lot of in an earlier life.[34]

He continued:

> My reverie was rudely interrupted by the sudden heart stopping appearance of a veritable flare path of exploding golden anti-aircraft fire. There was no doubt about it; it was very well predicted flak — dead ahead and at the same height as we were. My reaction was instinctive — throttles wide open and haul the aeroplane round on its starboard wing tip until the gyro compass pointed west ... We had about a thousand miles to go and I urged Mac [the co-pilot, Flight Lieutenant McAlistair Furze] to keep his eyes peeled for fighters which might pick us up outside the flak pattern. Much later I learned that there were fighters about with orders to ram us on sight. Maximum speed was essential. I flew the aeroplane just on the right side of the buffet; it sort of trembled affectionately. I had time to reflect that the earlier flashes we had seen below us had been ground fire and that our stately progress as ordered by [Flight Lieutenant] Rex [Sanders, navigator] had given even the dimmest battery commanders time to track us and fire. The early attempts had ALL misjudged our height — and, thank God, the Kiev defence had misjudged our speed; they had chucked everything up a few hundred yards ahead of us.[35]

Anglo-American cooperation on aerial photo-reconnaissance continued through the 1950s: three of the United States' new high-altitude U2 spy planes were initially based in the United Kingdom, but after the Crabb affair (p. 125) Anthony Eden quickly rescinded this approval, fearing further embarrassments. That the U2 set off the United Kingdom's nuclear early warning system every time it flew was another unfortunate factor that led to the transfer of the U2s to West Germany.[36] RAF crews were nonetheless trained to fly the U2, one being killed accidentally while training in the Nevada desert.[37]

It was becoming increasingly difficult for NATO aircraft to overfly the Soviet Union without being detected, a fact dramatically highlighted in 1960 by the shooting down over the Soviet Union of both Gary Powers' U2 aircraft and a British-based US RB-47D north of the Kola peninsula.[38] The Americans developed a successor to the U2, the SR-71 'Blackbird' strategic reconnaissance aircraft, capable of flying at Mach 3.5 at heights in excess of 80,000 feet. Operating from airfields in the USA and Britain, the SR-71 had a range of 3,000 miles and overflights of the Soviet Union remained possible. It was also used for photographic reconnaissance sorties over the Middle East and other local hotspots.

The RAF continued to have a strategic photographic reconnaissance role until 1974 operating modified Victor bombers, which were also used to gather air samples for analysis after nuclear explosions. Radar reconnaissance, particularly in the maritime environment, continued with the Victors, and later with Vulcans, when shipping could be plotted and the locations and dispositions of naval task forces passed to attacking aircraft formations. During the Falklands campaign in 1982, Nimrods carried out extensive radar, photographic and visual reconnaissance sorties searching for the Argentinian fleet.

It is in the tactical field that photographic reconnaissance continues. Thousands of photographic sorties were flown during the Vietnam War by dedicated aircraft equipped with specialized photographic, radar and infra-red sensors. This capability was also extensively used in the recent Middle East wars, while in Afghanistan unmanned reconnaissance vehicles, capable of data-linking information to a ground exploitation and intelligence centre, are playing an increasingly important role.

Ever since the Second World War, electronic reconnaissance has formed an important part of intelligence gathering. Over the years the RAF has used modified bombers to 'eavesdrop' on all types of electronic emissions, gathering and recording signals for later analysis. It can be considered as the equivalent of an airborne Y Service, and today the RAF operates a small fleet of specially modified Nimrod aircraft in the electronic reconnaissance role. Information collated with other SIGINT sources provides valuable strategic and tactical information

on an enemy. As technology advances for the development of platforms, sensors, communications and real-time analysis, gathering
intelligence from airborne platforms is becoming increasingly important in the modern battlefield.

Satellite intelligence in the Cold War

In 1964 the decision was taken to combine the three services' intelligence organizations with the Joint Intelligence Bureau to create a single Defence Intelligence Staff (DIS). In reality, the service splits between
air, land and sea were retained for some years within the new organization, but air intelligence was itself changing under the impact of new
technology. As photographic intelligence—particularly (from the
1970s onwards) from satellites—became more important, the DIS split
between two main areas: the analysis of intelligence from open and
covert sources, including MI6, MI5 and GCHQ (currently undertaken
by the defence intelligence assessment staff), and the work carried out
by its Intelligence Collection Group, whose role is essentially that of
interpreting satellite photo, radar and other information, most of
which is provided by the United States.

The rather laboriously titled JARIC (Joint Air Reconnaissance
Intelligence Centre, known as the National Imagery Exploitation Centre) is in fact the linear descendent of the PIU, created from the AOC
on its purchase by the RAF and integration into Cotton's organization
in 1940 (p. 146). JARIC, responsible for the assessment of imagery—
photography, infra-red and radar—rather than radar intercepts,
employs over 500 staff and was incorporated into the DIS in 1996; it
later merged with the Military Survey.[39] In addition to the central
organizations for photographic intelligence, the RAF has also created
its own intelligence specialization for officers to provide intelligence
information for pilots at the squadron level. From this specialization
come many of the RAF servicemen now working in the DIS.

The use of satellites for reconnaissance purposes was first considered in the early 1950s. President Eisenhower approved development of
such a satellite in 1955, at the same time as the British were undertaking their first feasibility studies.[40] Aside from the increasing danger to
pilots, air reconnaissance could only cover limited areas and photograph areas of specific interest—in other words, those considered
important enough to merit a dangerous reconnaissance mission. At
the same time, the development of nuclear missiles meant that exact

geographical data was now required to guide nuclear weapons to their targets. The Soviet habit of deliberately distorting publicly available maps, keeping whole cities and research establishments secret and naming research centres and military bases after cities hundreds of miles away, made acquiring such data particularly important.[41]

The story of British photo-reconnaissance satellites is relatively unknown. However, files at the National Archives show that serious consideration was given to their development between 1955 and 1964, culminating in a full feasibility study for a reconnaissance satellite programme in 1962. Options discussed in the study included a brace of five photographic satellites with a 10–14 day life (dropping their film in canisters at the end of the period) or a longer-lasting single television satellite transmitting its images to receiver stations. Such images would have had a survey resolution of 25 metres and a detailed reconnaissance functionality of down to five metres. GCHQ insisted that the satellite system should include electronic listening capabilities so that images could be matched up with signals—thus helping to pinpoint Soviet anti-ballistic missile radar systems as well as other signals such as air-to-ground voice communications, missile telemetry and VHF radio relay. It was recommended that the satellite be given a cover story—leading to the suggestion that some space should be set aside for meteorological payloads, while either the US Thor or the British Blue Streak would be used as the launch vehicle.[42]

The defence planning staff on satellite development finally produced two reports, now in a file in the records of the Ministry of Defence at the National Archives. In these it was argued that, of the various missions satellites could perform, the reconnaissance role was the most important for British strategic interests.[43] However, the second report also recommended the prior development of communications satellites —what would eventually became the Skynet system. Private organizations could contribute to their production, thus helping to share the costs, whereas reconnaissance satellites were much less likely to fit in with commercial satellite needs. The same report pointed out that civilian surveying satellites then under development—project SECOR, for example, which would become Landsat—required at least one ground station to be in the country being surveyed. This was, of course, out of the question for reconnaissance of Soviet territory.

The defence planners thus regarded Skynet as a precursor to the reconnaissance satellite. The papers went to the chiefs of staff, chaired by Admiral of the Fleet, Lord Mountbatten. He approved the communications satellite and decided to shelve the reconnaissance version, for quite different reasons from the defence planners. He disagreed that reconnaissance satellites were the most important for British interests, stating instead that 'from a purely British point of view and in the light of our widespread responsibilities short of general war, the use of space satellites for communications was of greater importance and should be given priority in any British development programme'.[44] Mountbatten was referring to Britain's commitments across the globe, particularly in South-East Asia, the Persian Gulf and the Indian Ocean, where Britain still retained a considerable military and naval presence. Allowing ships, aircraft and bases across these regions to communicate with each other was deemed more important at the time than a surveying and reconnaissance capability over the Soviet Union.

Service considerations might also have had something to do with Mountbatten's attitude: a report by the Admiralty the year before had been dismissive of the benefits of reconnaissance satellites for naval purposes.[45] Mountbatten at this time dominated the chiefs of staff and was not afraid to push for his own service's interests. He had also been instrumental in creating the 'East of Suez' strategy, emphasizing Britain's role outside the NATO area. The demise of the reconnaissance satellite is an interesting 'might have been', as only four months later a new government limited Mountbatten's power and started to shift strategy away from Britain's overseas commitments. By the time Skynet eventually appeared, after years of problems and misadventures, its original justification seemed no longer relevant: Britain had withdrawn from most of its commitments in the Persian Gulf and South-East Asia by 1971 and in the Mediterranean by 1975. Interestingly, the GCHQ requirement for independent air intelligence still remained in the mid-1970s, when the organization ensured that its requirements were added to Royal Aircraft Establishment feasibility studies for an (ultimately abortive) unmanned air surveillance system. Not unlike an unmanned helicopter or light aircraft, the system was being developed by Westland and other defence contractors.[46]

With no indigenous satellite photo-reconnaissance capability, Britain became wholly dependent on photographic imagery generated by American satellites, which in the early days of development had its limitations. The first US photo-reconnaissance satellites had very short lifespans of only three or four days, dropping capsules of exposed photographic reels to be picked up by US forces. In the pre-digital world, sending signals conveying the details of even a single image would have taken many hours and was therefore impractical; as a result, the recovery of films dropped by the satellites was the only effective alternative until the 1970s.[47] (In fact, the Soviets never managed to move beyond reel-retrieval satellites, still being wholly dependent upon them at the dissolution of the USSR in 1991.) Recovery was achieved by snagging the parachute cords on the capsule, bringing the reels to earth on paravanes fitted to specially adapted military aircraft.

The first US photo-reconnaissance satellite programme, run by the US Air Force and known as the WS 117L, had to be cancelled in early 1958 after USAF had leaked its existence. The reason was to counter press and public concerns, following the flight of the Soviet Sputnik satellite, that the US had been overtaken in military technology by its Cold War enemy. However, the development programme was relaunched in immense secrecy the same year under the auspices of the CIA. The system was codenamed Corona, after the brand of typewriter on the desk of the CIA director running the programme, and the first camera systems were given the designations Keyhole (KH) one to four. The very first satellite system (KH 1) lasted only three to four days with a resolution of 25 feet, but by the time the KH 4B had been launched the effective life had been extended to 19 days, resolution had reduced to 6 feet and the satellite contained two reel capsules, one to be ejected in the middle of the mission and the other at the end. Further developments of the KH programme in the 1960s and 1970s (Argon—KH 5, Lanyard—KH 6, Gambit—KH 7/8, Hexagon/Big Bird—KH 9) gradually increased the resolution down to 2 feet, the lifetime to 275 days, the number of cameras to two and the number of film-return capsules to four.[48]

The KH 10 was an abortive manned photo-reconnaissance satellite laboratory, superseded by the next great step forward in photo-reconnaissance technology: the KH11 (Kennan/Crystal) television-image data-linked satellite system. Film retrieval was no longer needed, as images were transmitted using digital technology via data link to relay satellites and then down to a series of ground stations. The first KH 11 system was launched in 1976—its first real-time images being shown to President Jimmy Carter on the day of his inauguration—and the last of nine in the original KH 11 programme was launched in 1988. These satellites had a lifespan of between three and ten years, with two remaining active in the mid-1990s. The KH 11 brought resolution down to less than one metre, with the resolution on detailed images down to 15–18 centimetres in very good weather.[49] Embarrassingly, the capabilities of the early KH 11s were revealed when images from the satellites were found in the wreckage of the US helicopters carrying special forces sent to rescue the Iranian embassy hostages following the fall of the Shah.[50] It is perhaps ironic that the failure of this mission was an important factor in causing Carter—the first president to have seen the images—to lose the 1980 election to Ronald Reagan.

The next generation of Advanced KH 11s was launched in the early and mid-1990s, and was in turn superseded by the Enhanced Image System (EIS) KH 11s, launched between 2001 and 2005. The Advanced KH 11s provided even greater improvements in image resolution; they also increased fuel capacity to evade attacks from enemy satellites and are believed to have included infra-red imaging and real-time television (rather than still) images. The EIS KH 11s were developed in response to requests from military commanders following the 1990–91 Gulf War for images to be produced in quicker time and for individual images to cover a wider area. In effect, photo-reconnaissance satellites had moved away from the old Cold War requirements of providing pencil-sharp images to allow detailed analysis of new military or technological installations. Instead, they produced near-instantaneous images of use to mid-level tactical commanders on the ground during a conflict situation, losing some image resolution in the process. Such a development shows how modern technology has telescoped the uses of intelligence from the strategic to the low-level tactical sphere. It is also notable—in a climate of concern about the state's all-seeing eye— that the proverbial ability to read car number plates from space seems to have been superseded by the need to provide more immediate battlefield intelligence for military commanders. Developed as a strategic tool, the photo-reconnaissance satellite has become an operational and tactical piece of technology.[51]

The new generation of Future Image Architecture (FIA) satellites has been under protracted development since the late 1990s. Over $10bn has reportedly been spent, with the work moving from the traditional specialist in this area, Lockheed Martin, to Boeing, and then back to Lockheed again in 2005. The first launch is expected in 2009.

In addition to the KH family of photo satellites, the US has developed a range of other complementary surveillance satellite systems. The Lacrosse system—first launched in 1998—provides radar images for similar surveillance purposes to the KH photo satellites; its solar panels are so large that they are visible from earth using amateur telescopes. The Misty system is designed to look 'sideways' at targets in

order to reveal details under cloud cover—and underneath the camouflage nets and foliage increasingly used by the Soviets and others to
counter the KH photo-reconnaissance satellites. The first Misty was
launched in 1990.[52]

The US Navy has also developed a family of ocean surveillance satellites to pick up radar or radio signals from maritime vessels and use
these to pinpoint their location, providing the navy with a picture of
enemy shipping 'over the horizon' and enabling the tracking of merchant shipping along sea routes. The first Poppy satellites of this type
launched between 1962 and 1977. They were followed by the Naval
Ocean Surveillance System (NOSS 1) White Cloud/Parcae launched
between 1977 and 1982, the NOSS 2 launched between 1990 and 1996,
and the NOSS 3 Gemini/Libra launching from 2001 onwards.[53]

What access do the British get to these various systems? A definitive
answer cannot be given, but it is probable that it is quite considerable,
given the long-standing reciprocal links between the US and UK in the
sphere of communications satellites, anti-ballistic missile tracking,
signals intelligence (such as Echelon and the abortive Zircon) and the
US use of UK-based or UK-run ground stations. There was also the
strong post-war cooperation between USAF and the RAF in aerial
photo-reconnaissance in the 1950s. The fact that JARIC, the organization within the DIS that analyses satellite images, employs more than
500 staff gives another indication of the quantity of imagery supplied
by the US, although one suspects that there are certain areas, such as
Israel and Palestine, where image transfer might be more circumspect.
It is perhaps also notable that during the period when the United Kingdom was considering developing its own reconnaissance satellites US
cooperation was suspended. Documentation released to the National
Archives gives no indication that the Ministry of Defence was aware
that the first Keyhole surveillance satellites had been launched.[54]

During the Falklands War US photo-reconnaissance satellites were
made available, but the US, mindful of Latin American opinion, was
keen to keep its aid surreptitious. Thus surveillance assistance that
would have been detected by the Soviets and others—such as sending
an SR-71 high-altitude, high-speed surveillance jet (the successor to
the U2) or diverting a KH 11 satellite off its standard orbit—was
apparently not possible. Cloud cover during large parts of the campaign meant that the surveillance satellite cover that was available
often did not produce useable images. Communications satellites were
available, and were heavily used by the Task Force to communicate

with London and the joint Naval/RAF Coastal Command Headquarters in Northwood, but limitations on these resulted in the rebirth of the Skynet system.[55]

Finally, US surveillance satellite imagery would have been (and still is) essential to Britain in, perhaps, an unexpected way: to ensure effective targeting for Polaris and Trident ballistic nuclear missiles introduced in the 1960s and 1990s respectively. Similarly, the data downlinks needed to provide targeting information for Tomahawk-equipped submarines can probably only come from US satellite systems.

In terms of the overall impact of satellite images on the intelligence community, the defence analyst Norman Friedman noted in 2000:

> The advent of the photo satellites drastically changed the US intelligence community. Suddenly there was a flood of images which had to be interpreted. Photo interpreters came to dominate intelligence simply by their sheer numbers. Moreover, imagery seemed to offer objective information. Traditional kinds of intelligence, even signals intelligence, were far more ambiguous and required far more interpretation. It had always been preferable to have hard information about an enemy's equipment and strength, but now that sort of information in effect seemed to drive out more traditional efforts to discover enemy intentions and the quality of enemy forces.[56]

Friedman, writing before the 9/11 attacks, then cites the US over-estimate of Iraqi capabilities in the build up to the 1990–91 Gulf War as an example. US intelligence agencies were able to provide highly accurate figures on Iraq's order of battle in terms of equipment, but they missed out on how 'hollow' these forces were due to poor morale, training and upkeep, and under-manning. Friedman's conclusions could also be said to apply to the more recent intelligence assessments prior to the current Iraq war.

Above all, the history of air reconnaissance—from the days of Colonel Renard to today's spies in the sky—demonstrates the enormous impact that technological growth has had on intelligence gathering. Satellite reconnaissance has resulted in a huge step forward in intelligence capabilities in the last 40 years, but an over-reliance on it, as on any single intelligence source, carries the risk of misinterpretation. The illusion that images can reveal all that there is to know about an enemy or potential adversary is a dangerous one, to be indulged at our peril.

6 | The Special Operations Executive

Launched in 1940 with Churchill's vivid exhortation to 'set Europe ablaze', the Special Operations Executive has been a source of fascination for many years. Its dramatic missions ranged from the leadership and support of resistance units across Europe to the planned assassinations of Hitler and his henchmen, feats of incredible endurance in the jungle and the sabotage of plants making material necessary to build atom bombs. The SOE's successes were balanced, inevitably, by some embarrassing failures—the collapse of the Carte and OCM rings in France and the highly successful *Englandspiel* operations that ensnared the SOE for more than 18 months in a German double cross in the Netherlands. More than 50 agents were sent to their deaths through the *Englandspiel* alone, and the dangers of such service—isolated, exposed and in civilian clothes behind enemy lines—cannot be exaggerated.

The mixture of extreme peril, individual courage and daring missions has ensured lasting interest in the SOE's work. More information on their activities has emerged in recent years, with the first files from the Public Record Office (now the National Archives) being released in the 1990s and digested into accessible pamphlet resources by Louise Atherton. Michael Foot's acclaimed official history of French special operations, published in 1966, and W.J.M. Mackenzie's top-secret account, completed shortly after the war and published in 2000, have been joined by both academic and popular accounts of SOE action. Most recent releases from the National Archives include investigations into the fortunes of individual 'pickaxes'—Soviet agents discreetly dropped into occupied Europe by the SOE—during and after the war, as well as the extraordinary story of Louis de Wohl, an astrologer of uncertain origins who offered regular advice and predictions to the military and intelligence services. The recent death of Pearl Cornioley (Flight Officer Pearl Witherington MBE, CBE, CdeG) has also enabled her heroic war record to be revealed, with new insight into activities in

France. But only by exploring the SOE's involvement in countries across Europe, Africa, the Middle East, Far East and Southeast Asia can the full extent of its contribution to Britain's war effort be appreciated.

The origins of SOE

The SOE was a hybrid organization, with its roots in both section D (of the Secret Intelligence Service) and MIR (the research section of military intelligence, run by the War Office). The first of these, section D of the SIS, had been created as the threat from Nazi Germany mounted in the late 1930s and was first headed by Major Lawrence Grand. In the 18 months before the war it had evolved into a 'service within a service', running agents for sabotage and paramilitary activities. Prior to its integration into the new SOE, it had consisted of four main divisions: Administration, Plans, Supplies and Execution. Little is known about the first two aside from the fact that Guy Burgess briefly headed up a unit in Plans, D/U, in the early years of the war. Supplies and Execution had quite substantial organizations, often working separately from—but in parallel to—the rest of the SIS structure. Supplies included four subdivisions covering propaganda, communications, technical and personnel, the last dealing with German refugees and the 'D School'—what would become the SOE training camp, where SIS agents were also trained.[1] Execution, split into geographical sections, dealt with the 'sharp end' of operations on the ground: building and keeping contact with local opposition and exile groups, handing over materials or explosives, carrying out operations and even, as historian Philip Davies has noted, developing local propaganda operations. Together these two divisions provided the core of future SOE overseas networks. Omens seemed good; section D conducted a number of operations in the early months of the war, some of which were highly successful, such as the 'rescue' of £1.25 million worth of industrial diamonds from Amsterdam as the Germans advanced.[2]

SOE's other component, MIR, had been set up at the start of the war by the War Office. Reporting to the director of military intelligence, its remit was to investigate potential methods of guerrilla warfare, produce guidance on how to conduct such warfare, create and locate suitable equipment and destructive devices for use by guerrillas and saboteurs and—if necessary—undertake or lead guerrilla missions. Operating from a building next door to section D, there was considerable overlap between the roles of the two organizations, but

MIR proved to be the more vigorous and active. Its early research activities laid the seeds for several key developments. These included the creation of MI9, the organization to aid evaders and escaped prisoners; the establishment of MI10 and ISSB, the organizations tasked with strategic deception (whose greatest coup would be to convince Hitler that the main allied invasion would be in the Pas de Calais region); the foundation of the Independent Companies, the predecessors to the Commandos; and the establishment of the guerrilla training centre at Loch Ailort.[3] However, just like section D, such networks as MIR had put in place were swept away by the speed of the German invasion.

In the first few months of the war the realization by the War Office, Admiralty and Air Ministry that intelligence activities overseas were not being handled as well as they might be by SIS prompted that most common of Whitehall solutions: a 'review'. Led by Lord Hankey, the former cabinet secretary and now a minister without portfolio in the war cabinet, this recommended the combination of section D and MIR under a single minister. In particular, the review noted that networks of agents for sabotage and paramilitary activities needed to be kept separate, not only from each other but also from networks for pure intelligence collection—the latter requiring calm and complacency on the part of the enemy, not eye-catching explosions and assassinations. It took some months for Hankey's recommendations to be carried out, with the fall of France proving the catalyst that finally forced movement. After May 1940, stirring up resistance to the occupiers and supporting sabotage, assassination and black propaganda were (along with strategic bombing) among the few ways that Britain could have a direct impact on the continent of Europe.[4] Thus on 19 July 1940 section D and MIR were combined with Electra House, the Foreign Office's black propaganda outfit, to create a new 'special operations' organization, grouped together in three branches under the Ministry of Economic Warfare (MEW).

Moving SOE to a rather small and obscure wartime ministry was ostensibly a curious decision, blamed by some on coalition politics requiring that the Labour Party (whose Hugh Dalton ran MEW) was in charge of at least one intelligence organization. In reality, the location acknowledged that most of the organization's sabotage targets were to be selected by MEW rather than any other ministries. Placing SOE with its main 'customer' was therefore a logical decision, and in August 1941, after a hard fight with the Secret Intelligence Service (SIS) who wanted control of sabotage and covert operations, the new organization's structure was finalized. SO3 (planning) was essentially still-born, its manpower absorbed into SO2 (sabotage and covert operations), while the Ministry of Information launched an ultimately successful campaign within Whitehall to take control of SO1 (black propaganda), which became the Political Warfare Executive (p. 70). Now on its own under MEW, SO2 effectively became the SOE, with a primary mission to undertake sabotage, guerrilla war and paramilitary activities in enemy and enemy-occupied territory.[5] Intelligence gathering was a relatively minor part of their role, although inevitably much intelligence was gathered through their operations, even if it was principally confirming what worked or proved unsuccessful. The intelligence collected was thus most of value to SOE itself, and often modified plans for future operations.

SOE was to operate in almost every theatre during the Second World War — with, inevitably, varying degrees of success — as well as in neutral countries such as Spain and Turkey, where it also had an important role to play. The largest amount of SOE activity was in Europe, and France, unsurprisingly, was the most significant of the countries in which its operatives and networks flourished.

SOE in France

SOE's dealings with France were the most complex. Even when occupied by the Germans, France remained a great power, with a huge population and a large overseas empire. There were also many political factions, few of whom worked from the same agenda. France was also the most accessible of the occupied countries with long and open coasts facing the English Channel, the Atlantic and the Mediterranean. In addition, it had two land frontiers with neutral countries, Switzerland and Spain. The very large country provided a huge area for air operations, which included the air dropping of supplies and agents and the landing of small aircraft into fields for 'pick up' operations. Finally, until the Germans moved into the Vichy-controlled Unoccupied Zone in November 1942, certain political channels remained open and freedom of travel varied between the two zones. All these factors had an important bearing on the organization and execution of SOE's activities in France.

With the occupation of France in June 1940, and the closing of section D's office in Paris run by Major L. A. L. Humphreys, SOE had to make a new start in August 1940 when the difficult task of recruitment commenced. There were also long, and often difficult, negotiations with General de Gaulle and his representatives (p. 172).

One of the first issues to be resolved was the method of delivering, and recovering, agents. The most discreet was by submarine, but anti-shipping operations were their primary task and few could be spared. Although they were used occasionally, small boats provided the main source of sea insertions. The Germans prohibited fishing boats in the Channel, so fast naval vessels had to be used for the Channel crossings. A motley flotilla of fishing boats and feluccas, which became known as the Coast Watching Flotilla, was based in Gibraltar and proved very effective. Despite these efforts and the long French coastline, sea transport proved more limited than it first appeared. Land communications, by contrast, were more to do with getting agents out rather than in; the key route was through Spain where SOE had a vital interest.

For deliveries, the alternative to sea was to use aircraft. To deliver bigger payloads, bombers were required but they were scarce and Bomber Command was always reluctant to divert them from their primary task. Older types such as the Whitley were used initially and by 1941, two squadrons (Nos 138 and 161 Squadrons) had been formed specifically to support clandestine operations. No 161 Squadron included Lysander aircraft, and later the Hudson, able to land in small fields by moonlight, and they played a major role in dropping off and picking up agents and VIPs. To be successful, air operations needed a reception party to provide rudimentary lighting aids to mark the dropping zone or landing area; this put both the aircraft and the resistance workers on the ground at risk. As the war progressed more squadrons became available and very large quantities of supplies were air-dropped. In the first nine months of 1944 the number of successful sorties rose to 6,194.

The first agents to be dropped were a party of five Free Frenchman led by Captain Berge; they were parachuted successfully into Brittany on the night of 15 March 1941 in Operation Savanna A. They were unable to ambush their target, but three of them remained in the area and undertook a valuable reconnaissance until they were recovered by submarine in a hazardous pick up. They were the first of over 900 agents parachuted into France, in addition to 269 delivered by Lysanders and Hudsons.

The first successful sea operation occurred on 25 April 1941 when two agents were landed on the Mediterranean coast; one of the largest escape lines was established as a result of their activities. On the night of 11 May, three Free French officers were dropped near Bordeaux on Operation Josephine B. They made their way to the nearby power station at Pessac, and despite meeting some formidable obstacles, managed to place their demolition charges on the eight main transformers, six of which were totally destroyed. The sabotage team managed to return to England via Spain.

In September 1941, a major reshuffle of SOE's senior staff resulted in the arrival of Colonel Maurice Buckmaster as the head of the French section, a post he held until the end of the war. On his arrival he had a small staff and about a dozen agents, but under his outstanding leadership the French section became a major operational force. His ability to manage very difficult and sensitive political issues with the numerous factions involved in clandestine operations in France contributed significantly to operational effectiveness.

The first attempts to establish 'organizers' in the field started when Commandant Georges Begue (nom de plume 'George Noble') was dropped near Chateauroux on the night of 5 May 1941. He was in radio contact with London three days later, the first SOE wireless message from France, and his work led to the whole structure of 'circuits' that became one of the main features of resistance work. He was soon followed by Baron Pierre de Viomecourt (Lucas), later described as 'one of the most exceptional men ever to go to the field'. Lucas was also dropped near Chateauroux, but with instructions to work in the Occupied Zone—and by the middle of June the two men had organized the first supply-dropping operation. Such early organization and landmark operations launched SOE's operations in France, but the casualty rate was high. Many of the agents sent to France in 1941 were caught.

Splits in the Free French movement heavily affected SOE planning in France. This led to the creation of two parallel French organizations: F section, the 'independent French' section established in the summer of 1940, and RF section, which was established in 1941 to work with General Charles de Gaulle and his growing network of agents in France. In effect the latter became de Gaulle's organization, while F section offered SOE the chance to maintain separate links and networks outside de Gaulle's influence in case another leader materialized. A serious candidate for this role did in fact emerge before the primacy of de Gaulle, and thus RF section, was assured: General Henri Honore Giraud, whose dramatic escape from Germany in 1942 came some two years after de Gaulle's own from France. The United States initially gave Giraud their backing and only gradually and reluctantly came round to de Gaulle after he outmanoeuvred his rival. Described as a 'broken reed' by Michael Foot, in his official history of the SOE in France, Giraud was forced to resign his various positions.[6]

In the early years of German occupation the SOE tried to maintain contact with a number of resistance organizations. The results were not always encouraging, and two apparently promising groups, André Girard's 'Carte' and the Organisation Civil et Militaire dissolved, for very different reasons. The artist Girard emerged as a charismatic and initially convincing leader with highly ambitious plans for creating an enormous secret army, neither Communist nor Gaullist, ready for action when required. Unfortunately, Girard proved on closer acquaintance to be unstable and something of a fantasist, and the willingness of many of his potential 'resisters' to do active work was uncertain. Girard's personal file at the National Archives sums up his character: a man of 'great intellectual and artistic ability', he did not seek personal gain but was nevertheless a problematic egotist; 'he wanted to play the grand seigneur, and his downfall was the direct result of as bad a case of megalomania as we have ever seen'. The head of F section finished his report by stating: 'I am very sorry for him. He meant well.'[7]

The end was not edifying. Girard ended up in dispute with his British liaison officer, Major Peter Churchill, and one of his assistants, Major Frager. Marginalized, with his cover blown to the Germans, Girard was brought over to England in February 1943 where he came to be regarded as something of a liability. The remnants of his 'Carte' organization were taken over by Frager.SOE had held considerable concerns about the 'serious lack of security' of Girard's network and they were proved right. Frager was duped by an Alsatian colonel named Verbeck—in reality an Abwehr agent, Corporal Bleicher— resulting in the gradual disintegration, arrest and destruction of the Carte network. Churchill was arrested in April 1943, his replacement five months later and finally Frager himself in August 1944. The unfortunate Frager was sent to Buchenwald where he was quickly executed. It later emerged that two of his key subordinates, Roger Bardet and Jean Kieffer, were double agents working for the Germans.[8]

Another potentially vital organization, the Organisation Civil et Militaire, was well to the right of the Communist and Gaullist resistance groups. Dominated by lawyers and largely concerned with an orderly transfer of power at the end of the occupation, it was severely compromised when the Gestapo 'turned' a leader in the Bordeaux area during interrogation. The traitor, Colonel Grandclement, was an admiral's son of hard-right views; his aversion to Communists proved stronger than to Nazis, with the result that much of his circuit was rendered useless and the Germans obtained a large cache of arms and a number of parachuted supplies. Following the D-Day landings, Grandclement was tricked into believing he had safe passage to England; he was then summarily executed by an SOE agent.[9]

Despite these and other setbacks, such as the collapse of the 'Prosper' network and the arrests of key figures such as Charles Delestraint and Jean Moulin, a considerable French resistance network remained on the eve of the allied invasion of France. For example, up until December 1943 the resistance had—with the support of SOE agents providing explosives, training and other equipment—managed to damage an average of 40 locomotives a month, resulting in something close to 2.5 per cent of French rolling stock being out of action at any one time. This was a much better rate than that achieved by RAF bombing raids in the same period.[10]

Immediately before June 1944 the resistance network set up by SOE agents in R/F and F sections had grown to a considerable size, due in part to the policy of the occupiers. Increased German pressure on the Vichy government to provide forced labour for German industry resulted in men taking to the hills (becoming the 'Maquis') to avoid work akin to slavery. SOE and the resistance gradually took advantage of this situation, bringing almost every significant group of Maquis under some form of resistance control. This might involve parachuting in an SOE liaison officer. Significant Maquis power centres before the invasion included Savoy, which had three SOE liaison officers, and the mountainous Massif Central region, with a similar number of SOE representatives. Over 70 wireless sets were in communication with R/F section and another 45 with F section, and there were estimated to be close to 40,000 well-armed men in the Maquis, supported by over 300,000 unarmed supporters. With the addition of trade unionists and railwaymen, this figure would have increased to something over a million. Estimates of the weaponry at their disposal gave the resistance organizations a total of around 70,000 sten guns, 25,000 pistols, 16,000 rifles and 3,000 Bren guns, supplemented by hundreds of bazookas, Piats and mortars.

Some formidable resistance was thus held in an organization which, with its liaison officers and wireless links to London or North Africa, could be coordinated, at least in part, by the allied command. Key Maquis groups were forewarned of the allied invasion a few days in advance, and were ordered to prepare sabotage and other operations designed to delay or halt German reinforcements heading towards Normandy. There were over 450 rail cuts and 180 derailments in this period, which forced large parts of the German military to travel by road. Road travel was simultaneously hindered by ambushes, sabotage of vehicles, concealing horses and removing signposts. The allies also began to insert 'Jedburgh' missions into France just after the invasion to improve coordination in areas lacking specific sabotage skills and equipment. Nearly 300 British, American and French Jedburghs were parachuted into or landed in France in the few months after D-Day to assist in sabotage and disruption. At this time some of the areas with the greatest concentration of Maquis were actively taken from the Germans—most notably in the Savoy, Massif Central and Jura regions. Such attempts were perilous and often unsuccessful; the resistance at Vercors managed to take the town from the occupiers, to be later over-whelmed by a German counter-attack of over 11,000 troops. Reprisals following this and other uprisings were savage. After the main German divisions began to fall back to the Rhine, however, the resistance took bold steps to liberate major cities such as Lyon, Toulouse and Bor-deaux. Over 40,000 German prisoners were rounded up in the south, with nearly 20,000 Germans being taken in the Loire alone. In the areas of allied advance, resistance fighters informally acted as guides to the liberators, as well as being left to undertake any 'mopping up' operations against small units of German stragglers.

This considerable achievement in guerrilla warfare had a significant impact on the German ability to resist the allied invasion. Primarily the result of French resistance work and operations, SOE's role was less direct but important. It provided the training and equipment for the Gaullist resistance and, above all, the infrastructure of communi-cation and coordination that allowed the resistance network to be fit-ted into the allied command chain. Through the SOE's efforts the resistance could act, in effect, as a fourth arm of the invading forces.

Among those involved was French-born Pearl Witherington (plate 27), whose two SOE files were released by the National Archives after her death in February 2008.[11] Driven by a desire for action, Withering-ton had signed up to the SOE in June 1943, leaving her job as PA to the director of allied air co-operation and foreign liaison at the Air Min-istry. Although 'not naturally agile', she proved to be an outstanding shot and was judged as 'completely brave', her instructor noting 'this student, though a woman, has definitely got leader's qualities'. Witherington was despatched to Chateauroux on 22 September to act as courier for a circuit identified at the time as one of the largest and most active in central France.

Early assessments of her aptitude were borne out shortly after her arrival behind enemy lines; when her commanding officer, Maurice Southgate, was recalled to England she took an active part in running the 'Stationer' circuit and was responsible for the safe custody of several escaped airmen. When Southgate eventually returned some three months later, he was arrested by the Gestapo and Witherington again stepped into the breach, taking full control of one section of his circuit. Though apparently suffering from ill-health at the time, she nonetheless undertook perilous missions to warn outlying members of the danger. She also helped organize her own Maquis group in the Indre, for whom she arranged numerous supply drops. When this group was broken by the Germans, who launched an attack against it with some 2,000 troops backed by artillery, Witherington simply built it up again. This, according to her file, she did 'with great success', and her rearmed Maquis began a large-scale guerrilla campaign, 'causing havoc among German columns passing through the area to the battle front.'

Witherington displayed undeniable valour, gallantry and devotion to duty, something recognized by her superiors, but recognition of her achievements was hampered by the conservatism of her time. As the Military Cross was not then open to women, she was instead offered the civilian MBE in 1945. This she turned down, stating that she felt it did not 'give a true picture of my work or the spirit in which I undertook it'. In a letter of 20 October, preserved in her files, she wrote,

> It is not for me to criticise the rules for decorating H.M. Forces, but I do consider it most unjust to be given a civilian decoration. Our training, which we did with the men, was purely military, and as women we were expected to replace them in the field; women were parachuted as W/T operators, etc., and I personally was responsible for the training and organisation etc. of nearly three thousand men for sabotage and guerrilla warfare. The men have received military decorations, why this discrimination with women when they put the best of themselves into the accomplishment of their duties?[12]

Witherington accepted a military MBE. In France she was awarded the Croix de Guerre and Médaille de la Résistance, and created a Chevalier of the Légion d'honneur. Further recognition followed at the end of her life: in 2004 she was awarded a CBE and in 2006 she was finally given her parachute wings.

SOE in the Netherlands

If France showed a successful side of SOE, operations in the Netherlands were not so successful, as Michael Foot described in his 2001 official history, *SOE in the Low Countries*, on which the following section draws.[13] Problems had existed from the outset, although the first head of the Dutch section, R. V. Laming, was on the surface an extremely good choice. Dutch-born and from a family of Anglo-Dutch stockbrokers with considerable links to the Netherlands, Laming spoke perfect Dutch and was a diplomat with a background in blockade enforcement. He had a deep knowledge of Dutch culture, customs and commerce, as well as wide contacts within the Netherlands. Unfortunately he also brought with him a 24-year-old quarrel with probably the most influential Dutchman in the exile community, van't Sant—the Dutch queen's chief adviser, treasurer and head of her intelligence service. As a result the Dutch leadership in exile refused to cooperate with the SOE at all. This meant that the most likely people to undertake SOE operations—young, educated and perhaps of a military background—were excluded from recruitment, having already been warned off the SOE and directed towards other work or involved in van't Sant's own much smaller, less well-organized intelligence operation. Laming was replaced in due course, but the damage had been done; the quality of potential SOE recruits was much lower than for most other occupied countries. This, combined with a feverish wish to keep up with successes in other parts of SOE (probably engendered by the ferocious Hugh Dalton) and a lax approach to security on wireless communications, contributed directly to one of SOE's worst intelligence defeats during the war.

Operation Glasshouse parachuted two inexperienced agents (neither of whom had been properly trained in wireless, and who had spent only one week at the SOE training camp) into the countryside near Utrecht in September 1941. Cornelis Sporre went missing while trying to return to Britain some months later, but Albert Homburg, a garage mechanic, proved a surprisingly good agent. He escaped from the Germans after their interrogations had discovered little, and managed to return to Britain by fishing boat, bringing a wealth of important information back with him.

The second pair of agents sent into the Netherlands inadvertently started the *Englandspiel* deception. Dropped near Zwolle in November 1941, Thijs Taconis and H. M. G. Lauwers were woefully unprepared, having been given badly forged documentation, ill-fitting clothes and coinage no longer in circulation. Their capture, however, was due to none of these, but to a simple deception by a double agent. Taconis had been introduced by an apparently reliable contact to a man called Ridderhof who had offered to recover stores from a planned drop. Ridderhof was in fact a double agent in the pay of the Abwehr, and when Lauwers next sent a prearranged message by wireless to the British, on 6 March 1942, the Gestapo were waiting for him outside his transmitting site — the flat of a sympathetic reserve officer and his wife. Told that the code he had been transmitting in had been easily broken, Lauwers, poorly trained in dealing with interrogation, broke down, as did Taconis when he was told of his colleague's betrayal. In fact, the Germans were bluffing. The information they chose to reveal to show that they had broken the code — a false piece of intelligence that the cruiser *Prinz Eugen* was in dock at Schiedam — had in fact been planted by Ridderhof; but it served their purpose.

The Abwehr then began an 18-month deception which had disastrous consequences for the SOE's Dutch section. Lauwers and Taconis could only transmit messages with German intelligence agents at their side, deceiving the recipients and sending agent after agent to immediate capture. Their wireless sets were used in turn by the Abwehr to create a false network of intelligence operatives. Lauwers and radio operators captured in later months tried surreptitiously to alert their British handlers by using non-standard language, codes and terms when they could get away with it, but slack procedures by SOE operators on the other side of the Channel meant that such attempts were not acted on. Nor was the rather obvious fact that every wireless signal from the false network came from towns and cities in which the Abwehr had headquarters.

The list of compromised operations and lost agents over the next year and a half makes for depressing reading. SOE estimated that a total of over 200,000 guilders had been spent giving the betrayed agents cash for when they reached the Netherlands; nearly 3,000 sten guns were lost, as were 300 Bren guns, 500 pistols and 15,000 kilograms of explosives. When operation after operation (usually code-named after vegetables and including Operations Carrot, Turnip, Parsnip, Leek, Broccoli and Radish) failed, concerns increased. Over the months of the *Englandspiel* SOE's head, Major General Colin Gubbins, grew suspicious, as did senior figures in MI5, but none had any evidence to confirm their doubts. The Air Ministry also began to have reservations, suspending flights by 138 Squadron to drop agents into the Netherlands in mid-1943. Operational losses for such missions had risen to over 17.5 per cent, compared with 1.5 per cent for similar missions over France. Yet such action—and its reasons—failed to change the minds of some senior SOE officers, according to files in the National Archives. Professional pride and resentment could provide powerful blinkers, and one officer observed:

> I have the strong feeling that the AM [Air Ministry] are partly actuated by suspicion of the security of our Dutch organisation. I do not feel we can submit to this, since (i) it is not the Air Ministry's business to judge of this security, especially without advising us of their fears, and consulting the appropriate departments, and (ii) it is also certain that these fears were aroused not by any observations of their own, but by the ostensibly casual innuendos of the VCSS [vice chief of the security service], which have since been withdrawn.[14]

The deception was finally revealed when two SOE agents escaped from Haaren concentration camp and made it to Switzerland. Contacts with the compromised agents were maintained until March 1944 but all operations were suspended, so the Abwehr became increasingly aware that they had been found out. Once this had been confirmed, following the interrogation of some captured SIS agents, they signed off their last contact with London with the following message:

> Messrs. Blunt, Bingham and Successors, Ltd London. In the last time you are trying to make business in the Netherlands without our assistance. We think that rather unfair in view of our long and successful co-operation as your sole agents. But never mind, when-ever you will come to pay a visit to the Continent you may be assured that you will be received with the same care and result as all those you sent us before. So long.[15]

SOE in Scandinavia

In the early days, Stockholm provided the focal point for SOE's work in Scandinavia. One of the most important efforts after the German invasion of Norway and Denmark was to re-establish the Stockholm Mission following the debacle in April 1940 when Alfred Rickman, head of the Swedish station, was caught red-handed loading explosives into his car at the warehouse of the Windsor Tea Company. They had been intended for use in Operation Lumps, the destruction of the iron-ore loading facilities at Oxelosund, a plan conceived—according to the National Archives file dealing with his organization—through Rickman's connections with anti-Nazi Social Democrats. Along with the explosives, fuses, limpet mines, some £1,200 in Swedish kroner, guns, passports, stamps and address lists, it was feared that Rickman had been carrying all his organization's reports from the beginning of the year. There were also diplomatic repercussions to contend with; as the head of the Scandinavian section stated: 'this disaster could not have come at a more unfortunate moment.'[16]

Following this debacle, very little work could take place in Sweden. An attempt to set up a 'Danish Freedom' radio station in Sweden to broadcast into Denmark, for example, foundered due to concerns about infringing Swedish neutrality. In July 1940 an assistant military attaché was established, charged with opening 'lines' to Norway, and Charles Hambro, then head of SO2's Scandinavian section, put this arrangement on a more formal basis following a visit in October 1940. The most significant SOE effort in Sweden was Operation Rubble. Five Norwegian ships, totalling some 25–30,000 tons, escaped to England in January 1941 with cargoes valued at over £1,000,000.

The unusual situation in Denmark, which technically remained neutral though occupied by German forces since 9 April 1940, made it difficult for SOE to establish formal links in the country. However, through a series of Anglo-Danish negotiations, a vigorous armed movement strongly sympathetic to the allies was established and much valuable intelligence was obtained through a group of senior Danish intelligence officers codenamed the 'Princes'. A Danish office was set up in Stockholm.

In April 1943 a sabotage campaign was launched by the Danish resistance and over the next few months this began to have a more significant effect. In August the occupiers demanded that German courts should in future try Danish saboteurs under German law, those convicted having to serve their sentences in Germany. The recently elected Danish government refused to accept the proposal, but pressure grew as the acts of sabotage increased, resulting in the Danish leader's resignation. On 29 August 1943, the Germans seized control; Danish military units were disbanded and many officers fled to Sweden. The main impact on SOE was the loss of the 'Princes' organization, although Lieutenant Svend Truelsen was able to carry on and develop an intelligence network. Although this was not strictly SOE's domain, it was agreed not to disturb the effective arrangement and SOE acted as the sole agent for SIS in Denmark.

By the winter of 1943–4 some 50 agents were operating in Denmark, able to tap the great support of the Danish population. At the time of the D-Day landings, the Danish railway system went on strike for three weeks, effectively preventing any of the six German divisions in Denmark, and others in Norway, from being able to reinforce German forces in Normandy.

With sabotage and resistance growing in the summer of 1944, the Gestapo tightened its grip on the country. Documents and dossiers used to persecute the population were held in Gestapo headquarters, housed in buildings of Aarhus University in Jutland. With the aid of intelligence gathered by SOE agents, 24 RAF Mosquitoes mounted a spectacular pinpoint attack on 31 October 1944 and destroyed the buildings.

The situation in Norway was very different. From the outset the population came out fighting, none more strongly than the fisherman. SOE and the Norwegians were in touch from an early stage, and close relations were maintained throughout the war. The first raid mounted from Great Britain was made as early as 29 May 1940, when a party sailed for the Sogne Fjord. Two of the team remained for almost three weeks and sabotaged a number of industrial plants and communications targets, returning to the Shetland Islands on 18 June. This was the first allied raid into occupied Europe and the first of many similar activities into Norway. With British aid, a courier service was established between the Shetland Islands and the Norwegian coast using Norwegian fishing boats, and large quantities of arms and many agents were ferried across the North Sea to Norway by the 'Shetland Bus'.

One of the great coups of the war was brought off by SOE in Norway—the attack on the Norsk Hydro at Rjukan, which some believe may have changed the course of the war. Intelligence reports had indicated that 'heavy water' (deuterium oxide) was being produced at the plant, suggesting that the Germans might be trying to develop an atomic bomb. An earlier attempt by Combined Operations to destroy the plant had failed. It consisted of two parts: Operation Swallow, in which an advance party of four Norwegians, led by Captain Jens Poulsson, was dropped to prearrange stores and equipment and help guide the following commandos; and Operation Freshman, in which two Halifaxes flew the 340-mile crossing from RAF Skitten to Norway, each towing a Horsa glider containing 16 Royal Engineers. The first plane and glider could not locate the landing zone as the 'Rebecca' receiver fitted to the aircraft failed to operate. The pilot struggled to find the site through map reading, but the towing rope snapped and the glider crashed at Fylesdalen. Of the 17 men in the glider, eight were killed outright and four seriously injured; all were captured at the crash site, after which the injured were poisoned and the uninjured shot by the Gestapo on 18 January 1943—despite their military uniforms, which should have ensured treatment as prisoners of war. The second plane and its glider were also unsuccessful, crashing after crossing the Norwegian coast. The crew on the plane were killed on landing, and survivors from the glider were also captured and shot a few hours later. The summary executions were carried out by the *Sicherheitsdienst* (SD), the Nazi security service, following interrogations, and the testimony of an SD officer, now in the National Archives, describes the commandos' final moments:

> On arrival at Akershus [prison] the British soldiers were told by [Oskar] Hans [of the SD] with the help of the interpreter that they were to be seen by a special German delegation. For this purpose they would have to have their eyes bandaged. This was duly done, and when the supposed delegation was said to arrive they were called to attention. The actual word of command was 'Achtung'—which in fact was the fire order for the execution squad.[17]

After this tragic failure, SOE took the project over and another attempt, Operation Gunnerside, was approved in December 1942. This time the team consisted of six men of the Norwegian Independent Company, a special unit of the Royal Norwegian Army created by Captain Martin Linge, the liaison officer between SOE and the Norwegian military in exile. Led by Captain Joachim Renneberg, the Norwegians were dropped on the night of 16 February 1943 on a frozen lake 30 miles north of the Operation Swallow party. They rendezvoused a week later with Poulsson and his men. Despite the increased security around the plant after the Freshman operation, Renneberg managed to lead his team through the wire at the perimeter, across a precarious snow bridge, up a rock face, past German guards, through a funnel for cables and pipes and into the plant itself. At this point, according to Renneberg's report in the National Archives, they were seen by a Norwegian guard, but he offered no resistance and did not raise the alarm. The charges were successfully placed and detonated: besides heavily damaging the plant, over 3,000 pounds of 'heavy water' were destroyed.[18] Unlike the

Hollywood film, the real Telemark agents completed the mission without firing a shot.

Five of the Gunnerside team then escaped 250 miles across the snow to neutral Sweden, travelling on skis for a month in awful conditions. Leader Knut Haukelid stayed on with the Swallow party, one of whom, Claus Helberg, had had a lucky escape when he had been spotted by three German ski-troopers and pursued across the snow for nearly two hours—a chase described in thrilling detail in his report. Some hours later, exhausted and in difficult terrain, he fell over a snow cliff and injured his arm. The following morning he ran into a German patrol, but as they were looking for British commandos they accepted his story that he was an innocent skier injured in a fall, and sent him to a nearby hotel for medical treatment. With extremely bad luck following on good—the 'slings and arrows of outrageous fortune' that determined whether agents and saboteurs lived or died—the hotel was then taken over by the German governor of Norway, Reichskommissar Terboven, and his private staff, for a holiday. Terboven flew into a rage after an alleged slight by a female Norwegian guest, sending all the remaining Norwegians in the hotel, including Helberg, to the nearest detention camp. Although injured, he escaped en route by jumping from the guarded bus taking them to Grini, dodging bullets to escape yet again from German pursuers. He eventually found his way back to Britain.[19]

Substantial stocks of heavy water still remained, however, and Haukelid was tasked with destroying them before they could be transferred to Germany. He decided to destroy the heavy water while it was on the ferry over Lake Tinnsjo, on the first leg of its journey. Despite considerable numbers of German guards on the railway line to the lake, Haukelid was able to board the ferry, which had been left almost unguarded, with two fellow saboteurs. According to his report, the one guard who spotted the party was a Norwegian who did not raise the alarm, and the charges were successfully set in the bow area. The agents left before the ferry sailed and seven hours later the charges detonated, taking the ferry, its passengers and its cargo of heavy water to the bottom of the lake. Unlike in the film's sanitised version of events, the agents could not help save the lives of the passengers: 18 people on board were drowned, most of them Norwegian, including two brothers aged 14 and 15.[20]

As the war progressed, SOE activities with the Norwegian Milorg (military organization) continued. Unlike in other occupied countries, politics, rival factions or major dissensions did not plague Norwegian

resistance, which continued to play a major role in offensive operations, intelligence gathering and, in the latter days of the war, defending crucial installations once it became apparent that Germany could
no longer stave off defeat.

Balkans and Eastern Europe

SOE activities in the Balkans and Eastern Europe present a significant
contrast to those in Western Europe, in particular the impact of
volatile politics and the consequences when peace came to Europe.
The growing influence of Communism seemed to many the sole way
out of a life of poverty, oppression and lack of personal freedom, and
Communist politics became a very important constituent of partisan
activity in the region.

On the formation of SOE, British intelligence was already established in the Balkans and Eastern Europe with section D of the SIS.
The British were particularly concerned about German access to the
Romanian oilfields, and section D conducted a close examination to
identify targets for sabotage should Germany attempted to take over
the oil. These centred on the Ploesti refinery and an attempt to gain
control of the 'Schultz' fleet of 26 barges and six tugs operating on the
River Danube from Belgrade. In February 1940, a scheme was devised
to bribe Danube pilots to refuse German employment. As a file at the
National Archives on the 'Danube enticement scheme' describes, it
involved paying pilots two-and-a-half-years' salary up front, plus a
monthly payment of between £45 and £53, in return for leaving the
Danube with their families. Despite the unusual nature of this operation, it was surprisingly successful.[21]

Section D also developed a series of plans for blocking the Danube,
and three vital points were identified. A further initiative was to open
contacts with political parties in Bulgaria and Yugoslavia. However,
following their success in Western Europe in May 1940, the Germans
began to put pressure on the various governments in the Balkans and
the result was the withdrawal of most of section D's personnel from
the region. Not all were withdrawn, however, and a slender thread of
continuity remained in the Balkans, although the British presence was
weak. This continuity was most apparent in Albania, Greece and
Turkey, where section D's small beginnings were carried over intact
into the SOE organization.

Stern resistance checked Mussolini's invasion of Greece on 28

October 1940, and it soon became evident that German intervention was probable. With the insertion of British forces into Greece following Italy's invasion, and the likelihood of a wider Balkan conflict, SOE established T.S. Masterson in Belgrade in December. By January 1941 a new policy clearly identified the priorities for action as:

The Roumanian oilfields.

Preparation for the destruction of the Kazan defile on the Danube.

The destruction of Yugoslav, Bulgarian and Roumanian communications ahead of a German advance and guerrilla warfare behind it.[22]

SOE's activities over the next four years were complex and heavily influenced by political issues, none more so than in Greece.

After the Italian invasion through Albania was halted by stubborn Greek and allied action, the Germans poured through Yugoslavia and Bulgaria in April 1941, swiftly defeating the Anglo-Anzac forces. Like others, SOE was surprised by the swift German invasion and few arrangements had been made for a resistance movement. Few operations took place over the next year as the Foreign Office sought clarity on which of the resistance organizations to support.

Left-wing and anti-monarchist leaders, whose plans for the post-war period did not include the establishment of the pre-war political status quo—the restoration of the Greek king and his supporters—dominated Greek resistance groups. The Foreign Office favoured supporting the king's followers, almost certainly with a view to the post-war politics, but military chiefs in Cairo leaned towards the Communists as being the best equipped and most motivated to take action against the Germans. This placed SOE in an invidious position.

In early autumn 1942, SOE was tasked to destroy one of the viaducts on the main railway line that connected southern Greece with Europe, thus hindering the dispatch of reinforcements to Rommel through the port of Piraeus. The operation's timing was to coincide with Montgomery's offensive at El Alamein planned for late October. Colonel E.C.W. Myers, a regular sapper officer, was chosen to lead the raiding party, and he and his team were parachuted into Greece on 1 October 1942. One of his companions was Captain C.M. Woodhouse, and the two men would, in due course, become two of SOE's most successful officers. The six-man SOE team had strong support from the Greek resistance movements, but many difficulties with the terrain and supplies delayed the operation. On the night of 25 November they destroyed a key bridge over the Gorgopotamos River near Thermopylae. This was admittedly too late to assist the 8th Army in North Africa, but the operation was a resounding success with the local population.

As part of the allied deception plan prior to the landings in Sicily in July 1943, a plan known as 'Animals' was developed. It was a simultaneous attack on communications designed to assist the cover plan of an impending attack on the west coast of Greece, and in part to prevent the withdrawal of German troops elsewhere. An all-SOE team led by Major Gordon-Creed blew up the Asopos viaduct on the same railway line on the night of 21 June, resulting in the line being closed for months. As a result of the success of 'Animals', the Germans sent a spare division from France to Greece. Had they been better informed, it might have been sent to face the allied landings in Sicily.

In the autumn of 1943, Greece's various political factions—the Communist-supported ELAS movement and the republican EDES—turned on each other in a vicious civil war. Unfortunately, relations between the resistance groups and the British soured in the complex climate. EDES had received most aid from SOE, but ELAS secured many weapons when Italy collapsed and Italian military forces in Greece dissolved. After bitter fighting, SOE brokered an uneasy armistice (The Palka Agreement), which came into effect on 29 February 1944. Eventually, the British army occupied Athens and Piraeus in the aftermath of the German withdrawal, fighting a street-by-street battle to drive ELAS from these cities. SOE's last act was to evacuate several hundred disarmed EDES fighters to Corfu, preventing their massacre by ELAS.

SOE's role in Greece proved highly significant. Michael Foot's classic book *SOE* concludes its account of their activities in Greece with the observation that: 'From all the confusion, one plain political point can be made clear. Had it not been for SOE, ELAS would in all probability have been in charge in Greece when the Germans left; Greece would have gone Communist'.[23]

In Yugoslavia, another key theatre of SOE activity, German forces posed a far greater threat to the allies than they could in the more remote Greece. The politics of Yugoslavia were just as complex, but it eventually became apparent that the best way of defeating the Germans was to support the Communist partisans. From the time of the German occupation in April 1941 to the end of the war, SOE's efforts in support of the Yugoslav partisans was almost as great as the effort in France.

Britain had a small number of emmisaries in Belgrade before the Germans arrived, including members of section D and MIR. After the German invasion, the country virtually collapsed, apart from Croatia. At the end of August 1941 contact was made with a Croat officer, Colonel Dragolub Mihailovitch, and the submarine *Triumph* put ashore a British officer, D.T. Hudson, in Montenegro on 16 September 1941 to meet him. Arms were dropped to support him, but by the spring of 1942 it was becoming clear that Mihailovitch, who had started to achieve hero status, was becoming too closely aligned with Italy.

On first arriving in Yugoslavia, Hudson had also met Josip Broz, codenamed 'Tito', and had been favourably impressed, although Tito had been cautious about British aid. Hudson arranged for the two guerrilla leaders to meet, but it was soon apparent that they had very different agendas. Tito saw the guerrilla war as a means of creating a socialist revolution, but he also saw his activities as a means of taking pressure off the Russians, heavily engaged with massive German forces on the Eastern front. Mihailovitch, however, wanted to preserve his forces until a major allied landing could take place, when he would be well placed to secure power in a liberated Yugoslavia. Notwithstanding this, his Cetniks did disrupt German communications and, with SOE support, were responsible for the demolition of the railway bridge at Visegrad, a very important railway line supplying German industry.

Hudson's superior, Colonel S.W. Bailey, was sent into Yugoslavia in December 1942 to assess the situation. His report, and further intelligence about the activities and effectiveness of the two Yugoslav factions, started to swing British opinion towards supporting Tito and his People's Liberation Army (PLA). The debate culminated in a decree from Churchill that Tito was to be supported.

The Italian surrender on 7 September 1943 allowed the partisans to expand into the vacuum left by the Italians. Brigadier Fitzroy Maclean arrived at Tito's headquarters, and SOE Cairo established an advance headquarters at Bari in southern Italy (Force 133). This allowed better sea communications to the Dalmatian coast, and by early 1944 transport aircraft (based at the airfields in the region) were making many regular flights to drop arms and supplies. It was at this time that the SOE missions that had supported Mihailovitch had to be withdrawn, although it was not until May 1944, and after many significant problems, that the last of SOE's personnel were evacuated from Mihailovitch territory. The commitment to the 'new' Yugoslavia was now final.

Support for the developing guerrilla war in Yugoslavia increasingly became the responsibility of the operational commands based in Italy. British troops began to land on the Adriatic islands during January 1944, and the RAF supply-dropping squadrons became increasingly active. The Balkan Air Transport Service (BATS), manned by RAF personnel, had no fewer than 36 teams in Yugoslavia preparing airstrips with landing aids in remote areas. Complications arose in the chain of command between Cairo and the theatre commands, effectively limiting SOE activities. This was partly resolved by the formation of the Balkan Air Force in June 1944, which worked closely with Land Forces Adriatic and the naval forces of Flag Officer Taranto.

With Tito's forces, increasingly supported by regular allied forces, taking the war to the Germans door, the SOE organization based in Italy now remained responsible only for organizing supplies carried by sea and air to Tito. This was a major task, and by the end of the war almost 60,000 tons of supplies had been delivered by sea and 13,700 by air. Around 13,500 personnel had also been evacuated, most of them by air.

Only in Yugoslavia did guerrillas impose a serious strategic burden on Hitler—and there, as everywhere in the Balkans, the British found themselves entangled in a political imbroglio. SOE played a major role in the early days, and once Churchill decided to back Tito it had the difficult task of disengaging from support of Mihailovitch's forces and placing liaison officers with Tito's Communist guerrillas. From 1944, SOE's main responsibility was to organize the huge resupply operation that allowed Tito's forces to wage such a large scale war against the Germans and, some would say, against fellow Yugoslavs.

Operations in Albania were generally low-key until 1944, not least because, apart from the Albanian oilfield, there were no significant industrial or economic targets. When SOE intervention did step up, in 1944, it was in response to the increasing power and effectiveness of the Communist Albanian partisans, in particular in support of the coastal area of control they had carved out, resulting in a German counter-offensive and the loss of more than 100 German lives. Over the course of the war SOE and its predecessor organizations sent over 7,000 rifles, 5,000 sub-machine guns, 240 mortars and more than a million rounds of ammunition into Albania, as well as a hundred or more SOE agents. Whether SOE support for the Communists made their eventual takeover of the country any more likely is a contentious point, one on which even the SOE agents involved disagreed at the time and for many years afterwards. However, given the moribund nature of the non-Communist nationalist resistance, and the already growing strength of the Communists before British support increased significantly, it seems unlikely that British help was decisive.[24]

Bulgaria and Romania were very much secondary theatres for the SOE, although both were believed to form a potentially useful block to Axis expansion in the Middle East. Operations in Bulgaria, which had allied itself with the Axis from 1941, were hampered by rivalry between two of the SOE agents: Dr G. Dimitrov, leader of the Peasants' Party (agent John), and Padev, a former Bulgarian correspondent for *The Times*. The ability to mount operations was also limited, not only due to Bulgaria's distance from British- or US-controlled territory, but also by the lingering possibility that the country might be persuaded to swing behind the allies and by the lack of an effective resistance movement. The death of King Boris and the fear of a Soviet invasion helped to create a more effective resistance movement, but Operations Mulligatawny and Claridges, which aimed to capitalize on this, ended in disaster with the agents being surprised and almost all of them killed.[25]

The mission to Romania, allied to Germany from 1940, was forced to quit Bucharest in 1941, after which SOE maintained a tenuous link via a wireless set with the main head of the Peasants' Party, Dr Juliu Maniu. By mid-1944 Maniu was the leading player in the successful coup against the authoritarian General Antonescu, with King Michael as its figurehead, that followed the negotiation of an armistice with the allies. The SOE was vital in the transport of his negotiators to Cairo and in maintaining contact with Maniu as he gained support within Romania.[26]

Mediterranean and the African littoral

SOE operations in Africa and the Middle East centred on a number of missions. The first and largest, the SOE office in Cairo, covered not just North Africa and the Middle East, but also the Balkans and the Mediterranean. A large and elaborate organization, SOE Cairo attracted considerable bureaucratic opposition in London and in Cairo; turf wars with London over its reach in the Balkans and Eastern Europe were coupled with local British military concerns that SOE should be under direct military command. It was also subject to internal disputes and opposition from various regimes in exile. The exiled governments of Yugoslavia and Greece, for example, did not support it, while the question of who controlled subversive propaganda (which came under the PWE after it was split away from SOE in 1941) was another bone of contention. SIS and the Foreign Office were also hostile.

None of this made life easy for the organization, and SOE Cairo saw several heads of operations in rapid succession, as well as numerous staff imposed by SOE London. Arthur Goodwill of section D was replaced by the barrister Sir George Pollock, followed in less than ten months by the banker and industrialist Terence Maxwell, replaced in turn by another banker, Lord Glenconner. Glenconner was soon out of the revolving door, with the engineer Major General Stawell entering in late 1943. The Cairo operation came under sustained attack from all its enemies and, as records in the National Archives show, was saved from extinction only by the personal intervention of Churchill.[27] Despite such intrigue, little of which benefited the war effort, SOE Cairo and its associated missions undertook a wide range of operations throughout the Middle East and North Africa.

In Palestine SOE cultivated links with Zionists including Chaim Weizmann, and used its networks in the Balkans to help extract Jewish refugees, place them in reception bases and pick agents to send back into occupied Europe. Such work benefited both parties, the SOE clearly being aware that Weizmann and others used SOE exfiltration work to bring potential leaders and fighters over to Palestine to help create a future Jewish state. As the immediate threat of Axis attack faded, it soon became clear that while Hagana and other radical Zionist organizations might prove to be thorns in the side of post-war British rule in Palestine, the moderate organizations of a few years earlier, such as the Ichud movement, had lost any credibility they once held. SOE also tried to disengage from the situation to avoid being dragged into attempts 'to cope with the [expected] trouble' from Zionist armed groups.[28]

The SOE also operated in Algeria, Tunisia and Morocco prior to and during Operation Torch, the invasion of North Africa by Anglo-American forces in November 1942. Operations after the conquest of North Africa included sabotage and agent running in southern France and Italy (under the code name Operation Massingham), and the SOE also established a wireless base at Monopoli in southern Italy prior to the allied invasion of 1943.[29] The most notable mission in West Africa was led by Major M. Phillips in 1940; it successfully captured the Italian liner *Duchessa d'Aosta* and the German tug *Likomba*, both of which had sought refuge in the neutral Spanish colonial possession of Fernando Po. The night-time raid involved boarding parties taking over the vessels while senior Italian and German officers were ashore at a party and the local power station was temporarily shut down. The fortuitous power cut was achieved by bribing the chief electrician's wife with a diamond ring to persuade her 'admirer'—another of the other power station technicians—to switch off the power. According to the account in the files of the National Archives, this buccaneering adventure provided the British with a cargo worth over £200,000, more than making up for the mission's costs of £5,000.[30]

The SOE East Africa mission (based in South Africa and later renamed the South Africa mission) operated under various covers. Initially known as the East African Trade Mission, theoretically undertaking an economic survey of the region and looking for trading opportunities, it then became the Imperial Movements Control (Intelligence Section) mission and finally the Combined Headquarters SO (I) Office, Army Liaison section. Each of these esoteric titles hid the real purpose of the organization—sabotage, propaganda and the placing of agents. The East Africa mission was also heavily involved in the 1942 allied invasion of Madagascar, from reconnaissance to cutting telegraph lines and providing French-speaking guides.[31]

SOE in Eastern Europe

Operations in Eastern Europe were hampered by the difficulties in getting aircraft of sufficient range to parachute agents in safely. However, SOE remained in contact with the Polish resistance throughout much of the war and with anti-German politicians in Hungary until the German invasion of 1944.

The most successful operation in Czechoslovakia—and the only successful SOE assassination of a senior Nazi—was the killing of Reinhard Heydrich in May 1942. Planned by the Czech government in exile and named Operation Anthropoid, two former Czech paratroopers were trained by SOE and armed with just about every conceivable weapon—sub-machine gun, anti-tank grenades, explosives, a mortar and even a lethal syringe—to fulfil their mission. They managed to injure the Reichsführer of the Bohemia and Moravia protectorate so severely that he died in agony, of septicaemia, some weeks later: a fitting end for the man who had chaired the meetings that led to the adoption of the 'final solution' for the Jews. The two assassins were betrayed by a fellow agent, Karel Curda, and were killed fighting SS troops. Nazi reprisals involved the murder of 5,000 Czech civilians, including all the inhabitants of the villages of Lidice and Ležáky. A further consequence, revealed in files in the National Archives, was the disruption of part of the Czech resistance movement.[32]

Hungary's difficult political position—an increasingly reluctant ally of the Germans—resulted in considerable efforts to persuade its leaders and politicians to take Hungary out of the war. Links were established with the Kállay government, and in 1943 attempts were made to take advantage of Admiral Horthy's more pro-allied approach. Secret wireless contact was made using SOE equipment, but although the British chiefs of staff accepted that offers of cooperation with sympathetic Hungarian politicians acting as go-betweens were genuine, they requested the dispatch of a liaison mission to speak directly with the Hungarian government. The mission, named Operation Sandy, was not in fact dispatched until May 1944, partly due to Foreign Office concerns about possible 'unpleasant reactions on the part of the Russians'. By this time any role as a diplomatic liaison mission had largely disappeared because Germany had already invaded Hungary.[33]

Operation Foxley and the plan to assassinate Hitler

Despite the successful killing of Heydrich in 1942, surviving SOE files appear to show that the assassination of Hitler was given serious and sustained consideration only in 1944. (Documents in the National Archives show that some thought had been given to the subject in 1941, further work being vetoed for reasons unknown.)[34] An operation to assassinate the German leader was considered in June 1944 when an SOE representative in Algiers reported that a contact had proposed killing Hitler while he was staying at a château in Perpignan. The operation soon became a possible RAF bombing raid rather than an assassination and finally got nowhere, but the proposal did encourage the prime minister and the chiefs of staff to consider whether killing the Führer would be advantageous or not. Their conclusion was the open one that: 'from the strictly military point of view, it was almost an advantage that Hitler should remain in control of German strategy, having regard to the blunders that he has made, but that on the wider

18. (*below*) The Royal Navy identity card of Sub-Lieutenant David Bingham. He passed much significant information to the Soviets, not least the rules of engagement for maritime forces. (DEFE 69/199)

19. (*right*) A miniature map showing drop-off points for Bingham's intelligence near East Clandon and Ewhurst in Surrey. (DEFE 69/199)

20. (*bottom*) A request from Bingham's handler mixing pleasantries with demands for technical information. Of key interest were nuclear depth charges, used in anti-submarine warfare. (DEFE 69/199)

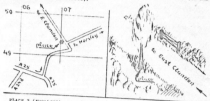

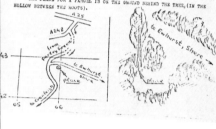

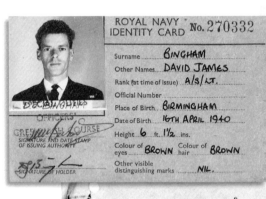

ROYAL NAVY No. 270332
IDENTITY CARD

Surname BINGHAM
Other Names DAVID JAMES
Rank (at time of issue) A/S/LT.
Official Number
Place of Birth BIRMINGHAM
Date of Birth 16TH APRIL 1940
Height 6 ft. 1½ ins.
Colour of eyes BROWN Colour of hair BROWN
Other visible distinguishing marks NIL.

DEAR FRIEND,

YOUR PARCEL RECEIVED. THANK YOU. FILMS ARE NOW O.K. MATERIALS ARE SUBSTANTIAL.

WE HOPE EVERYTHING IS ALL RIGHT WITH YOU AND YOUR FAMILY AND THAT AT YOUR PRESENT POSITION YOU WILL BE ABLE TO OBTAIN DOCUMENTS MENTIONED IN MARCH.

IN ADDITION THE FOLLOWING INFORMATION WILL BE APPRECIATED:

- NUCLEAR DEPTH CHARGE:
  = NAME, MARK AND CHARACTERISTICS (YIELD, DIMENSIONS, WEIGHT, FUZE, DEPTH OF EXPLOSION).
  = YEAR IT WAS ADOPTED INTO SERVICE, FOR WHAT UNITS AND WEAPONS.
  = TYPES OF AIRCRAFT AND HELICOPTERS DESTINED AND FITTED TO USE IT, ALTITUDE OF DROPPING.
  = MAKER AND MAKER'S CAPABILITY (ANNUAL PRODUCTION), QUANTITY ALREADY AVAILABLE IN THE NAVY.
  = PRESENT STATE OF DEVELOPMENT REGARDING NUCLEAR DEPTH CHARGE FOR "IKARA".
- DOCUMENTS ON THE RADIO-RADAR COUNTERMEASURES EQUIPMENT OF YOUR SHIP.
- CHARACTERISTICS OF SMK-6 MINE, ITS FUZE, DEVICES PROTECTING MINE FROM NATURAL HYDRODYNAMIC INTERFERENCE.

PLEASE KEEP US INFORMED ABOUT YOUR WAYS OF OBTAINING DOCUMENTS AND SOURCES OF INFORMATION. LET US KNOW IN GOOD TIME OF FUTURE PLANS FOR YOUR SHIP. OBSERVE TIME-TABLE AND EMERGENCY SIGNAL AGREED.

ENCLOSED IS £500. ALSO £100 FOR M.'S SERVICES.

ALL THE BEST TO YOU AND YOUR FAMILY.

OPERATIONAL INTELLIGENCE CENTRE SPECIAL INTELLIGENCE SUMMARY

June 1941 – Jan.1942	Completely available.
	June & July are current as result of captured documents.
	August onwards available with average delay of 24 – 48 hours.
Feb. – Nov. 1942	None.
Dec.1942 – Oct.1944	All traffic read with delays from a few hours to a week or more on the worst occasions. Occasional days were missed.
Nov.1944 – May 1945	During the previous period there had always been some extra delay in the reading of certain important signals which were specially encyphered. From November 1944 an additional difficulty was introduced in that many U-boats were provided with special individual cyphers (one time pads). These were used where U-boats were operating independently and the problem of breaking these messages was not properly solved. It related mainly to the U-boats operating in the U.K. inshore campaign but did not affect to any considerable extent the ocean routes. The basic U-boat traffic continued to be read with very little delay.

10 Special Intelligence undoubtedly played an
exceptional part in helping to defeat the U-boats.

The U-boats were slow off the mark. The
figure of operational U-boats had only reached 40
in May 1941 when Special Intelligence became completely available. This number steadily increased
for the next two years until it reached its peak
of/ 2̶5̶0̶ nearly 250 operational U-boats in A̶p̶r̶i̶l̶ May 1943. From
then on the numbers steadily declined.

/ It...

Wt. 42789/P7345 10m 12/44 D. & R. Ltd. Gp. 38-2
Wt. 60769/P8156 10m 4/45

21. (*above*) A Special Intelligence Summary written by the staff of the Operational Intelligence Centre (OIC). It details the 'exceptional part' played by special intelligence in the Battle of the Atlantic. (HW 11/38)

22. (*right*) A complaint forwarded from RFC HQ in France. In the early days of air intelligence there was a belief that photography was not a specialist role and could be fulfilled by the pilots. (AIR 1/895/204/5/710)

23. (*below*) An aerial reconnaissance photograph from November 1916. The two white patches visible on the road running from top to bottom of the picture are tank traps. (AIR 1/895/204/5/714)

C.R.F.C. 1838/11.Q.

Major Campbell,

M. A. 2.

Dear Campbell,

I have had a complaint from one of the photographic Officers who shall be nameless, that the instruction of Photography at Reading has got to such a pitch of efficiency, that the pilots know too much, and one of the questions apparently asked the pilot is:
" How do you adjust the lens of an aerial camera?", as also
" How do you use the plates for aerial camera? ".

Although all knowledge is valuable, yet the cause of complaint is that this knowledge is sometimes put into practice with dire results as far as the adjusting of lenses is concerned.

The complaint apparently is that many pilots arriving now from home are "trying to teach me my job and interfering very seriously with my arrangements as to cameras" to quote from photographic Officer who writes me.

Could I have sent me a 12" lens that will ...ver a whole plate. It need not be faster than F.6. ...uld you obtain this for me and send it direct, as I want ...try making a wide angle camera which I think sometimes is ...ted when photographing for maps rather than for detail.

No news of the big Camera as yet. I cannot ...k where this has got to. The Port Depot at Boulogne are ...ng it, but so far no results.

Yours sincerely.

...e Field,

...24th July, 1916.

24. (*bottom*) Camera with a new type of plate changer and release, designed by the photographic officer, 12 Wing, in January 1918. Camera designs constantly evolved in the early days of aerial reconnaissance. (AIR 1/901/204/5/761)

25. (*right*) A recommendation for a DSO for SOE's Freddie Spencer Chapman. Major Chapman headed up one of the very few British stay-behind groups in Malaya to undertake missions after the Japanese invasion. (HS 9/294)

26. (*below right*) Chapman in his days as an outward-bound master at Gordonstoun school before the Second World War.

27. (*below left*) Although 'not naturally agile', Pearl Witherington was judged 'completely brave' by her SOE tutors. She went on to organize and train some 3,000 maquis in the skills of sabotage and guerilla warfare. (HS 9/356)

D.S.O.

Major (temporary) Frederick Spencer CHAPMAN (94604)
5th Seaforth Highlanders

Major Chapman was last known to be operating against the enemy lines of communication during the Malayan campaign - a hazardous undertaking for which he had volunteered - and was not heard of after the Japanese occupation of Malaya.

He has now been contacted in that country and it has been learnt that for the last two years he has been visiting and instructing guerilla bands in Malaya and has visited some twenty-five different guerilla camps. There is no doubt that the continued resistance made by these guerillas to the enemy is due very largely to his individual efforts and inspiration.

Despite a long period of existence under the most difficult and arduous conditions living in tropical and malarial jungle country in constant danger of capture by the enemy, Major Chapman has kept himself physically fit and maintained his keenness and morale unimpaired.

He has now declared his wish to remain in the country in order to lead and fight with the guerilla bands he has helped to train.

Major Chapman has displayed outstanding qualities of endurance, courage and leadership, and his tenacity of purpose and enthusiasm under trying conditions are deserving of the highest praise.

October	Outstanding days seem the 10th and the 30th

October
Outstanding days seem the 10th and the 30th
At least the first part of the month is still good
for Hirohito
The days around the 10th are bad for Goebbels
                                    v.Papen
                                    Italy as a whole
                                    Timoshenko
                                    Adm.King
and very bad indeed for Pétain,should he then still
be alive.If he is alive,this aspect might easily kill him
The days around the 30th are good for France as a whole
and show fighting in the chart of the U.S.A.

Now at last General Eisenhower has very good aspects
and should win honours
Mussolini is badly aspected
Rundtedt shows strong mixed aspects,good and bad
Admiral King is still badly aspected
But the best aspects of all are found in the chart
of King George VI.
The first days are good for the Fuehrer,the rest is
neutral

November
Outstanding days:around the 13th
The month is not bad for the Fuehrer
It is bad for Mussolini
Not too good for Churchill
very good for Hirohito,especially around the 13th
but not so good 24-28th)
It is bad for Montgomery(3rd-24th)

December
Outstanding:the days around the 14th
These days are equally important for Roosevelt and
Hirohito and are likely to see action of the first
magnitude,in whi...   ...des gain advantages,although
very possibly in...   ...ohito it is
more likely to b...
In the second h...
depressive aspe...
matter
Churchills aspe...
Montgomerys asp...

Even with the greatest p...
for Hitlers astrological...
him in 1943.On the contr...
it will need/ a lot of s...
grave defeats.This is th...
strong good aspects are...
of Churchill,and a few...

28. (*left*) A page of astrological predictions for the key players in the Second World War by Louis de Wohl, one of the more unusual employees of the Special Operations Executive (SOE). (KV 2/2821)

29. (*below*) After the end of the Second World War questions were asked about the whereabouts of 'pickaxe' agents dropped by SOE into Western Europe on behalf of the Soviet Union. Kim Philby of MI6 took a particular interest. (KV 2/2877)

Top Secret and Personal.

dated 17th March, 1945.

Dear Roger,

I attach herewith a copy of a recent analysis of services known to
have operated or to be operating to France on Group 12 Division 1.

You will see that it is proved in the case of Service 168 and evident
in the case of 186 that the answer stations were manned by N.K.V.D. agents
dropped in France by S.O.E. between March 1942 and March 1944. It would seem
however, that Moscow had previously had wireless communication with Occupied
France for we know that the first agent sent to London under the S.O.E. and
N.K.V.D. agreement - one Anna Ouspenskaia by alias - was charged "to reach
Paris at all costs and there to visit certain Soviet agents, with one object -
re-establishing the wireless communication between Occupied France and the
U.S.S.R." She was landed at Lannion Bay, North France on 10.1.42 and took
no wireless equipment with her.

Incidentally 11 N.K.V.D. agents were put into France by S.O.E.
Ouspenskaia was probably Polish - at any rate not French, three others were
obviously Spaniards, the remaining 7, six men and a woman were French Communists
who escaped to Russia at the beginning of the war.

All these agents were put into France without the knowledge of the
French authorities although by 5.2.44 the French National Committee had agreed
to the landing of 5 agents for purely military purposes.

Guyot and there is just the possibility that he is identical with one Grigori
Rodionov who was parachuted into France by S.O.E. on 3.3.42. There is
nothing in the facts to disprove the theory, rather the reverse, but equally
there is no proof whatever in its support.

The material is not in itself particularly interesting, but the
analysis does prove that the N.K.V.D. in wartime were working in close cooperation with elements of the dissolved Comintern. It also proves that the
N.K.V.D. agents parachuted into France by S.O.E. were given political rather
than intelligence assignments - a conclusion which S.O.E. had themselves arrived
at.

Yours sincerely.

for H.A.R. Philby.

R. Hollis, Esq.,
M.I.5.

30, 31. (*right*) In Operation Backfire British scientists battled to build V-2 rockets from captured materials. The first successful launch of a reconstituted V2 (*below right*) was at Cuxhaven on 2 October 1945.
(WO 219/5335)

32. (*bottom right*) Klaus Fuchs passed atomic secrets to the Soviets, arguably aiding their development of the H-bomb.
(KV 2/1288)

33. (*bottom*) A note to Anthony Eden from his minister of defence. The Soviets had tested their RDS-37 hydrogen bomb the previous day.
(DEFE 13/414)

---

stores (including batteries) which are unobtainable from German sources.

| 43. | 7th August, 1945. | U.S. DEMANDS AND LACK OF TECHNICAL ADVICE | 43/Training/3548 73A (1A) |

Extract from letter from General Cameron to DRA –

"I think I should warn you that a crisis is boiling up in the affairs of BACKFIRE. I had a visit to-day from Colonel Toftoy of the US Ordnance Dept., who is now in charge of all the rocket development in the States. He says that he needs 27 of the German civilians I am using here. I am reaching a state where I find I lack the technical advice necessary to overcome the problems involved in the assembly of rockets from the mass of miscellaneous parts."

| 44. | 7ᵗ August 1945 | | |
| 45. | 9th August, 1945 | GENERAL DIFFICULTIES – SUGGESTION | 43/Training/3548 74A (1A) |

Extract from letter – General Cameron to Prof Ellis

"Assembly of rockets which will fire is turning out to be a lengthy process and more difficult than we had expected. We are using components, some of which have come out of Nordhausen, but many of which have been collected from farms, holes in the ground, railway sidings, and so on, all over Germany, and even our Nordhausen components have suffered from exposure to the weather. We have found that even such assemblies as we have cannot be accepted as workable and must be dismantled and put together again. We are short of working drawings, wiring diagrams, etc. The state of our equipment is such that we must test everything and we have not got the testing apparatus. I am unhappy that no one from the War Office has yet had an opportunity of coming out here and seeing for themselves what facilities are available, and the state of our resources. I think it is important that that should be done before decisions are taken."

TOP SECRET

MINISTRY OF DEFENCE, S.W.1.

PRIME MINISTER

The Russians let off the biggest explosion they have yet made on Tuesday morning at the usual test site. So far as we can ascertain, this appears to have been detected at all the acoustic and seismic stations, both American and our own.

2. Admiral Strauss has informed our Ambassador that he may find it necessary to make an announcement some time tomorrow. We are taking steps to ascertain the terms of the announcement.

3. For ourselves, we should have preferred to have deferred any announcement until we had captured debris samples, but this cannot be done for some days yet. We have asked the Americans to let us know in what terms they propose to make the announcement, and can then decide our own action.

4. I am sending a copy of this note to the Foreign Secretary.

(Sgd.) SELWYN LLOYD

23rd November, 1955.

EMIL JULIUS KLAUS FUCHS, with aliases Dr. Karl Fuchs, Klaus Fuchs, Klaus Emil Fuchs

Name	
Residence	Wormwood Scrubs Prison, England
Occupation	Research physicist
Born	12/29/11 Russelsheim, Germany
Citizenship	Naturalized British citizen
Height	5'11"
Build	Thin
Complexion	Dark and sallow
Hair	Brown, receding at temples and decidedly balding
Eyes	Brown (wears glasses)
Features	Medium, high forehead given to wrinkling when in thought or study, cleanshaven. Has noticeable vein running from left eye level across temple to level of hair line.

K-22

7

430

Copies to:
Mr. E. C. Williams (1)
Sir R. Powell (1)
C.D.S. (1)

SIR FREDERICK BRUNDRETT

1. In view of the recent Russian success in hitting the moon with a rocket, I think that we should review our current assessment of Russian progress in rocketry.

2. In particular, I should like to know what deduction can be made from this about the probable accuracy of their military rockets.

Duncan Sandys

October, 12th, 1959.

Inland cable on american soil – this was the one handed to Dr Page and exposed by the President. Washington to Mexico.

7.

No 3.

16·1·17

Berlin telegram.

We intend to begin on the first of February unrestricted submarine warfare. We shall endeavour in spite of this to keep the U.S.A. neutral. In the event of this not succeeding we make Mexico a proposal of alliance on the following basis:-

MAKE WAR TOGETHER
MAKE PEACE TOGETHER

Generous financial support and an understanding on our part that Mexico is to reconquer the lost territory in Texas, New Mexico and Arizona. The settlement in detail is left to you.

You will inform the President of the above most secretly, as soon as the outbreak of war with the U.S.A. is certain and add the suggestion that he should on his own initiative invite Japan to immediate adherence and at the same time mediate between Japan and ourselves.

Please call the President's attention to the fact that the ruthless employment of our submarines now offers the prospect of compelling England in a few months to make peace.

36. (*right*) In September 1940 Churchill asked 'C' – MI6 head Stewart Menzies – to send him summaries of the most important military and diplomatic decrypts. Distribution of this top-secret intelligence was otherwise confined to the directors of intelligence for the army, navy and air force. (HW 1/1)

37, 38. (*below*) An example of Churchill's 'Golden eggs'. One of five Ultra decrypts, with its précis (*below right*), that Menzies passed to Churchill on 31 August 1944. (HW 1/3196)

HW 1/1

10, Downing Street,
Whitehall.

MOST SECRET.

September 27, 1940.

Dear C.

In confirmation of my telephone message, I have been personally directed by the Prime Minister to inform you that he wishes you to send him daily all the ENIGMA messages.

These are to be sent in a locked box with a clear notice stuck to it "THIS BOX IS ONLY TO BE OPENED BY THE PRIME MINISTER IN PERSON".

After seeing the messages he will return them to you.

Yours ever,

Stewart Menzies

...e will be no check possible here,
...ou please institute a check on receipt
...rned documents to see that you have
...n all back.

A.M. FORM No. 1 **TOP ~~MOST~~ SECRET ULTRA**
TO BE KEPT UNDER LOCK AND KEY AND NEVER TO BE REMOVED FROM THE OFFICE.
THIS FORM IS TO BE USED FOR AIR INTELLIGENCE MESSAGES ONLY.

| HR. No. | | GR. No. | | OFFICE SERIAL. No. | |
| DATE | TIME OF RECEIPT | | TIME OF DESPATCH | SYSTEM | |

TO:

FROM:

SENDERS No.

(T.O.O. 1400/30/8/44)

CX/MSS/T293/20

(ZTPGM/87836)

XL 8702 (TIME OF DESPATCH 2 am. 30.8.44)

S O U T H E A S T   E U R O P E.

FROM DOCUMENTS DATED 30/8:

ACCORDING ADMIRAL AEGEAN AFTERNOON 30TH SITUATION REQUIRED NEW CONCENTRATIONS. INVOLVING CERTAIN WITHDRAWAL MOVEMENTS IN PELOPONNESE AND MOVE OF SINGLE TROOP UNITS FROM CRETE TO MAINLAND. PERSONNEL BY AIR, EQUIPMENT BY SEA. TRANSPORT PRIORITIES FROM CRETE ARE SECOND BATTALION 22 INFANTRY DIVISION, 1 PANZER ABTEILUNG, FORTRESS ENGINEERS, G.A.F. CONSTRUCTIONAL BATTALION. HEAVY EQUIPMENT TO BE BROUGHT UP AT ONCE AND EVERY KIND OF SHIPPING SPACE EXPLOITED. IN IMMEDIATE FUTURE FOLLOWING AVAILABLE IN CRETE : HEIDELBERG, ERPEL, PELIKAN, ALSO TORPEDO BOAT AND CAIQUE SPACE.

THE ABOVE HAS BEEN PASSED AT 10.44 am /31/8/44 A8:

XL 8702/LG/FR/RJ/NCA/AL/CO/PK

| DISTRIBUTION: BB/AM/ADY/WO | | B2B/2NB/BBD SIGNATURE OF ORIGINATOR, NOT TO BE TELEPRINTED | 1208/31/8/44Z OPERATOR'S RECEIPT RD |
| DEGREE OF PRIORITY | | TIME OF ORIGIN | |

CX/MSS/T293/20
(ZTPGM/87836).

GERMAN ADMIRAL AEGEAN, afternoon 30th August :-

Situation necessitates new concentrations, involving withdrawals in PELOPONNESE and troop movements (personnel by air, equipment by sea) from CRETE to Mainland.

point of view, the sooner he was got out of the way the better'. This gave SOE head Major General Colin Gubbins enough encouragement to ask his senior officers for their views on a possible assassination. Most were in favour, the head of the German section being one of the few who opposed such an operation. Gubbins therefore gave the go-ahead for the planning of an assassination codenamed Operation Foxley.[35]

The plans, which can be found among the SOE files held at the National Archives, centred on Hitler's alpine retreat, the Berghof, near the town of Berchtesgaden in Bavaria. Three options were considered: first, the assassination of Hitler by snipers as he took his regular daily walk to the tea house in the grounds (as a back-up, the assassins would be armed with bazookas to kill Hitler if they missed him and he sheltered in the tea house); second, a bazooka attack on Hitler's car as it rounded the corner of one of the lanes leaving the Berghof; finally, the parachuting into the area of a battalion of SAS to 'swamp' any guards and defenders, thus ensuring that Hitler could be captured and executed.[36] Each of these options had large elements of uncertainty — perhaps even fantasy — about them. Detailed plans could not really be made until forward teams had reconnoitred the area, nor was it clear how often Hitler spent time at the Berghof or how many guards were in the area. Given that most of the information used to collate the draft plan was pre-war, the three proposals almost inevitably posed more questions than they answered. Some planning also went into destroying Hitler's train, but the lack of any up-to-date knowledge of Hitler's itinerary or security measures on the train made this a difficult option. Without solid information, a variety of far-fetched schemes were considered. For example, it was thought that an operative, possibly a German or Austrian prisoner of war with a well-developed hatred of Hitler, might hurl a suitcase of explosives in front of Hitler's train while it was passing through a station. The assassin, it was noted, would 'be prepared to take the consequences'. It was also suggested that poison might be introduced into the train's water or milk supplies, a scheme flawed because of the lack of certainty that the Führer would be the first to taste the water or milk, even if the supplies could actually be contaminated.[37]

By October 1944 such planning as there was on Operation Foxley had ground to a halt. Reports in the National Archives show that SOE officers had begun to believe that any assassination would lead to a martyr cult, the last thing they wanted with the war approaching its final stages: 'Any attempt by the allies, successful or otherwise to assassinate Hitler would be simply playing into Germany's hands. We should immediately have a modern version of the Kyffhauser nonsense [the 12th-century Holy Roman Emperor, Frederick Barbarossa, who died on the crusades, was said in German nationalist myth to be still alive deep in the mountain of Kyffhauser, awaiting the call to save Germany in its hour of need], offering every incentive to German rebirth. Besides, how do we know that we assassinate the right Hitler? There are said to be at least three.'[38]

The assassination of other senior Nazis—Foxley II—was also considered, but again much of the planning seems not to have been anchored in reality, in part because the movements of these senior figures were virtually unknown. One SOE planner even suggested hypnotizing Rudolf Hess—Hitler's former deputy who had secretly flown to Britain in 1941 to negotiate a peace—and employing him to assassinate Himmler. The practicality of the plan is doubtful: Hess's sanity had been questioned following his unauthorized and eccentric flight to Britain, he would probably have had little chance of getting close to Himmler if he returned to Germany, and above all he was still an avowed Nazi even if a disowned one.[39]

'Our tame astrologer'

Another attempt to probe Hitler's defences was even more bizarre than the implausible assassination plots. It involved Louis de Wohl, an eccentric astrologer of uncertain background who arrived in England from Germany in 1935, whose file has been recently released to the National Archives.[40] According to this, some intelligence officers thought he was a Nazi sympathizer but others thought he was a Jew. He claimed to be of Hungarian aristocratic stock but was unable to speak a word of the language; hostile sources claimed he was a homosexual, others that he was consorting with a flame-haired 'harlot', a Mrs Self, with a suspicious German background. Another assessment, by sceptical MI5 officer W.T. Caulfield, summed him up as 'extraordinarily clever' and 'exceedingly vain ... with the mentality of a prima donna'.

The SOE's connection with de Wohl seems strange, but his influence stemmed from the years before the Second World War. De Wohl had established a high-profile clientele for his astrology readings, including a group of grateful and indulgent clients among senior members of the intelligence services. He claimed in an early draft of his autobiography that Lord Halifax, Neville Chamberlain's foreign secretary and later ambassador to the USA, and the heads of both naval and military intelligence, as well as Charles Hambro of SOE, all attended his readings. That the MI5 officers vetting his autobiography towards the end of the war explicitly stated that the reading public 'did not need to know' this indicates that his claims were not wholly divorced from the truth. They ensured, for example, the omission of a passage that stated that John Godfrey, the head of naval intelligence, had read out to de Wohl the names and birth dates of admirals.

Initially it seems to have been de Wohl's 'psychological insight' into the German mind and character—plus his alleged knowledge of the sort of astrological predictions Hitler could have received—that made him useful to Charles Hambro of SO2 (the future SOE) and to Electra House. According to Caulfield, de Wohl argued that Hitler's consulting of astrologers was more significant than the validity of individual predictions; if an attack were made by the allies when Hitler felt that his 'aspects were bad', the Führer would be more prone to defeatism. Certainly, de Wohl claimed near-absurd proportions for the influence of astrology on the German Reich, reporting that even 'units of the German navy carry devices of an astrological nature'. An example from de Wohl's file of his astrological predictions for November 1943 (plate 28) reveals the information passed to Hambro and others:

> Outstanding days [in this month]: around the 13th
> > The month is not bad for the Fuehrer
> > It is bad for Mussolini
> > Not too good for Churchill
> > Very good for Hirohito, especially around the 13th, but not so good 24–28th
> > It is bad for Montgomery (3rd–24th).[41]

In reality it certainly was a bad month for Mussolini—he had been reduced to the status of a German puppet by November 1943. However, 'not bad' hardly begins to describe Hitler's month: his armies in the east lost the battle for Kiev and fell back from the river Dneiper, while the RAF started a major bombing offensive on Berlin. Nor was Hirohito's November especially good: the allies landed at Tarawa and the Japanese came off worst in the naval battle of Cape St George, effectively breaking Japanese supply lines to the Solomon Islands. Montgomery's advance up the Italian peninsula continued, with Castiglione being taken—not an especially bad month for the British field marshal. And the Cairo declaration that the British, Americans and

Chinese would attack Japan, and the Teheran conference, which agreed on a Western invasion of German-occupied Europe in 1944, would not have displeased Churchill either.

Predictions of dubious accuracy aside, MI5 also seem to have extracted information from de Wohl on his wide range of clients. De Wohl had claimed a minor diplomatic coup in persuading the Romanian ambassador and his chargé d'affaires to stay in Britain rather than return to German-occupied Romania as instructed, and even if exaggerated, MI5 took this seriously enough to ask for a full list of his contacts. We do not know if this was supplied, but de Wohl certainly travelled to the US on behalf of SOE prior to the American declaration of war. His brief was to produce a series of astrological predictions suggesting troubled times ahead for Hitler, which were placed in US papers as a propaganda initiative. A letter written to Oswald Harker — the deputy head of MI5 — in February 1942 and preserved in de Wohl's file described his work in America as 'quite satisfactory'.

De Wohl's friends in high places were to prove useful as the war progressed. Head of military intelligence Frederick Beaumont-Nesbitt managed to push for his naturalization as a British subject, despite a sceptical MI5, and in 1941 Charles Hambro arranged for him to be made a captain in the army. Whether de Wohl could legitimately describe himself as captain or not, it ruffled many feathers, especially among émigrés working in the intelligence services, most of whom were denied an army commission. The sceptical Caulfield was not impressed, noting that 'he struts about in the uniform of a British army captain and gives every reason for believing that he is in some secret employment'. Earlier accusations of Nazi sympathies were also resurfacing; de Wohl's partly estranged wife, living in Chile, was accused of consorting with German nationals and Nazis while receiving remittances of cash from her husband from his SOE salary. The opportunity was taken to search his flat, which revealed scrapbooks of German newspaper cuttings prior to 1935 showing predictions apparently praising the Nazi leadership. An exasperated Caulfield suggested three ways of 'dealing with him'. Unfortunately, the lines of the note outlining the first two of these are still closed to the public, but a third involved 'compel[ling] him to live in some remote part of the country and restrict[ing] his movements'.

Neither this fate nor anything more drastic descended upon de Wohl, but as the tide of war began to turn, even Hambro, his greatest patron, began to distance himself. De Wohl's 'commission' was rescinded and MI5 took to intercepting his mail, at the request of MI6, with some glee: 'I am always very glad to receive reports on the activities of individuals who, like the subject of your letter, were once employed by one of the British propaganda organisations,' stated a Major Alley of MI5 to his correspondent at SIS. The intercepted letters include rather desperate attempts to gain funds from Hambro after his work at SOE and the PWE dried up, but after the war de Wohl faded completely from the world of British intelligence, dying in Switzerland in 1961.

SOE and the Soviet Union

Another file recently released by the National Archives reveals the SOE's role in dropping agents, codenamed 'pickaxes', into occupied Europe on behalf of the Soviet Union.[42] The agreement between the SOE and the NKVD (the KGB's predecessor) was negotiated in September 1941 by Lieutenant Colonels Guiness and Hill of SOE. Formally signed on 30 September, it instituted the stationing of liaison officers in Britain and Russia, and committed the SOE to infiltrating agents provided by the Soviet Union into Axis-occupied Europe. This usually involved parachuting agents into France, Germany or Austria, but one instance shows the landing of a Communist agent — Alexandra Filipov — in Italy from a submarine.

Lieutenant Colonel Hill was the SOE liaison officer in Moscow, and his NKVD counterpart in London was Colonel Chichaev. Chichaev appears to have been unusual for a Soviet official in the United Kingdom during the war, a section on 'NKVD personalities' in the pickaxe file describing him in the following terms: 'he is a man of 42, probably of Siberian stock. He is inclined to be effeminate, with a passion for roses, one of which he usually carries in his pocket. He drinks little and has a dislike for vodka.' Chichaev's unusual manner — apparently 'wanting to behave in a western way' — belied his background as a guerrilla fighter in the Russian civil war, a bullet wound injury to his hand confirming his credentials as a Soviet revolutionary.

A total of 34 Soviet agents were dispatched to Britain, usually on ships via Sweden or Murmansk, but only 25 were successfully infiltrated into occupied Europe. Six were returned to the USSR and three were lost either on the way to Britain or while being infiltrated. All were French, Spanish, Italian, German or Austrian Communists who had emigrated to the Soviet Union in the 1930s. From the SOE's perspective the arrangement was not a success. An official account contained within the above file and written a few years after the war noted that:

> Pickaxes caused a great deal of trouble, waste of time and energy on our part, a fact which never seemed to be properly appreciated by our Russian colleagues, who were forever carping at our slowness and inefficiency. These complaints, though perhaps in some cases well founded, seem nevertheless rather unfair in view of stories which had since reached us on Russian organisations and dropping of agents—all of which tend to prove that the Soviet methods are, to say the least of it very rough and ready.[43]

Compared with SOE agents, Soviet agents' covers were often rudimentary, with cover names often close to the agents' real names, false identity papers sometimes of a low standard and equipment that could be faulty. The agents generally came from one of two organizations: the NKVD itself or the Comintern (Comintern agents were considered particularly ill-equipped and ill-trained). NKVD agents were of two sorts: those collecting intelligence or undertaking general subversion, who would report by wireless to the 'Zentrum' or centre in Moscow, and who might have to wait days or weeks for replies; and those who would report directly to the 'Direktor' and would receive near-immediate responses. These latter would often belong to special assassination or sabotage groups; few if any of these were parachuted into Europe via Britain.

A number who were parachuted from Britain were Comintern agents with specific orders to lie low and undertake political subversion primarily after the war had finished. Members of the Russian section of SOE tasked with shepherding such agents soon began to have suspicions of this political rather than military agenda. This was especially the case with regard to a group of three Comintern agents code-named 'Coffee Party': Wilhelm Wagner, Hilda Uxa and Alvin Mar, due to be dropped into their native Austria by SOE in 1943. It soon became clear that the agents had received malfunctioning radios and shoddy false passports, which were returned to the Soviet Union and replaced with only marginally better equipment and documents. In the process it seemed that the three were now viewed as 'politically suspect' in Moscow, a shift they sensed from contact with Chichaev's officers. All three, as a report in the pickaxe file reveals, gradually turned from ardent Communists to displaying 'an intense dislike of the Soviet system'. Uxa in particular believed that the 'Russians have something against her, and that they were deliberately being sent away with faulty documents as a subtle method of liquidation'. Their mission was abandoned and the three began to discuss their backgrounds and training with their SOE handlers. Each had little idea of the mission, due to be explained when they arrived in Austria, but to the SOE their relative lack of training, their Comintern background and their past roles as Communist or left-wing activists in Austria all suggested a post-war political role. Eventually the NKVD ordered their return to the Soviet Union and it was decided to send them via the Panama Canal to the Pacific coast of the Soviet Union. Fearing for their lives if they returned, the agents requested asylum in Britain, but this was not granted. Despite being accompanied by one of Chichaev's men, they somehow managed to escape during a stopover on the west coast of North America. It appears that Wagner, Uxa and Mar were given protection by the US authorities and granted leave to remain in the US.

SOE suspicions of intended political infiltration were confirmed in September 1944 when interrogation of a German prisoner revealed that the Germans had captured a Soviet agent, known to the British as Elena Nikitina (a German, real name unknown). Dropped over Austria by the British, she had tried to poison herself when the Gestapo raided her flat but, according to a letter written by Guy Liddell in September 1944, survived to reveal under interrogation her 'instructions to stay in Germany even after the US army had entered the country'. Such plans were confirmed by her possession of significant quantities of British, French and US currency. Nikitina's eventual fate is not known, a note in the 'pickaxe' file merely stating that she 'may have been shot' by the Gestapo.

The fates of Soviet agents dropped into Europe were largely unknown to the British until the end of the war. The very first 'pickaxe' dropped over Europe, Szyfra Lipseyc, was captured soon after landing and shot, although this was only confirmed as late as 1955. The interrogation in June 1945 of Johann Sanitzer, the senior Gestapo officer who had himself interrogated numerous Soviet agents, 'turning' a number of them to operate as double agents and feed false information to their Soviet masters, yielded details on some of the 25.

The stories, such as those of Comintern agents Gregor Kersche, Louise Soucek and Hildegard Mraz, make disturbing reading. All three were dropped in Poland by SOE in August 1943, and Sanitzer noted that they had been badly trained, with few documents to support their cover and no parachute training. On arrival in Austria they had built their own radios and started transmitting using Russian recognition signals. Their transmissions were picked up by Sanitzer because they often interfered with signals his own double agents had been sending to the Soviet Union. After their arrest, Sanitzer managed to 'turn' the three who continued to send signals to Moscow under Gestapo control. Sanitzer soon realized that signals from Moscow included some directly from the general secretary of the Comintern, Dimitrov, and the leader of the Austrian section of the Comintern, Kopienig. The three pickaxes' mission had been to 'observe political fluctuations' and to build up a resistance movement of Austrian trade unionists and sympathizers. Sanitzer kept these three double agents in 'play' to discover more information about Soviet intentions—Moscow Comintern signallers even revealed the constitution of the Austrian legion of Tito's partisans—and send out erroneous and misleading information. Sanitzer sustained the pretence until only two days before the Russians entered Vienna, when, he claimed, he let the agents go free. Kersche and Soucek were quickly rearrested by Smersh, the NKVD's front-line counter-espionage unit, and disappeared into the gulags, where Soucek died in 1950. Kersche was released in 1956, but the fate of Mraz is not known.[44]

Some pickaxes undoubtedly survived the war. Eugene Nesper, for example, who was turned by the Gestapo but later escaped to Switzerland, was reported in 1950 to be active as an arms dealer operating out of Tangier. Some agents, whose real names the SOE did not always know, seemed to disappear entirely once they landed in occupied Europe. After the end of the war, the head of counter-espionage at MI6 began to be concerned that surviving agents were now being used against the West. In particular, he highlighted a number of radio signals picked up by the Radio Security Section, indicating Communist cells operating in France and possibly consisting of former 'pickaxes'. This was politically a difficult issue, as the SOE had not informed the Free French of these insertions during the war.

Such concerns might be justified as Europe began its descent towards the Cold War, but the identity of the MI6 officer—Kim Philby—gives a further twist to these post-war investigations: was Philby, a Soviet spy from before the Second World War who later defected to the USSR, planting dissent within the intelligence services by suggesting that agents put in place by the SOE were now operating against Britain? Was this an attempt to blacken SOE's name as it fought for its institutional life against MI6, or was this merely a routine and legitimate investigation into an adversary's agents? Philby indicated to Roger Hollis of MI5 that signals picked up from an agent in France—known as 'Service 21'—could be the pickaxe Raymond Guyot (known to SOE by his Russian cover name of Grigori Rodionov), parachuted into France in March 1942 (plate 29). Philby admitted that he had no evidence, however, and the pickaxe link could not be maintained.

In 1954 Philby resurrected the issue of the SOE–NKVD link again, this time in very different circumstances. Partially implicated in Burgess and Maclean's defection and dismissed from MI6 (p. 82), he was questioned intensively to discover whether he was the 'Third Man'. During these discussions Philby mentioned links between Major Hill of the Russia section of SOE and Chichaev of the NKVD, and implied that Chichaev and Kislytsin, another NKVD officer at the embassy in London, had been Burgess and Maclean's handlers during the Second World War. This could well have been an attempt to shift suspicion away from the real handler, Yuri Modin, but it also had the advantage of linking the Soviet penetration to the SOE Russian section's links with the NKVD during the war, exploiting SOE's reputation for recruiting more officers with 'left-leaning' or progressive politics than either MI6 or MI5. Philby's suggestive comments certainly encouraged an unnamed MI6 officer to contact E. MacBarnet of MI5 asking whether that service had any evidence of links between Burgess and Chichaev. Here, unfortunately, the National Archives file finishes, so we cannot know whether links between the SOE's Russian section and the NKVD were investigated further.

SOE in the Far East

With the war against Japan some 18 months away, SOE had been established to meet the perceived needs of fighting the European war. However, the Far East had not been forgotten and by late 1940 terms of reference for establishing an SOE group in Singapore had been drawn up. This led to the formation of the 'Oriental Mission' in May 1941 under the C-in-C Far East and directed by Valentine Killery. The area to be covered by this small organization was vast, stretching from Manchuria to the Philippines and from the Dutch East Indies to northern Burma.

Shortly after Killery's arrival in Singapore, the secretary of state for India sent Colonel Joyce of the Indian Political Service to meet him. The men held discussions and shortly afterwards the 'India Mission' (later to be known as Force 136) was established under Colin Mackenzie.

The directives to the two organizations were based on the SOE activities in Europe, yet the Far Eastern theatre had nothing in common with it. In Europe, the various resistance groups had a common enemy, but in the numerous countries in the Far East there was often doubt as to who the real enemy was. Many local factions had their own agendas for the way ahead and how to align their efforts—some wanted nothing to do with the 'foreigner's conflict' at all. Another factor that complicated Far East operations was the vast distances involved, far greater than anything experienced in Europe; this had two particularly severe impacts on SOE. Suitable transport to deploy and support clandestine groups over the huge distances was in very short supply and the remoteness of the headquarters from 'field' locations created major administrative and control problems. Last but by no means least, few Europeans had any kind of command of the many local languages and dialects, and it was virtually impossible for them to travel and operate unnoticed among Orientals, whether in major cities or remote jungle locations.

Before exploring some of SOE's work in the region, it is worth recording Lord Selbourne's observation that 'the collection of secret intelligence is not a function of SOE, although it inevitably obtains it in the course of its other activities'. The main intelligence-gathering organization in the Far East was the Inter-Services Liaison Department (ISLD), a founder member of the intelligence club in the Far East (and a cover name for SIS in a number of theatres). ISLD and SOE never fully cooperated with each other—ISLD's operations were highly secret and often unknown to SOE—and this generated much rivalry and competition for scarce assets, particularly sea and air transport, and was often counter-productive. On one occasion the same submarine was tasked to drop a party from each organization, but after the SOE party leader deemed it unsafe to land his team, he vetoed the landing of the ISLD party in case it compromised his own operation. This was not an isolated incident.

The first of the SOE organizations to become involved in the fight against the Japanese was the Oriental Mission, and their heroic efforts are worthy of recording. The Oriental Mission of SOE, established in May 1941 and based in Singapore, was largely unprepared for the Japanese army's rapid advance down the Malay Peninsula: few 'stay-behind' units had been created in time. SOE operations in the Far East subsequently centred around the SOE organization in India, operating alongside Special Operations Australia (SOA) and the US Office of Strategic Services (OSS). Retaining some responsibility for propaganda, the SOE also set up and ran the Eastern Warfare School at Poona and the School of Jungle Training at Trincomalee. The enormous size of the theatre of operations, US hostility to colonial empires, the poor transport facilities in many of these areas and the inability to use Western agents made subversion and sabotage operations difficult to undertake. Much work concentrated on maintaining links with and supporting local resistance movements, often of a Communist or nationalist/anti-colonial nature.[45]

One of the very few 'stay behind' officers to survive the Japanese occupation was Major Freddy Spencer Chapman (plates 25 and 26). Before the war he had been the outward-bound master at the famously robust public school Gordonstoun. His adventures included shooting a rampaging polar bear while on an expedition in Greenland for the British Arctic Air Route, taking part in an intelligence mission to Tibet across the Himalayas and becoming the first to scale Mount Chomolhari in Bhutan; he was considering an attempt on Everest when the war began. An unconventional and charismatic leader (according to one his colleagues 'he talked like a liberal and acted like an anarchist'), he was quickly snapped up by SOE. After a spell instructing recruits at the Loch Ailort training school, he was dispatched to Singapore in April 1941 to set up and run the Singapore SOE training camp: 101 Special Training School (101 STS).[46]

Only after Singapore had been bombed by Japanese forces in late 1941 did the colonial authorities finally agreed to arm non-white groups within Singapore and Malaya to act as paramilitary or guerrilla forces. Chapman lamented the lost opportunity in a report now in the National Archives:

> If only we had had even a small means of support from Malaya command and had been allowed to start preparations even a few weeks earlier then, instead of three individuals working from hastily improvised bases, there would have been a large number of B.O.s [British officers] backed up by hundreds of trained Chinese operating under ideal circumstances, and it is possible that the Japanese advance might have been very considerably delayed.[47]

The chance was missed, but eventually the authorities agreed to enter into negotiations with the Malayan Communist Party (MCP) to arm some of their members as stay-behind groups. If nothing else, the Communists could be guaranteed to be hostile to the invading Japanese.

Chapman attended the initial meetings with Li Tek of the MCP, along with a representative of police Special Branch, and it was agreed to train a selection of MCP members at 101 STS. The aim was to create 15 teams each consisting of 10–15 trained men to provide the core of a regional resistance organization. Each team would be given five machine guns, 15 pistols, 70 grenades and explosives 'on a generous scale' to provide them with an initial supply of weapons, augmented by strategically placed arms dumps. The teams would then be free to recruit locals in the areas to which they had been assigned. Two sorts of locals were required: those to form the Anti-Japanese Forces (AJF), a core guerrilla group living in the jungle, conducting operations and evading Japanese forces; and those to form the Anti-Japanese Union (AJU)—essentially sympathetic locals able to provide food and assistance for the guerrillas when necessary, with a number able to act as unarmed auxiliaries.

What was planned was therefore a classic insurgency which—had it been in place in time—would no doubt have created a useful resistance organization. Such was the speed of the Japanese advance that few of the trained teams reached their allocated areas, and nearly all failed to find their arms dumps. They had no trouble recruiting locals as they progressed up the country, although the MCP was almost entirely composed of ethnic Chinese, with ethnic Malays and Indians largely excluded. The teams therefore recruited from the Chinese communities of timber workers, tin-miners and rubber tappers—a powerful force which after the war came home to roost. In the immediate term they became the nucleus of active resistance to the Japanese, although their ulterior motive—the creation of a people's republic of Malaya— remained the ultimate goal. Such British-created resistance cells became the core of the Communist insurgency in Malaya during the 1940s and 1950s (p. 104).

Chapman headed up one of the very few British stay-behind groups able to undertake any missions after the Japanese invasion. He led a team of 10 men, one of only three teams to head into the jungle, but they discovered the assigned dump had been raided by bandits and much of the weaponry taken. Chapman's party then decided to move 18 miles across the jungle to the town of T Malim, an apparently straightforward journey on the map. The difficult terrain—including a number of 5,000-foot mountains hidden in the jungle canopy, 20-foot boulders strewn across the valley floor, swamps and intense humidity —turned the journey into a 12-day epic. As Chapman recounted:

It was a nightmare journey. The rain was almost continuous and our matches were so wet that after the 2nd we were unable to light a fire. For the last 5 days each man's ration was only two spoonfuls of raw oatmeal twice a day. The leeches were so bad that when we took our clothes off at the end of the day we found at least 30 of them on our bodies. At night we were always soaked through and bitterly cold, and in the morning our faces were so distorted from insect bites that we could scarcely open our eyes until we had bathed them. Our face, hands and legs were a network of scratches.[48]

Having finally reached T Malim, Chapman's diminished team (three had lost contact, heard rumours of Japanese troops in the vicinity and become caught up in the general retreat) set about a highly effective campaign of sabotage. His report in the National Archives describes nine bridges destroyed, three trains made unserviceable and over 400 telephone wires cut, although his estimate of more than 500 Japanese casualties proved over-optimistic. Having exhausted their gelignite, his unit decided to make for the nearest Chinese resistance group in the Batu caves, where they discovered six British army stragglers and a large number of Chinese resistance, led by Ah Wan, one of the 101 STS trainees. The group, consisting of nearly 100 AJF members, had also failed to locate their weapons dumps, and only a small number were properly armed. Almost all the British were in various states of illness: two were on the verge of death, one had fallen into madness and none survived more than another year, while Ah Wan and most of the leadership were killed after a member betrayed the group and led the Japanese to a meeting in September 1942. Chapman himself suffered badly from malaria and soon was the only surviving member of his original team. When recovered he moved from resistance camp to resistance camp in search of the elusive MCP headquarters, always apparently one step ahead of him.

Over the next year Chapman visited most of the Chinese camps across Malaya; he saw no other European at all during this time, and his isolation and recurring bouts of malaria caused him to feel impotent. The AJF consulted him, having great respect for his skills, but they were fighting their own war and had little interest in working to any British agenda. Eventually, in December 1943, Chapman met up with the SOE Operation Gustavus group of John Davis and Richard Broome, sent to regain contact with the Malay resistance. He was captured by the Japanese in early 1944, escaping death only by easing himself out under the awning of the tent he was held in and vanishing into the jungle. Reunited with the Gustavus team he continued his work, surviving the war as the very last European stay-behind agent.[49]

India Mission

Initially the India Mission's activities were mainly defensive, aimed at coping with a possible Japanese invasion of India or the failure to prevent any German advance through the Caucasus. A small training centre was established at Kohima and four companies of the Assam Rifles were instructed in the art of guerrilla warfare. They were later to form V Force, administered by SOE, and tasked with operating along the 800-mile mountainous eastern frontier of India—running from the Himalayas to the Bay of Bengal. Documents in the National Archives chart its varied missions and funds.[50] In the event of a Japanese invasion, V Force was to remain behind enemy lines to patrol the occupied territory and carry out sabotage and gather intelligence.

Once Japan had occupied most of Burma, much of the Indian Mission's Burma Country Section activities were directed to operations behind enemy lines and the various Force 136 parties with their locally recruited Karen and Kachin tribesmen. However, although there was a limited role to play in the early days, it was not until the XIVth Army began its advance southwards in late 1944 that they began to play a major role in harassing the Japanese.

By the beginning of 1945, Force 136 had over 70 officers and nearly 12,000 men under arms, mainly in the area along the route from Maymo to Rangoon. Attempts were made at this time to direct the activities of Force 136 to long-range intelligence collection, and it was agreed that they should combine with Z Force, whose role was to gather intelligence up to 60 miles inside enemy territory. Although agreed, this plan was never fully implemented. However, amongst Force 136's more traditional guerrilla warfare activities it did conduct specific operations to report traffic levels on roads and railways in the Sittang valley between Mandalay and Toungoo, and later they established teams in the Pegu Yomas Range to watch the valley between Rangoon and Prome. As the XIVth Army advanced, Force 136 was tasked to continue gathering intelligence on enemy movements and to reconnoitre possible enemy escape routes.

Operations Nation and Character were by far the biggest and most important operations carried out by the Burma Country Section. Nation was implemented during February and March 1945 and a number of Jedburgh teams were dropped behind enemy lines. The majority were given the task of reporting traffic movements and some very successful bombing attacks, based on the intelligence sent back by the team's W/T operators, were made by the RAF. Once the Japanese were in full retreat, the teams established observation posts.

One team under a very capable officer was dropped near the road from Maymyo to Mandalay. The object was to disrupt traffic with a series of ambushes but, while settling in, they started to report the daily movements of the Japanese, who had at least one division in the Shan States. This information proved to be so valuable that the army ordered the team not to attempt the traffic disruption, but to report daily troop movements instead—a procedure that was continued until the capture of Mandalay.

Operation Character had the same objectives in the Karenni area. Here the main railway line was kept under constant surveillance and a constant watch maintained on possible escape routes to Siam. The teams were also tasked with raising guerrilla groups from the local population; one of them managed to raise a group of 2,000 Karens to harass, and in some cases destroy, the enemy.

As the advance to Rangoon progressed, the RAF relied increasingly on intelligence passed by the Force 136 teams. In the weeks before the fall of Rangoon, almost all their long-range fighter-bomber sorties were employed on Force 136 targets. By this time there were so many high-grade reports that it had become impossible to react to them all. One of a number of notable successes was an attack on the railway station at Pyu; a raid by the RAF coincided with a troop train's arrival and the enemy suffered more than a thousand casualties. A measure of the RAF's satisfaction at the intelligence reports passed from the field can be judged by their request that, for the forthcoming landings into Malaya, at least one squadron would be held on standby to carry out immediate air strikes when targets were identified by Force 136 teams.

Following the abrupt end of the war in the Far East, SOE had one important task remaining. Joining with other organizations, it would play a crucial role in the identification of prisoner of war camps and repatriation of the prisoners there. This joint enterprise was known as the Repatriation of Allied Prisoners of War and Internees (RAPWI). Following a series of leaflet drops to the camps, 54-man teams were briefed to go to the camps, and SOE's W/T network, already on the ground in some areas, was a vital element in the communications plan. Some of the camps, particularly those in Sumatra, proved difficult to locate, and Indonesian guerrilla forces were a constant threat.

The final days of SOE

With the end of the war, SOE faced an uncertain future. The chiefs of staff baldly stated that the organization had 'no future task', but parts of SOE itself lobbied hard for a post-war role, particularly given its performance in comparison to SIS. Two committees were established to decide SOE's fate: the chairman of the Joint Intelligence Committee (JIC) led the first, while the second was created under the auspices of the chiefs of staff. Both committees concluded that greater coordination between SIS and SOE was required, but neither directly advocated shutting SOE down. The report of the first committee recommended that both organizations be placed under a single head, creating a Special Operations Branch and a Special Intelligence Branch. At first it appeared that an autonomous successor to SOE was being contemplated within a single overseas intelligence structure. However, when the Foreign Office took over control of SOE the bureaucratic battle in Whitehall shifted decisively in favour of SIS, and in the process SOE lost its former protector and advocate, the MEW (which had been wound up). It was then decided that Menzies, the head of SIS, would lead the new combined organization. By early 1946 it was clear that any combination would be on the terms of SIS, and this meant subsuming SOE completely within SIS—in effect returning to the situation prior to 1940, before section D had been separated and placed into a new service.[51]

Thus ended the SOE, one of the most successful intelligence organizations of the Second World War. If it had not quite set Europe ablaze, it did manage to place and maintain networks of agents in a host of occupied countries. They had undertaken many significant operations, the effect and outcome of which—in most instances—outweighed the investment in people, equipment, money and time. Where there had been failures, most notably in the Netherlands and in Singapore and Malaya, there had also been successes, such as vital and spectacular operations in Norway and the pre-D-Day networks of agents in France (whose work made German military movements extremely difficult in the months after the allied invasion). Nor in reality did the SOE influence cease, as its staff and ethos dominated SIS's training in the post-war years. Early Cold War operations in Soviet-occupied Europe—Hungary and the Baltic states—also had the hallmark of SOE, and were led by former SOE staff.[52]

The legacy of SOE

A little-known camp run by SOE developed an undeserved notoriety after the war and influenced *The Prisoner*, the cult television series of the 1960s. The camp at Inverlair, given the cover name of the 'Number 6 Special Workshop School' but nicknamed the 'cooler' by SOE in London, was set up to house prospective agents deemed unsuitable for operations after initial training. The secret information acquired during training meant that they could not be released into general society; they therefore needed to 'live in retirement'—the camp at Inverlair—until the end of the war.[53]

Those placed there were generally foreign nationals, and although they were housed in some comfort and could leave the camp during the day to mix with locals, the situation naturally caused frustration. Some of the failed agents had difficult personalities; others were physically unsuitable for secretive work, such as the man who, according to the camp's head, 'couldn't have made an agent because he was so outstandingly ugly. He'd be recognised anywhere—once seen, never forgotten. He had no teeth at all, except two gold tusks, two incisors.'[54] Needless to say, the reality was much more mundane than the programme's depiction of Patrick McGoohan's character ('Number 6') trying unsuccessfully to escape from 'the village'.

Yet it is the individuals themselves who have secured SOE's lasting legacy. Young, clever and undeniably brave, the agents knew that their chances of survival were slim, and many were captured through no fault of their own—victims of double agents, poor equipment, hostile terrain or simply the arbitrary fortunes of war. Among the most celebrated are Odette Hallowes and Violette Szabo (both commemorated in classic films), Noor Inayat Khan, Francis Cammaerts, Christine Granville, George Starr and Pearl Witherington. Their fates, revealed in their National Archives files, were varied. Hallowes was captured along with Peter Churchill when the Carte network collapsed, and was cruelly tortured before being sent to Ravensbruck concentration camp, which she survived; the less fortunate Szabo was executed at the same camp at the age of 23. Khan—the first female radio operative dropped into France—worked for the Prosper network, but was eventually betrayed after its leaders were arrested and executed in Dachau in December 1944. Granville, a member of the Jockey network in France, was recruited by the SOE after her activities in Hungary and Poland; she went on to secure the release of Cammaerts, the network's leader, from the Germans in 1944. Cammaerts himself headed up a huge force prior to the D-Day landings, overcoming initial concerns by the SOE authorities about his distinctive, 6ft 4in height, while George Starr—under the cover of a retired Belgian mining engineer—ran the Wheelwright network. He established the 'Armagnac Battallion' and proved particularly successful in uniting the factions that were the bane of SOE, bringing Communist and anti-Communist resistance groups together to fight against the Germans. They, and many others like them, became legends after the war and have remained sources of fascination ever since, their extraordinary stories revealing the human cost of 'setting Europe ablaze'.

7 | Scientific and Technical Intelligence

The 20th century witnessed a revolution in the military application of both science and technology. The ironclad warship was replaced by the Dreadnought and the submarine, and the dirigible gave way to the fighter plane and bomber. Mounted cavalry were replaced on the battlefield by the machine gun, poison gas and tank regiments. The need to keep abreast of technological advances, and to monitor the developments of potential adversaries, became a critical aspect of military strategy in the new industrial age. New forms of intelligence were required: scientific intelligence, responsible for evaluating scientific techniques and processes with potential military application; and technical intelligence, more narrowly focused on advances and limitations in weapons and equipment. The division between these two areas is not always clear-cut, and advances in one can lead to developments in another. Nevertheless, in a modern industrial state a strong scientific and technological infrastructure is an essential component of economic and military power.

Defence research establishments

In the early 20th century the responsibility for gathering scientific and technical intelligence was undertaken by individual service ministries. The information gathered was of two types, open source and covert. To gather open source material, military attachés posted abroad simply attended army parades, visited training establishments and monitored reports on the deployment of new military equipment. Information gained in this manner was forwarded home for collation and analysis. By convention, military attachés were not involved with covert intelligence, obtained by more clandestine means—usually by agents, willing to pass over information for a price, and defectors, able to provide details of military hardware and research programmes.

Once acquired, the information was passed to government research establishments to evaluate its potential.

All three services (navy, army and air force) operated a range of experimental establishments. Some of these had been established in the 19th century, but it was not until the outbreak of the First World War that the research establishments began systematically to investigate the military implications of science and technology.[1] A major concern for the British army was the Germans' use of poison gas in the trenches, which began in April 1915 at the start of the second Battle of Ypres. The gas should not have surprised the allies, as its imminent use on the Western front had been revealed by captured German soldiers. Their warnings, however, were dismissed as alarmist, and no further action had been taken. In 1916 an experimental company of the Royal Engineers was formed to develop countermeasures at Porton in Wiltshire. Known as the Trench Warfare Department, its early work centred on the release and dissemination of gas from cylinders, artillery shells and grenades. Analysing intact shells from abandoned or overrun German positions was an important source of intelligence in developing more effective respirators. Gaining intelligence on the types and volumes of gases possessed by Germany, and indications of their intended use, also helped lower the casualty rate by reducing the risk of surprise upon which gas attacks relied.[2]

Away from the battlefield, a further concern was the threat posed to British naval supremacy by the newly developed U-boat, able to sink ships with its torpedoes while remaining undetected beneath the waves. The development of some form of submarine detection device was therefore a priority, and in July 1915 the Admiralty established the Board of Invention and Research with the aim of producing a workable solution to this and other problems. Though the secretariat of the board remained mainly naval, its creation marked the beginning of civilian scientific participation within the Admiralty. Many fellows of the Royal Society, including Sir Ernest Rutherford, Sir Oliver Lodge and Sir William Crookes, were members of its Scientific Panel.

By 1916 the board had developed an active sound detection device using quartz piezoelectric crystals. Records in the National Archives show that a prototype was produced for testing in mid-1917 and housed in a metal dome beneath a ship's hull. High frequency beams—audible 'pings'—were sent out and bounced back when they hit a submarine. The time that passed before an echo was received allowed the range of the submarine to be determined and the pitch of the echo revealed whether it was approaching or moving away.[3] The work was undertaken in utmost secrecy, with care being taken not to alert the Germans to the use of quartz. The word used to describe the early work was given the cover name ASD, from which came the British acronym ASDIC. In response to a question from the *Oxford English Dictionary*, the Admiralty concocted the story that the letters stood for 'Allied Submarine Detection Investigation Committee'. This is still widely believed, although no committee bearing this name has ever been found in the Admiralty archives.

In 1918 the functions of the board were transferred to the newly created Scientific Research and Experiment Department, responsible for coordinating the activities of all the various naval experimental stations that had sprung up during the war.[4] Similar establishments were created for the army and air force. A particular concern during the inter-war years was the rapidly increasing size and sophistication of Germany's armed forces—especially its air force—and the scale of development was closely monitored by air intelligence. In 1934 they produced a report, jointly written with the Industrial Intelligence Committee, stating that the monthly output of aero engines by German industry had risen from 60 to 100. More worryingly, it contended that the German government was developing 'types of sports and commercial aircraft which in time of war may be rapidly converted into efficient fighter, reconnaissance and bombing aircraft'.[5] Following the report, a large-scale exercise was conducted to test the effectiveness of Britain's air defences, with mock raids carried out on London. Even though the routes and targets were known in advance, well over half the bombers reached their intended targets with little difficulty. To address these deficiencies, the Air Ministry increased the priority given to air intelligence and announced increases in both finance and suitably trained staff.

To improve cooperation between scientists and the intelligence community, the Air Ministry appointed a scientific liaison officer, Dr R. V. Jones, to work within the air intelligence section of the Secret Intelligence Service (SIS), headed by Group Captain Frederick Winterbotham. In making the appointment, the ministry expressed the hope that other service departments would join it to form a combined scientific section. However, the increased priority now given to scientific intelligence stood in stark contrast to the fate of technical intelligence. Both the Air Ministry and the War Office relied on their geographical departments to provide them with updates on military technology.

Only the Admiralty's Naval Intelligence Department possessed a technical section, and that consisted of just one officer. It would take the shock of war to remedy these deficiencies.

Developments in the Second World War

On the evening of 28 October 1939, a Heinkel He-111 bomber of the German Luftwaffe strayed off course and crash-landed in Scotland. It was to prove valuable for scientific intelligence, as hidden among the wreckage was a Lorenz blind landing receiver. Developed in the 1930s for use by commercial airliners, the Lorenz system was the forerunner of the modern autopilot, allowing aircraft to take off and land at night or in bad weather. On further analysis by air intelligence, it was discovered that the German device was far more sensitive than standard models, which usually had a range of 30 miles, and was capable of being used for long-range navigation. In March 1940, a scrap of paper retrieved from a second downed He-111 was found to contain enigmatic reference to a navigation aid called Knickebein.[6]

Further information on Knickebein was obtained from a variety of sources, including prisoner interrogations and signals intelligence.[7] As the evidence mounted, it began to point to an alarming realization: the German air force had perfected a long-range radio navigation system to direct bombers to their targets. It was guessed that Knickebein itself (translated as 'crooked leg') referred to the 'ZZ' course of an aircraft homing in along a beam, but in fact the system consisted of a pair of transmitters located at separate sites. The beams from these transmitters intersected over the intended target; German bombers travelled along the first beam, dropping their bombs as soon as the beams intersected. According to a report on Knickebein, now held among the Air Historical Branch papers at the National Archives, two frequencies and two transmitter sites had been pinned down by the end of June. This was largely due to the retrieval of a number of W/T logs, such as that recovered from a German wireless operator shot down on 19 June. Realizing that he still had his notebook with him, and desperate to prevent it from falling into enemy hands, 'he tore it up into small pieces (a figure of 3,000 is given) and attempted to bury them. He was observed to do this, and the pieces were recovered and sent to A.I.1.(k) [Air Intelligence Branch], who spent till 3 a.m. the following morning piecing them together.'[8]

The news of the discovery was passed to Churchill, who demanded solid proof. To provide the necessary evidence, three aircraft from the recently formed Wireless Intelligence and Development Unit were modified to carry the American Hallicrafters S-27 wideband radio receiver. On the evening of 21 June 1940, one of the aircraft picked up a signal from one of the Knickebein transmitters. Under heavy cloud and in darkness, the flight crew then followed the beam until they received a signal from the second transmitter. To Churchill's consternation, the point where the two beams crossed was directly above the Rolls-Royce aero engine factory at Derby.[9]

The evidence was conclusive, and the unnamed author of the Knickebein report finished by stating:

> The possibility that Knickebein is an elaborate hoax may be discounted. At least sixteen independent sources have been obtained, and while some of them could conceivably have been inspired, the physical evidence of the sharpness of the beam, which would never have been gratuitously revealed, and of the increased sensitivity of the Lorenz receiver, are too subtle even for German thoroughness to have executed.
>
> The writer trusts that an expression of his appreciation of having worked with the group of officers mentioned in this report, as well as with others whose contributions are nameless but necessary, will be accepted. If our good fortunes hold, we may yet pull the Crooked Leg.[10]

To disrupt the German bombing offensive, countermeasures designed to nullify the Knickebein system were quickly developed: the battle of the beams had begun. The organization with the most expertise in this area was the Telecommunications Research Establishment (TRE) at Malvern. Staff at TRE soon produced a range of equipment that either jammed the signal or deflected the beam away from its true course. The Germans then deployed an improved system, but this too was countered by TRE. Scientific intelligence had demonstrated its worth.

The revelations about Knickebein appeared to confirm the validity of the so-called Oslo report. Delivered to the British embassy in Norway by 'a German well wisher', its receipt and history are described in a document written by R. V. Jones, an early supporter of this 'casual source'.[11] His work is now preserved at the National Archives, along with the report itself. According to Jones, a letter had been received by the British naval attaché in Oslo asking whether the British would be interested in receiving information on new German scientific developments—if so, they were to alter the normal preamble to their German news broadcast on one particular evening. This was done and the document duly arrived, along with parts of a high-tech proximity fuse then under development in Germany. The seven-page report contained a wealth of information concerning the latest advances in German military technology. However, the information in the report was so detailed and seemed so far-fetched that British intelligence was initially extremely sceptical, believing it to be a plant. According to Jones, their argument—'given here as a warning for the future'—ran that since

> '(i) the few portions which could be checked were accurate and (ii) no one man in Germany could possibly know so much so accurately in so wide a field as was covered by the report, then either (iii) the unconfirmed portions were well-meaning but inaccurate, or (iv) they were planted by a wily enemy who calculated to make them more convincing by virtue of the accuracy of the checkable items.' In fact, the information the report contained proved to be accurate in nearly every respect. It was a goldmine, and Jones later contended that 'no other single report contained so much valuable material and gave such an early warning'.[12]

The Oslo report also indicated that the Germans were attempting to develop radio-controlled missiles and long-range rockets. The first concrete evidence concerning German rocket development occurred in December 1942, when intelligence reports from Poland indicated that the German army had test-launched a five-ton rocket with a range of 120 miles. In January 1943 air reconnaissance highlighted unusual objects at the German experimental research station at Peenemunde on the Baltic coast. These included tower-like structures and a number of cylindrical objects approximately 35-feet long, with fins protruding from one end. Further reports from Polish intelligence described the launch of pilotless planes that made a noise 'as if an empty iron barrel was being rolled on a hard surface'. It was also confirmed that Peenemunde was a construction and research centre for rocket aircraft and 'houses a factory employing some 8,000 persons, laboratories and an experimental airfield. All the roads are closed within a distance of some kilometres from the Peenemunde station, and access is possible with special passes only.'[13]

To evaluate the intelligence, Churchill established the Crossbow committee under Duncan Sandys, his son-in-law and parliamentary secretary to the Ministry of Supply.[14] It soon became clear that the Germans were developing two types of rocket weapon: a pilotless aircraft (V-1) and a ballistic missile (V-2). On the night of 17–18 August, Peenemunde came under sustained attack from a force of 597 RAF heavy bombers. The attack forced the Germans to move production of the rockets underground in the Hartz mountains near Nordhausen. Air intelligence also revealed the construction of what appeared to be a number of ski ramps in northern France. Intelligence from a variety of sources revealed that these were launching sites for the V-1 flying bomb. A review of the available intelligence, now in the National Archives, came to the following conclusion:

> There is good reason to believe that for some time past the enemy have been investigating the possibilities of pilotless aircraft for use as offensive weapons. More recently there have been indications that the experimental work has borne fruit, and that one or more types of these aircraft may have passed the development stage and be ready for operation.[15]

The launch sites so far identified were targeted in a series of bombing raids, which succeeded in destroying many of the installations. However, although the bombing delayed the threat from the V-weapons, it did not eliminate it: the first V-1 attack was launched against London in June 1944, killing eight civilians. In the following months a total of 2,419 V-1s exploded in London, killing about 6,184 people and injuring 17,981. The attacks only stopped when allied troops overran the launching sites in France. The V-1 attacks were soon followed by the V-2s, with the first rocket slamming into Chiswick on 8 September 1943, killing three people and devastating an entire street. In the weeks that followed, 518 V-2 rockets were fired at London, killing 2,724 people and injuring over 6,000 more.

To avoid panic, the government announced that the first V-2 explosion had been caused by a ruptured gas main. It was only on 10 November 1944, after Hitler had publicly proclaimed the existence of the V-2 rocket, that Churchill informed parliament and the world that England had been under rocket attack for the last few weeks. Unlike the V-1, which could be brought down by fighter planes and anti-aircraft batteries, the V-2 rocket was impossible to intercept in flight. The only effective defence against the V-2 was to destroy the launch sites. However, 'as the firing points are virtually invisible from the air until they have fired', this proved virtually impossible.[16]

The fight against the new German super weapon was aided by the receipt of vital technical details of the V-2 guidance system from Polish resistance agents who had recovered an intact missile from the banks of the river Bug in May 1944.[17] Within Britain, deception was employed in the concoction of false impact reports sent through a network of double agents. The reports, which were compiled by the Twenty

Committee, were so convincing that one of the Double Cross agents, codenamed Garbo, was awarded the Iron Cross (p. 42). Tricked into believing their aim was true, the majority of V-1s and V-2s targeted at London fell in less populated areas east of the city. It is estimated that the deception saved the lives of 1,300 Londoners, prevented a further 10,000 injuries and avoided the destruction of over 23,000 properties. The German rocket attacks continued until March 1945 when the allied advances into Western Europe overran the missile batteries or forced them beyond the range of the United Kingdom.[18]

The hunt for German scientists

The technological advances made by Germany during the war were impressive. In addition to the ballistic rocket, German scientists and technicians had developed the world's first operational jet fighter, the Messerschmitt Me-262, a guided anti-aircraft missile—the *Wasserfal* —and the world's first air-to-air missile, the Ruhrstahl X-4. Many of these weapons were in their early stages, and if Germany had had the time to develop them further the outcome of the war could well have been different. At the end of the war, with Hitler on the verge of defeat, allied governments began to scramble over the ruins of the Third Reich to uncover the Nazis' military secrets. The stakes were high—whoever managed to seize the technology would have a signifi-cant military advantage in the post-war world. To prevent the bulk of Germany's scientific and technological know-how falling into the hands of the advancing Russian forces, allied intelligence officers were rapidly despatched to the front line. The advance guard was the Field Information Agency, Technical (FIAT), established in May 1945 to recover and exploit Germany's scientific and military technology.[19] FIAT was divided into a British and American element but tended to work as a single entity, with its headquarters located at Hochst, near Frankfurt. The British element was directed by the British Intelligence Objectives Sub-committee (BIOS), originally part of the Ministry of Economic Warfare, but later absorbed into the German section of the Foreign Office. Records and reports of their varied work are now held in the National Archives.[20]

Tracking down Germany's scientists, engineers and technicians (especially those with specialist knowledge of ballistics, radar and nuclear physics) was the role of FIAT's Enemy Personnel Exploitation Section (EPES).[21] The responsibility for seizing scientists and technicians fell to a specialized, highly mobile army unit known as T-Force that raced ahead of British troops, tracking down individuals and technical artefacts.[22] Once located, the captured scientists underwent interrogation at Garmisch and Witzenhausen, and if considered sufficiently important were offered jobs in Britain or the United States. These people were valuable commodities and sometimes more drastic measures were required. In a series of operations, codenamed Matchbox and Top Hat, small 'snatch squads' were assembled to recover scientists from the Soviet-occupied zone of Germany and to smuggle them—sometimes against their will—into allied-controlled territory.[23] In July 1945 the combined chiefs of staff agreed the terms of a secret agreement that provided for the 'exploitation' of a certain number of German scientists by the United States. They would not be allowed to take their families, who would be taken care of by authorities in the West. The only stipulation was that no war criminal was to be included in the transfer.

In terms of hardware, the majority of the spoils went to the Americans, with over 300 trainloads of V-2 parts shipped to the US. The principal design staff, including Wernher von Braun and Walter Dornberger, were also in American hands after surrendering to units of the US 44th Infantry Division in the Bavarian resort of Oberjoch, near the Austrian border. Following their surrender, von Braun and his colleagues were flown to the United States as part of Operation Paperclip, a programme that sanctioned the employment of many German scientists on US military projects. The German rocket engineers were stationed at Fort Bliss in Texas and made significant contributions to the US ballistic missile programme, which in its early years relied on information derived from the V-2 system.

The British also gained valuable scientific intelligence by exploiting German sources. In Operation Backfire, a team of German engineers, 'supervised by British technical experts', assembled a number of V-2 rockets using captured plans and equipment. The programme proved to be something of a challenge (plate 30), as the following report from General Cameron, the commander of Operation Backfire, to Professor Charles Ellis, scientific adviser to the War Office, reveals:

> The assembly of rockets which will fire is turning out to be a lengthy process and more difficult than we had expected. We are using components, some of which have come out of Nordhausen, but many of which have been collected from farms, holes in the ground, railway sidings, and so on, all over Germany, and even our Nordhausen

components have suffered from exposure to the weather. We have found that even such assemblies as we have cannot be accepted as workable and must be dismantled and put together again. We are short of working drawings, wiring diagrams, etc. The state of our equipment is such that we must test everything and we have not got the testing apparatus. I am unhappy that no one from the War Office has yet had an opportunity of coming out here and seeing for themselves what facilities are available, and the state of our resources.[24]

A further difficulty encountered by Cameron was America's continued insistence on the lion's share of the spoils. The issue came to a head in August, when Colonel Toftoy, the director of all rocket development in the United States, demanded the 'return' of 27 German technicians currently deployed by the British on Operation Backfire. Cameron stood firm, insisting that without the technicians he would soon reach the stage where 'I lack the technical advice necessary to overcome the problems involved in the assembly of rockets from the mass of miscellaneous parts'. The Americans eventually relented, and on 2 October 1945 a V-2 rocket was successfully launched across the North Sea from a site at Cuxhaven on the German coast (plate 31), 'landing within 3 miles of the aiming point'.[25] The British also secured documents and equipment on the German guided weapons programme under Operations Surgeon and Abstract.

The recruitment of German scientists was overseen by a panel of experts under Sir Charles Darwin, scientific adviser to the War Office and director of the National Physical Laboratory.[26] Compared to the Americans, the British acquired only a small number of German scientists, with approximately 100 relocated to Britain by 1947. On arrival, most of the scientists were put to work by the RAF at the Rocket Propulsion Department at Westcott.[27] A significant number of German scientists were captured by the Red Army and sent to various secret locations throughout Russia to assist in the organization of missile production and the design of the R-1, the Soviet Union's first ballistic missile, which was a direct copy of the V-2.

A major concern for the allies was to determine Germany's progress in exploring atomic energy. Scientific literature showed that the Germans had started uranium research prior to the war, but little was known about wartime developments. A small team of technicians and military personnel was assembled to discover the secrets of Hitler's nuclear programme. Known as the Alsos mission and headed by Samuel Goudsmit, professor of physics at the University of Michigan, the team raced through Germany with the advancing US army. For Goudsmit, the lack of intelligence on the German nuclear programme was obvious: 'No ordinary spy could get us the information we wanted for the simple reason that he lacked the scientific training to know what was essential. Only scientifically qualified personnel could get us that and a Mata Hari with a Ph. D. in physics is rare, even in detective fiction.'[28]

The fear underpinning the Alsos mission was that the Nazis had developed a crude nuclear device and would be prepared to use it in a last-ditch defence of the German homeland. Another concern was that, even if the Germans had not yet perfected a viable nuclear weapon, their advances in atomic science would fall into Russian hands, greatly assisting any future Soviet nuclear weapons programme. In early 1945 the Alsos team examined research laboratories and interrogated scientists and technicians involved in Germany's atomic bomb project. It soon emerged that Nazi Germany was not close to creating a viable weapon, a result that Goudsmit attributed—rather simplistically—to the inability of science to function under a totalitarian state.[29] A further team, known as the Target Intelligence Committee (TICOM), undertook a similar mission to gather information on German developments in cryptography.[30]

Post-war planning

During the Second World War, the military application of science and technology was essential to allied success. This convergence presented the government with opportunities as well as challenges, as the development of radar, the ballistic missile and the atomic bomb placed new demands on an already overstretched defence budget. The need to address the strategic reality of the modern age was expressed succinctly in the 1946 Defence White Paper:

> In the design and development of weapons and equipment, in the study of tactical methods, and in foreseeing and counteracting the enemy's technical progress, scientists played an invaluable part. Experience during the war showed that any future development of our central organisation for defence would be incomplete if it did not provide throughout for the closest possible integration of scientific and military men.[31]

If no one questioned the need to maintain a strong scientific base, the best ways to achieve this were not yet certain. To examine the post-war organization of scientific and technical intelligence, the Joint

Intelligence Committee (JIC) assembled a small committee of experts chaired by Professor Patrick Blackett, a future Nobel laureate and the wartime director of naval operational research at the Admiralty. Other members included Professor Charles Ellis and Dr R.V. Jones of the Air Ministry (p. 213), assistant director of intelligence (science) within SIS.[32] This latter post, established as a separate section from Air Intelligence in 1941, was responsible for providing scientific and technical intelligence to all Whitehall departments and not just the Air Ministry. Predictably, Blackett and Jones did not see eye to eye; they held radically different visions concerning the future organization of scientific and technical intelligence. Blackett favoured a decentralized system with each service retaining its own scientific and technical sections; Jones pressed for a fully integrated scientific and technical service with all elements centralized within SIS.[33]

The JIC accepted Blackett's recommendations. As a result scientific and technical intelligence was not contained in one central organization, but spread across Whitehall. SIS retained its Scientific Intelligence Section, while each of the three service departments had its own scientific intelligence staff headed by a scientific intelligence adviser. Technical intelligence was treated in a similar manner. In an attempt to foster inter-service collaboration, all six sections (the scientific and technical sections of army, navy and air force) were housed together in the same building in Bryanston Square. They met collectively as the Joint Scientific and Technical Intelligence Committee (JS/JTIC), the rotating chairmanship held by each service for three months at a time.

The sections' base at Bryanston Square, which also housed the recently established Joint Intelligence Bureau (JIB), was less than auspicious. Located north of Marble Arch and far away from its main customers in Whitehall, its main claim to fame was a pervasive smell of rotting linoleum. The service was viewed as a dumping ground for misfits. Moreover, in an attempt to preserve Anglo-American nuclear collaboration, atomic intelligence was not transferred to JS/JTIC, instead remaining the responsibility of the Directorate of Atomic Energy under the control of Commander Eric Welsh (SIS) and Michael Perrin (Ministry of Supply). As a result, one of the most crucial elements of post-war defence was separated from the rest of Britain's scientific and technical intelligence effort.

The primary role of JS/JTIC was to produce assessment reports, relying on a steady stream of scientific and technical information gathered from both open and clandestine sources.[34] Russia was the primary target, with information sought on the location and activities of defence research establishments, atomic energy, biological and chemical warfare, guided weapons, and radio and radar development. The Intelligence Division of the Control Commission for Germany (British Element) and its Scientific and Technical Intelligence Branch (STIB) was a major source of raw intelligence.[35] Valuable information was also provided in the early post-war period by repatriated German prisoners of war. Many of them were scientists, engineers and technicians who had been forced to work in the Soviet Union and defected to the West on their return to East Germany. To exploit this intelligence, STIB initiated a systematic interrogation programme, codenamed Dragon Return.[36] Once collated the various reports, the majority now in the National Archives, were forwarded to London for evaluation.

Intelligence machinery

The continued effectiveness of scientific and technical intelligence soon came under question. Sir Henry Tizard, the government's chief scientific adviser, dismissed the JS/JTIC as a waste of money, believing that it had contributed no worthwhile intelligence to help Britain's research and development. He came to this scathing assessment for straightforward reasons: JS/JTIC was neither a producer nor consumer of intelligence; it had no fixed chairman and attempted to direct a staff of some 20 scientists and 40 technicians without a central secretariat. Tizard demanded improvement in both the quality and quantity of scientific and economic intelligence from potential enemy countries, with priority given to scientific programmes and planning. 'The clearer our picture of the nature of the attack we have to face the more effectively we can plan our defence programme.'[37]

Tizard took up his concerns with the minister of defence, A.V. Alexander, who initiated a full-scale review of the UK intelligence organization, 'to enable the intelligence services to provide as comprehensive a cover as possible of foreign countries, and particularly of Russia, and to ensure the necessary degree of coordination of intelligence requirements'. The review was undertaken by Air Chief Marshall Sir Douglas Evill, the former head of the RAF delegation in Washington during the war. His findings were presented to the chiefs of staff in July 1947.[38] Evill paid particular attention to the organization of scientific and technical intelligence, which he considered had serious weaknesses especially on the scientific side. He recommended that the Joint Scientific Intelligence Committee (JSIC) should be disbanded and reconstituted with a new chairman and secretariat to coordinate work throughout the whole scientific field. The chairman should be a first-rank scientist and sit as a regular member of the JIC. To emphasize the importance attached to the position, he recommended that the new chairman should have an office within the Ministry of Defence and get full access to atomic intelligence.

The first occupant of this new post was Professor David Brunt, a former president of the Royal Meteorological Society and member of the Chemical Warfare Committee at Porton Down. The appointment was apparently not a success, with Brunt retiring from the role in less than a year, citing ill health. Brunt believed the job was impossible and that whoever was persuaded to take up the position 'was either a saint or a fool'. His successor, Dr Bertie Blount, was a former Special Operations Executive (SOE) scientific adviser who had been a member of the secret wartime team tasked with examining ways of assassinating Hitler (p. 192). After the war, Blount was appointed director of the Research Branch in the Control Commission for Germany. A chemist by training, he was largely responsible for transforming the Kaiser Wilhelm Laboratory, one of the most dynamic scientific research laboratories in Germany, away from its wartime past and into its peacetime role as the Max Planck Institute.

On assuming the chairmanship of JSIC in September 1949, Blount embarked on a similar transformation. He broke down the old military divisions, based on service departments, and replaced them with functional sections studying electronics, chemistry and hydrodynamics. The JIC broadly welcomed these developments, but believed they should go further, with the JSIC being replaced by a Directorate of Scientific Intelligence based in the Ministry of Defence. This would give Blount greater autonomy over the future direction of work and remove scientific intelligence from military control, the military being served directly via the Joint Technical Intelligence Committee (JTIC), emerging from Evill's review largely unscathed. In approving the changes, the prime minister expressed disquiet about progress in the field of scientific intelligence. In responding to the criticism, the minister of defence contended that the new arrangements under Blount would produce much better results, but with one significant caveat: 'It has to be borne in mind, however, that the task of the scientific intelligence organisation is not only something quite new, but is particularly difficult when the country about which information is required is a totalitarian state like Russia, where every one is under the closest super-vision and all foreigners are treated with suspicion and hostility.'[39]

The Directorate of Scientific Intelligence (DSI) was eventually established in April 1950, the three service scientific intelligence sections amalgamating under Blount who was given the title of director of scientific intelligence. These reforms reflected developments in America where the newly formed CIA, quick to realize the importance of scientific developments, had established the Special Office of Scientific Intelligence. In December 1950 Blount visited Washington and met with his US counterpart and fellow research chemist, Dr Harris Marshall Chadwell. The two organizations were soon exchanging assessments with many reports routinely exchanged. The reports, now in the National Archives, covered a broad spectrum of work and included such diverse topics as the development of Soviet guided weapons and electronic research in the USSR to an evaluation of a Russian transistorized hearing aid.[40]

The increased emphasis now being placed on scientific intelligence led some to question the continued validity of traditional espionage operations. One prominent critic of the latter was Air Chief Marshal Sir William Elliot, head of the British Joint Services Mission in Washington. Writing to Sir Norman Brook, the cabinet secretary, in October 1951, Elliot expressed his 'misgivings' on the current state of the SIS. Brook defended the agency and cautioned against placing faith exclusively in scientific advances.

> I do not share your view that the days of the agent are over. It is true that the more 'scientific' methods of collecting intelligence have pro-duced, from time to time, some spectacular results; and they are at the moment producing a greater volume of valuable intelligence than the older methods. But like those older methods, they depend to some extent on a lucky break; and the luck may at any time turn against them. It would be a fatal mistake to rely exclusively or too much on any one method of collecting intelligence: we must keep our lines out in all directions, and by all available means, so that we may be in a position to exploit a lucky break when it comes. I believe that the distribution of our resources between the various methods, scientific and other, is about right.[41]

In October 1951 Attlee's Labour Party was defeated in the general election, with the Conservatives under Winston Churchill returning to power. Blount soon found himself out of favour and resigned to become deputy secretary at the Department of Scientific and Industrial Research

(DSIR). His replacement at the DSI was R. V. Jones, who had spent the post-war years as professor of natural philosophy at Aberdeen University. Jones took up his position in 1952, but resigned at the end of 1953 —primarily due to the government's continued policy of separating atomic energy from scientific intelligence, as ridiculous to him as isolating the jet engine from air intelligence. After Jones's resignation, the post remained unfilled, and following a critical report by Sir Frederick Brundrett, the government's chief scientific adviser, the DSI was absorbed into the JIB as the Division of Scientific Intelligence.[42] Eventually, in 1957 atomic energy intelligence was transferred to the JIB, becoming the Division of Atomic Energy Intelligence (DAEI).[43] The centralization process was completed in 1964 when, following the creation of the unified Ministry of Defence, DSI and DAEI were merged with the single-service technical intelligence branches. They formed the Directorate of Scientific and Technical Intelligence (DSTI) of the Defence Intelligence Staff (DIS) under General Kenneth Strong, who became director general of intelligence, Ministry of Defence, until his retirement on 9 May 1966.[44]

The Russian bomb

For the British and American authorities after 1945 the paucity of intelligence meant that analysis assumed a critical role. The resources and expertise of Soviet counter-espionage presented formidable challenges to Western operations within Russia, operations further compromised by the penetration of intelligence services by men such as Kim Philby and George Blake. It is now clear that the Soviet bomb took the British and American scientific and intelligence communities by surprise; nobody doubted the Soviets would develop it, but the timescale was difficult to gauge and opinions differed. The first British estimate—in 1945—was of a Soviet-produced bomb in three to four years, and this eventually proved closest to the truth. The planning assumption of the chiefs of staff was that the Soviets would have deployed atomic and biological weapons by 1956 to 1957. The JIC believed that, while it was possible that the Soviets might have a crude bomb by January 1951, the earliest date for the production of a fully deliverable weapon was January 1954.[45]

On 23 September 1949 Britain's prime minister, Clement Attlee, stood on the steps of 10 Downing Street and read out a brief statement that, within recent weeks, evidence had emerged that an atomic explosion had occurred within the Soviet Union. The evidence was provided by a joint Anglo-American programme that routinely monitored air samples from around the periphery of the Soviet Union. On 3 September 1949 a specially converted B-29 belonging to the US Air Force Office of Atomic Energy (AFOAT) collected samples at 18,500 feet over the Kamchatka peninsula. They were found to contain a radioactive fingerprint obtainable only from a nuclear explosion. The British were informed that the radioactive cloud was about to pass over Scotland and the RAF immediately scrambled a Lincoln bomber, specially adapted to monitor radioactivity in the atmosphere. The British results proved beyond doubt that there had been an atomic explosion, most probably caused by a plutonium bomb detonated between 26 and 30 August 1949.[46] To ensure that the Russians could not identify the method of detection, public confirmation of the explosion was delayed until the end of September.

News of the Soviet explosion forced Anglo-American intelligence to reassess their assumptions. Evidence that the Soviets had tested a bomb followed the arrest of the atomic scientist Allan Nunn May and preceded that of Klaus Fuchs (plate 32), both of whom had worked on the US bomb project. The espionage activities of Nunn May, code-named Primrose, were first drawn to the attention of the British authorities following the defection of the Russian diplomat Igor Gouzenko in September 1945. The information provided by Gouzenko included over 100 documents on Soviet espionage activities. These identified Nunn May as the Soviet agent ALEX who had been passing details of the US bomb programme to his handler, the Soviet military attaché Colonel Zabotin. In March 1946 Nunn May was arrested and charged under the Official Secrets Act. Following his trial, he was sentenced to 10 years in prison.[47]

Nunn May's espionage did not inflict damage on the same scale as that of Klaus Fuchs, who had worked on both the American and British atomic programmes, including the development of the more powerful hydrogen bomb. Fuchs, a German-born scientist with links to the Communist Party, later confessed that between 1942 and his arrest in February 1950 he had volunteered atomic information to Soviet intelligence. This included key data on the production rates of uranium-235 and plutonium, from which the Soviets could calculate the number of atomic bombs possessed by the United States. Assessing how far this information had accelerated Soviet research was an immediate worry. However, Sir Henry Tizard was so dismissive of Russian scientific and technical capability that he attributed the recent Soviet test to the acquisition of complete blueprints from its overseas spy network, even wondering whether the Soviets had stolen some plutonium from the Americans. Files in the National Archives show that the JIC concurred with this analysis of Russian inventiveness, concluding:

> It seems certain that the scientific potential of the USSR although immense in numbers, is in fact less formidable than it appears. It is perhaps a reasonable deduction that, while much competent and original work is being done and will continue to be done, Soviet scientists are unlikely to rise to the greatest heights of scientific thought and imagination, from which the major advances in human knowledge proceed.[48]

The Soviet Union was a closed society and obtaining human intelligence on its bomb project proved difficult. Indirect methods were thus often adopted in order to assess the progress of Soviet nuclear research, for example monitoring the atmosphere around the Soviet Union's perimeter for radioactive particles. By monitoring these gases, particularly krypton, it was possible to determine a crude measure of Soviet plutonium production. In 1953 a collaborative Anglo-American project was undertaken to measure the levels of atmospheric krypton. Known as 'Music', the project was used to estimate the production of plutonium and hence the size of the Soviet nuclear arsenal.[49] This information was supplemented by analysing the output of uranium ore, believed to be a limiting factor in the production of nuclear weapons. It was known that high-grade ore was being mined in Czechoslovakia, with production also taking place in the Uzbek and Khazak regions of central Asia.

The size of the Soviet atomic stockpile was a crucial factor in estimating their capabilities and intentions. By 1952 the agreed Anglo-American estimate of the Soviet stockpile was between 70 and 100 atomic bombs, rising to 190 weapons by 1954. Lacking hard intelligence, these early estimates were based on educated guesswork, with the realization that the actual figures could be as low as half or as high as twice that amount. Such uncertainty over the stockpile's size was due to the difficulty of running agents within a police state. According to Sir Frederick Brundrett, the Soviet security apparatus was at a higher level than had previously been known in the world, making all intelligence extremely sketchy.[50] The head of scientific intelligence in the Admiralty, G. L. Turney, was particularly scathing of the methods employed by atomic intelligence, believing that far better results would be available 'from a messenger or labourer in the right place than from any number of Professors of physics swanning round Europe, or even in Moscow'. It was not until the early 1960s, when other technical sources came on stream, that the British and Americans finally agreed on the size of the Soviet stockpile.

While the Soviet Union was the major target for Western intelligence, the nuclear potential of other states was also a concern. Estimating when others would join the nuclear club became a matter of great significance to diplomatic efforts to constrain the proliferation of nuclear weapons. In their 1961 estimate the JIC concluded that India could explode a nuclear device by 1964 to 1965, and that China was the only country within sight of a nuclear test, expected to take place in 1962 to 1963. Both assessments, while correct in predicting the testing of an atomic capability, were pessimistic with regard to timing: China actually tested in 1964, India in 1970.[51] The advent of satellite technology in the 1970s (see p. 160) increased the reliability of technical data and offered a means of verifying the size and disposition of Soviet nuclear forces. This in turn paved the way for a stabilization of the arms race and the beginning of détente.

Soviet rockets

While the Soviet development of the atomic bomb was an important Cold War milestone, the means of its delivery were equally critical (plates 33 and 34). The capacity to strike the US mainland was of enormous political and strategic consequence, particularly for America's European allies. The question was stark but simple: in a stand-off with the Soviet Union, would the US be prepared to sacrifice Chicago for London? It was recognized as early as 1949 that the Soviets had bombers capable of reaching US territory. The Tu-4, a copy of a captured American B-29 bomber and the only Soviet aircraft that could carry an atomic bomb, was capable of mounting one-way missions (p. 157), and Western intelligence believed that the Soviet Union possessed 150 of them. Initial estimates of Soviet ballistic missile capability reflected the important role of German scientists coopted by the Soviets—the expectation was that early Soviet models would be based on the German V-2 programme. The Soviets were known to have captured significant quantities of rocket parts, along with production and test facilities. While German expertise offered them a good start, the Russians were believed to lack the modern electronics necessary for a successful ballistic missile programme. Yet the paucity of hard intelligence was all too apparent, with the chiefs of staff concluding that there was insufficient information to estimate how many guided missiles the Soviets might have in stock by mid-1954.[52]

The US intelligence community exhibited less caution than its British counterpart and often inflated the progress made by Moscow. In 1954 it concluded that Moscow had undertaken an extensive guided weapons programme, giving highest priority to air defence missiles. By October 1955 the US believed that the Soviets had a capacity to produce missiles with a range of 600–700 miles and would most probably have an Inter Continental Ballistic Missile (ICBM) capability by 1963. The British remained more phlegmatic, Brundrett believing that the Soviets were extremely unlikely to mount a serious threat against the US mainland until 1970 at the earliest. This view was supported by Kenneth Strong, director of the JIB, who observed that intelligence estimates were repeated year to year 'and like advertisements take root. We should not forget the lack of evidence and keep open minds.'[53] Intelligence gained from U2 reconnaissance flights over the Soviet Union, which began in 1956, tended to confirm the British position and cast doubt on the numbers of front-line bombers and missiles that were claimed to be deployed by Soviet forces.

In August 1957 the Soviet Union successfully test-launched its first ICBM. This was followed on 4 October by the launch of Sputnik I, the first earth satellite, a visible demonstration that the Soviets could now strike at intercontinental distances. To assess the consequences for Western strategy, the JIC began a systematic study of Soviet missile capability. It concluded that a force of 100 missiles, each equipped with a nuclear warhead, would be deployed in the next three years. The US intelligence community was more alarmist and estimated that the Soviets would have 140–200 ICBMs by mid-1961, rising to 350–450 by mid-1963.[54] The lack of hard evidence on which these estimates were based was soon to be rectified. In the early 1960s Oleg Penkovsky began to supply the West with considerable information on the operational characteristics of the Soviet rocket forces, confirming in 1961 that the SS-4 was in serial production, but that the SS-5 was experiencing production problems. Penkovsky also contended that Khrushchev's bellicose statements on the capability of Soviet missile forces were a bluff. He believed that the Soviets possessed no more than 25 ICBMs, with an operational capability of less than 10. Images obtained from the Corona spy satellite confirmed this position, and in 1963 the figure for Soviet ICBM deployment was revised downwards to between 75 and 125. The 'missile gap', which had formed a major part of President Kennedy's election campaign, had been revealed as a myth.

Bugs and germs

In addition to its ballistic missile programme, British intelligence believed that Moscow would give high priority to biological and chemical weapons. It was known that the Red Army had both captured a Japanese bacteriological weapons facility in Manchuria and seized over 6,000 tons of German nerve gas. Intelligence received from returning German scientists also suggested that the Soviets had dismantled a full-scale manufacturing plant in Silesia and transported the entire facility back to central Russia. Prior to the war, Soviet biologists had conducted experiments using the plague virus and had established a research facility on a remote island in the Aral Sea. In reviewing the consequences for future warfare, Tizard concluded that within 10 years there would be a hundredfold increase in the effectiveness of biological weapons and that, weight for weight, 'biological warfare may be as devastating as atomic weapons'.[55]

In the face of the potential Soviet threat, Britain adopted a dual strategy: modernization of its chemical and biological warfare stocks, and development of a defence mechanism against both methods of warfare for the military and civil population. The centre for these studies was at Porton Down in Wiltshire, Britain's experimental research station. Initial work and trials were conducted using the German nerve agents Tabun and Sarin, with the majority of the research directed towards defensive measures. However, proper assessment of the effectiveness of countermeasures would require both knowledge of Soviet activity and the possession of limited amounts of potential agents, both chemical and biological.[56]

Top priority was given to countering the possible military use of nerve agents by Soviet forces. Odourless and colourless, they can be absorbed through the skin, with one drop usually sufficient to kill. Details on the Soviet programme were sparse; they were based primarily on information provided by the former Nazi scientist Walter Hirsch, forced to work on the Soviet chemical weapons programme at the end of the war. British intelligence believed that the Red Army had weaponized its stocks of Tabun, estimating the Soviet stockpile in 1952 to be around 18,000 metric tonnes. A new type of agent was discovered in the mid-1950s, 100 times more potent than previous stocks.

Known collectively as V-agents, as little as 200 micrograms was enough to kill an average person. The V-agents also possessed a similar viscosity to motor oil, and so did not degrade or wash away easily, remaining on clothes and other surfaces for long periods. It is believed the Soviets began industrial production of V-agents in 1972, with storage facilities located in Volgograd, Zaporozhye and Volsk. It is also reported that Moscow had developed a third generation of nerve agents under a top-secret programme codenamed Foliant.

In addition to nerve agents, the Soviets were also developing biological weapons. Interest in biological warfare began during the Second World War, based on fears that Nazi Germany was developing 'germ' weapons. Following the fall of France in 1940, Lord Hankey—chair of the Bacteriological Warfare Committee, among other roles—advised Churchill that the practicality of biological weapons should be investigated 'so as to put ourselves in a position to retaliate if such abominable weapons should be used against us'. Churchill agreed, and a small group of scientists went to Porton to work secretly on determining both the means and methods of British retaliation in the event of a German biological attack. The use of anthrax was considered feasible and small-scale trials were conducted on Gruinard Island on the north coast of Scotland and Penclawdd on the Welsh coast.[57]

The trials showed that, weight for weight, anthrax could be 100 times more potent than chemical munitions. In January 1942 the war cabinet sanctioned the large-scale production of anthrax and approved its use in retaliation in the event that Britain came under attack with biological weapons. By 1943, an operational stockpile of 5 million cattle cakes infected with anthrax spores had been produced at Porton. The project, codenamed Operation Vegetarian, envisaged a single raid consisting of a dozen Lancaster bombers scattering their infected cargo over the north German countryside. Had the operation taken place, it is estimated that the German beef and dairy herds would have been wiped out, with the bacterium subsequently spreading to the human population. With no access to antibiotics, the death rate would have been in the tens of thousands, perhaps even millions. Apart from two boxes of infected cattle cake, the British stockpile was incinerated at the end of the war. Reports in the National Archives show that anthrax spores in the retained material were still viable in 1955.[58]

Following the end of the war, the British established a number of committees to oversee its biological research programme. Foremost among these were the Inter-Services Sub-Committee on Biological

Warfare (ISSBW). This was a mixed military-civilian body operating under the aegis of the Defence Research Policy Committee (DRPC) tasked with 'the formulation of all aspects of BW policy, both offensive and defensive', and the Biological Warfare Sub-Committee, reporting directly to the chiefs of staff. Both of these subcommittees were served by a scientific advisory panel, the Biological Research Advisory Board, chaired by Lord Hankey, which provided independent technical advice.[59]

The British believed that the Soviet research programme would follow similar lines to that which was being pursued in the West, concentrating on anthrax, botulinum toxin and plague. In 1946 the chiefs of staff approved a set of planning assumptions that stated that 'up to 1951 attacks may be carried out by existing and improved types of bombers using orthodox and biological bombs; thereafter these attacks may be augmented by high performance bombers carrying atomic or biological bombs'.[60] Following the Soviets' first atomic bomb test in August 1949, it was widely believed that biological weapons would be their next strategic priority. An American report issued in 1951 confirmed that the Soviets had a long-standing interest in biological research and that it would 'be foolhardy' to believe that they had not developed an offensive capability in the field of biological warfare. These assumptions appeared to be confirmed in 1956 when Marshal Georgy Zhukov, in a speech to Twentieth Congress of the Soviet Communist Party, declared that if attacked by the West, the Soviets would respond with all means at their disposal including atomic, chemical and bacteriological weapons. However, Zhukov's rhetoric aside, the West believed that Moscow did not possess sufficient delivery systems and that the Soviet military command would be unlikely to use biological weapons as their effects were delayed, unpredictable and less destructive than those of nuclear weapons.

In November 1969 President Richard Nixon made a surprise declaration renouncing biological weapons. Unilaterally, the US suspended research and development on all biological agents and associated delivery systems. The decision had the support of the US joint chiefs of staff who believed that biological weapons—in comparison with nuclear forces—were militarily ineffective, and that a unilateral decision to halt production would help to establish a non-proliferation regime. The primary concern was that biological weapons were relatively cheap compared with nuclear weapons, and could become the poor man's nuclear bomb. The ambition to halt proliferation was realized

in 1972 when both the United States and the Soviet Union signed the
Biological Weapons Convention (BWC).[61]

The explicit intention of the BWC was to prohibit the possession
and use of all biological weapons. Unfortunately, the reality — revealed
in October 1989 when Dr Vladimir Pasechnik, a leading Soviet bio-
chemist, defected to Britain — was rather different. Pasechnik's information stunned Western intelligence. He disclosed that far from halt-
ing biological research, as obliged to do under the terms of the BWC,
the Russians had established a vast research organization known as
Biopreparat as a cover for its secret weapons programme. Biopreparat
employed over 25,000 people in a network of 20–30 military and civilian laboratories and research institutions, and was involved in developing new types of biological weapons against which the West was
defenceless. Top priority had been given to the development of a super-
plague to be packed into munitions and rocket warheads. Key targets
included London, New York and Los Angeles.

Rather than go public with the revelations, the British and Americans decided to issue a private warning to Moscow demanding an end
to the Soviet's biological weapons programme. In a meeting between
the Soviet president Mikhail Gorbachev and Margaret Thatcher in
June 1990, the British prime minister threatened to put Pasechnik on
television if the Soviet leader did not halt biological weapons development. In the end, political events took a hand. The Soviet Union collapsed in December 1991, with Boris Yeltsin replacing Gorbachev as
head of the newly formed Russian Federation. Expectations in Washington and London were high — optimism apparently justified by a
secret message from Yeltsin to US president George Bush in January
1992. The message informed Bush that the continued development of
all illegal biological weapons within Russia had been halted. In April
Yeltsin issued a decree banning biological programmes and mandating
Russia's compliance with the BWC.

The West now demanded full disclosure of all former Soviet activities, but the final document produced by the Russian authorities had
some significant omissions. In September 1992 Kanadjan Alibekov, a
former senior deputy director of Biopreparat, defected to the United
States. His information clearly showed that, although some stocks had
been destroyed, the Russian military were unwilling to cooperate fully
with Western demands. The total stockpile of biological pathogens
now within Russia is unknown, and there remain doubts that Russia
has completely dismantled the old Soviet programme.[62]

UFO sightings in the Cold War

The focus of scientific intelligence was not solely directed upon developments within the Soviet Union. In October 1950, the *Sunday Express* captured public imagination by serializing *The Riddle of the Flying Saucers* by Gerald Heard—an exploration of the recent spate of mysterious objects sighted over Britain. The book became a best-seller and another newspaper, the *Sunday Dispatch*, carried extracts from a variation on the theme, Donald Keyhoe's book *Flying Saucers Are Real*. Both books contained eyewitness accounts of unexplained objects, often travelling at vast speed, seen in the skies over Britain and abroad.[63] In public, the government dismissed the sightings as products of overactive imaginations, but in private it was more circumspect. Sir Henry Tizard for one believed that the subject should not be dismissed without proper investigation, and in October 1950 it was agreed to establish a joint working party, consisting of members of both DSI and JTIC, to examine the matter. The Flying Saucer Working Party, as the body became known, was given the following terms of reference: to review the available evidence in reports of 'flying saucers'; to examine the evidence on which the reports of British phenomena were based; and to liaise with the American authorities where relevant.

The Flying Saucer Working Party included five intelligence officers from the three services and was chaired by G. L. Turney, head of scientific intelligence at the Admiralty. In their final report, issued in June 1951, the working party examined the sightings over Britain and dismissed them as either optical illusions, misidentifications of ordinary aircraft or hoaxes. The report concluded that all sightings of unidentified objects could be explained scientifically and that 'no further investigation of reported mysterious aerial phenomena should be undertaken, unless and until some material evidence becomes available'. It was further agreed that the working party should be disbanded without further meetings.[64]

In compiling their report, the working party was appraised of similar occurrences under investigation in the United States. These had begun in 1948, following a spate of unexplained sightings, including reports from both military and civilian pilots. The United States Air Force (USAF) was concerned that these sightings may have been caused by Soviet secret weapons attempting to penetrate US airspace. To investigate the reports, the air force established Project Sign, under the Technical Intelligence Division of the Air Material Command. Project Sign concluded that the sightings were real, but could be explained by one of three causes: misinterpretation of known objects, hoaxes or mass hysteria. In order to allay growing public disquiet concerning unidentified flying objects (UFOs), the air force initiated Project Grudge, seeking to explain the UFO sightings as the result of natural phenomena or misidentified aircraft. The fact that the air force took the issue seriously tended to increase public interest rather than diminishing it, and the project was terminated in December 1949.

Air force interest in UFOs was soon reactivated, however. In 1952, following an increase in the number of sightings, Major General George Cabell, USAF director of intelligence, initiated Project Bluebook. Undertaken by the Air Technical Intelligence Centre, this became the primary air force study of all UFO phenomena throughout the 1950s and 1960s. Its investigation into UFOs was closely studied by the CIA, concerned that Moscow might seek to exploit UFO hysteria as a method of psychological warfare, or that the Soviets might use UFO sightings to overload the US early warning system, allowing them to launch a surprise nuclear attack. The CIA formed a special study group within the Office of Scientific Intelligence (OSI) to review current developments; responsibility for coordinating its work was given to OSI's Physics and Electronics Division. Harris Marshall Chadwell, the assistant director of OSI, was also involved with the British investigation. Seriously concerned that 'something was going on', Chadwell forwarded a report to the US National Security Council suggesting that the investigation of UFOs should be a priority project for the scientific intelligence and defence research community.

In January 1953, in response to Chadwell's request, CIA director Walter Beddell Smith agreed to establish a panel of independent scientists. Their remit was to review and appraise all available evidence related to UFOs, and to consider the possible dangers to US national security. Chaired by H. P. Robertson, an eminent physicist from California Institute of Technology, the body became known as the Scientific Advisory Panel on UFOs. It also included Lloyd Berkner, director of the Brookhaven National Laboratories, Thorton Page, deputy director of the Johns Hopkins Operations Research Office, Luis Alverez, a high-energy physicist, and Samuel Goudsmit, the former head of the Alsos mission (p. 220). The panel met between 14 and 17 January 1953, publishing its report at the end of that period. The panel concluded that there were no grounds to suggest a direct threat to national security, nor any evidence that UFOs were extraterrestrial. Anxieties remained, however, and the panel was worried that potential enemies might exploit UFO phenomena to mount a surprise attack against the US. The Robertson Panel report, which effectively ended the CIA's interest in UFOs, recommended that the National Security Council should begin a campaign to inform the public that UFOs were natural phenomena and not to be taken seriously.[65]

Although the Flying Saucer Working Party had been disbanded, the UK was no less subject to Cold War fears than the US. With tensions growing between East and West, it is understandable that evidence that UK airspace was being penetrated would at least receive cursory attention, however far-fetched it might seem. In 1953 it was decided that all sightings of UFOs by RAF personnel should be reported to the Air Ministry. This interest was understandably balanced by a desire to keep public interest in the subject in check, orders preserved at the National Archives stating,

> It will be appreciated that the public attach more credence to reports by Royal Air Force personnel than to those by members of the public. It is essential that ... information should be examined at Air Ministry and that its release should be controlled officially. All reports are, there-fore, to be classed 'Restricted' and personnel are to be warned that they are not to communicate to anyone other than official persons any information about phenomena they have observed, unless officially authorised to do so.[66]

The collection of reports continued after the absorption of the Air Ministry into the Ministry of Defence in 1964; to date some 11,000 have been amassed. The Ministry of Defence began the first in a series of releases of these files to the National Archives in May 2008, coinci-dentally a month that also saw the head of the Vatican Observatory, Gabriel Funes, acknowledge the possibility of extraterrestrial life.

The future of scientific intelligence

Following the collapse of the Soviet Union in 1991, a primary concern for the West was that nuclear materials, biological agents or scientific expertise could leak out of former Soviet countries and find their way into the hands of terrorists or rogue states. In the late 1980s, the possi-bility that terrorists might seek to use weapons of mass destruction was considered remote. In its assessment of the possible dangers undertaken in 1989, the JIC concluded that even the most sophisti-cated terrorist organization was 'unlikely to be able to steal and then detonate a nuclear weapon within the foreseeable future' and that the most likely scenario would be a credible hoax. The situation regarding the use of chemical and biological weapons was more equivocal, in that terrorist organizations could obtain 'without insurmountable difficulty, suitable bacteria, viruses and certain toxins', but would be deterred from using such agents because it would alienate both the public and their own supporters.[67] Following the attacks on the World Trade Center and the Pentagon conducted by al-Qaeda, however, this analysis was brought into question. In September 2001, in its first assessment following the attacks, the JIC noted that in the context of global jihad 'casualties and destruction could be an end in themselves'. Even more worryingly, it was believed that 'from the early 1990s Osama bin Laden has sought to obtain nuclear and chemical materials for use as weapons of terror'.

The focus of scientific intelligence has shifted in the 21st century towards supporting the global war on terrorism and countering the proliferation of weapons of mass destruction. The British government acknowledges the spread of such nuclear, chemical and biological weapons—and their delivery systems—as a major threat to strategic interests, and a danger to which all intelligence services have to respond. To date there is only one known case of terrorists using chemical weapons. It occurred in 1995 in Japan, when the Aum Shinrikyo sect released Sarin gas in a coordinated attack on five trains in the Tokyo subway system—killing 12 commuters, seriously injuring 54 and incapacitating 980 others. Ensuring that Tokyo remains an isolated incident ultimately depends on the effectiveness of Western intelligence, but the odds are not in our favour. To thwart such an attack using chemical, bacteriological or nuclear weapons requires a 100 per cent success rate for the indefinite future. In contrast, a determined terrorist network needs to be lucky only once.

8 | Communications Intelligence

The world of intelligence is driven by communications—the ability to transmit information to your allies and penetrate that of your opponents. It is an area of constant change, from the days of Post Office surveillance of enciphered letters to the interception of telegrams in the First World War and the highly sophisticated/complex Enigma codes of the Second. Code-breaking activities of the Cold War era saw multinational cooperation among Western powers as the potential of signals intelligence (SIGINT) became apparent, not least in unmasking some of the era's most successful agents.

The Secret Office

In 1657 parliament established the General Post Office (GPO). It also gave the secretary of state the right to open all letters so as to discover any 'wicked designs' against the Commonwealth. The GPO consisted of an Inland Office, subsequently known as the Private Office, which was responsible for the interception of domestic mail; and a Foreign Office, subsequently known as the Secret Office, for the interception of overseas correspondence. Housed in a series of three rooms adjoining the Foreign Office in Whitehall, the Secret Office was staffed by Isaac Dorislaus, a translator and linguist of Dutch extraction, and Dr John Wallis, a clergyman and professor of geometry at Oxford University. The office's purpose was twofold: to intercept and read coded correspondence from abroad, and to provide codes and ciphers for the safe transmission of messages to British officials overseas. The difference between the two is essentially one of technique. A coded message substitutes the original words in the message for a random string of characters or numbers, according to a code book. A cipher relies on well-defined instructions, known as an algorithm, and the selection of a key before using a cipher to encrypt a message. Wallis's knowledge of mathematics allowed him to construct complex algorithms, making his ciphers almost unbreakable.

Wallis was succeeded in his post by his grandson, William Blencowe, who in 1703 became England's first official decipherer, with an annual salary of £100. When the Elector of Hanover acceded to the British throne as King George I in 1714, the Secret Office's focus shifted to continental Europe. It was a time of change in communications practice; the forgery of newly introduced seals, broken when correspondence was opened, posed particular problems. In 1732 John Ernest Bode, an expert forger of seals, was brought to Britain from Hanover to assist the Secret Office. Other members of the office included the clergyman and chief decipherer, Edward Willes, who had learnt his cryptography skills from Blencowe when he was studying at Oxford. Fluent in Latin, French, Spanish, and Swedish, Willes soon established his credentials by deciphering a series of pro-Jacobite messages between the Swedish diplomat George Heinrich von Görtz and the ambassador in London, Count Karl Gyllenborg. In all, over 300 pages of cipher were translated, resulting in Gyllenborg's arrest for conspiracy. Willes also successfully decoded communications between the bishop of Rochester, Francis Atterbury, and leading Jacobites abroad. He was awarded the deanery of Lincoln in appreciation, and ended his days as the Bishop of Bath and Wells. Due to the work of the Secret Office, Hanoverian monarchs and their governments had access to the majority of incoming and outgoing diplomatic correspondence from the London missions of Austria, France, Prussia, Russia, Spain and the smaller European states—a happy situation that was not to last.[1]

In 1742, following Sir Robert Walpole's fall from power, the Secret Office's existence was made public. Walpole had made many enemies during his long time in office, and they used his resignation as an opportunity to investigate alleged corruption in his administration. Particular concern centred on the award of government contracts and misappropriations of the Secret Vote. To investigate the charge of maladministration, Parliament established a Committee of Secrecy; it began taking evidence in March 1742. In the course of its investigations, the committee discovered that between 1732 and 1742 an allowance of £45,675 had been secretly transferred from the Treasury to the Post Office. Anxious to determine how this money had been used, the committee cross-examined John Barbutt, the secretary to the Post Office. Papers in the National Archives show that Barbutt—questioned under oath—revealed that the allowance was used 'for defraying the expense of a private office for inspecting foreign correspondence' which acted under the direction of the secretary of state. He further disclosed the names of the individuals who worked in the Secret Office and their annual salaries:

> To the chief decipher Mr Willes, for himself and his son, £1,000; to the second decipherer, Mr Corbiere, £800; to the third decipherer, Mr Lampe, £500; to the fourth decipherer, Mr Zolman, £200; to the chief clerk, Mr LeFebre £650; to the four other clerks, Messrs Bode, Thouvois, Clark, Hemmitt, £300 each; to the Comptroller of the Foreign-Office, Mr Day £60, to the doorkeeper £50; and to Mr Lavalade, formerly the alphabet keeper, but now superannuated £40.[2]

The committee considered the establishment of the Secret Office 'extraordinary', but found no evidence of corruption or misuse of public funds. Other damage had been done, however, as foreign governments—now aware of the Secret Office—knew that the British were intercepting their communications and changed ciphers accordingly. They occasionally used the opportunity to deceive, sending misleading communications to be intercepted and deciphered. A further change came following the creation of the Foreign Office in 1782, when financial responsibility for administering the Secret Office's affairs, including its deciphering office, was given to the Foreign Secretary.[3]

By the early 19th century states' interception of communications was so widespread that important messages were usually enciphered, with their delivery entrusted to king's messengers. Despite such safeguards, communications were often compromised. In 1825 the Russians gained unauthorized access to the cipher of the British delegation in Moscow, a fact that the British only realized the following year, when the Duke of Wellington visited Russia to negotiate an agreement on Greek independence from Ottoman rule. On learning the news, the Post Office immediately introduced a new system of ciphers.

The Mazzini affair

In 1844 Tsar Nicholas I of Russia visited Britain ostensibly to meet the young Queen Victoria and Prince Albert—a stateroom at Buckingham Palace was renamed the 1844 Room in honour of the visit—but primarily to reach a 'gentleman's agreement' on the future of the Ottoman empire and the territorial distribution between Russia and Britain. Prior to the Tsar's arrival, the British government received information from the Russian authorities that Polish émigrés living in London were plotting to assassinate him. A warrant to intercept the correspondence of two named individuals (Stolzmann and Grodicki) was signed by the home secretary, Sir James Graham. The power to issue a warrant was sanctioned by the Post Office Act, passed by parliament in 1837, which consolidated the 140 Acts that had been passed since 1657.

The interception of the Polish émigrés' correspondence soon became subsumed in the Mazzini affair, which cast a shadow over Sir Robert Peel's government. In March of that year, at the same time as he was investigating the plot to assassinate the tsar, the home secretary also approved a warrant authorizing the Post Office to intercept the correspondence of Giuseppe Mazzini, an Italian nationalist and revolutionary believed to be involved in subversive activity in Austria's Italian provinces. Over 60 letters were intercepted, with their details passed to the Austrian embassy in London. During the course of the investigation, Mazzini became convinced that his mail was being intercepted and voiced his suspicions to Thomas Duncombe, radical MP for the London borough of Finsbury. Duncombe proceeded to raise the issue in the Commons in July. In the ensuing debate, the government refused to confirm or deny the specific allegation, contending that it was 'not the duty of the royal post to propel the correspondence of wicked and designing men from Shetland to Scilly for the price of a penny'.[4] The episode generated a flurry of critical reports in the press, prompting the Earl of Radnor, a fellow radical, to express the view that the government's behaviour 'brought shame and disgrace' on the British people.

To curtail further revelations, the government agreed to establish two secret committees: one in the Commons, to examine the legal position in respect of detaining and opening letters, and one in the Lords, to adjudicate on the government's conduct. The two committees took evidence throughout July 1844 and presented their reports, now in the National Archives, to parliament in August.[5] In a thorough investigation, it was discovered that 101 warrants had been issued between 1712 and 1798, rising to 372 between 1799 and 1844. The warrants divided into two classes: those issued in connection with criminal justice and those issued for 'discovering the designs' of individuals engaged in activity of danger to the state or involving British interests overseas. In relation to the latter, the committees found that the power to intercept letters had been sparingly exercised and that every case examined appeared to be necessary 'to prevent a disturbance of the public tranquillity, or otherwise to promote the best interests of the country'. The report found no evidence to support the contention that the home secretary had abused his powers, and approved his action in intercepting the correspondence of Stolzmann, Grodicki and Mazzini. The episode was summed up by *The Times* which believed that, while the practice reading of other people's mail was difficult to reconcile with English habits, 'it is far better that one or two dozen letters should be opened than that the nation should be shocked and its character sullied by some madbrained tumult or some monstrous outrage'[6]—a position as relevant today as it was in the mid-19th century.

In the aftermath of the Mazzini affair, the government scaled back the Secret Office's work. In part to distance itself from further revelations, this was primarily due to the growing sophistication of ciphers, which were proving increasingly difficult to break. The work of the deciphering office was gradually scaled back and in February 1845 the decision was taken to close down the Secret Office. This decision was contested by Henry Addington, under-secretary at the Foreign Office, who believed that the Secret Office offered a source of great advantage and utility to the state in difficult times. Documents in the National Archives show that William Bode, the head of the Secret Office, was equally alarmed, believing that:

> Whatever opinions may be entertained in this country, Foreign Governments will not desist from a practice which they all follow; nor will they believe that the English Government has abandoned all control over the Post Office. The motive of State necessity, which can alone justify the practice, will accordingly still exist. As, however, the existence of an office of such an exceptional nature can hardly be avowed, or sanctioned by Parliament, it seems absolutely necessary to devise some Mask for it.[7]

Bode was equally concerned about the future of his staff, 'who make some sacrifices in the performance of a service which can only with safety be entrusted to men of honour and integrity'. These views carried little weight and in 1847, following the fall of the Peel government, the new foreign secretary, Lord Palmerston, abolished the Secret Office, pensioning off Bode and the remaining eight members of staff. Thus at a time when Morse code and the electric telegraph were poised to replace mail as a rapid means of international communication, Britain deprived itself of one of its most useful sources of intelligence.

The advent of the telegraph, soon followed by wireless telegraphy, revolutionized communication in the 19th century. The world's first telegraph line was established in May 1844 by the American inventor Samuel Morse; it was owned by the Ohio Railroad Company and ran between Baltimore and Washington. Morse himself transmitted its first message—a short message from the Book of Numbers: 'What hath

God wrought'. The new Morse code was unique in that it provided a standard system of signals that could be transmitted over great distances and read by ear or eye, offering a potential new source for gathering intelligence. It was soon realized that the telegraph line carrying the message could easily be tapped anywhere along its length by unsophisticated listening equipment. The same applied to underwater international cables, vulnerable to eavesdropping at their terminals.

The security of the message could be improved by employing a cipher, and two methods of enciphering were included in the first *Manual of Instruction in Army Signalling*, issued by the War Office in 1876. The manual also candidly admitted that no message transmitted electronically was secure and that 'the most accurate way of transmitting intelligence is by means of an orderly carrying a written message'.[8] The Boer War was the first time that interception techniques were used systematically by the British, when the country used its dominance of the global telecommunications network to intercept and decipher communications of enemy and neutral states. Britain achieved this by monitoring the two main submarine cables that linked South Africa to Portugal and Aden. However, British landline communications in South Africa were also intercepted by the Boers. Aware of this, the commander in chief of British forces, Field Marshal Lord Roberts, directed the first recorded military use of signal deception. Messages giving false orders were transmitted in order to misinform Boer fighters and to draw them into well-prepared ambushes. These operations were conducted by a special unit of the War Office known as Section H, under the command of Major James Edmonds. Files in the National Archives show how, operating from offices in Cape Town and Durban, Section H was also responsible for intercepting the mail of suspected Boer sympathizers.[9] The perceived vulnerability of communications led the British to develop sophisticated ciphers and codes. In 1904 parliament passed the Wireless Telegraphy Act, which outlawed the use of radio broadcast equipment without first obtaining a licence from the postmaster general.

Room 40 and the Zimmermann telegram

The outbreak of the First World War led to considerable advances in both the interception of enemy signals and the development of countermeasures to ensure secure communications. British efforts were headed by the Admiralty's Naval Intelligence Department and its communications section (NID 25). The director of naval intelligence, Rear Admiral Henry Oliver, soon realized the importance of cracking the encoded communications of the German fleet, and tasked Sir Alfred Ewing, the director of naval education, to begin work immediately. Ewing, who had an interest in codes and ciphers, seized the opportunity offered by Oliver and began to assemble a small team of linguists from the Royal Naval Colleges at Dartmouth and Osborne.

The novice code-breakers worked out of Ewing's cramped office and soon began to produce results, helped in October 1914 by a code book taken from the SMS *Magdeburg*; the German cruiser had run aground on the island of Odensholm, near the Estonian coast. This windfall was later supplemented by another code book captured from a German merchant ship off Melbourne, Australia. On 30 November a British trawler recovered from a sunken German destroyer a chest containing a copy of the *Verkehrsbuch* (traffic book)—the German navy's primary cipher system. So important was the recovery of code books that the Admiralty organized a small group of experienced divers to locate and recover material from sunken ships. The code-breakers' work was dependent on a steady stream of raw intercepts from a network of wireless tracking stations situated around Britain, codenamed Y Stations.

In November 1914 Oliver was succeeded as director of naval intelligence by Reginald 'Blinker' Hall, who expanded the code-breakers' work and provided them with new offices in Room 40 of Whitehall's Old Admiralty Building. Room 40's greatest success was to ensure that the US entered the war in the spring of 1917. On 16 January the German foreign minister, Arthur Zimmermann, sent a coded message to Count Johann von Bernstorff, his ambassador in Washington. The message gave advance warning that the Kaiser's supreme command had taken the decision to intensify the U-boat campaign in the Western Atlantic. Unrestricted submarine warfare (including the sinking of neutral US ships crossing the Atlantic) would commence on 1 February, breaking previous undertakings given to President Woodrow Wilson. Bernstorff was directed to forward the message to Heinrich von Eckhardt, the German ambassador in Mexico, and it included proposals urging the Mexicans to attack the US from the south. In return for Mexican support, the Germans promised the return of Mexican territory in Texas, New Mexico and Arizona.

This dramatic piece of intelligence was obtained through Britain's tapping of the transatlantic cable which used a relay station at Portcurno in Cornwall, enabling them to intercept all of the diplomatic traffic that passed between Berlin and Washington. Zimmerman's encoded telegram was duly intercepted and passed to Room 40 for interpretation. The code used to encipher German diplomatic messages, known as 0075, had only been partially cracked by the British, so Room 40's code-breakers could produce only a garbled version of the telegram. The significance of the message was nevertheless clear, leaving the British with the challenge of informing Washington of its contents without revealing that it was reading the messages of neutral countries, including the United States.

Gradually, a strategy to inform the Americans without revealing Britain's knowledge of the encryption system began to emerge. It was known that Zimmermann's telegram had been forwarded from Washington to the German legation in Mexico City—and it was also believed that on this leg of its journey, it would most probably travel by an older encryption system, known as 13040 and already broken by Room 40. In early February Hall ordered one of his agents in Mexico City, known only as Mr H., to bribe an employee of the commercial telegraph company to give him a copy of the message. A few days later the encoded telegram was in British hands. Hall's hunch had proved correct: the telegram had been encoded using the simpler cipher, allowing Room 40 to read the message in full (plate 35). It ran:

> We intended to begin on the first of February unrestricted submarine warfare. We shall endeavour in spite of this to keep the U.S.A. neutral. In the event of this not succeeding, we make Mexico a proposal of alliance on the following basis:-
>   Make war together
>   Make peace together
>   Generous financial support and an understanding on our part that Mexico is to reconquer the lost territory in Texas, New Mexico and Arizona. The settlement in detail is left to you.
>   You will inform the [Mexican] President of the above most secretly, as soon as the outbreak of war with the U.S.A. is certain and add the suggestion that he should on his own initiative invite Japan to immediate adherence and at the same time mediate between Japan and ourselves.
>   Please call the President's attention to the fact that the ruthless employment of our submarines now offers the prospect of compelling England to make peace within a few months.[10]

The British were still unsure about passing the telegram to the United States, but Germany's resumption of U-boat attacks on British shipping allayed their concerns. On 22 February Hall passed the decoded telegram to the US ambassador in London, using the cover story that it had been obtained by British authorities in Mexico. Initially reluctant to believe the story, the Americans were soon convinced of its authenticity. Files in the National Archives reveal that Britain's conduct was commended in the following terms:

> Please convey to Mr Balfour a message of thanks for this information of such inestimable value and add that the President has asked me to express his very great appreciation of so marked an act of friendliness on the part of the British Government. For your information, Ambassador Fletcher has been instructed to take up the matter confidentially with General Carranza and preliminary reports indicate that perhaps it has not yet been presented by the German Minister. If the telegram is (published) the source will be most carefully guarded. You will be kept informed.[11]

The full text of the telegram was subsequently released to the Associated Press without any indication as to its source. On 1 March 1917 the *Washington Post* carried the banner headline 'German Plot to Conquer the United States with Aid of Japan and Mexico Revealed', with Zimmermann's telegram reproduced in its entirety. The story caused a sensation, resulting in a violent swing of public opinion against the Kaiser, although a number of senators opposed to American involvement in the war believed it to be a British hoax. The Mexican president, Venustiano Carranza, issued a vehement denial of involvement, but on 3 March Zimmermann confirmed that he was indeed the telegram's author and that the story was genuine. The foreign minister defended Germany's position by stressing that the proposals were only intended to come into force if America attacked Germany, and that it was now more important than ever that the United States remain neutral. Zimmermann's statement further inflamed anti-German opinion within America, and barely a month later, on 6 April 1917, the United States declared war on Germany. In asking Congress to support a declaration of war, Wilson cited the telegram as proof that Germany was a direct threat to the peace and security of the American people.

In the course of the First World War, over 20,000 messages were decoded in Room 40, thus making the Admiralty aware of most major movements of the German navy.[12] The intelligence provided by Room 40, however, was not always acted upon—sometimes with unfortunate results. In the Battle of Jutland, for example, the only major engagement between the British and German fleets, Britain lost the opportunity of inflicting a major defeat on the German navy. Intercepts gathered before the engagement had allowed Room 40 to monitor the deployment of the fleet and its intended plan of attack; but the intelligence was either ignored as unreliable, misinterpreted or failed to reach the intended recipients in time. Only three of the 16 decoded messages sent to the Admiralty in London were received by Admiral Jellicoe, the commander of the British fleet. When Jellicoe finally learned of the true position of the German fleet at 04.15, it was too late for the battle to be resumed. While the British had lost more ships, and had not destroyed the German fleet as intended, the Germans had retreated to port, effectively ending any threat to the Royal Navy's control of the North Sea.

The Government Code and Cipher School

After its success during the First World War, the Admiralty was anxious to consolidate its work in code-breaking and ciphers. The cabinet's Secret Service Committee, chaired by Lord Curzon, agreed and recommended that a peacetime code-breaking agency should be created. The task of creating the new agency and coordinating its activities was given to the new director of naval intelligence, Commodore (later Rear Admiral) Hugh Sinclair. On 1 November 1919 the Government Code and Cipher School (GC&CS) was established, with premises in the former headquarters of Marconi at Watergate House, near the Savoy Hotel, in London. The first recruits to the new agency consisted of staff from Room 40 and its army equivalent MI1b, which dealt with military ciphers. GC&CS was initially placed under the control of the Admiralty, with Alastair Denniston—a veteran of Room 40 who had also played hockey for Scotland in the pre-war Olympic games— appointed as its operational head.[13] The acknowledged function of GC&CS was 'to advise as to the security of codes and ciphers used by all Government departments and to assist in their provision'. It also, as records in the National Archives acknowledge, had a secret directive 'to study the methods of cipher communications used by foreign powers'—an activity that absorbed most of its resources.[14]

The primary target for GC&CS was the interception of diplomatic traffic, which, in contrast to postal interception, required no warrant. The 1920 Official Secrets Act carried a little-noticed clause that explicitly granted the British government authorization to obtain copies of any telegram transmitted by cable on imperial territory. Given that by the 1920s most of the global telecommunications network was either owned by British companies or passed through the territory of the British Empire, GC&CS had unrivalled access to the vast majority of diplomatic cables. Just how far that authority extended was discovered in December 1920, when Western Union president Newcomb Carlton shocked a Senate subcommittee with the revelation that the British government secretly required that his company turn over to naval intelligence every incoming and outgoing telegram received in Britain. Although the British denied the accusations, it was later revealed that when censorship ceased in 1919, the government had insisted that commercial cable companies be required to hand over all telegrams received in Britain no later than 10 days after they were sent.

During this early period GC&CS intercepted and deciphered the diplomatic messages of France, Italy, Germany, Turkey and America. The volume and quality of the intelligence was such that in 1922 GC&CS was placed under the administrative and budgetary control of the Foreign Office. Further reorganization occurred in 1923, when GC&CS was placed under the operational control of the Secret Intelligence Service (SIS), with its newly appointed head, Hugh Sinclair, redesignated chief of the secret service and director of GC&CS, while Denniston assumed the title of deputy director. The service departments initially objected to these changes, but eventually relented on the understanding that GC&CS would establish separate sections for the navy, army and air force, which could be relocated to the operational commands on the outbreak of a future war. In 1924, to coordinate the work of these various sections and determine priorities, GC&CS established a Cryptography and Interception Committee (later renamed the Co-ordination of W/T Interception Committee), chaired by the head of GC&CS and containing representatives of the three services and the GPO. In 1925 the two organizations became even closer when SIS and GC&CS moved to new offices in Broadway Buildings in Westminster, sharing separate floors of the same building.

Throughout the 1920s the main priority for GC&CS was Soviet Russia. The responsibility for intercepting and deciphering diplomatic traffic between Moscow and London was given to GC&CS's Russian section, headed by Ernst Fetterlein, a former cryptographer for Tsar Nicholas II who had fled Russia following the 1917 revolution. The task proved relatively straightforward as the Soviets had adopted simple ciphers, with most communications transmitted by radio. The most valuable intercepts were diplomatic telegrams sent by Soviet foreign minister Georgi Chicherin to the Soviet trade delegation in London. These messages spelt out in detail the negotiating position to be adopted by the Russians in the Anglo-Soviet trade negotiations aimed at restoring diplomatic relations between the two countries—immensely useful insight for the British.

Further successes occurred in July 1920 when GC&CS intercepted a series of radio messages between Chicherin and the deputy commissar for foreign affairs, Maksim Litvinov. The messages concerned the activities of the *Daily Herald*, a Soviet-funded newspaper, and detailed its active role in spreading subversion within the British trade union movement. On receiving the information, the cabinet's initial response was to expel the entire Russian delegation, but after reflection it was considered that such action would cause more damage than good. Instead, the government took the surprising decision to make the intercepts public by releasing them to sympathetic newspapers. Even more surprisingly, the Russians either failed to notice the story or did not appreciate its full significance, and took no immediate action to change their ciphers.

This position was soon to change. In May 1927, a team of Special Branch officers and members of the security services raided the offices of the All Russian Cooperative Society (ARCOS), which shared its offices in Moorgate with the Soviet trade delegation. The raid sought to prove that ARCOS was being used by Moscow to conduct espionage operations within the UK and to spread subversion throughout the British Empire, but, poorly planned and badly executed, it failed to discover any incriminating evidence (p. 30). Although portrayed to parliament and public as a success, its far-reaching consequences included the expulsion of the Soviet trade delegation and the severing of diplomatic relations between the two countries. In order to justify its actions, the government was forced to make public incriminating documents— not from the raid but, as files in the National Archives show, previously intercepted by GC&CS.[15] In contrast to the revelations of 1920, the Russians soon recognized the source of the documents; they immediately abandoned their diplomatic ciphers in favour of one-time pads that were virtually impossible to break. The episode meant that GC&CS could no longer decipher Soviet diplomatic traffic and deprived Britain of an important source of intelligence, with little to show in return.

The arrival of Enigma

By the mid-1930s, Nazi Germany began to replace Soviet Russia as the main target for GC&CS. To encode their messages, the Germans relied on the use of the Enigma machine, developed in the 1920s by Arthur Scherbius, an electrical engineer from Düsseldorf. The Enigma machine resembled a typewriter, with each letter connected to an illuminated display board via a system of electromechanical rotors. To add further complexity, the rotors were connected to a series of electrical cables which could be set in a variety of positions. This design feature meant that each letter was encoded using a different cryptographic transformation. To decode the message, usually transmitted in Morse code, the operator needed to know the exact setting of the rotors and cables on the original machine. As these settings were changed on a daily basis, the task of intercepting the message and deciphering it was believed to be impossible. The Enigma machine was soon adopted by the German military, with the navy taking possession of its first machine in 1926. By 1934 the Enigma had become the Germans' main means of encoding both their diplomatic and military communications.

Unknown to the Germans, the Polish Cipher Bureau had managed to obtain a commercial version of the Enigma machine, and by 1933 had devised a method enabling them to read German radio messages enciphered using Enigma. The Poles used this information to build several replicas of the Enigma machine similar to those used by the German navy and air force, but in 1938 the Germans added further refinements to the Enigma, making the Poles' work considerably more difficult. Aware that a German attack was imminent, the Poles decided to share their knowledge of the Enigma with Britain and France. In January 1939 the first meeting of the three countries' code-breakers took place in Paris: participants included the head of GC&CS, Alastair Denniston, his French counterpart, Captain Gustav Bertrand, and the head of the Polish Cipher Bureau, Lieutenant Colonel Gwidon Langer. A further meeting was held in Warsaw in July, where the Poles finally revealed how they had cracked the German codes and handed over a replica of the Enigma machine to the British. The machine was secretly spirited from the country and on 16 August, two weeks before the outbreak of the Second World War, it was presented to Stewart Menzies, then deputy head of SIS.

Station X

A month before the outbreak of war, to escape the expected air attacks, GC&CS was relocated to Bletchley Park, formerly part of the manor of Eaton, in Buckinghamshire. To disguise its function,

GC&CS was renamed the Government Communications Headquarters (GCHQ) and was known variously as Station X, Room 47 Foreign Office and BP. As the war progressed, staff numbers increased from fewer than 100 in 1939 to almost 10,000 by 1945, accommodated in prefabricated wooden buildings erected in the courtyard. These soon became known as 'Huts', with each specializing in a particular area of expertise. The most important were Huts 3 and 4, responsible for the analysis and distribution of army, air force and naval decrypts, Huts 6 and 8, responsible for breaking the Enigma codes, and Hut 11, which housed the main computing section. The volume of work soon proved impossible to manage and in January 1942 GC&CS was split in two. Diplomatic and commercial sections operated from 7–9 Berkeley Street in London, with Denniston as deputy director (C), while the service sections remained at Bletchley Park under Commander Edward 'Jumbo' Travis, previously Denniston's assistant, as deputy director (S).[16]

The wartime recruits at Bletchley Park were usually selected for their knowledge of mathematics and computing, but they also included a mix of chess players, linguists and crossword enthusiasts. (The ability to solve the *Daily Telegraph* crossword in less than 12 minutes was often used as part of the recruitment test.) Among the staff working at Bletchley during the war were Alan Turing, the mathematician and crypt-analyst who invented the world's first programmable computer; Tommy Flowers, the designer of Colossus, the world's first electronic computer; Jim Rose, the future literary editor of the *Observer* and chairman of Penguin Books; and Harry Hinsley, who would later become vice chancellor of Cambridge University and official historian of British intelligence during the Second World War. Family ties were also important. Nigel de Grey and Dillwyn Knox, both veterans of Room 40, recruited their sons; and Evelyn Sinclair, the sister of Hugh Sinclair, the former chief of SIS, joined the staff at Bletchley in the summer of 1940.

The enciphered messages broken by Bletchley were cracked at out-stations in Adstock, Gayhurst, Wavendon, Stanmore and Eastcote at which high-speed computing machines known as 'bombes' were used. Intercept stations including the War Office Y Group, stationed at Beaumanor Hall, and its RAF equivalent, sited at Chicksands in Bed-fordshire, provided the raw material. Once intercepted, the raw messages were forwarded to Bletchley for decryption and analysis. The intelligence was then finally relayed to 'consumers' in the military and other branches of government. To protect its source, distribution was confined to the chief of SIS and the directors of intelligence for the army, navy and air force. Further to disguise the fact that Britain was reading German communications, records in the National Archives show that intelligence derived from Bletchley Park was given the code name Boniface, to suggest that SIS had a secret agent operating at the highest levels within the German military establishment.[17] This could backfire, however, as reports were often ignored as unreliable or misleading because of SIS's poor reputation.

In the early 1940s the signals intelligence produced by Bletchley Park was given the security classification 'Ultra'. To emphasize its importance, a daily digest of Ultra material was delivered personally to the prime minister, Winston Churchill (plate 36). The intelligence in the digest, selected directly by Menzies, consisted of summaries of the most important military and diplomatic decrypts, the so-called 'golden eggs'. The digest was delivered personally to the prime minister by Desmond Morton, his trusted intelligence adviser, in a locked briefcase to which Churchill and Menzies had the only keys. The 'golden eggs' (plates 37 and 38) were avidly devoured by Churchill, whose estimation of Menzies and SIS increased considerably.[18]

Radio Security Service

The interception of radio communications was not the sole preserve of GC&CS. In the late 1930s MI5 created a small unit, known as MI8c, to intercept and locate any illicit radio transmissions sent by enemy agents operating within the United Kingdom. It was soon established that no such transmissions existed. Following the outbreak of war, the unit was renamed the Radio Security Service (RSS) and turned its attention to German radio communications. Headed by Colonel J. P. G. Worlledge, who had commanded the No 2 Wireless Company in Palestine, and operating from headquarters at Arkley in north London, RSS was soon to justify its new role.

In December 1939 it intercepted a series of transmissions emanating from a German ship in the North Sea. The ship belonged to the Abwehr, the German intelligence service, and was being used as a mobile communications platform directing operations in Norway. The transmissions were of two distinct types: communications between the Abwehr and its overseas stations, which were encoded using Enigma; and messages to individual agents, which were encoded by hand using a book cipher. The key to breaking the Abwehr codes was provided by a double agent, known as SNOW, who had been recruited by MI5 in

1938. Unaware that SNOW had been turned, the Abwehr provided him with a copy of its cipher so that he could relay messages back to Germany. The cipher was immediately passed on to the analysts at Arkley who were soon able to read all of the Abwehr's traffic transmitted by radio. The unit responsible for reading the hand ciphers was headed by Oliver Strachey—brother of the writer Lytton Strachey—and was given the code name ISOS (Intelligence Service Oliver Strachey). The Morse-encoded messages were decoded by Dillwyn Knox and in similar fashion were given the code name ISK.

The success of the RSS in reading the traffic of the Abwehr soon came to the attention of SIS, who were concerned that the security service was encroaching on the work undertaken at Bletchley Park. Menzies was adamant that all signals intelligence should be placed under GC&CS and took the issue to Churchill. The prime minister agreed, and in May 1941 RSS was placed under the operational control of SIS. New working arrangements were established, with Major Ted Maltby replacing Worlledge as head of RSS. The interception of Abwehr communications was now the responsibility of SIS's section VIII (Special Communications Unit) with facilities at Hanslope Park, near Milton Keynes, and Whaddon Hall, near Bletchley. Once the messages had been intercepted they were sent to GC&CS for decryption, with the raw intelligence then forwarded to the staff at Arkley for analysis. To determine priorities a Joint Signals Intelligence Committee was established with representatives of SIS, GCHQ, MI5, RSS, GPO and the military. The committee's secretary was Hugh Trevor-Roper, the future Regius professor of modern history at Oxford University, who was also responsible for liaison with Russia and the United States.[19]

BRUSA

On 11 December 1941, four days after the Japanese attack at Pearl Harbor, Hitler declared war on the United States. The American entry into the war heralded a new era of closer Anglo-American cooperation in code-breaking and signals intelligence (SIGINT). Prior to the US entry into the war, the British had sought an agreement with the Americans covering the exchange of information on cryptography and ciphers. In February 1941 a small group of military officers, headed by Captain Abraham Sinkov of the US army's Signals Intelligence Service, visited Britain and were shown around Bletchley Park. In return for details of the Enigma machine and a substantial amount of information on German, Italian and Russian ciphers, the Americans delivered an American clone of the Japanese diplomatic service's cipher machine—codenamed Purple—together with details of naval codes and ciphers. In June the Anglo-American relationship in the Far East was further strengthened with agreement reached to exchange intelligence between the British base at Singapore and the US Pacific Fleet.

In August 1941 Alastair Denniston, the head of GC&CS, visited Washington to discuss further assistance. It was not until America's entry into the war, however, that full-scale cooperation between the two countries was formally established. The impetus behind the agreement began in February 1942, following the German navy's introduction of a new cipher system for communicating with its U-boat fleet in the North Atlantic. In order to find the key and break the cipher, a new generation of 'bombes' was required. Only the United States possessed the necessary resources to undertake such a programme in the timescale required. In August 1942 the US navy informed Captain Edward Hastings, GC&CS's liaison officer in America, that it was soon to embark on an extensive research programme to develop a high-speed bombe, with an allocated budget of over $2m. Fearing that the US was planning to go its own way unless the British had something to offer in return, the new head of GC&CS, Commander Travis, immediately set off for Washington. The result was the so-called Holden Agreement named after the US director of naval communications, Captain Carl Holden, which was signed between the two countries on 2 October 1942.[20]

The Holden Agreement provided for a 'logical division' of labour covering the interception and exploitation of allied SIGINT, and the Americans were the main beneficiaries. In return for full collaboration against German naval ciphers, the US navy was given sole control over Japanese communications, with Britain agreeing to disband the British-Australian naval unit at Melbourne and to 'withdraw from active crypto-analytical work in the Pacific area'. In addition—and against the wishes of Menzies—the British also agreed to provide the US with raw naval Ultra material. The agreement soon came to the attention of the US army, which demanded a similar stream of raw Enigma intercepts. For reasons of security, Travis informed the Americans that, in order to receive the raw intelligence, the US army would first need to establish an operational contingent at Bletchley Park. Negotiations continued until May 1943, when agreement was reached between Travis and the head of US military intelligence, General George V. Strong, providing for the complete exchange of SIGINT material. In the agreement spoils were divided: the United States was given primary responsibility for reading Japanese army and air force ciphers, and the British for reading German and Italian army and air force codes and ciphers. On 14 January 1944 allied SIGINT cooperation was further strengthened with the signing of the BRUSA agreement, which established a global network of stations located in Washington, Bletchley Park, Pearl Harbor, Melbourne and Colombo. The agreement also contained provisions covering the exchange of personnel, security regulations for the handling of the Ultra material and methods for its distribution.[21]

The BRUSA agreement resulted in a series of conferences involving not only Britain and the United States but also the code-breaking agencies of Canada and Australia. In March 1944 the second Joint Allied Conference was held at Arlington Hall, the headquarters of the US Signal Security Agency (SSA). The participants included Colonel W. Preston Corderman, Commander Edward Travis, Lieutenant Colonel Edward M. Drake and Captain S. R. I. Clark, respective heads of the US, British, Canadian and Australian SIGINT organizations. Others in attendance were Leonard James Hooper, a future director of GCHQ, and, from the United States, William F. Friedman and Solomon Kullback (later to become chief cryptologist and chief scientist at the National Security Agency). A notable, if unsurprising, absentee from the conference was Soviet Russia. To what degree Moscow was aware of allied advances in signals intelligence is as yet unknown.

A peacetime role

GCHQ's successes during the war had been overshadowed by the fact that it was controlled by SIS, an arrangement that rankled with senior staff. In September 1944, following the liberation of Paris, GCHQ assembled a small group of senior officials to study its post-war future. Led by Gordon Welchman, the head of Hut 6—which was responsible for breaking German army and air force Enigma ciphers—the group advocated creating an independent body to become the unchallenged headquarters for all signals intelligence in the UK. It also recommended that, rather than devoting time against Japan, which was primarily an American concern, GCHQ should focus its resources on developing new computers and the latest communications equipment. While it was clear that SIGINT was likely to play a significant role in the post-war world, a primary concern was that GCHQ's budget would be reduced, preventing it from attracting the top-rate engineers and scientists it required. In this regard, as records in the National Archives reveal, the secret nature of GCHQ's work also proved a handicap, since very few people in government were aware of the true scale of its achievements.[22] This perennial 'Catch 22' faced by intelligence organizations was also to impact after the fall of the Berlin Wall in 1989.

The chiefs of staff, however, were well aware of GCHQ's contribution to the allied victory. Meeting in November 1945, they gave top priority to signals intelligence and recommended complete cooperation with the United States. Despite receiving priority status, GCHQ underwent a reduction in staff numbers, with army SIGINT collection units falling from a peak of 4,000 personnel in December 1945 to fewer than 1,000 by the following March. In April 1946, to offset these reductions, GCHQ relocated its main headquarters from Bletchley Park to Eastcote in north-west London, where it was able to share the facilities of the Post Office Research Department at Dollis Hill.[23] That year saw GCHQ achieve one of its primary aims, when it became independent from SIS and was placed directly under Foreign Office control, taking the wartime cover name of GCHQ as its official title.[24]

Its first director was Commander Travis, who set about establishing a network of listening stations throughout the Commonwealth. In January 1947 Travis chaired a Commonwealth SIGINT conference in London, attended by representatives of Australia, Canada and New Zealand. In addition to establishing a Commonwealth network, he was keen to foster a good working relationship with the United States. Throughout 1947 a series of meetings were held between GCHQ and its American counterparts, aimed at establishing a global division of responsibilities. In 1948 these talks came to fruition with the signing of the UK–USA Security Agreement—better known as the UKUSA agreement. This brought together under a single umbrella the SIGINT organizations of the United States, Britain, Canada, Australia and New Zealand, with each nation assigned specific geographical targets. The signatories to the agreement also agreed to standardize their terminology, security caveats and intercept handling procedures. To cement the relationship, special liaison officers were seconded to the headquarters of each participating nation.[25]

Operation Venona

The signing of the UKUSA agreement facilitated the joint exploitation of Soviet diplomatic communications that had been intercepted but not yet deciphered. The majority of the traffic had been intercepted between 1944 and 1945, and contained messages transmitted between Moscow and its embassy in Washington. It was soon realized that the traffic contained details of Soviet intelligence operations conducted in the United States. The messages had been encoded using one-time pads, which meant that they were almost impossible to crack. That situation was soon to change. On careful analysis it was discovered that some of the messages had been encrypted using the same one-time pad. This discovery, when used in conjunction with a copy of a Soviet code book obtained by the US Office of Strategic Services in 1945, provided the key that the code-breakers required. Throughout 1947 a proportion of the most significant messages were decoded and revealed that someone working on the US atomic bomb project had passed highly classified information to the Russians. The revelation appeared to substantiate the claims made by Whittaker Chambers, a former Communist, that the Soviets had a network of spies operating at the highest levels of the American government. In 1948 the FBI appointed special agent Robert Lamphere to investigate the claims and, if possible, to uncover the identities of other Soviet agents mentioned in the decoded messages.

Codenamed Venona, the operation soon began to produce results revealing the identities and clandestine activities of Julius and Ethel Rosenberg, Harry Gold, David and Ruth Greeenglass, and Klaus Fuchs. Details of the Venona messages were also passed to Britain, where they were handled under the codename Bride. The decoded messages did not name individuals directly, but contained cryptonyms which related to specific individuals. One message indicated that the Soviets had a source in the British embassy known as Homer. The list of possible suspects was soon narrowed down to a small handful of individuals, with the final breakthrough occurring in April 1951. A decoded message revealed that during 1944 Homer had contacted his Soviet controller in New York, travelling from Washington under the pretext of visiting his pregnant wife. The profile matched only one person: Donald Maclean. The news that Maclean was about to be unmasked as a Soviet agent soon found its way to the desk of Kim Philby, the SIS liaison officer in Washington. Philby informed Guy Burgess, who immediately returned to Britain to alert Maclean of his impending fate. On the evening of 25 May both men boarded the night ferry to France, never to return.[26] Files in the National Archives describe the close cooperation between British and American cryptologists, leading to

Maclean's identification as a Soviet agent, in the following terms:

> On 30 March 1951, Mr House transmitted to England the suggestion
> that letter group G was Homer ... This identification if true allowed
> the placing of G in New York in June 1944. On 7 June 1951, the press
> reported the disappearance of Donald Maclean and Guy Burgess. On
> 26 June 1951, the FBI reported to AFSA that Homer and G were
> believed to be identical in Donald Maclean.[27]

GCHQ in Cheltenham

The facilities at Eastcote were only intended as a temporary measure
and in September 1949 GCHQ moved to new premises in Cheltenham,
occupying two sites at Oakley and Benhall. GCHQ's budget was also
increased, with over 600 new staff joining the organization at its Cheltenham headquarters. The primary target for GCHQ was the Soviet
Union, with the Joint Intelligence Committee directing Britain's code-
breakers to focus their efforts on the Soviet Union's atomic, biological
and chemical warfare programmes.

The new influx of staff allowed GCHQ to expand its remit into
other related areas. In March 1954 the organization gained administrative control of the London Communications Security Agency,
responsible for providing advice and assistance to other government
departments and the armed forces on the security of their communications and cipher systems. GCHQ was given additional responsibility
for advising on technical translations and in 1955 took over the Joint
Technical Language Service (JTLS). The 1950s also saw GCHQ taking
control of electronic intelligence (ELINT). Initial work in this area
had been undertaken by the Central Signals Establishment at RAF
Watton, with intelligence provided by a fleet of specially equipped
Lincoln bombers—known as 'ferrets'—which patrolled the Soviet perimeter. The purpose of such flights was to obtain as much electronic
information as possible to develop countermeasures against enemy
radar sites and missile systems. To facilitate this work, GCHQ formed
the Composite Signals Organization (CSO), which eventually took over
control of the various networks run by the armed forces.[28]

Throughout the Cold War, GCHQ supplied a steady stream of
intelligence to its customers in government and the armed forces. Its
operations during this period, however, are still classified. To remain at
the forefront of cryptography, GCHQ invested heavily in computing
technology, taking the lion's share of the intelligence budget. A major

achievement was the development of what is now known as public-key encryption, which greatly increased the security of government communications. In 1966 staff numbers at GCHQ totalled 11,500—a figure equal to the combined workforce of SIS, MI5 and the Foreign Office diplomatic service. The reason for this growth was simple: SIGINT was regarded as more accurate, easier to verify and less risky than conventional espionage.

In addition to the covert interception of communications, Britain has continued to monitor and distribute open source intelligence (OSINT). This function is currently undertaken by BBC Monitoring located at Caversham, near Reading, and founded in 1939. BBC Monitoring selects and translates information from radio, television, the print media, news agencies and the internet; its global reach—like that of GCHQ—covers over 150 countries and 70 languages, with customers including the Foreign Office, the Defence Intelligence Staff and other government bodies and agencies.[29] The task of global OSINT collection is shared with its US counterpart, formerly the Foreign Broadcast Information Service and now known as the Open Source Center, a division of the CIA. The information gathered from open sources is pooled under an intelligence-sharing agreement dating from 1946 and made available to a variety of foreign governments via the Open Source Information System (OSIS). In July 2005, during a review of BBC Monitoring, the security and intelligence coordinator highlighted the continuing importance of such information: 'Open source material derived from overseas media is a rich resource, which can be mined at a low cost relative to the benefits it yields.'[30]

In July 2004 GCHQ moved into a purpose-built building at Benhall. Known locally as the Doughnut, due to its shape, the building was completed in June 2003, with the various directorates completing the move by the summer of 2004.[31] For purposes of continuity, it was decided temporarily to retain the upper part of one of GCHQ's existing sites to ensure that a round-the-clock service was maintained. The new building reflected the enduring role of GCHQ, as new threats have emerged to take the place of the old and the prevention of terrorism has become a priority. In its work GCHQ and the other agencies operate under the terms of the Regulation of Investigatory Powers Act 2000 (RIPA) which authorizes the covert interception of telephone calls, either by landline or mobile, emails, faxes and letters. The information gained in this way can only be used for intelligence purposes and under section 17 of RIPA is inadmissible in court. To complicate the issue, this does not apply to intelligence gained by the use of bugging devices, or to telephone conversations on an internal network where one of the people on the line is an undercover officer.

The inadmissibility of intercept evidence in court has recently come under criticism. In 2003 the prime minister ordered a review of existing legislation to examine the risks and benefits of using intercepts as evidence to secure more convictions of terrorists and criminal gangs. Following the review, the government concluded that the time was not right to change the law, and that the impact of new technology needed to be properly considered and factored into the decision-making process. The position was supported by the home secretary, Charles Clarke, who contended that intercept evidence would make little difference because so much evidence depends on other forms of surveillance and that technology is changing so fast that any regime put in place would soon be outdated. In expressing his view, the home secretary articulated the concerns of the intelligence community, who feared that allowing intercept evidence to be heard in court could reveal its secret operational methods. Baroness Ramsey, a former SIS officer, was particularly concerned, believing that even the slightest hint of interception techniques would compromise operations, especially where the material was encoded or enciphered. In light of recent terrorist trials, the government's position is evolving. In September 2006 the attorney general, Lord Goldsmith, stated that he now favoured allowing intercept evidence to be used in court provided that it did not compromise operational capabilities, personnel or future plans. The recent Chilcott report on the use of intercept evidence in court supported this view.[32] It recommended that intercept evidence should be used in criminal trials provided that there is no risk to national security and that the agencies retain ultimate control over its use.

In the 21st century, the vast potential of the internet and electronic methods of communication pose enormous challenges to those seeking to control or monitor intelligence. The sheer pace of technological change, and the sophistication of professional agents, criminals or terrorists in its use, have transformed traditional operational methods, while the expectation placed on GCHQ and other intelligence services have dramatically increased. Surveillance raises other concerns too. Issues such as intercept evidence illustrate the delicate balance to be struck between society's need for privacy and security—a debate that protestors in the Mazzini affair over 100 years ago would have recognized only too well.

9 | Intelligence in a Changing World

On 9 November 1989 the Berlin Wall, the symbol of the post-war division of Europe, was torn down. Two years later, in December 1991, the Soviet Union itself was dissolved and the Cold War, which had dominated international politics for over half a century, was consigned to history. The new strategic environment raised significant questions concerning the role and size of the various intelligence agencies. New roles were sought and found with the drugs trade and organized crime soon emerging as priority targets. One important immediate consequence, however, was greater transparency. The notion of political oversight emerged strongly, as did the need to reassure the public that operations were being conducted both ethically and effectively. The carte blanche secrecy enjoyed during the Cold War era was over.

In 1994 parliament passed the Intelligence Services Act which placed both SIS and GCHQ on a statutory footing and created the Intelligence and Security Committee (ISC). Composed of nine members drawn from the Houses of Commons and Lords, the role of the ISC is to examine the administration, policy and expenditure of MI5, SIS and GCHQ. The ISC reports annually to the prime minister on a variety of subjects and is given access to ministers, the agencies and government departments. Although the ISC does not have formal oversight of the Defence Intelligence Staff, the chief of defence intelligence has given evidence to the committee when required. The ISC also examines the work of the JIC and the assessments staff, and takes evidence from the chairman of the JIC and the chief of the assessments staff. The first chair of the ISC was Tom King, the former secretary of state for Northern Ireland.[1]

The ISC has recently been criticized in certain quarters for its apparent failure to take a more robust line with the various agencies. Particular concern has centred on its report dealing with the London terrorist attacks on 7 July 2005, in which it concluded that there were no culpable failures by the security and intelligence agencies. In May

2007, however, following the trial in which five Islamic terrorists were found guilty of conspiring to cause explosions, it was revealed that MI5 had placed two of the 7 July bombers under surveillance a year before the attacks, as part of Operation Crevice, tailing their car from Crawley in the south-east of England to West Yorkshire and bugging their conversations. This information was logged, but no further action was taken as it was believed that the individuals were peripheral to the main investigation. This revelation increased calls for a public inquiry and raised questions concerning the ISC's work; in response the recent Green Paper on constitutional reform has proposed a number of changes to the ISC's role. These include making the appointment of committee members more transparent, giving the committee the option to meet in public and strengthening the secretariat by appointing an independent investigator clearly separable from the staff of the Cabinet Office. In conjunction with these reforms, the government has also announced its intention to establish a National Security Committee, under the chairmanship of the prime minister, to ensure that policy development and implementation are coordinated and appropriate to the changing nature of the risks and challenges facing the United Kingdom in the 21st century.

Counter-terrorism is clearly a major challenge, with an 'unprecedented' number of investigations into extremist groups undertaken in the years before the London bombings in 2005. The security services' new focus was underlined on 2 October 2006, when Special Branch merged with the Anti-Terrorist Branch to form a new Counter Terrorism Command, and has since been reinforced with the appointment of Jonathan Evans as the new director general of MI5 in April 2007, whose expertise is in counter-terrorism. In a tactical move, recruitment into the services has become more open and deliberately draws from a wider ethnic base; Arabic and Urdu versions of the MI5 website were launched in May 2005. The substantial influx of recruits after 9/11 has been accompanied by a boost in financial resources for the intelligence services. The 2004 spending review announced the government's intention to provide MI5 with funds for a 'significant expansion' of its counter-terrorism capabilities, with a further increase, phased over three years, announced the following year.

Intelligence history is also becoming more accessible, with numerous documents now available at the National Archives. An interdepartmental advisory group on security and intelligence records was established in 2004, under Cabinet Office chairmanship, with representatives from the intelligence agencies, Foreign and Commonwealth Office, Ministry of Defence, Home Office and the National Archives. The advisory group also includes representatives of the academic community: Professor Christopher Andrew of the University of Cambridge and Professor Peter Hennessy of the University of London. The purpose of the group, as set out in its terms of reference, is 'to facilitate scholarly development and use, by historians and other researchers, of security and intelligence records that are already available, and to facilitate and identify other security and intelligence records which might be made publicly available'. Details of the group's activities are posted on the Cabinet Office's website.[2]

The last 100 years have witnessed a transformation in the size of intelligence organizations, and the need to manage and coordinate all the disparate elements is consequently even more acute. In the 1920s, for example, the number of officers employed by MI5 totalled fewer than 50, with a cost to the taxpayer of £90,000. Today, the number of staff is approximately 2,800, with a budget running into millions of pounds. The same increase has been enjoyed by the other agencies, and such growth in numbers has required an innovative approach to organization. The creation of the Joint Intelligence Committee (JIC) in 1936 saw the first step in this direction. Over the years, the authority of the JIC has gradually increased, with the chairman of the JIC now solely responsible for providing ministers with assessments that have been formulated independently of the political process.

Such an emphasis on political independence is one of the consequences of the Butler report, commissioned in response to the failure of the Iraqi Survey Group (ISG) to find any weapons of mass destruction in Iraq after coalition forces had deposed Saddam Hussein. The 1,400-strong international team of scientists and technicians, operating under the control of the Pentagon and CIA, conducted an intensive search of Iraq's research facilities and military bases, but failed to find any stocks of chemical, biological or nuclear weapons in a state fit for deployment or any developed plans for their use. It was still believed, however, that the former Iraqi regime had been determined to maintain the intellectual capital necessary for the reconstruction of nuclear, biological and chemical weapons programmes once sanctions had been removed. Nevertheless, the failure to find any weapons of mass destruction—the ingredients that had played a key part in the British decision to invade Iraq—has called into question the government's use of intelligence in support of its Iraq policy. On 3 February 2004 the foreign secretary announced in the House of Commons an inquiry into the intelligence relating to Iraq's weapons of mass destruction. The five-member committee of inquiry, headed by the former cabinet secretary Lord Butler of Brockwell, included senior parliamentarians and civil servants with military and intelligence backgrounds. Its terms of reference were *inter alia* to investigate the accuracy of intelligence on Iraqi weapons of mass destruction, to examine any discrepancies between the intelligence gathered, evaluated and used by the government, and to make recommendations on the future use of intelligence. The committee held its first meeting on 5 February and published its final report *Review of Intelligence on Weapons of Mass Destruction* on 14 July 2004.[3]

The main conclusion of the Butler report was that key intelligence used to justify the war with Iraq had been unreliable and that judgements had stretched available intelligence 'to the outer limits'. The committee, however, found no evidence of deliberate distortion or of culpable negligence. To guard against any recurrence, the committee made a number of observations. First, steps should be taken to integrate the work of the Defence Intelligence Staff (DIS) more closely with the rest of the intelligence community. Second, SIS validation procedures cast doubt on the reliability of human intelligence reports. Third, there was a strong case for the post of chairman of the JIC being held by an individual with experience of dealing with ministers in a very senior role, and who was 'demonstrably beyond influence'. Fourth, the resources allocated to the assessment staff were insufficient to cover the volume and range of work required, and it lacked a proper career structure for specialized staff. Last, JIC assessments should not give undue weight to intelligence reports over wider analysis of historical, psychological or geopolitical factors.

The government accepted these recommendations and established the Butler Implementation Group, under the direction of Sir David Omand, the security and intelligence coordinator, to oversee the necessary changes.[4] To integrate the DIS more fully into the work of the other agencies, a procedure was agreed between DIS and SIS to extend the distribution of sensitive reports. To ensure that human sources received effective scrutiny, SIS introduced new procedures and appointed a senior assurance officer to oversee the evaluation of sources, the quality of reporting and the underlying intelligence processes. To enhance the role of chairman of the JIC, the government established the post of permanent secretary, intelligence, security and resilience (PSISR) reporting directly to the prime minister. The PSISR is responsible for ensuring the effective coordination of intelligence within government and with partners both in the UK and internationally, and for providing the intelligence community with a clear strategy. The PSISR is also principal accounting officer for the single intelligence vote, chair of the Permanent Secretaries' Committee on the Intelligence Services and chairman of the JIC. The first holder of the post is Sir Richard Mottram, who took up his position in November 2005.[5]

The size of the assessments staff was also expanded, with a new team established to provide internal review of JIC assessments and additional resources provided to the team dealing with weapons of mass destruction. The chief of the assessments staff was also given the additional role of overseeing all assessments across government dealing with the security, defence and foreign relations. The post of professional head of intelligence analysis was also established within the Cabinet Office's Security and Intelligence Secretariat to advise on the recruitment of analysts, their career structures and training needs. To ensure the evaluation of all available sources, instructions were issued to the assessments staff to review past judgements and historic evidence when producing reports. In addition, all assessments teams were provided with research analyst support to ensure the more effective use of open source intelligence.

The global 'war on terror'

In response to the terrorist attacks in New York and Washington, Madrid, Bali and London, intelligence resources are now focused on countering the threat posed by Islamic extremism. A major concern expressed by the JIC was that terrorist networks would attempt to gain access to weapons of mass destruction, and in July 2002, in an attempt to address this concern, the government established the Counter-Proliferation Committee (CPC). Chaired by the head of the Defence and Overseas Secretariat within the Cabinet Office, the CPC is responsible for coordinating policy on counter-proliferation and brings together all policy and operational issues which had previously been dispersed throughout Whitehall. The policy decisions agreed by the CPC are put into action by the Counter-Proliferation Implementation Committee which coordinates the tactical and technical policy initiatives and sets the priorities of individual Whitehall departments. To assist in this work, a new IT system called SCOPE has been developed which allows intelligence information to be pooled and shared across government. The SCOPE system links together ten government departments and agencies and became operational in October 2007. The UK government has also promised to use its presidency of the Financial Action Task Force, the intergovernmental policy-making body established by the G7 in 1989, to deter, detect and disrupt terrorist financing and to hold to account those countries that are undermining the international effort through insufficient terrorist financing controls.

The drive for greater coordination was exemplified in the government's decision to set up the Joint Terrorism Analysis Centre (JTAC).[6] Established in 2003, JTAC is the focal point for the handling and dissemination of intelligence in response to the international terrorist threat. Based in Thames House, the home of MI5, JTAC is a multi-agency unit, staffed by members seconded from the three intelligence agencies and the DIS and including representatives from the Foreign and Commonwealth Office, the Home Office and law enforcement organizations. In the four years of its existence, JTAC has become widely recognized as an authoritative and effective mechanism for analysing all-source intelligence on the activities, intentions and capabilities of international terrorists who may threaten UK and allied interests anywhere in the world. It sets threat levels, issues warnings and provides in-depth assessments on trends, terrorist networks and capabilities. The head of JTAC is accountable directly to the director general of MI5, who in turn reports to the JIC. An oversight board, chaired by the Cabinet Office, has been established to ensure that JTAC meets customer requirements by monitoring the effectiveness of JTAC's systems for engaging with customer departments.

JTAC has no powers of arrest and works closely with the Counter Terrorism Command (CTC) of the Metropolitan Police, which was established in October 2006. The new command, which is also known as SO15, brings together intelligence analysis and the coordination of operational support activity. Its overriding objective is to bring to justice those involved in terrorism or extremist activity. To achieve this, CTC gathers and exploits intelligence on potential terrorist activity within London and is the single point of contact for all overseas law enforcement agencies engaged in counter-terrorism. The first head of CTC is deputy assistant commissioner Peter Clarke, who also holds the position of national co-ordinator of terrorist investigations.

The need for organizations to adapt to the demands imposed by international terrorism is not confined to the intelligence community and law enforcement agencies. In March 2007 the Home Office was effectively split into two: a slimmed-down Home Office, dealing with national security; and a Ministry of Justice, which combines the Home Office's criminal justice remit with the functions of the Department of Constitutional Affairs. Under the reorganization a new Office for Security and Counter-Terrorism was established within the Home Office with responsibility for developing and supporting the UK's overall counter-terrorism strategy.[7] In conjunction with these changes, a new ministerial committee on security and terrorism, chaired by the prime minister, was established. The home secretary also chairs a national security board which meets weekly to investigate potential threats to the UK. The work of the board is supported by a new inter-departmental research, information and communications unit housed in the Home Office to support 'the struggle for ideas and values'. To a lesser extent, these changes mirror events in the United States where the Bush administration has established a National Counterterrorism Center and begun attempting to meld together the work of 22 separate intelligence agencies into the all-embracing Department of Homeland Security. The similarity of these responses is no surprise. It is clear that in the ongoing fight against international terrorism, the effective co-ordination of intelligence assets will be a crucial dimension.

Notes on the Text

INTRODUCTION

1 See Cradock, P.
2 Omand, D., 'Reflections on Secret Intelligence' in Hennessy, P. (ed.), *The New Protective State* (Continuum Books, 2007).

CHAPTER 1

1 *The Times*, 14 December 1867.
2 TNA MEPO 2/1297.
3 Ibid.
4 See French, D., p. 355–70, for further details.
5 TNA CAB 16/232.
6 TNA KV 1/5.
7 See Wilkinson, N.J., for further details.
8 TNA KV 1/6.
9 TNA KV 1/32–40 also notes that the *onus probandi* now lay with the accused and not the prosecutors.
10 Andrews, C., p. 175.
11 TNA KIV 1/21.
12 See TNA KV 2/1–2 and MEPO 3/2444 for Mata Hari and KV 2/6–10 for Casement.
13 TNA CRIM 1/683–685 and CRIM 1/153/4. See also DPP 1/38.
14 There are a number of files on Lody including TNA DPP 1/29 and HO 144 /3324.
15 See TNA CAB 127/355–65 for the records of the Secret Service Committee. See also Bennett, G.
16 Stafford, D., p. 130.
17 TNA CAB 24/166 and PRO 30/69/220–221 provide examples of these reports.
18 TNA KV 2/1398. See also KV 2/997–999.
19 See TNA KV 2/1034–1047 for files on Pollitt.
20 There are dozens of files relating to the ARCOS raid including TNA KV 3/15, which contains a Photostat of the British military manual, the possession of which led to the raid, KV3/16–17, KV 2/818 and HO 144/8403. See also MEPO 38/70–72.
21 TNA CAB 127/366.
22 TNA KV 2/2699.
23 Ibid.
24 See TNA KV 4/227 for a history of MS

Section from 1939 to 1945.
25 See TNA KV 2/1020–1023 for further information on Glading and KV 2/1237–1238 and KV 2/1003 for his co-defendants George Whomack and Albert Williams.
26 KV 2/816.
27 KV 2/815.
28 KV 2/815.
29 TNA KV 2/815–816.
30 TNA KV 2/802–805. See also KV 4/228.
31 TNA KV 4/111.
32 TNA KV 4/241 gives a useful summary of MI5's knowledge of the BUF.
33 See TNA KV 4/170 for a note on Pulitz's role between 1936 and 1939.
34 See TNA PREM 3/418/1 for the foundation of the HD(S)E.
35 Further details of Hankey's report are in TNA CAB 63/192–193. See also CAB 127/383.
36 TNA HO 45/25568–25572.
37 TNA KV 2/2106–2107.
38 See TNA KV 4/339–444 for policy and procedure for detaining subjects at the RPS and HO 215/485–489 for welfare arrangements at the LRC. See also KV 4 /142–144. KV 4/344 contains a typical example of an alien interrogation at the LRC.
39 TNA KV 4/201. See also KV 4/208.
40 TNA KV 4/5 contains the original transcript.
41 Hinsley, F.H., and Simkins, C.A.G., vol. 5, p. 19.
42 See TNA KV 2/41 for a summary of the Garbo case written by his case officer; KV 2/42 for a comparison of ISOS product with MI5 deception material; and KV 2/63–71 for Garbo's communications with the Nazis. The importance of his role in Fortitude can be gleaned from KV 2/39.
43 TNA KV 4/195.
44 TNA KV 2/1500–1501.
45 TNA HO 325/17.
46 See TNA MEPO 2/10736–10739 for the police investigation into his escape; HO 278/7 for photographs and reports; and PREM 13/952 for prime ministerial reaction.
47 Some of the case against 'Gordon Lonsdale and others' can be found in TNA CRIM 8/31.
48 Bennett, G. and Hamilton, K. (eds.), doc. No. 66.
49 TNA PREM 15/1935.

50 Ibid.
51 For further details, see Hughes, G. in *Cold War History*, 6 (2006), pp. 229–49.
52 TNA PREM 15/1935.
53 *http://www.opsi.gov.uk/acts/acts1989/Ukpga_19890005_en_1.htm.*

CHAPTER 2

1 See Budiansky, S.
2 TNA SP 53/18/55 and SP 53/22.
3 TNA SP 94/2. For further details of Standen's espionage activities, see the online exhibition at *http://www.nationalarchives.gov.uk/spies/spies/standen/default.htm.*
4 TNA WO 1/87.
5 TNA HD 2/1.
6 Henderson, G.B. in *English Historical Review*, 53 (1938).
7 TNA AO 19/122–123. See also PRO 30/60/13.
8 TNA HD 3/65.
9 TNA FO 1093/37.
10 Bethell's letter and Cumming's response can be found on the SIS website: *www.mi6.gov.uk/output/Page557.html.*
11 TNA FO 1093/25. See also WO 106/6292.
12 For details of this early period, see Judd, A.
13 TNA FO 902/1.
14 TNA CAB 37/158.
15 Zaharoff never communicated directly with the British government but used an intermediary, usually Sir Vincent Caillard, who later became the financial director of Vickers. See TNA FO 1093/47–57 for details of the correspondence between the two.
16 TNA FO 1093/56.
17 Bennett, G., p. 55.
18 TNA KV 2/827.
19 The records produced by the Ministry of Information are in TNA INF 4.
20 The records of the Political Intelligence Department are in TNA FO 371/4352–4387.
21 For further details see Goldstein, E. in *Review of International Studies*, 14 (1988).
22 The records of the Secret Service Committee are in TNA CAB 127/355–365.
23 For details, see West, N.
24 See Bennett, G.
25 The records of the Indian Political Intelligence Service can be found in the India Office Records, British Library.
26 TNA T 160/860.
27 For details, see Read, A. and Fisher, D.
28 See Best, S.P.
29 TNA FO 371/23107 and KV 2/2106–2107.
30 See Brown, A.C.
31 TNA FO 366/2382.
32 The papers of the Future Operations (Enemy) Planning Section are in TNA CAB 81/64. See also CAB 79/8/7.
33 The records of MEW are in TNA FO 837. See also PRO 30/95.
34 TNA PREM 1/374.
35 TNA FO 954/23A. After the war, Leeper was instrumental in establishing the British Council.
36 The records of PWE are in TNA FO 898.
37 For further details, see Howard, M., pp. 89–92. See also TNA CAB 154/67and WO 208/3163.
38 CAB 154/112.
39 Ibid.
40 Dahl, who was serving as assistant air attaché in Washington, later claimed that he had been recruited into BSC by the novelist C.S. Forester.
41 For details, see *British Security Coordination*, an internal history of BSC written shortly after the end of the Second World War.
42 For details of Stephenson's career, see Hyde, H.M.
43 See KV 3/350–351.
44 KV 3/351.
45 TNA CAB 163/7.
46 For details see Dorrill, S.
47 IRD records can be found in TNA FO 1110 and FCO 95.
48 TNA CAB 21/3878 and PREM 11/1578. See also Hamrick, S.J.
49 TNA FO 953/2165. For Philby's own account, see Philby, K.
50 For details of Blunt's activities, see Boyle, A.
51 See Modin, Y.
52 Janet Chisholm's obituary, *Daily Telegraph*, 8 May 2004.
53 For details see Wynne, G.
54 For details see Gordievsky, O.
55 *Falkland Islands Review.*
56 *www.sis.gov.uk.*

CHAPTER 3

1 TNA WO 43/292.
2 TNA WO 37/10/5.
3 TNA WO 37/1/13 contains the original. Details of Grant's escapades can be

found online at *http://www.national archives.gov.uk/spies/spies/grant/default .htm*.

4   See TNA FO 38 for records relating to the British Secret Service during the Napoleonic era.

5   TNA WO 106/6149.

6   TNA WO 32/7290.

7   *The Times*, 23 June, 1855.

8   TNA WO 32/6053.

9   TNA WO 32/6054.

10 TNA WO 108/356.

11 *Report of the Commissioners*. See also TNA WO 108/415.

12 TNA WO 279/537.

13 TNA WO 158/962.

14 TNA AIR 1/895/204/5/712. See TNA AIR 10/200 for examples of photographs taken from the air.

15 See TNA WO 106/1510–1517 for MacDonogh's career at DMI.

16 TNA INF 4/1B, WO 106/45 and WO 106 /6290.

17 TNA WO 158/961.

18 TNA WO 106/1594A.

19 TNA WO 287/82.

20 The Davidson papers are at the Liddell Hart Centre for Military Archives, King's College London, Reference code: GB99 KCLMA Davidson F H N.

21 TNA WO 204/1038–1042.

22 TNA WO 167/1384.

23 See TNA WO 208/4410–4418 for the 'Birley Bible'. For Annan's own account of his time in MI14, see Annan, N. For intelligence reports on Germany, 1938– 40, see TNA WO 208/4607–4611.

24 See TNA WO 208/4307–4319 and WO 208 /5482–5489 respectively for MI14's weekly and daily intelligence reports.

25 TNA WO 208/5192–5194.

26 TNA WO 165/42.

27 TNA WO 208/3242.

28 TNA WO 208/3268.

29 TNA WO 208/3460.

30 TNA WO 208/3663–3748. This series of records contains numbered interro- gation reports of alien civilians and refugees from friendly countries arriving in the United Kingdom from abroad. The reports generally include the names and nationalities of the individuals being interviewed and some biographical detail together with infor- mation regarding where the individuals had been in enemy or enemy-occupied territory, what was their occupation in those places, and what period of time they had spent in those occupations and places. Some reports include sketch maps and diagrams, and occasionally photographs. See also WO 208/5494.

31 TNA WO 208/5619.

32 Ibid.

33 TNA CAB 150/36.

34 TNA WO 258/92.

35 See, for example, TNA FO 371/104561.

36 TNA WO 208/5566.

37 TNA FO 1305/129.

38 TNA WO 208/5271.

39 *The Times*, 26 March 1985.

40 Geraghty, T., pp. 208–11.

41 TNA WO 208/5270.

42 See TNA WO 208/4978–5003 and 5248– 5271 for BRIXMIS intelligence reports.

43 TNA WO 216/494. By 1956, five SAS squadrons with a total strength of 560 men were operating in the Malayan jungle.

44 TNA CO 1022/11–12.

45 TNA CO 1022/51, CO 1035/6 and CO 1035 /38.

46 TNA WO 216/806 and CO 1022/103.

47 TNA FO 371/101223–101225. See also Cloake, J.

48 TNA AIR 23/8559.

49 TNA CO 1022/50.

50 TNA WO 291/1786 and CO 875/71/6.

51 TNA DO 35/5992–5993.

52 TNA WO 276/231–243 and WO 276/384.

53 See TNA WO 276/387–408 for Intelli- gence Committee and Special Branch summaries and reports from districts.

54 TNA CO 822/455, WO 276/62 and CO 1035/30.

55 TNA WO 276/231.

56 TNA CO 822/796, DO 35/5352 and WO 276/513–514.

57 See, for example, Elkins, C.

58 TNA CO 822/1219.

59 TNA KV 2/1787–1789, CO 822/453, PREM 11/3413 and CO 822/1909–1914.

60 TNA WO 33/2736.

61 TNA FO 371/123897.

62 TNA CO 1035/98 and FO 371/117632.

63 TNA FO 371/123924. See also FO 371 /123897.

64 TNA WO 967/320–321.

65 See Holland, R., for a definitive account of British operations in Cyprus.

66 Further details of the role and respons- ibilities of DIS are at: *www.mod.uk/ DefenceInternet/AboutDefence/What WeDo/SecurityandIntelligence/DIS.htm*.

CHAPTER 4

1 Remark books can be found in ADM 346 and drawings and maps in ADM 344.
2 Maffeo, S., p. 10.
3 *Report on the Finch Manuscripts*, pp. cxxxvii–cxxxviii, 744–50. I am indebted to Sonia Anderson for her research into the career of Fontaines, published in the introductory essay to her edition of the Finch papers. I have relied on it extensively in what follows.
4 Ibid, p. 745.
5 TNA ADM 1/3935–3969. The letters are in French.
6 Andrew, C., pp. 12–15.
7 Lambert, A. (ed.) pp. 71–3.
8 This account is based on the pen portrait of Hall given in the best published account of First World War naval intelligence: Beesly, P., pp. 34–7.
9 Beesly, P., pp. 37–8, 43–4, 123–7. See TNA ADM 137/3956–3962 and ADM 137 /4057–4189 for Room 40 records.
10 Hinsley, F.H., vol. 1, pp. 9–10.
11 Andrew, C., p. 455.
12 The section that follows owes much to Syrett's two Navy Records Society volumes and Beesly's *Very Special Intelligence*. It should be noted that 'Ultra' applied only to the intelligence yielded from the breaking of the most complex ciphers (including but not only those from Enigma and Lorenz machines). SIGINT also yielded much non-ULTRA intelligence, from unenciphered material and from low-level ciphers. Many coded communications (including German naval ones) were exploited, whose intelligence did not merit ULTRA protection.
13 Syrett (ed.), *U-boat Situations and Trends*, pp. 33–4.
14 TNA HW 3/147;see also document 172 in Syrett, D. (ed.), *U-boat Tracking Papers*.
15 TNA ADM 223/463; see also document 170 in Syrett, D., *U-boat Tracking Papers*.
16 TNA HW 11/38; see also document 1 in Syrett, D., *U-boat Tracking Papers*.
17 Syrett, *U-boat Situations and Trends*, pp. xix, xx, xxv, xxvi.
18 Beesly, *Very Special Intelligence*, pp. 100–1.
19 This section draws on Dorril, S., p. 290–9, for information on these Baltic operations.
20 The recommendations for awards to Crabb are set out in TNA ADM 1/14531.
21 Dorril, *MI6*, pp. 617–20.
22 Records relating to the Crabb incident can be found in TNA ADM 1/28941, ADM 1/28946, ADM 1/29240 ADM 1/29241, PREM 11/2077, PREM 13/2919, PREM 15 /1316, FO 371/122885, CAB 21/2887 and CAB 163/207. The later of these files relate to attempts in the 1970s to prevent the filming of a documentary on the fate of Crabb.
23 The records of Operation Sandstone in ADM 326 and include hundreds of beach surveys with annotated maps of the coast, depth measurements at different tide levels and details of potential landing places for military equipment. Reference is made to the original US request in ADM 326/1314.
24 TNA ADM 326/413.
25 TNA ADM 326/1314 and ADM 326/1323 provide histories, and the former also contains an explanation of how the teams operated; ADM 326/1325 gives the terms of reference of the survey in 1961; and ADM 326/1320 provides details of the afterlife of the survey in the merged DIS.
26 ADM 326/1315 relates to negotiations with the Irish for starting a survey while ADM 326/1313 and ADM 326/1319 cover the Suez area and the Mediterranean. Note that these files state that details of such surveys themselves were placed with the Army Historical Branch.
27 The gradual downgrading and dissolution of the survey can be tracked in TNA ADM 326/1316– a 1954 review of their operations states that the survey does not have sufficient importance to warrant the attachment of scientists; ADM 326/1318 provides options for the survey team following the end of Sandstone; ADM 326/1324 covers absorption by DI32; and ADM 326/1326 gives earlier proposals for a merger with the Hydrographic Office. ADM 326/387–388 are the hovercraft landing-slip surveys.
28 Brown, D.K. and Moore, G., pp. 116–17.
29 Aldrich, R.J., p. 526–9.
30 Brown D.K. and Moore, G., pp.115.
31 Aldrich, R.J., pp. 539–40.
32 TNA PREM 13/1382.

33 Aldrich, R.J., p. 530.
34 TNA ADM 223/875. The list of details to be collected is in enclosure 8.
35 Dorril, *MI6*, pp. 524–5.
36 Files dealing with the *Gaul* incident include: TNA FCO 76/950 and FCO 76/1157, PREM 16/31, AY 23/121 and HO 331/30. The last of these is the initial Home Office wreck enquiry.
37 Hackmann, W., pp. xxvii–xxix, xxix.
38 Bud, R. and Gummett, P. (eds.), pp. 169–70.
39 Ibid.
40 See the US SOSUS veterans website: *http://www.iusscaa.org*.
41 Ibid.
42 Moore, J.E., pp. 122–8.
43 Brown D.K. and Moore, G., p. 155.
44 Prezelin, B. (ed.), p. 512.
45 The lack of a market economy made it immensely difficult for the Soviet leadership to stimulate innovation. The best short account of the working (or non-working) of the Soviet military-industrial complex can be found in Odom, W., pp. 223–43.
46 The Vassall case records are in TNA ADM 1/27370 and ADM 1/30091–30092.
47 The records of the Houghton case, Portland spy ring and security reviews following the trial are in: TNA ADM 1/27831, ADM 1/27832, ADM 1/28308, ADM 1/28160, ADM 116/6296–16/6297. Tom Wright's essay in Bud, R. and Gummett, P. (eds.), pp. 175–8, gives a good summary of the spy ring and its capture.
48 TNA ADM 116/6296.
49 Wright in Bud, R. and Gummett, P. (eds.), pp. 175–8.
50 TNA DEFE 69/196–200 covers the Bingham case.
51 TNA DEFE 69/196.
52 Ibid.
53 FOTIs 404, 410, 412 (all Nimrod), 702 (jammer), 704 (jamming counter measures), 802 (anti-ship missile defence), 901 (Valiant class), 912 (Ikara).

CHAPTER 5

1 TNA AIR 1/686/21/13/2244.
2 TNA AIR 1/797/204/4/1002.
3 Raleigh, W., p. 250.
4 TNA AIR 1/749/204/3/76.
5 TNA AIR 1/686/21/13/2244.
6 Raleigh, W., p. 343; Jones, A.H., vol. 2, p. 87.
7 Jones, A.H., vol. 2, pp. 88–91.
8 TNA AIR 1/2182/209/15/17.
9 Ibid.
10 AIR 1/1254 204/8/25.
11 AIR 34/735.
12 AIR 1/686/21/3/2244.
13 See Hinsley, F.H., vol. 1, pp. 10, 14 26–9, 498–9. See also chapter 13 of Winterbotham, F.W., and Stanley, R.M., pp. 40–3.
14 AIR 1/895/204/5/710.
15 Stanley, R.M., p. 40.
16 Winterbotham, pp. 199–200.
17 This section draws on Hinsley, F.H., vol 1, pp. 29–30, 104, 169–72.
18 AIR 34/89.
19 AIR 34/715.
20 *http://www.defence.gov.au/news/raaf news/EDITIONS/4616/history/story02. htm* [accessed 5 June 2007]; Andrew, p. 470.
21 *Air Intelligence, A Symposium*, chapter 4, pp. 7–8; Hinsley, F.H., vol. 1, pp. 284–5.
22 Hinsley, F.H., vol. 1, p. 15.
23 CAB 81/95.
24 This section draws on Hinsley, F.H., vol. 1, pp. 162–3, 173–4, 177–82, 315–23.
25 Clayton, A., p. 30.
26 Ibid., pp. 32–49; see also Stubbington, J., chapter 7, in particular p. 50.
27 This section draws on Hinsley, F.H., vol. 1., pp. 237–40, 252–68, 517–19.
28 TNA AIR 2/7689.
29 Ibid.
30 Stubbington, J., chapter 5, in particular pp. 27–34.
31 AIR 20/1568.
32 Aldrich, R.J., p. 397.
33 Ibid., pp. 394–7.
34 *Air Intelligence: A Symposium*, pp. 118–127.
35 Ibid.
36 Aldrich, R.J., pp. 526
37 Ibid., pp. 530–1.
38 Ibid., p. 534–8.
39 *http://www.mod.uk/DefenceInternet/ AboutDefence/WhatWeDo/Securityand Intelligence/DIS/ICG/JaricTheNational ImageryExploitationCentreHistory .htm*.
40 Friedman, N., p. 91.
41 Ibid, pp. 87–8.
42 TNA AVIA 6/25034.
43 See DEFE 11/574.

44 Ibid.
45 ADM 1/28880.
46 AVIA 6/25027. See also Baker, D., 'Military Communications Satellites' (United Kingdom section).
47 Friedman, N., pp. 89–91.
48 Ibid, p. 91–4.
49 Ibid, pp. 95–8.
50 West, N., pp. 82–3.
51 Friedman, p. 97–8; Baker, D., 'Military Ocean Surveillance' (United States section).
52 Baker, D., 'Military Ocean Surveillance' (United States section).
53 Ibid.
54 DEFE 11/574.
55 West, N., pp. 80–4.
56 Friedman, N., pp. 98–9.

CHAPTER 6

1 Davies, P.H.J., pp. 115–17, 124.
2 Foot, M.R.D., *SOE in France*, p. 5.
3 Mackenzie, W.J.M., pp. 38–55; for achievements, see p. 54.
4 Foot, M.R.D., *SOE in France*, pp 8–9.
5 Davies, P.H.J., pp. 120–1.
6 Mackenzie, W.J.M., pp. 558–62 for de Gaulle–Giraud rivalry and pp. 243–80 for early operations of F and R/F sections and creation of R/F section; Foot, M.R.D., *SOE in France*, p. 136 for quotation.
7 TNA HS 9/273/2.
8 Foot, M.R.D., *SOE in France*, p. 97; Mackenzie, W.J.M., pp. 267–8, 566–9.
9 Mackenzie, W.J.M., pp. 569–571; Foot, M.R.D., *SOE in France*, pp. 360, 249–50
10 The following statistics are drawn from Mackenzie, W.J.M., pp. 586, 599, 602.
11 TNA HS 9/355/2, 356.
12 TNA HS 9/356.
13 Foot, M.R.D., *Low Countries*, pp. 103–14, 116–97.
14 TNA HS 6/727.
15 Mackenzie, W.J.M., p 307.
16 TNA HS 2/264.
17 TNA HS 2/184. The execution was the consequence of a direct 'Führer order' dated 20/10/43 which stated that 'prisoners taken as a result of contact with British or British Empire Commando troops' should be 'handed over without delay to the nearest SD unit; this SD unit will be responsible for the execution of the prisoners.' It also stated: 'Wherever possible such Commando troops will be killed to the last man during the action; only where this is not practicable will the procedure laid down above be followed.' Under interrogation the SD officer stated that the four had been executed under an earlier version of the Fuhrer order, but no copy of an earlier order was found. Although the interrogators were inclined to believe the officer, it is possible that the four were executed without formal authorisation.
18 TNA HS 2/186.
19 Ibid.
20 TNA HS 2/188.
21 TNA HS 5/206.
22 Mackenzie, W.J.M, pp., 25, 100.
23 Foot, M.R.D., *SOE*, p. 237.
24 Bailey, R., pp. 316–20.
25 Atherton, L., *Balkans*, pp. 14–16.
26 Ibid., pp. 28–30.
27 Atherton, L., *Africa*, pp. 2–3, 17–18; TNA HS 3/153.
28 Atherton, L., *Africa*, pp. 20–1; TNA HS 3/165 and HS 3/207.
29 Ibid., pp. 9–10.
30 TNA HS 3/14.
31 Ibid.
32 TNA HS 4/18, HS 4/19, HS 4/22, HS 4/24 and HS 4/39; Atherton, L., Eastern Europe, pp. 4–5, 22; Seaman, M., pp. 10–11.
33 TNA HS 4/132.
34 Seaman, M. p. 13 (referencing TNA HS 6/623).
35 Seaman, M., pp 13–15.
36 TNA HS 6/625.
37 TNA HS 6/624 and HS 6/625.
38 TNA HS 6/625.
39 Seaman, M. pp. 24–8.
40 TNA KV 2/2821.
41 Ibid.
42 TNA KV 2/2827.
43 Ibid.
44 *http://en.doew.braintrust.at/db_gestapo_6107.html* and *http://en.doew.braintrust.at/db_gestapo_9348.html*.
45 Atherton, L., *Far East*, pp. 2–4.
46 Smith, C., p. 79.
47 TNA HS 1/109.
48 Ibid.
49 Ibid.
50 See TNA HS 1/21, WO 172/4585, WO 203/1064 and CAB 106/178.
51 Davies, P.H.J., pp. 199–204.
52 Davies, P.H.J., pp. 205–9.
53 See Murphy, C.J., chapter 2. I would

like to thank Chris Murphy for drawing my attention to this.

54 Ibid., p. 36.

CHAPTER 7

1 Main research establishments included: the Royal Aircraft Establishment, the Royal Radar Establishment, the Admiralty Research Laboratory, the Admiralty Surface Weapons Establishment, the Admiralty Experiment Works, the Trench Warfare and Chemical Warfare Department and the War Office Proof and Experimental Establishment. Records for these establishments are found in: TNA AIR 1, AIR 5, AVIA 6, AVIA 7, AVIA 13, AVIA 14, AVIA 26, AVIA 36, ADM 204, ADM 212, ADM 204, ADM 220, ADM 226, WO 142 and WO 186.

2 TNA WO 142/20, WO 142/212 and WO 142/314.

3 TNA ADM 116/3451.

4 See TNA ADM 283 for the records of the Admiralty's Department of Scientific Research and Experiment.

5 TNA CAB 48/4.

6 TNA AIR 20/1623.

7 TNA WO 208/3506–3507.

8 TNA AIR 20/1623.

9 For details, see Jones, R.V.

10 TNA AIR 20/1623.

11 TNA AIR 40/2572 contains a copy of the original Oslo report. This can be found in its translated form in Hinsley, F.H., vol. 1, Appendix 5.

12 Ibid.

13 Monthly reports of Home Army GHQ in *The Report of The Anglo-Polish Historical Committee*, p. 475.

14 Minutes and reports of the Crossbow Committee are in TNA CAB 98/36–38; see also CAB 21/775 and AIR 40/2517–2531.

15 TNA DEFE 40/15.

16 TNA AIR 40/2887.

17 *The Report of The Anglo-Polish Historical Committee*, p. 478.

18 For details, see Hinsley, F.H., Vol. 3, pp. 357–455.

19 See TNA FO 1031 for the records of FIAT, including reports on the evacuation of equipment, interrogation of enemy personnel and captured enemy documents. See also FO 1078, which contains FIAT reports of the interrogation of Albert Speer and other civilian personalities.

20 BIOS records are in TNA FO 935. See also FO 1005/1602, WO 219/1984 and AIR 40/1555.

21 EPES records are found in TNA FO 1031/52, FO 1031/75 and FO 1031/89–95.

22 TNA WO 219/1985, WO 219/2694, FO 1032/1471 and FO 1031/49.

23 TNA DEFE 41/109–111, FO 371/70952–70958, DEFE 41/122, DEFE 41/130–32, FO 1032/1018–1019 and FO 1032/1231A.

24 TNA WO 219/5335.

25 TNA WO 33/2554–2561 and WO 231/22–26.

26 TNA FO 1032/296–306, FO 940/108 and AVIA 22/936.

27 The British also secured documents and equipment on the German guided weapons programme under Operations Surgeon and Abstract. See TNA AVIA 12/82, FO 1062/114, AVIA 54/1849, FO 1031/12 (interrogation of von Braun) and FO 1031/13.

28 See Goudsmit, S.A., for Goudsmit's own account of the Alsos Mission.

29 TNA AVIA 10/70.

30 TNA HW 50/71.

31 'Central Organisation for Defence', Cmd. 6923, 1946.

32 TNA CAB 81/130.

33 For Jones' account of events, see Jones, R.V., pp. 492–8.

34 The Charters of the JSIC and JTIC are found at TNA DEFE 40/24.

35 STIB records are in TNA DEFE 41; see also FO 1039/672 and FO 1050/67.

36 Dragon Return records are in TNA DEFE 41/2-6. Further progress reports are located at DEFE 21/25–27.

37 DRPC records are in TNA DEFE 10/18–40.

38 TNA CAB 163/7.

39 TNA PREM 8/952.

40 TNA DEFE 44/1.

41 TNA CAB 21/3878.

42 The Brundrett report is in DEFE 32/4.

43 The records and reports of these divisions are in TNA DEFE 21, DEFE 44 and DEFE 63.

44 See Strong, K. for details of his early career.

45 JIC reports for the period 1947–68 are located at CAB 158.

46 For details, see Ziegler, C. and Jacobson, D.

47 A series of 20 files from the Security Service on Nunn May's activities are at TNA KV 2/2209–2226, 2563–2564.

48 TNA CAB 81/130.

49 TNA DEFE 13/60.

50 TNA DEFE 13/414.

51 FCO 37/116–117 and PREM 11/4672 give details of the Indian and Chinese nuclear programmes.

52 Chiefs of staff records are in TNA DEFE 4.

53 TNA DEFE 13/342.

54 For further details, see Aldrich, R.J., chapter 24.

55 See TNA CAB 137 for the records of the JTWC.

56 See TNA WO 188 and 189.

57 See Carter, G. and Balmer, B, in Bud, R. and Gummett, P. (eds.).

58 TNA WO 188/698.

59 TNA WO 188/659–666, DEFE 10/261–266 and WO 188/667–672.

60 TNA CAB 79/52.

61 TNA PREM 15/1264.

62 For details see, Mangold, T.

63 Heard, G.; Keyhoe, D.

64 See TNA DEFE 44/119 for the working party's conclusions. Related material is found at DEFE 10/496, DEFE 41/74, 75.

65 For details, see the articles by Ziegler, C. and Haines, G., in *Intelligence and National Security*, 14, No. 2 (1999).

66 TNA AIR 20/9994.

67 'Review of Intelligence on Weapons of Mass Destruction', Report of a Committee of Privy Counsellors, HC 898, July 2004.

CHAPTER 8

1 See *'My Purdah Lady'* for the early history of the Secret Office.

2 TNA HD 3/17.

3 Records describing the work of the Secret Office can be found in the following files: TNA HD 3/2, HD 3/8, HD, HD 3/35.

4 HD 3/17

5 *Report from the Secret Committee on the Post Office*, House of Commons, 5 August 1844, No. 582; *Report from the Secret Committee of the House of Lords relative to Law in respect to opening and detaining letters at the Post Office*, 7 August 1844, No. 601. See also Smith, F.B., 'British Post Office Espionage, 1844', *Historical Studies*, 14 (1970).

6 Editorial, *The Times*, 25 June 1844.

7 TNA HD 3/35.

8 *Manual of Instruction in Army Signalling* (Stationery Office, 1876).

9 TNA WO 33/198, WO 32/8112, WO 106

/6149. See also Fergusson, T.

10 TNA HW 7/8. This file and HW 3/176–82 contain the most important papers relating to the Zimmermann telegram.

11 TNA HW 3/179.

12 See TNA ADM 231, ADM 137, ADM 233 and HW 7 for the records of naval intelligence and Room 40 during the First World War.

13 See Denniston, R. for details of his father's career.

14 Records of GCCS are in TNA HW 3, HW 12, HW 42 and HW 43. The personal papers of Alexander Guthrie Denniston are at the Churchill College Archives, Reference GBR/0014/DENN.

15 Along with the files mentioned above in note 20 under chapter 1, see the government white paper on the affair (Cmd 2874) 1927.

16 Second World War policy papers are found in TNA HW 14. Establishment branch records, which contain correspondence on accommodation, personnel, staffing, pay and conditions at Bletchley Park, are found in HW 64.

17 See for example, TNA HW 1/323, 1306, 1689.

18 For the signals intelligence seen by Churchill see series TNA HW 1. The request for access is at HW 1/1. For Morton's correspondence, see PREM 7.

19 Records of the Radio Security Service are located in TNA HW 19 and HW 34. Records describing the relationship between RSS and SIS are in KV 4/97–98.

20 The Holden agreement is reproduced in full in *Intelligence and National Security*, 14 (1999), 192–95. For details of Anglo-American cooperation see TNA HW 50/13.

21 TNA HW 50/37. The BRUSA agreement is reproduced in full in 'The BRUSA Agreement of May 17, 1943', *Cryptologia*, 21 (1997).

22 TNA HW 3/169.

23 TNA HW 14/164, HW 64/68, FO 366/2221.

24 Menzies continued as 'director general' until his retirement in 1952 and the title was retained by his successor. When Sinclair retired in 1956, the title and GCHQ role for the chief of SIS lapsed.

25 For details of UKUSA, see Richelson, J. and Ball, D.

26 Records relating to Venona are found in TNA HW 15. See also *www.nsa.gov/venona/*.

27 TNA HW 15/58. AFSA was the Armed Forces Security Agency, the forerunner of the National Security Agency.

28 There is very little in the public domain detailing the activities of GCHQ in the post-war period. For details, see Bamford, J.

29 Details of BBC Monitoring are on its website at *www.monitor.bbc.co.uk/*.

30 Intelligence and Security Committee, *Annual Report, 2005–06*, Cm 6864.

31 Details of GCHQ's site are detailed on its website at *www.gchq.gov.uk/*.

32 *Privy Council Review of Intercept as Evidence*, report to the prime minister and the home secretary, 30 January 2008, Cm 7324.

CHAPTER 9

1 Details of the ISC can be found at *www.cabinetoffice.gov.uk/intelligence/*.

2 *www.cabinetoffice.gov.uk/about_the_cabinet_office/other_bodies/horuintel.asp*.

3 *The Butler Report*, HC 898, 14 July 2004.

4 The position of security and intelligence coordinator was created in the summer of 2002. It was designed to allow the cabinet secretary to hand over his responsibility for the security and intelligence functions, and for the new task of developing resilience and crisis management capability within the civil service, to an experienced permanent secretary.

5 In April 2005, Sir David Omand retired as the security and intelligence coordinator and was replaced by Bill Jeffrey from the Home Office. In August 2005, William Ehrman moved on from his post as JIC chairman to take up a new posting as ambassador to China. In September 2005, the cabinet secretary announced that Bill Jeffrey was to succeed Sir Kevin Tebbit as permanent secretary at the Ministry of Defence and that Sir Richard Mottram was to take up the post of SIC and assume, in addition, the role of chairman of the JIC.

6 For details, see *www.intelligence.gov.uk/agencies/jtac.aspx*.

7 *http://security.homeoffice.gov.uk/counter-terrorism-strategy*; see also *www.cabinetoffice.gov.uk/reports/government_changes/*.

Intelligence Records and Sources

Intelligence records transferred to the National Archives are located in a variety of record series. Descriptions of records can be found in the online catalogue at *www.nationalarchives.gov.uk/catalogue*. The National Archives website also houses an online exhibition on security and intelligence history at *www.nationalarchives.gov.uk/securityhistory*.

DOMESTIC INTELLIGENCE. Prior to the creation of the Security Service (MI5) in 1909, the responsibility for gathering intelligence on individuals and organizations within the UK was vested with the Metropolitan Police Special Branch. Its registered files can be found in MEPO 38, but some sensitive information is not available. CO 904 contains records of the British administration in Ireland prior to 1922, including material on various Nationalist movements such as Ribbonism, United Irish League, Sinn Fein and Ulster Unionists.

Security Service records are in department code KV, which comprises six discrete series. KV 1 contains First World War Historical Reports. KV 2 contains selected personal files from the First and Second World War and the inter-war years on suspected spies, double agents and Communist sympathizers. KV 3 consists of subject files and includes documents seized in police raids on the Communist Party Headquarters in 1925, the German secret services during the Second World War and the activities of British Fascist groups. There are also files relating to various Jewish and Zionist groups during the Second World War and in the last years of the Palestine mandate. KV 4 contains policy files setting out the Security Service's policies, chiefly from the inter-war and Second World War periods. It includes the Curry report, a three-volume top-secret wartime history commissioned by the then director-general, Sir David Petrie, covering 1908–45.

Files on organizations studied by the Security Service including ARCOS, the Anglo-German Society and Friends of Republican Spain can be found in KV 5. List files, relating to investigations carried out on related individuals or organizations (for example, investigations into SOE personnel forming part of the SOE 'list') are in KV 6. Some records are reconstituted files copied from microfiche, the original file having been destroyed. During the Second World War a number of temporary bodies were established to gather domestic intelligence. Records of the two most important, the Ministry of Home Security and the Ministry of Information, can be found in HO 199 and HO 262. Daily Intelligence Reports are in HO 203.

INTERNATIONAL INTELLIGENCE. Following the creation of the Foreign Office in 1782, the foreign secretary was responsible for administering the Secret Service Fund. Records relating to the fund's administration 1791–1909, are in four series. HD 1–4 consists of correspondence, accounts and letterbooks. HD 5 outlines the establishment and history of the Polish 'Deuxieme Bureau' network in France during the Second World War. Records relating to the British Secret Service in the Napoleonic era are in FO 38; they contain secret communications, originally from agents on the frontier of Holland and France, but later from agents in northern Germany and Sweden. The FO 1093 series consists of miscellaneous unregistered papers from the Permanent Under-Secretary's Department (PUSD) 1873–1939. The files deal with Secret Service matters such as estimates, expenditure and accounts as well as pensions and operations abroad. Records covering First World War activities are in a number of series. Most relevant are those created by the War Trade Intelligence Department, FO 902 and TS 14; the Foreign Office's Political Intelligence Department, FO 371/4357-87; and the Ministry of Information, INF 4. Records covering the Second World War can be found in CAB 154, the London Controlling Section; FO 837, the Ministry of Economic Warfare; and FO 898, the Political Warfare Executive. Records created by the Information Research Department are in FO 1110 and FCO 95.

MILITARY INTELLIGENCE. The majority of records relating to military intelligence are to be found in four major record series: WO 78, which contains maps and plans from intelligence gathering operations 1627–1953; WO 106, which consists of records created by the Directorate of Military Operations and Intelligence 1837–1960; WO 157, which contains intelligence summaries 1914–1921; and WO 208, which consists of records created by the Directorate of Military Intelligence as established in 1939, plus material inherited from the former Directorate of Military Operations and Intelligence. The intelligence records created by the major commands during the Second World War are in the following series; WO 201, Middle East Forces; WO 203, South East Asia Command; WO 204, Allied Forces Mediterranean Theatre; WO 219, Supreme Headquarters Allied Expeditionary Force. The minutes of the Inter Services Security Board, responsible under the direction of the Joint Intelligence Committee for the coordination of all security measures 1939–45 are in WO 283. A small collection of post-war intelligence material can be found in DEFE 65.

NAVAL INTELLIGENCE. Records relating to naval intelligence can be found in four main series: ADM 137, documents forming material for the official history of the First World War; ADM 223, intelligence reports and papers created by the Admiralty's Naval Intelligence Division and Operational Intelligence Centre; ADM 231, reports on foreign naval strength and coastal defences from the Naval Intelligence Department and its predecessor, the Foreign Intelligence Committee; ADM 326, United Kingdom Beach Intelligence Records produced by the Naval Intelligence Division and Defence Intelligence Staff.

AIR INTELLIGENCE. Records are in two main series: AIR 1, the records of Air Historical Branch, which contains scattered intelligence papers of the First World War; and AIR 40, which consists of various intelligence reports, narratives and photographs of enemy capabilities and reports of operations against enemy installations. The series has interrogation reports of prisoners of war and files relating to the air forces and commands of the United States Army Air Force. Also included are some records of the Joint Intelligence Bureau of the Ministry of Defence.

SPECIAL OPERATIONS. The vast majority of SOE operational files have not survived. Many were destroyed in a fire at SOE's headquarters shortly after 1945 or were destroyed at the end of the war. Surviving SOE records can be found in department code HS, which contains 20 series covering operations in various theatres, headquarters files and card indexes. SOE Personnel Files (PFs) were transferred to the National Archives in 2003 and can be found in series HS 9. As with SOE operational records, many files were destroyed, particularly those of junior SOE staff, whilst others were damaged, or contain extracts that continue to be retained. Because of the sensitive nature of many of these files, the lord chancellor has stated that SOE personnel files will remain closed for the lifetime of the individual concerned. If a researcher can demonstrate that the individual is deceased, or is a living SOE agent wishing to see their own file, the National Archives will make the relevant record available.

SCIENTIFIC INTELLIGENCE. The files in series DEFE 21 include a number directly related to the activities of the Scientific and Technical Intelligence Branch (STIB), which worked in the British Zone, Germany, under the technical direction of DSI and JTIC. Subjects covered include the capture of German scientists, liaison with other countries and the Soviet atomic energy programme. Related files can be found in DEFE 41, comprising the records of the Scientific and Technical Branch and Overseas Liaison Branch of the Foreign Office and Ministry of Defence. These records detail the procedures and the results of scientific and technical intelligence gathering in Germany following its occupation by the allies. Included are minutes of and correspondence with the JIC (Germany) and reports of interviews of German scientists.

Further material is contained in DEFE 44, which contains reports, notes and memoranda, together with a range of other intelligence products generated by the Ministry of Defence Directorate of Scientific Intelligence (DSI) and, after 1964, the Defence Intelligence Staff (DIS) Directorate of Scientific and Technical Intelligence (DSTI). These branches were responsible for the collation, analysis, assessment and dissemination of scientific and technical intelligence about foreign countries. The records of T Force and Field Information Agency Technical are found in FO 1031. They deal with such matters as evacuation of equipment, interrogation of enemy personnel and captured documents. The Papers of R.V. Jones, director of scientific intelligence, are located in DEFE 40. The papers in this series mainly concern German radio direction finding equipment, long range rockets and pilotless aircraft (Operation Crossbow) as well as later technical intelligence, conference, visits and research. The papers and technical reports produced by the Chemical and Biological Defence Establishment at Porton are found in WO 188 and 189.

COMMUNICATIONS INTELLIGENCE. The main source of material is located in department code HW which contains over 75 separate record series. The most relevant are HW 1, which contains summaries of selected signals intelligence reports, issued by the Government Code and Cypher School and sent by the head of MI6 ('C') to the prime minister during the Second World War. Other important series include HW 5, the German section; HW 15, the Venona Project records and HW 75, Soviet Bloc reports between 1945 and 1950. The records of early Admiralty work can be found in ADM 137 which includes papers produced by the Naval Intelligence Department and Room 40. A related series is ADM 233, which contains copies of Wireless News—summaries of intercepted wireless signals between 1918 and 1921. The series DEFE 3 also contains some decrypted signals and intelligence summaries related to naval activity during the Second World War.

OTHER SOURCES. Those records released by American intelligence agencies can be found at the US National Archives *www.archives.gov*. Further material released under Freedom of Information Legislation is available at the National Security Archive *www.gwu.edu/~nsarchiv*. Material declassified by the Central Intelligence Agency can be found at *www.cia.gov/library*.

Bibliography

BOOKS
Adams, J., *The New Spies* (Hutchinson, 1994).
Air Intelligence, A Symposium, Bracknell Paper No.7 (RAF Historical Society 1997). Especially chapter 4: 'The Organisation and Sources of Air Intelligence' by Cox, S. and chapter 11: 'RB-45 Operations' by Crampton, Squadron Leader J.
Aldrich, R.J. *The Hidden Hand, Britain, America and Cold War Secret Intelligence* (Overlook Press, 2002).
Andrew, C., *Secret Service: The Making of the British Intelligence Community* (Heineman, 1985).
Atherton, L., *SOE Operations in Scandinavia* (PRO, 1994).
Atherton, L., *SOE Operations in the Balkans* (PRO, 1994).
Atherton, L., *SOE Operations in Western Europe* (PRO, 1995).
Bailey, R., *The Wildest Province: SOE in the Land of the Eagle* (Cape, 2008).
Baker, D., *Jane's Space Directory 2005–06* (Janes, 2005).
Bamford, J., *The Puzzle Palace: The American NSA and its special relationship with Britain's GCHQ* (Sidgwick & Jackson, 1983).
Beesly, P., *Room 40, British Naval Intelligence 1914–18* (Hamish Hamilton, 1982).
Beesly, P., *Very Special Intelligence* (Hamish Hamilton, 1977).
Bennett, G., *Churchill's Man of Mystery: Desmond Morton and the World of Intelligence* (Routledge, 2007).
Bennett, G. and Hamilton, K. (eds), *Documents on British Policy Overseas, Series III, Vol. 1: Britain and the Soviet Union, 1968–72* (The Stationery Office, 1997).
Best, S.P., *The Venlo Incident* (Hutchinson & Company, 1950).
Bower, T., *The Perfect English Spy* (Heinemann, 1995).
Boyle, A., *Climate of Treason* (Hutchinson, 1980).
Brown, D.K. and Moore, G. *Rebuilding the Royal Navy* (Chatham Publishing, 2003).
Bud, R. and Gummett, P. (eds.), *Cold War Hot Science: Applied Research in Britain's Defence Laboratories 1945–1990* (Harwood Academic Press, 1999).

Budiansky, S., *Her Majesty's Spymaster: Elizabeth I, Sir Francis Walsingham and the Birth of Modern Espionage* (Viking, 2005).
Clayton, A., *The enemy is Listening: the Story of the Y Service* (Hutchinson 1980)
Craddock, P., *Know Your Enemy: How the Joint Intelligence Committee saw the World* (John Murray, 2002).
Cruickshank, C.G. *SOE in the Far East* (OUP, 1983).
Cruickshank, C.G. *SOE in Scandinavia* (OUP, 1986).
Davies, P.H.J., *MI6 and the Machinery of Spying* (Cass, 2004).
Denniston, R., *30 Secret Years: A.G. Denniston's Work in Signals Intelligence* (Polperro Press, 2007).
Dorril, S., *MI6: Inside the covert World of Her Majesty's Secret Intelligence Service* (Free Press, 2000).
Dorrill, S., *MI6: Fifty Years of Special Operation,* (Fourth Estate, 2000).
Fergusson, T.G., *British Military Intelligence, 1870-1914,* University Publications of America, 1984.
Foot, M.R.D., *SOE* (BBC, 1984).
Foot, M.R.D., *The SOE in France* (HMSO, 1966).
Foot, M.R.D., *The SOE in the Low Countries* (St Ermins Press, 2001).
Friedman, N., *Seapower and Space* (Chatham Publishing, 2000).
Geraghty, T., *BRIXMIS: The Untold Exploits of Britain's Most Daring Cold War Spy Mission* (Harper Collins, 1997).
Gordievsky, O., *Next Stop Execution* (Macmillan, 1995).
Goudsmit, S.A., *Alsos: The Failure of German Science* (Sigma Books, 1947).
Gudgin, P., *Military Intelligence: The British Story* (Arms and Armour, 1989).
Hyde, H.M, *The Quiet Canadian: The Secret Service Story of Sir William Stephenson* (Constable, 1962).
Hackmann, W., *Seek and Strike* (HMSO, 1984).
Hamrick, S.J., *Deceiving the Deceivers: Kim Philby, Donald Maclean, and Guy Burgess* (Yale University Press, 2005).
Heard, G., *The Riddle of the Flying Saucers* (Bantam Books, 1950)
Hennessy, P. (ed.), *The New Protective State: Government, Intelligence and Terrorism* (Continuum Books, 2007).
Hennessy, P., *Whitehall* (Secker, 1989).
Hinsley, F.H., *British Intelligence in the*

Second World War, vols. I-V (HMSO, 1979-).

Jones, H.A. *The War in the Air*, vols. 2-5 (Clarendon, 1931-7).

Jones, R.V., *Most Secret War: British Scientific Intelligence 1939-1945* (Hamish Hamilton, 1978).

Judd, A., *The Quest for C: Mansfield Cumming and the founding of the Secret Service* (Harper Collins, 1999).

Keyhoe, D., *Flying Saucers Are Real* (Fawcett, 1950).

Lambert, Andrew (ed.), *Letters and Papers of Professor Sir John Knox Laughton 1830-1915*, Navy Records Society, vol. 143 (Ashgate, 2002).

Mackenzie, W.J.M., *The Secret History of the SOE* (St Ermins, 2000).

Maffeo, S.E., *Most Secret and Confidential, Intelligence in the Age of Nelson* (Chatham Publishing, 2000).

Mangold, T., *Plague Wars: A True Story of Biological Warfare* (Macmillan, 1999).

Modin, Y., *My Five Cambridge Friends* (Hodder, 1994).

Moore, J.E., *Jane's Naval Review 1982-3* (Janes, 1983).

Murphy, C.J., *Security and Special Operations, SOE and MI5 during the Second World War* (Palgrave, 2006).

'My Purdah Lady': *The Foreign Office and the Secret Vote 1782-1909*, FCO History Note, No. 7 (1994).

Odom, W.E., *The Collapse of the Soviet Military* (Yale University Press, 1998).

Prezelin, B. (ed.) *The Naval Institute Guide to Combat Fleets of the World* (Naval Institute, 1993).

Raleigh, W *The War in the Air*, vol. 1 (Clarendon, 1922).

The Report of The Anglo-Polish Historical Committee: Intelligence Co-operation between Poland and Great Britain during World War II (Vallentine Mitchell, 2005).

Report of the Commissioners Appointed to Inquire into the Military Preparations and Other Matters Connected with the War in South Africa (1904), Cd. 1789.

Report on the Finch Manuscripts, vol. 5 (Historical Manuscripts Commission, 2004).

Richelson, J. and Ball, D., *Ties That Bind: Intelligence Cooperation between the UKUSA Countries* (Allen & Unwin, 1985).

Seaman, M. *Operation Foxley, the British Plan to Kill Hitler* (PRO, 1998).

Smith, C., *Singapore Burning, Heroism and Surrender in World War II* (Penguin, 2005).

Stafford, D., *Churchill and Secret Service* (Constable, 1997)Stanley, Roy M. *World War II Photo Intelligence* (Sidgwick and Jackson, 1981).

Stanley, R.M., *World War II Photo Intelligence* (Sidgwick and Jackson, 1981).

Strong, K., *Intelligence at the Top: The Recollections of an Intelligence Officer* (Cassell, 1968).

Stubbington, J., *Bletchley Park Air Section, Signals Intelligence support to RAF Bomber Command – Combined Bombing Offensive 1943-45* (Minerva, 2007).

Syrett, D. (ed.), *The Battle of the Atlantic and Signals Intelligence, U-boat Situations and Trends, 1941-45*, Navy Records Society, vol. 139 (Ashgate, 1998)

Syrett, D. (ed.), *The Battle of the Atlantic and Signals Intelligence, U-boat Tracking Papers, 1941-47*, Navy Records Society, vol. 144 (Ashgate, 2002).

West, N., *MI6: British Secret Intelligence Operations 1909-45* (Weidenfeld & Nicolson, 1983).

West, N., *The Secret War for the Falklands* (Little, Brown, 1997).

Wilkinson, N.J., *Secrecy and the Media: The Official History of the D-Notice System* (Routledge, 2008).

Winterbottom, F.W. *The Nazi Connection* (Harper & Row, 1978).

Wynne, G., *The Man from Moscow: The Story of Wynne and Penkovsky* (Atheneum, 1968).

Ziegler, C. and Jacobson, D., *Spying without Spies: The Origins of America's Secret Nuclear Surveillance System* (Praeger, 1995).

ARTICLES

Goldstein, E., 'The Foreign Office and Political Intelligence', *Review of International Studies*, 14 (1988).

Haines, G., 'The CIA's Role in the Study of UFOs, 1947-1990', *Intelligence and National Security*, 14, No. 2 (1999).

Henderson, G.B. 'Lord Palmerston and the Secret Service Fund', *English Historical Review*, 53 (1938).

Hughes, G. 'Giving the Russians a Bloody Nose: Operation Foot and Soviet Espionage in the United Kingdom, 1964-71', *Cold War History*, 6 (2006).

Ziegler, C. 'UFOs and the US Intelligence Community', *Intelligence and National Security*, 14, No. 2 (1999).

Index

The authors and publishers would like to thank the staff at The National Archives, including LOUISE ATHERTON, Head of Corporate Planning and author of numerous guides to the Special Operations Executive; HOWARD DAVIES, Head of ICMU for his guidance on the latest document releases; WILLIAM SPENCER, Principal Specialist, Military Records, for sharing his expertise; and HUGH ALEXANDER and PAUL JOHNSON in the Image Library. The authors and publishers would also like to thank JOHN CRAMPTON and the RAF Historical Society Journal for kind permission to reproduce the quotations reproduced on page 158; FCO HISTORIANS for their useful comments on earlier drafts; GRAHAM PITCHFORK for his assistance and contributions to the Air and Special Operations Executive chapters; and KEN WILSON for his attention to detail and design skills.